෪ What Is History For? ෫

MAKING SENSE OF HISTORY

Studies in Historical Cultures

General Editor: Stefan Berger

Founding Editor: Jörn Rüsen

Bridging the gap between historical theory and the study of historical memory, this series crosses the boundaries between both academic disciplines and cultural, social, political and historical contexts. In an age of rapid globalization, which tends to manifest itself on an economic and political level, locating the cultural practices involved in generating its underlying historical sense is an increasingly urgent task.

For a full volume listing please see back matter

WHAT IS HISTORY FOR?

*Johann Gustav Droysen and
the Functions of Historiography*

Arthur Alfaix Assis

berghahn
NEW YORK · OXFORD
www.berghahnbooks.com

First published in 2014 by

Berghahn Books
www.berghahnbooks.com

Library of Congress Cataloguing-in-Publication Data

Assis, Arthur Alfaix.
What is history for? : Johann Gustav Droysen and the functions of historiography
/ Arthur Alfaix Assis.
    pages cm. — (Making sense of history ; Volume 17)
Includes bibliographical references and index.
ISBN 978-1-78238-248-5 (hardback) — ISBN 978-1-78533-334-7 (paperback)
— ISBN 978-1-78238-249-2 (ebook)
    1. Historiography—Philosophy. 2. Historiography—Political aspects.
3. Droysen, Johann Gustav, 1808–1884. I. Title.
    D16.8.A727 2014
    907.2—dc23

2013017832

British Library Cataloguing in Publication Data

A catalogue record for this book is available from the British Library.

ISBN: 978-1-78238-248-5 hardback
ISBN 978-1-78533-334-7 paperback
ISBN: 978-1-78238-249-2 ebook

Contents

Acknowledgements

I am indebted to a good number of people who throughout the different phases of this project's development, from its inception to the preparation of the manuscript, provided me with scholarly advice, spiritual support and friendly encouragement (and frequently all these together). They are, at least: David Aires Neto, Dermeval de Sena Aires Jr., André Araújo, Shadia Husseini de Araújo, Marcelo Balaban, Diana Brenscheidt, William Brito Jr., Hannah Busch, Aaron Bustamante, Maria Filomena Coelho, Vicente Dobroruka, Francisco Doratioto, Marten Düring, Kira Funke, Jean-Claude Gens, Christian Gudehus, José Otávio Guimarães, Luís de Gusmão, Lizette Jacinto, Theo Jung, Oliver Kozlarek, Jordino Marques, Henrique Modanez de Sant'Anna, Sérgio da Mata, Fabiano Menke, Sebastião Nascimento, Marcos Aurélio Pereira, Peter Hanns Reill, Norma Reynolds, Marlon Salomon, Noé Freire Sandes, Judith Schildt, Gunter Scholtz and Mário Silva, as well as my brothers, Fred and Gustavo O. A. Assis. I am also very grateful to my former teachers Carlos Oiti Berbert Jr., Estevão de Rezende Martins, Jörn Rüsen and Luiz Sérgio Duarte da Silva. My option to dedicate a good part of my time to walk the fascinating field between history and theory is largely due to the great impression their classes and texts left on me.

Horst Walter Blanke, Pedro Caldas, Chen Chih-hung, Christiane Hackel, Friedrich Jaeger and Stephan Paetrow share my interest in Droysen's historical theory. They imparted their expertise and knowledge at many crucial moments, and I would like them to know how much I have appreciated their advice and criticism. In the case of Horst Blanke, I am doubly thankful, since he gave me access to the text of the second volume of the critical edition of Droysen's *Historik* almost two years before its publication.

Throughout the research and writing processes, I was associated with the Institute of Advanced Studies in the Humanities (KWI) in Essen and to Witten/Herdecke University, both in Germany, and later to the University of

Brasília. I would also like to thank the organizations that all along this project provided me with funding: the Brazilian Ministry of Education, through its funding agency, CAPES; the German Academic Exchange Service (DAAD); the Stiftung Mercator, through the research project Humanism in the Era of Globalization; the Center for Seventeenth- and Eighteenth-Century Studies of the University of California, Los Angeles; Brazil's National Council for Scientific and Technological Development (CNPq) and finally the History Graduate Program at the University of Brasília. At Berghahn Books I am particularly thankful to Elizabeth Berg, Adam Capitanio and Ann DeVita for their competent assistance. I am also thankful to the two anonymous peer reviewers who very much helped me in giving the text its final shape, as well as to Jaime Taber, who did an excellent job copyediting the manuscript.

I owe special thanks to my wife, Vânia Carvalho Pinto, not only for her lovely companionship but also for having helped immensely in converting the manuscript into passable academic English. Last but not least, I would like to thank my parents, Marly Oliveira Assis and Eduardo Augusto Alfaix Assis, for all the love and support they have always given me. This work is dedicated to them.

Introduction

In many cultures, the practice of historiography has often been attended by reflections on its general value and function. In the Western world since classical antiquity, some rhetoricians, philosophers and historians have attempted to explain why writing narratives referring to the past (and reading them) happens to be a worthwhile venture. Throughout the centuries a great variety of explanations emerged, most of them stressing that the issue goes far beyond the recognition that reading histories is sometimes a pleasant experience. In this regard, one explanatory *topos* had a very significant impact: Cicero's (106–43 BC) metaphor comparing history to a '*magistra vitae*' (life's teacher, guide to life).[1] Up until the beginnings of modern times, very few scholars would disagree with the argument condensed in Cicero's metaphor, namely, that the historian's task is to convey to an audience the lessons that can be extracted from past events and experiences. Even today, one could still easily uncover metaphors and arguments similar to Cicero's in several cultural realms. However, historians on duty at the beginning of the twenty-first century – unless they wished to commit professional suicide – no longer resorted to such a discourse when justifying the significance of their work and their academic discipline.

The origins of this change in how the work of historians is justified are traceable to the period from the late eighteenth to the mid nineteenth century, when criticism of historiography's exemplary function took shape. A modern discourse on the function of historiography only arose when (German) intellectuals such as August Ludwig Schlözer (1735–1809), Wilhelm von Humboldt (1767–1835), Georg Wilhelm Hegel (1770–1831) and Leopold von Ranke (1795–1886), to quote only the most widely known, began challenging what can be called the 'exemplar theory of history'.

In this work, I assume that Johann Gustav Droysen's (1808–1884) texts on historical theory can be read as very important marks on the intellectual path leading to the critique of historical exemplarity. Part of their significance is due

Notes for this section begin on page 14.

to his extraordinary attempts to think out a new positive justification for historiography. Basically, he proposed that we should not study, research and write history in order to learn or produce universally valid examples. Instead, he suggested that historiography is better conceived of as a vehicle through which authors and readers learn and improve mental skills that he himself addressed as 'historical thinking'.[2]

Droysen's claim that history should teach how to think historically points to the capacity by which human beings become able to really understand the present world they live in. This is as skill that should enable one to see one's lifeworld through the lens of a genetic perspective, a perspective centred on the temporal evolving of current things. In other words, it is the capacity to mentally re-enact the history of the present and, hence, to unveil the historicity of oneself and one's surrounding world. But in no way did Droysen see historical thinking only as a means for contemplating the past, for it was directly linked to human agency in a given present. According to him, historical thinking can provide an understanding of the generative process of a given lifeworld that is crucial for someone willing to reasonably make decisions, act and interact within that world.

Such an argument elicited a new approach to the relationship between historical knowledge and human action. Previous historical theorists had defined the function of historiography as the conveyance of examples worked out of past events related to the actions of either memorable or despicable men, thus presupposing historical knowledge as general knowledge of human nature. Accordingly, histories were supposed to communicate substantive maxims of action whose exemplary validity would transcend temporal and spatial contexts – maxims that actors in each given present would be able to apply if they judged it convenient. Droysen, for his part, regarded this way of referring historical knowledge to action as largely insufficient. He proposed instead that historical knowledge should function as a formal support for subjective reflection, action and suffering. Unlike the theorists who focused on historical learning from examples, Droysen assumed that the kind of learning sponsored by historical thinking related neither to a substantial set of recommendations nor to the ability to decide which example to follow in each given circumstance. For him, historical thinking was not a ready-made solution to the problem of human agency, but a capacity that agents could develop and improve so as to be able to find adequate, feasible, responsible and original paths of action in every specific case.

As can be seen, Droysen's theoretical texts reflected and promoted the stabilization of a genetic and non-exemplary sense of history. Nevertheless, they reveal not only a rejection of the old meta-historical pragmatism, but also a special concern not to isolate historiography from either ethics or politics. In fact, what Droysen proposed was a reconstruction of the very pragmatic link between history and life that Cicero had placed at the core of his formula. This was, however, only one of the paths nineteenth-century historians and philosophers followed in their attempts to either formulate a non-exemplary justification for historiography or put into practice a non-exemplary form of historical writing. Leopold von Ranke, as we will see in Chapter 1, constantly pled in favour of isolating historical knowledge from any kind of immediate practical application.[3] Conversely, Friedrich Nietzsche (1844–1900) would later argue for a radically pragmatic use of historiography to counter what he regarded as the paralysing effects of excessive historical knowledge on the human capacity to act.[4] Like Nietzsche, Droysen believed that history should be a practical, somehow life-assisting and life-enhancing knowledge. But he could at once agree also with Ranke that history no longer had examples to teach. What Droysen proposed, then, was a redefinition of the practical value of history. For him, historical knowledge could be a legitimate source of cultural, moral or political orientation, but only if it were relocated to a temporalized, historicized, atmosphere that he found lacking in all previous exemplar theories of history.

In its broadest sense, the term historicism (*Historismus*)[5] gives a name to the general framework within which a genetic (and non-exemplary) approach to history emerged. According to Ernst Troeltsch, historicism refers to the 'fundamental historicization of our thinking on human beings, their culture and values'.[6] It is thus a way of perceiving the human world that assumes that history is the most important concept for the understanding of human beings. To embrace a historicist perspective thus means to accept that the present world is indissolubly and dynamically linked with past worlds. It also means to acknowledge that a privileged way to understand the present is by looking into its becoming, into the gradual changes undergone by the past situations and frameworks that set up a given present context. Historicism hence directs attention to formative processes, qualitative changes and morphologies, and the adjective 'genetic', which I frequently use to define Droysen's conception of historiography, refers precisely to this attitude of spotlighting the complex linkage (made of changes and continuities) that every present retains with its preceding pasts.

As such a world view, historicism opposes both theological and mechanistic views of social life: it attempts to understand why the world is the way it is, but not by equating current reality with an order determined by God or resorting to natural patterns or laws. Historicism comprises a special kind of consciousness of time that stresses the singularity of every historical epoch and subject, and is structured by individualizing, developmental and genetic concepts. Historicism, which originated in late eighteenth-century Europe among German and Scottish historical thinkers especially,[7] had the work of Italian Giambattista Vico (1668-1744) as its most significant precursor.[8] It is an (originally Western) intellectual phenomenon that can only be understood in connection with other major modern developments, such as the Enlightenment, the political revolutions of the late eighteenth century, the industrial revolution and many accomplishments in natural sciences and technique.[9]

In this sense of a specifically modern historical outlook, historicism frequently went hand in hand with the German historiographical movement that established history as a professional and autonomous discipline. The word historicism commonly refers also to this process, so it is important to differentiate it from the more general meaning of historicism as a genetic approach to human life, as mentioned above. In fact, the latter extends to several academic fields beyond historiography: jurisprudence, theology, philology and philosophy, among others. In addition, historicism in a broad sense is not limited to the academic world, for it comes close to being a world view. In a narrower sense, however, historicism frequently refers to the professionalization of historical studies as first accomplished in some German universities between the late eighteenth and first half of the nineteenth centuries.[10]

Justifications and Functions

Droysen's texts are rife with attempts to define which impacts the kind of genetic historiography composed by professional historians have or should have on then contemporary culture, society or politics. He frequently expresses these attempts in sentences opening with 'Our science's task is…' or 'The task of historians is…'. In general in this kind of sentence (and here I am thinking not only about Droysen's case), it is difficult to differentiate descriptive from ascriptive content. Drawing a line between Droysen's assessment of the actual function performed by historiography and his ideas about what this function should really be is an unworthy task. But as we survey the particular sentences in which Droysen describes functions or ascribes them to historiography, a more fruitful conclusion strikes us: depending on the context, Droysen filled the ellipses in sentences like 'the task of historians is…' with relatively differing arguments. This point can be illustrated by a collection of quotes extracted from some of his texts.

In 1843, in a preface printed in only a few copies of the second volume of his *History of Hellenism* – the so-called Private Preface – Droysen expatiates on the ultimate presuppositions of his interpretation of ancient history. Within this context, he states that that 'our science's highest task is the theodicy'.[11] Later on, in 1846, he further develops this same argument on the religious value of history as follows: 'Faith offers us the consolation that a hand of God bears us.… And the science of history has no higher task than to justify this faith.'[12] Nonetheless, in the 1855 opening of his multi-volume *History of Prussian Politics,* Droysen claims that the essence of historical studies is 'to learn how to understand by means of research'.[13] In his first lecture course on historical theory in 1857, that definition undergoes a slight change, for there he claims that 'the task of historical studies is to stimulate one's learning of historical thinking'.[14] Shortly after, in 1858, while opening his lectures on contemporary history, he advocates that 'more than ever, history is the interpreter of the present, its *gnothi seauton* (γνῶθι σαυτον), its conscience'.[15] Further, in the last edition of his *Outlines of Historical Theory* (*Grundriss der Historik*), of 1882, he reminds us that '[t]he great practical significance of historical studies lies in the fact that they, and they alone, hold up before the state, or people, or army, its own picture. It is the study of history – and not the study of law – which is the basis for political and administrative instruction and qualification'.[16] Finally, in the same *Outlines,* he also proposes that history is 'humankind's knowledge of itself, its self-awareness'.[17]

As the quotes reveal, Droysen's argues that the function(s) of historiography comprise, at least, serving as humankind's self-awareness; training politicians and bureaucrats to qualify them to properly deal with state affairs; interpreting the contemporary world; stimulating the development of historical thinking; learning to understand the world by means of research; justifying the religious faith that God directs the movement of history; and, finally, providing an explanation for the theological issue concerning the existence of evil in a world supposedly created by a good god. This multiplicity of answers might indeed lead today's readers to the opinion that Droysen's entire theory of history is either ambiguous or vague. Even if this opinion could be proven correct with regard to certain passages of his texts, one should from the very beginning take into account Droysen's highly dialectical way of thinking and arguing. In dialectics, as it is well known, contradiction plays the role of a constructive principle for reasoning and exposition; therefore, it does not necessarily indicate a vice of thought. Most of the ambiguities featuring in Droysen's theoretical texts can be understood in this manner.

Moreover, with regard to Droysen's style of thought, it is interesting to recall a dictum by Hegel, who alongside Karl Marx (1818–1883) is the most obvious modern philosopher associated with the term dialectics. Characterizing his own philosophical system, Hegel is quoted as having said that as he uttered its first word he also uttered its last.[18] The image of the mutual interrelatedness of all concepts and ideas evoked here also serves as a good description of the way Droysen structured his own historical theory. In fact, Droysen never clarified a single sector of his theory without referencing all others: his methodological and epistemological concepts imply notions related to a substantive philosophy of history, his didactic arguments imply ethical and religious assumptions, and so on. In addition, Droysen many times delivered more or less the same message by using different key terms and introducing peripheral changes to subject matter.[19] All these repetitions, of course, raise the correct impression of circular thought, but again, in most of the cases, circularity does not necessarily correspond to vagueness or tautology. It can largely be seen as a stylistic mark accruing much less from Droysen's personal choice than from his affiliation to the hermeneutic tradition, a tradition that is no stranger to the image of knowledge and understanding emerging from circles or spirals of thought.

Indeed, Droysen's proposition that histories are meaningful because they serve to support the development of someone's historical thinking is not the only functional definition that can be extracted from his work. However, it is probably his strongest, most general, and consistent definition. First of all, historical thinking, as Chapter 2 will show, is very much akin to the formula 'understanding by means of research'. Nevertheless, as it points to not only historical understanding as performed by researchers but also that of readers and agents, historical thinking much better highlights Droysen's opinion that the value of history reaches far beyond the academic world. Secondly, Droysen's argument on history as the interpreter or conscience of the present is also highly compatible with the notion of historical thinking, though again the latter conveys a didactic orientation that the former lacks. In addition to that, and especially because of its close link with the parallel notion of *Bildung,* historical thinking underscores the idea of history as humankind's self-awareness. Finally, the notion of historical thinking also accords with Droysen's theological assumptions: it does not disallow the presupposition that God directs the course of history, and it can also be harmonized with an ultimately teleological conception of the historical process.

In any case, Droysen speaks of functions of historiography that definitively transcend his plea for historical thinking – even though there is, as mentioned, a high level of compatibility between many of them. It is also important to keep in mind that arguments justifying historiography's value are commonly contradicted by the actual functions concrete historical texts perform. Droysen's case unequivocally illustrates this disjunction between theory and practice, which abounds in the history of historical thought. As will be shown in Chapter 4, his theoretical argument against historical exemplarity largely conflicts with the recurrence, in his texts on Prussian history, of characters and stories that can function as examples to be followed by the audience. To be more specific: Droysen's commitment to the cause of German national unification led him to infuse many of his historical texts with the very same exemplarity that his theoretical reflections once condemned.

Outline of the Book

This study places Droysen's notion of historical thinking in the limelight. I have attempted to investigate many of his texts in search of the existing connections between this notion and three of the main sectors of his general world view: his theory of historical method, his representations regarding the totality of the historical process, and his political beliefs and agenda. The book deals, therefore, with Droysen the theoretician of historiography; Droysen the holder of a necessitarian sense of history; and Droysen the political historian and utopist.

This last circumstance and of course also the comprehensiveness of Droysen's intellectual interests necessarily turn every consequent survey of his ideas into an enterprise falling within several academic fields. These include, among others, history of German nineteenth-century politics, ideas and intellectuals; theory and philosophy of history; history of philosophy and hermeneutics; and history of historiography. My text combines concepts, analyses and insights accruing from all these fields, and I only hope that its hybridized perspective will turn out to be more enriching than confusing for the readers.

I am starting with an outline of the history of the discourse on the function of historiography. Up until its last paragraphs, Chapter 1 does not directly address Droysen, but rather the diachronic context in which his historical theory came about. First, I will attempt to substantiate the general thesis that premodern meta-historical discourses were importantly marked by exemplar theories of history. Here my references to ancient, medieval and early modern authors are supposed to disclose a fundamental structure of thought that could be treated as a *longue durée*. However, since it is unrealistic here to extensively consider the over 2,000-year-old corpus of literature containing reflections on historiography, I will have to restrict the analysis to some well-known classics and rely heavily on secondary sources. Then, in this chapter's second half, I will discuss some of the critiques levelled against the exemplar theory of history by German historical thinkers of the late eighteenth and nineteenth centuries, as well as different types of arguments advanced as alternative justifications for the practice of historiography.

The proper analysis of Droysen's ideas related to the issue of the function of historiography begins in Chapter 2, where I will focus on his texts on historical theory and methodology. The chapter delivers an analysis of what was at stake in Droysen's claim that 'the task of historical studies is to stimulate one's learning of historical thinking',[20] considering methodological, epistemological, didactical and pragmatic aspects involved therein. It will track the roots of Droysen's new didactics, both in his opposition to the historiographical positivism of facts,[21] and in the hermeneutical methodology of historical science that he developed as a consequence thereof. In that way, I will reconstruct Droysen's theory of historical thinking and analyse the concepts it envelops, particularly historical understanding and interpretation, sense of reality, *Bildung* and identity.

Subsequently, Chapter 3 will turn to the way Droysen's theory of historical thinking materialized into a substantive philosophy of history, that is, a concrete and long-ranging meta-narrative that, taken as a whole, ascribes a meaning to the process of history. There I will attempt to show that his notion of historical thinking is strongly linked to a genetic interpretation of his own present age, in which the latter features as an intermediary stage within the historical development of the idea of freedom – a long-term development initiated by the ancient Greeks and to be continued in the future. The chapter cuts into some significant cross-sections of Droysen's genealogy of the present, concentrating especially on its contemporary phase.

As already pointed out, Droysen's theory of historical thinking remained in tension with his commitment to a set of ideas regarding German national politics and Prussia's role in it. Chapter 4 will delve into Droysen's application of historical thinking to politics. I will characterize there the main aspects of his political standings, identifying the interrelationship between them and Droysen's actual historiographical oeuvre. Furthermore, I will argue that a good deal of the universalism that characterizes Droysen's theory of historical thinking was lost in the application. In addition, I will show that with this instrumentalization of historiography, Droysen eventually fell back into the very kind of historical practice suggested and justified by the old exemplar theories of history.

Finally, since Droysen is not among the most obvious authors within the English-speaking meta-historical debate, I have prepared a biographical sketch and a brief characterization of his historical theory, which are both to be found in the Appendix. This text can provide some initial orientation to those who are encountering Droysen's ideas for the first time, and may as well serve as a reminder that Droysen's *Historik* reaches far beyond the themes and concepts at the centre of the study at hand.

Having just mentioned the German term *Historik,* I shall take the opportunity to make note of the meaning and the translation of some of the vocabulary used throughout the present text. Droysen developed many of his theoretical considerations on history and historiography within the context of lectures he gave between 1857 and 1882–83.[22] Droysen's own advertisements for his theoretical lectures employed different combinations of terms, such as historical encyclopaedia and historical methodology, but sometimes he also resorted to the term *Historik*.[23] The latter ended up becoming a widespread way for editors and commentators to refer to Droysen's theoretical project. The semantics of the term *Historik* is rather ambiguous; Droysen and his editors and commentators use it to refer to his theoretical lectures as well as to the arguments and points of views they communicate. The realm of the term's meanings is amplified by the fact that *Historik* (as *Geschichtstheorie* and *Theorie der Geschichte*) has also been generally used in Germany to designate the academic field that deals with theoretical and methodological issues related to historical knowledge.[24] The ambiguities of *Historik* are, moreover, only furthered by the ambiguities of the term history itself, which simultaneously means, at least, a given succession of past events, the account of such events and the academic field specializing in historical research and writing.[25]

Taking all that into consideration, I am translating *Historik, Geschichtstheorie* and *Theorie der Geschichte* as 'theory of history' or 'historical theory'. Sometimes I will also employ the term *Historik* in its original form, but only as a special reference to Droysen's theoretical lectures and ideas. I am thus differentiating between 'theory of history' and '(substantive) philosophy of history'. In the following, philosophy of history will be used only as a reference to the many kinds of conceptions related to the course and the general meaning of the historical process,[26] whereas theory of history will point to a general reflection on the historians' professional practice.[27] In the English-speaking world, this distinction is rather unusual, since a more general meaning is linked to philosophy of history, and as a result the term has come to cover also the semantic field that I ascribe to historical theory.[28] All in all, as Droysen's case will illustrate once again, it should not be forgotten that historical theories are often related to substantive philosophies of history. Meanwhile, I try to employ the word 'historiography' exclusively when referring to the writing of history, as a way to avoid setting it into concurrence with terms like 'historical theory' or 'philosophy of history'.

Neither the language of my main primary sources (German) nor the language of my own text (English) is my native language (Portuguese). Because of that, during the research (for) and the writing of this book, I have always felt translation as a critical issue. My strategy to cope with this difficulty consists in privileging paraphrases rather than translations when referencing primary sources and secondary literature. Even so, several passages and expressions had to be translated into English. In translating, the transparency of the translated text was at least intended, sometimes to the detriment of fidelity to the source's language. To compensate, most of the quotes appear in the notes in their original version.

Background

In order to situate the general theses on the history of historical thought that the present study is premised on, one could retrocede at least as far as to the differentiation of the kinds of historiography Hegel developed in the earlier versions of his philosophy of history. Hegel distinguished between the philosophical world history that he took on as his subject matter and older forms of historiography that he called 'original history' and 'reflective history', respectively. He conceived of one of the variations of this latter as 'pragmatic history', insisting that the genre was possibly suitable to the moral instruction of children, but over time it had definitely revealed itself of no help for the management of current affairs related to the life of peoples and states.[29]

Decades later, Ernst Bernheim would outline a similar scheme of the evolution of historical studies. According to him, history of historiography was marked by three different and increasingly more complex stages, namely 'narrative (or referential) history', 'exemplar (or pragmatic) history', and 'developmental (or genetic) history'.[30] Bernheim accentuates that none of the newer stages had cancelled the effects of their forerunners, and that in his time all three co-existed more or less peacefully. But he notes that since the early nineteenth century, the greatest German historians had professed themselves to the genetic conception of history, and then argues that thenceforth the other two forms of history were subordinated to it.[31]

Curiously, these two nineteenth-century interpretations resemble several general arguments and formulations on the function of historiography that I have borrowed from more recent authors, especially Reinhart Koselleck, George Nadel, Ulrich Muhlack, Peter Reill and Jörn Rüsen. In this regard, maybe the most important case is the expression 'exemplar theory of history', which I have imported from Nadel's 1964 essay on 'philosophy of history before historicism'.[32] This text argues that one of the decisive features of Western premodern historical thought was the ascription of an exemplary function to historiography. The term exemplar theory of history is precisely the conceptual label Nadel uses to address that feature. Analysing texts dating from classical Greece to the time of the European Enlightenment, he correctly locates the roots of the exemplar theory of history in classical rhetoric, tracing its decline back to the late eighteenth century and to the outset of historicism. Nevertheless, he also suggests that the exemplar attitude was only superseded by the claim that historical knowledge should be entirely segregated from practical imperatives.

This debatable conclusion is frequently drawn by many of the most important authors who have addressed the function of historiography in the German historical thought of the nineteenth century. Another case in point is Ulrich Muhlack's 1990 essay on '*Bildung* between Neo-humanism and Historicism'.[33] Muhlack focuses on the incorporation of nineteenth-century *Bildung*-philosophy into the problematic of the value and function of historiography. He appropriately stresses that the historicist orientation towards *Bildung,* that is, historicism's *Bildungsanspruch,* embodied both a refusal of and an alternative to the exemplar theory of history. Even so, precisely like Nadel, Muhlack ends up concluding that historicism as a whole was marked by an autotelic[34] definition of the function of historiography, that is, by the notion that historical knowledge is a purpose in itself rather than a means for other purposes.[35] Here Muhlack overlooks that the works of many important late eighteenth- and nineteenth-century historians hold no evidence of the kind of autotelic definitions that are to be found, for instance, in Ranke's texts.

An additional problem exhibited by Muhlack's interpretations is that, by crediting Wilhelm von Humboldt as the first historical theorist to have resolutely rejected the validity of the motto '*historia magistra vitae*', he entirely downplays the efforts a few earlier historians had made towards rethinking historiography's function.[36] Contrariwise, Peter Reill has shown that even though German late-Enlightenment historians kept conceiving history as pragmatic knowledge, they were in fact re-signifying historical pragmatism.[37] The same can be said about Droysen and some other important figures of nineteenth-century historical thought. In this regard, the thesis I want to develop is that the establishment of a critical attitude towards historical examples in the early nineteenth century did not automatically imply discarding historical pragmatism. This was so not only because a good part of historical culture remained untouched by the mentioned criticism of historical exemplarity, but also because a group of historical thinkers – of whom Droysen is representative – combined a refusal of historical examples with an insistence on history's pragmatic value.

Reinhart Koselleck has, in my opinion, correctly grasped the real meaning of this refashioned historical pragmatism. I have therefore resorted to arguments he developed, especially those from his 1967 essay on 'the dissolution of the topos *historia magistra vitae* into the perspective of a modernised historical process'.[38] Koselleck's reference to the topos *historia magistra vitae* equals Nadel's use of 'exemplar theory of history'. Like Bernheim and Nadel, Koselleck points to the strong connections between the critiques of exemplar justifications for historiography and what he presents as the emergence of a modern concept of history, a process that for him would have taken place during the period from 1750 to 1850. In recent years, Koselleck's interpretation of the origins of the modern concept of history has been subjected to some meticulous critical assessments that have undermined some of his conclusions.[39] But still, regarding the particular issue of the discourse on the functions of historiography, I think Koselleck introduces several good clues. First, he avoids the mistake of postulating that the downfall of the exemplar theory of history meant the total disappearance of historical pragmatism. At the same time, he accurately identifies (though without exhaustively analysing) the onset of a new way of justifying the pragmatic function of historiography in German-speaking historical thought, by connecting it to the notion of *Bildung*. In this regard, what Koselleck shows is that in the late eighteenth and the first half of the nineteenth centuries the idea of 'learning from history' was undergoing an important change. This change corresponds to the emergence of a new definition of historical learning, one that departed from the old convention that historiography is the source of a moral and political kind of wisdom that could be immediately applicable to decision-making and action. At the core of this new perspective is the idealistic concept of *Bildung*. Reconceived as a special facet of individual *Bildung,* historical learning, according to Koselleck, then began to be seen as a vehicle that leads human subjects to a mediate and self-reflexive relationship with their past and that of humankind.[40]

It is, in any case, symptomatic that Koselleck's conclusion refers to a passage in Droysen's *Historik* that argues that whereas history offers no examples to be imitated it conveys ideas that can nourish the individual's *Bildung:* 'History provides agents with a plethora of ideas, with a material, which they have to bring into the melting pot of their judgement in order to refine it.'[41] Clearly, this new definition of the purpose of historiography is in no way equivalent to the notion of history as a purpose in itself. Droysen's claim that the main point of studying history is the development and enhancement of the ability to judge – in other words, of historical thinking – condenses thus a still pragmatic though no longer exemplary definition of the function of historiography.

The general architecture of my interpretation of Droysen's historical theory evolved in a critical dialogue with the mentioned views on the history of historical thought. As I have recalled, analysts have long recognized that by the beginning of the nineteenth century, the old exemplary function of historiography had been destabilized by the reinforcement of a genetic model of historical explanation. For scholars like the ones mentioned above and many others, modern historical discourse distinguishes itself from its predecessors because it is much more decisively structured by a dynamic, historicized or genetic perspective. In the main, I do subscribe to this general thesis, though it is at least my intention to avoid the frequent mistake of rigidly opposing a modern, dynamic, temporalized consciousness of time to a supposedly static and transtemporal 'premodern' one.

On the beaten track of scholarship on modern historical thought, my investigation concentrates on a particular issue not hitherto subject to intensive exploration. Despite the goodly number of works dedicated to both the crisis of exemplary historiography and the emergence of modern historical thought, to my knowledge no analyst has really focused on the kind of justifications that replaced the exemplar theory of history. How was the modern genetic historiography justified? What kind of non-exemplary functions were then ascribed to history? These questions remain, I think, insufficiently answered. Indeed, Koselleck, for one, correctly points out that a special kind of educative function took the place of historical examples. At that point, he has argued, the function of historiography started to be defined in terms of a *Bildungsfunktion*. However, neither he nor the scholars whose texts I have surveyed delved deeply into the way this new function was conceived. None of them focused on how a few nineteenth-century historical thinkers, such as Wilhelm von Humboldt, Droysen, Jacob Burckhardt (1818–1897), Wilhelm Dilthey (1833–1911), Nietzsche and maybe a few others, attempted to theoretically establish a non-exemplary function for historical knowledge.

My interpretation also engages in dialogues with the much more specific scholarship on Droysen's historical theory and historiography.[42] In particular, it proceeds on the assumption that Droysen's *Historik* can be taken as an important culminating point in the trajectory of the conceptions of history and historical knowledge originated since 1750.[43] The most pre-eminent contemporary defence of that point of view is undoubtedly the one advanced by Jörn Rüsen, an author who, by the way, also agrees in not seeing the autotelic solution as the only modern answer to the problem of the function of historiography. According to Friedrich Jaeger and Rüsen, Droysen's *Historik* is 'historicism's most significant achievement as regards the discussion on the fundaments of historical science'.[44] Furthermore, I also draw on Rüsen's publications with regard to particular analyses of Droysen's texts. I have especially tried to follow Rüsen's suggestion that one should understand Droysen's *Historik* not as a purely theoretical hermeneutics, but as a theory embedded in concrete historical interpretations and entirely intermingled with practical motives.[45] In his *Begriffene Geschichte,* published in 1969, Rüsen shows how Droysen's historical and political texts presupposed several of the theoretical ideas that he systematically developed in his *Historik*.[46] Rüsen's basic claim is that it is not adequate to isolate Droysen's methodology from other segments of the historical cosmos within which it evolved.[47] To a good extent, this volume's Chapter 3 (on Droysen's substantive philosophy of history) and Chapter 4 (on his politics of historical thinking) are attempts to further validate that claim.

Nonetheless, although Rüsen has succeeded in demonstrating the interdependence between Droysen's hermeneutical reflections and his substantive historical interpretations, he has not sufficiently explored the connections between Droysen's theoretical arguments and Droysen's political creed and positions. In this regard, Rüsen follows a general trend in Droysen research. Actually, most scholars who have produced detailed analyses of Droysen's texts and ideas have usually leaned towards separating the author's theory of history from his political historiography, engagement and beliefs. This situation has given rise to a scholarly division of labour, according to which one approaches either Droysen's meta-historical ideas or his political activism, but very seldom tries to prove how the two could be interrelated. Even though scholarship on Droysen has resulted in a great many high-quality studies, the tendency to separate the theoretician from the political actor has led to only an incomplete picture of Droysen as an intellectual. The consequent research gap is worth reducing.

To some extent, bridging this gap was one of the main goals pursued by the most prominent book on Droysen published in recent years, namely, Wilfried Nippel's *Droysen: A Life between Science and Politics*.[48] Nippel's book undoubtedly represents a new step towards a critical assessment of Droysen's biography and texts, but one clear shortfall is his interpretation of Droysen's historical theory. His argument is that Droysen's *Historik* must be regarded as both a justification for Droysen's political creed and a tactical device providing support to Droysen's presumably inflated career ambitions. On this sole basis, and hence without having properly analysed Droysen's theoretical arguments, Nippel condemns Droysen's *Historik* for not being a 'pure theory'.[49] By doing this, Nippel misperceives some of the aspects that, according to many other scholars, make Droysen's *Historik* almost compulsory reading for anyone interested in exploring the field of historical theory and methodology. Examples include the trailblazing notions and arguments found in Droysen's texts, such as his threefold methodology focused on the formulation of research problems and on interpretation rather than on source criticism; his perspectivist and, to a good extent, constructivist approach to the nature of historical knowledge; his sensitivity to the issue of historical representation, which even led him to articulate the notion of 'narrative' in a meta-historical context; as well as his phenomenological insights on the historicity of both human action and historical sources.[50]

I think, hence, that the relationship between historical theory and political commitment in Droysen's works is far more complex than Nippel's analyses indicate. To come to a more nuanced approach, I propose that we should avoid looking at Droysen's theory of historical thinking as a spurious rationalization of his political beliefs. In the same vein, however, we also have to cope with the fact of his theory being much more than a pure epistemological construct, for undoubtedly it interacts with strong political motives and assumptions. I have therefore decided to take both historical theory and politics, as developed in Droysen's writing, very seriously. Contrasting them with one another, I have often come across internal tensions and contradictions, some of which Droysen ultimately was unable to solve. Like many other intellectuals throughout history, Droysen attempted to integrate his ideas into a coherent world view. He only found mixed success in that, not least because coherence in the history of ideas is at best relative coherence. My aim of providing a critical account of Droysen's ideas entails, among other things, the need to point out and understand such contradictions. By this means, I hope to arrive at a realistic picture of Droysen as an intellectual without diminishing his status as a classical author who, in his theoretical reflections on history and historiography, posed questions that are still worth asking and provided some answers that remain valid.

Notes

1. Marcus Tullius Cicero. 1942. *De oratore,* books I–II, London: Heinemann; Cambridge, MA: Harvard University Press, 224–225.

2. At this point, let me refer to only one clear (and perhaps the most elucidative) example of Droysen's usage of 'historical thinking': 'Die Aufgabe der historischen Studien ist, daß man

historisch denken lerne'. Johann Gustav Droysen. 1977. *Historik,* vol. 1: *Rekonstruktion der ersten vollständigen Fassung der Vorlesungen (1857); Grundriß der Historik in der ersten handschriftlichen (1857/58) und in der letzten gedruckten Fassung (1882),* Stuttgart: Frommann-Holzboog, 5 [Vorlesungstext, 1857].

    3. Leopold von Ranke. 1990. 'Vorwort zu den ‹Geschichten der romanischen und germanischen Völker von 1494 bis 1535›', in Wolfgang Hardtwig (ed.), *Über das Studium der Geschichte,* Munich: DTV, 44–46; Leopold von Ranke. 1859. *Englische Geschichte, vornehmlich im 16. und 17. Jahrhundert,* vol. 1, Berlin Duncker und Humblot, iii–xvi. That Ranke succeeded in satisfying that theoretical plea in his actual history writing is dubious.

    4. Friedrich Nietzsche. 2000. 'Von Nutzen und Nachteile der Historie für das Leben', in Friedrich Nietzsche, *Unzeitgemäße Betrachtungen,* Frankfurt am Main, Leipzig: Insel, 95–184.

    5. It is important to note that here I am not addressing what Karl Popper meant by historicism. In Popper's understanding, historicism is a fallacious approach to the social sciences that assumes their primary aim is to predict the course of future events based on knowledge of history's putatively underlying laws or patterns of evolution. See Karl Popper. 2002. *The Poverty of Historicism,* London: Routledge, 3.

    6. Ernst Troeltsch. 1961. *Der Historismus und seine Probleme,* book 1: *Das logische Problem der Geschichtsphilosophie,* Aalen: Scientia, 102: 'Es ist das Problem der Bedeutung und des Wesens des Historismus überhaupt, wobei dieses Wort von seinem schlechten Nebensinn völlig zu lösen und in dem Sinne der grundsätzlichen Historisierung alles unseres Denkens über den Menschen, seine Kultur und seine Werte zu verstehen ist'. It is noteworthy that Troeltsch – like Karl Heussi, Friedrich Meinecke and Benedetto Croce after him – ascribed to *Historismus* a positive meaning that it lacked when it was initially popularized in the last quarter of the nineteenth century. For more recent comprehensive studies on the history of historicism, see Frederick Beiser. 2011. *The German Historicist Tradition,* Oxford: Oxford University Press; Friedrich Jaeger and Jörn Rüsen. 1992. *Geschichte des Historismus. Eine Einführung,* Munich: C.H. Beck.

    7. Jaeger and Rüsen, *Geschichte des Historismus,* 12–14; Murray Pittock. 2003. 'Historiography', in Alexander Broadie (ed.), *The Cambridge Companion to the Scottish Enlightenment,* Cambridge: Cambridge University Press, 258–279; Peter Hanns Reill. 1975. *The German Enlightenment and the Rise of Historicism,* Berkeley: University of California Press.

    8. Benedetto Croce. 2000. *History as the Story of Liberty,* Indianapolis: Liberty Fund, 69. Croce, while emphasizing Vico's role as a pioneer of historicism, would nonetheless stop short of crediting late-Enlightenment intellectuals with being historicists.

    9. Otto Gerhard Oexle. 1996. *Geschichtswissenschaft im Zeichen des Historismus: Studien zu Problemgeschichten der Moderne,* Göttingen: Vandenhoeck und Ruprecht, 17–18.

    10. Scholars frequently trace the beginning of the professionalization process back to the late eighteenth-century University of Göttingen, where the term 'history' was mentioned in the designation of some academic chairs, historical journals were edited and historical seminars held. See, e.g., Horst Walter Blanke. 1991. *Historiographiegeschichte als Historik,* Stuttgart: Frommann-Holzboog, 111; Robert Harrison, Aled Jones, and Peter Lambert. 2004. 'The Institutionalisation and Organisation of History', in Peter Lambert and Phillip Schofield (eds), *Making History: An Introduction to the History and Practices of a Discipline,* London: Routledge, 11; Georg Iggers. 1994. 'Ist es in der Tat in Deutschland früher zur Verwissenschaftlichung der Geschichte gekommen als in anderen europäischen Ländern?' in Wolfgang Küttler et al. (eds), *Geschichtsdiskurs,* vol. 2: *Anfänge modernen historischen Denkens,* Frankfurt am Main: Fischer, 75–76. Nevertheless, Jeremy Telman calls attention to the fact that the late eighteenth-century University of Göttingen was an exceptional case within the German academic landscape. According to him, the professionalization of the historical discipline only caught on during the nineteenth century. See Jeremy Telman. 1994. 'Review Essay', *History and Theory* 33(2): 249–265.

    Professionalization means first of all that historical research and teaching found an institutional anchor – namely, in most cases, the universities, which in the course of the nineteenth century showed a mounting number of history professors. Beyond that, the professionalization of historical research and writing was also buttressed by several other related developments, including the establishment of a system of archives, libraries and historical museums; the growth of historical journals and associations; the proliferation of seminar classes designed to convey research techniques to young historians; and the emergence of attempts at a theory of historical method, which formulated the principles of research and surely strengthened historians' professional identity. See Friedrich Jaeger. 2007. 'Historismus', in Friedrich Jaeger (ed.), *Enzyklopädie der Neuzeit*, vol. 5, Stuttgart: J. B. Metzler, 532–539; Jaeger and Rüsen, *Geschichte des Historismus*, 8–10; Matthew Jefferies. 2006. 'The Age of Historism', in Stefan Berger (ed.), *A Companion to Nineteenth-Century Europe*, Malden, MA: Blackwell, 316; Georg Iggers. 1997. *Historiography in the Twentieth Century: From Scientific Objectivity to the Postmodern Challenge*, Middletown, CT: Wesleyan University Press, 27–28; Zachary Schiffman. 1985. 'Renaissance Historicism Reconsidered', *History and Theory* 24(2): 170–182; Rolf Torstendahl. 2003. 'Fact, Truth and Text: The Quest for a Firm Basis for Historical Knowledge around 1900', *History and Theory* 42(3): 308–310.

11. Johann Gustav Droysen. 2007. *Historik*, vol. 2: *Texte im Umkreis der Historik (1826–1882)*, Stuttgart: Frommann-Holzboog, 228 [‹Privatvorrede› zu Band 2 der Geschichte des Hellenismus, 1843]: 'Die höchste Aufgabe unserer Wissenschaft ist ja die Theodicee'.

12. The translation of this quote from the *Lectures on the Wars of Freedom* (1846) was borrowed from Robert Southard. 1979. 'Theology in Droysen's Early Political Historiography: Free Will, Necessity, and the Historian', *History and Theory* 18(3): 379 (here the translation is slightly modified). Original quote in Johann Gustav Droysen. 1846. *Vorlesungen über die Freiheitskriege*, vol. 1, Kiel: Universitäts-Buchhandlung, 5.

13. Johann Gustav Droysen. 1868. *Geschichte der Preußischen Politik*, part 1: *Die Gründung*, Leipzig: Veit, v: 'Es gibt mancherlei Ansicht über die Art und Aufgabe der historischen Studien. Vielleicht darf man Alles zusammenfassend sagen, ihr Wesen sei forschend verstehen zu lernen'.

14. Droysen, *Historik* 1: 5 [Vorlesungstext, 1857]: 'Die Aufgabe der historischen Studien ist, daß man historisch denken lerne'.

15. Droysen, *Historik* 2: 379 [Einleitung in die Vorlesung über das Zeitalter der Revolution, 1858]: 'Mehr als je ist die Geschichte eine praktische Wissenschaft geworden. Sie ist die Deuterin der Gegenwart, ihr γνωσι σαυτον, ihr Gewissen'.

16. Johann Gustav Droysen. 1893. *Outline of the Principles of History*, Boston: Ginn, 56 [translation slightly modified].

17. Droysen, *Outline of the Principles of History*, 49.

18. The dictum was transmitted by Droysen himself in a paraphrase and without any further reference. I could not find any other source for the statement. See Droysen, *Historik* 1:382 [Vorlesungstext, 1857].

19. A good example is the interrelationship between the notions of understanding, interpretation, historical thinking, sense of reality, historical *Bildung* and identity. Chapter 2 will present more details on this.

20. Droysen, *Historik* 1: 5 [Vorlesungstext, 1857].

21. Chris Lorenz clarifies the meanings evocated by the term positivism while used in historiographical discussions as a resource to disqualify a work, an author or a school of historians. He distinguished between the 'positivism of facts', or empiricism, on the one hand, and 'the positivism of the covering-law model of explanation', i.e., the model implicated in attempts to demonstrate that historical explanation follows somehow the pattern of more evidently nomothetic sciences. See Chris Lorenz. 1998. 'Can Histories Be True? Narrativism, Positivism and the "Metaphorical Turn"', *History and Theory*, 37(3): 310–311.

22. For more details on the lectures, as well as on the published and translated texts related to them, see the Appendix.

23. Peter Leyh. 1977. 'Vorwort des Herausgebers', in Droysen, *Historik* 1: ix, fn. 2. According to Leyh, Droysen designated his theoretical lectures as follows: *Encyclopaediam et methodologiam historiarum* (1857), *Encyclopaedia historiarum* (1858, 1859), *Historische Methodologie und Enzyklopädie* (1860–61 [winter semester], 1863–64, 1865, 1868, 1870, 1872, 1879, 1881), *Hi-*

storik oder Methodologie und Enzyklopädie der historischen Wissenschaften (1862–63), *Methodologie und Enzyklopädie der Geschichtsstudien* (1875), *Methodologie und Enzyklopädie der historischen Wissenschaften* (1876), *Methodologie und Enzyklopädie der Geschichte* (1878, 1882–83).

24. *Geschichtstheorie* or *Theorie der Geschichte* are currently more common denominations for the field in question. *Historik* tends to be a less frequent term, not least for a structural reason: in German it is impossible to derive an adjective from the substantive *Historik*. The only possibility would be *historisch*, but this already means historic or historical. See H.-W. Hedinger. 1974. 'Historik, ars historica', in Joachim Ritter (ed.), *Historisches Wörterbuch der Philosophie*, vol. 3, Basel: Schwabe, 1132; Hans-Jürgen Pandel. 1990. *Historik und Didaktik. Das Problem der Distribution historiographisch erzeugten Wissens in der deutschen Geschichtswissenschaft von der Spätaufklärung zum Frühhistorismus (1765–1830)*, Stuttgart: Frommann-Holzboog, 130–162. One alternative denomination is, moreover, *Historiologie*. Indeed, this could be a universal label, and registers of equivalents to it are found in other languages (historiology-en, historiologie-fr, historiogía-es, historiologia-pt, etc.). These denominations, however, have never been widely used.

25. See, e.g., Reinhart Koselleck. 2003. *Zeitschichten. Studien zur Historik*, Frankfurt am Main: Suhrkamp, 130.

26. Karl Löwith's definition is still very much worth recalling. He used the term philosophy of history to define 'a systematic interpretation of universal history in accordance with a principle by which historical events and successions are unified and directed towards an ultimate meaning'. See Karl Löwith. 2004. *Meaning and History: The Theological Implications of the Philosophy of History*, Chicago: University of Chicago Press, 1.

27. See a further justification of this basic differentiation by José Guilherme Merquior. 1988. 'Philosophy of History: Thoughts on a Possible Revival', *History of the Human Sciences* 1(1): 23–24.

28. More usual distinctions are those between speculative philosophy of history and analytic philosophy of history (see Michael Lemon. 2003. *Philosophy of History: A Guide for Students*, London: Routledge); or between speculative philosophy of history and critical philosophy of history (see William Dray. 1964. *Philosophy of History*, Englewood Cliffs, NJ: Prentice-Hall).

29. Georg Hegel. 1955. *Die Vernunft in der Geschichte*, Hamburg: Felix Meiner, 18.

30. Ernst Bernheim. 1908. *Lehrbuch der historischen Methode und der Geschichtsphilosophie*, Leipzig: Duncker & Humblot, 22. Bernheim's original terms are 'erzählende oder referierende, lehrhafte oder pragmatische (im weiteren Sinne), entwickelnde oder genetische Geschichte'.

31. Bernheim, *Lehrbuch der historischen Methode*, 26–27.

32. George H. Nadel. 1964. 'Philosophy of History before Historicism', *History and Theory* 3(3): 291–315.

33. Ulrich Muhlack. 1990. 'Bildung zwischen Neuhumanismus und Historismus', in Reinhart Koselleck (ed.), *Bildungsbürgertum im 19. Jahrhundert*, part 2: *Bildungsgüter und Bildungswissen*, Stuttgart: Klett-Cotta, 80–105.

34. The term autotelic (from the Greek autotelés, complete in itself) was introduced into the English language in the 1920s as a way to refer to the belief that a work of art (or literature) is an end in itself or is its own justification. Its meaning is equivalent to that of the aestheticist formula 'art for art's sake'. Though the term is not commonly used in meta-historical contexts, I have opted to employ it on certain occasions, as it simplifies the reference to the point of view according to which historiography has a purpose in itself.

35. Muhlack agrees that the notion of *Bildung* did not entirely fit into this autotelic justification of historiography, for the former entails a practical and also in many cases a political moment. He deals with this problem by arguing that the historicist ideal of *Bildung* was actually subordinated to the scientific ideal of objectivity. Such an explanation is not entirely suitable to the case of the historians connected to the so-called Prussian School, and thus also to Droysen. See Muhlack, 'Bildung zwischen Neuhumanismus und Historismus', 89: 'Der Historismus negiert die praktische Zwecksetzung der Geschichte, erklärt vielmehr die historische Erkenntnis zum Selbstzweck.... Er [der Historismus] verkündet, daß die in seinem Zeichen erneuerte Geschichte zugleich gebildet mache und daß allein diese durch die erneuerte Geschichte vermittelte Bildung

praktisch nützlich sei. Er gelangt damit zu einer eigentümlichen Trias von Geschichtswissenschaft, Bildung und ethisch-politischer Praxis. Nach der Systematik des Historismus kommt die Geschichtswissenschaft vor der Bildung und die Bildung vor der ethisch-politischen Praxis.'
   36. Muhlack did it quite consciously. His book on 'historicism's prehistory', i.e., on historiography and historical thought between Renaissance Humanism and Enlightenment, comprises several detailed analyses of the most important authors of the German historical *Aufklärung*. See Ulrich Muhlack. 1991. *Geschichtswissenschaft im Humanismus und in der Aufklärung. Die Vorgeschichte des Historismus,* Munich: C.H. Beck. Muhlack's argument on the fundamental cleavage between Enlightenment and historicist historical thought can be clearly read in the following quote (Muhlack, *Geschichtswissenschaft im Humanismus,* 44): 'Über den Zweck der Geschichte haben humanistische und aufklärerischen Historiker eine einhellige Meinung «historia magistra vitae»'.
   37. Reill, *The German Enlightenment and the Rise of Historicism,* 41–43.
   38. Reinhart Koselleck. 2003. *Vergangene Zukunft. Zur Semantik geschichtlicher Zeiten,* Frankfurt am Main: Suhrkamp, 38–66.
   39. In Chapter 1, I will go into some detail on Koselleck's interpretation of the emergence of the modern concept of history, as well as on the critiques it has recently undergone.
   40. Reinhart Koselleck. 2004. *Futures Past: On the Semantics of Historical Time,* New York: Columbia University Press, 41: 'However much the German Historical School conceived itself as concerned with a science of the past it did nonetheless fully exploit the dual meaning of the word Geschichte and seek to elevate history into a reflexive science. Here, the individual case lost its politico-didactic character. But History as a totality places the person who has learned to understand it in a state of learning [*Bildung*] that should have an indirect influence on the future.' The quote here is modified, as an error in the translated text seriously affects understanding of Koselleck's argument. Where the author writes '… Zustand der Bildung, der *mittelbar* auf die Zukunft einwirken soll', the translated text uses 'directly' where the correct term is 'indirectly'. The original quote is from Koselleck, *Vergangene Zukunft,* 65.
   41. Johann Gustav Droysen. 1971. *Historik. Vorlesungen über Enzyklopädie und Methodologie der Geschichte,* Munich: R. Oldenbourg, 300: 'Also die Geschichte bietet eine Fülle von Ideen, und diese sind dem, der handeln soll, ein Material, das er in den Schmelztiegel seines eigenen Urteils tun muss, um es zu läutern.'
   42. Droysen's notion of historical thinking has been little explored by either historians of nineteenth-century historical discourse or interpreters of his *Historik.* Pedro Caldas's Portuguese-language Ph.D. dissertation is surely the main exception in this landscape. See Pedro Caldas. 2004. *Que significa pensar historicamente: uma interpretação da teoria da história de Johann Gustav Droysen,* Ph.D. thesis: Pontifícia Universidade Católica do Rio de Janeiro. Caldas addresses the issue of historical thinking in Droysen's works throughout three enriching chapters dedicated to the issues of teleology, hermeneutics and *Bildung.* But even though he correctly points out that historical thinking is simultaneously implicated with these three dimensions, he leaves their interrelationship rather unexamined.
   43. See, for instance, Blanke, *Historiographiegeschichte als Historik,* 111; Alexandre Escudier. 2006. 'Theory and Methodology of History from Chladenius to Droysen: A Historiographical Essay', in Christopher Ligota and Jean-Louis Quantin (eds), *History of Scholarship: A Selection of Papers from the Seminar on the History of Scholarship Held Annually at the Warburg Institute,* Oxford: Oxford University Press, 476–477.
   44. Jaeger and Rüsen, *Geschichte des Historismus,* 54. See also Jörn Rüsen. 2005. 'Droysen heute – Plädoyer zum Bedenken verlorener Themen der Historik', in Lutz Niethammer (ed.), *Droysen-Vorlesungen,* Jena: Universität Jena, Philosophische Fakultät, Historisches Institut, 179.
   45. Jörn Rüsen. 1969. *Begriffene Geschichte. Genesis und Begründung der Geschichtstheorie J. G. Droysens,* Paderborn: Ferdinand Schöningh, 14–15.
   46. Rüsen, *Begriffene Geschichte;* see also Jörn Rüsen. 1968. 'Politisches Denken und Geschichtswissenschaft bei J. G. Droysen', in Kurt Kluxen and Wolfgang Mommsen (eds), *Politische Ideologien und Nationalstaatliche Ordnung. Studien zur Geschichte des 19. und 20. Jahrhunderts*

(Festschrift für Theodor Schieder), Munich: Oldenbourg. Rüsen has also been one of the main promoters of the contemporary reception of Droysen's theory of history and has attempted to reintroduce it into contemporary meta-historical discussion at the international level. The importance of Rüsen's interpretations lies furthermore in the fact that he largely incorporated Droysen's theoretical insights into his own theory of history, which originated from an explicit effort to refresh and renew Droysen's Historik. With regard to this last aspect, see Jörn Rüsen. 1983. *Historische Vernunft. Grundzüge einer Historik I: Die Grundlagen der Geschichtswissenschaft,* Göttingen: Vandenhoeck & Ruprecht; Jörn Rüsen. 1986. *Rekonstruktion der Vergangenheit: Grundzüge einer Historik II: Die Prinzipien der historischen Forschung,* Göttingen: Vanderhoeck & Ruprecht; Jörn Rüsen. 1989. *Lebendige Geschichte: Grundzüge einer Historik III: Formen und Funktionen des historischen Wissens,* Göttingen: Vanderhoeck & Ruprecht.

47. Some of the main ideas featuring in my analyses of the historical-philosophical implications of Droysen's notion of historical thinking are also largely based on interpretations by Robert Southard, who has outstandingly demonstrated how Protestant philosophy of history, diagnosis of the present, and political expectations intertwine in Droysen's early political historiography. See Robert Southard. 1995. *Droysen and the Prussian School of History,* Lexington: University Press of Kentucky; Southard, 'Theology in Droysen's Early Political Historiography'.

48. Wilfried Nippel. 2008. *Johann Gustav Droysen. Ein Leben zwischen Wissenschaft und Politik,* Munich: C.H. Beck.

49. Nippel, *Johann Gustav Droysen,* 227.

50. In addition, Nippel also completely ignored the religious foundations of Droysen's political thought and practice. For critical views on Nippel's book, see Joachim Eibach. 2008. 'Rezension zu: "Nippel, Wilfried: Johann Gustav Droysen. Ein Leben zwischen Wissenschaft und Politik. München 2008"', *H-Soz-u-Kult,* 12 December 2008; Jörn Rüsen. 2008. 'J. G. Droysen, Dämon der Machtbesessenheit. Rezension zu Wilfried Nippels "Johann Gustav Droysen: Ein Leben zwischen Wissenschaft und Politik"', *Die Welt,* 5 April 2008; James Sheehan. 2009. 'A Political Professor: A New Biography of J.G. Droysen', *German History* 27(4): 580–582; Thomas Welskopp. 2009. 'Der "echte Historiker" als "richtiger Kerl". Neue Veröffentlichungen (nicht nur) zum 200. Geburtstag von Johann Gustav Droysen', *Historische Zeitschrift* 288(2): 385–407.

CHAPTER 1

Functions of Historiography until the Mid-nineteenth Century

A Short History of the Problem

The Rise of the Exemplar Theory of History

Long before Droysen began to systematize his ideas on the nature, methods, specificity and relevance of the science of history, the Greek historian Diodorus of Sicily in the first century BC included in the preface to his *Historical Library* a kind of catalogue in which he listed all the uses of history that came to his mind. According to him,

> It is an excellent thing to be able to use the ignorant mistakes of others as warning examples for the correction of error, and, when we confront the varied vicissitudes of life, instead of having to investigate what is being done now, to be able to imitate the successes which have been achieved in the past.... One may hold that the acquisition of a knowledge of history is of the greatest utility for every conceivable circumstance of life. For it endows the young with the wisdom of the aged, while for the old it multiplies the experience which they already possess; citizens in private station it qualifies for leadership, and the leaders it incites, through the immortality of the glory which it confers, to undertake the noblest deeds; soldiers, again, it makes more ready to face dangers in defence of their country because of the public encomiums which they will receive after death, and wicked men it turns aside from their impulse towards evil through the everlasting opprobrium to which it will condemn them.[1]

To sum up: in Diodorus's view, histories remind us of the actions of notable and failed men, thereby establishing models for present agents to either imitate or avoid. Histories multiply the experience already possessed by the old and, moreover, convey to the young the wisdom accumulated in the past. Histories teach lessons on leadership and inspire leaders to perform great deeds, and they stimulate soldiers' patriotism by offering them the hope of posthumous praise.

Notes for this section begin on page 51.

Finally, they dissuade bad persons from evil by threatening them with perpetual disrepute.[2] Diodorus's arguments weave what might be called an 'exemplar theory of history'. Exemplar are those theories of history that hold that the major task of historians is to locate in the past timeless models of action to be immediately applied or avoided in the present.

One of the striking things about Diodorus's catalogue is the number of centuries through which it lingered as a valid description of the value and functions of historiography. At least until the second half of the eighteenth century, nobody dared seriously question the assumption that history is written to underscore moral and/or political virtues and discourage vices. Throughout the centuries in between, those who thought historians do or should cater for the public's demand for historical examples were also acknowledging that historians do not do their work merely to advance knowledge about the human past, or for the sake of arousing pleasant feelings in their readers. The assumption behind the exemplar theory of history was that histories straightforwardly exert influence over the way readers make decisions and act. Accordingly, historians were supposed to resort to the past in search of cases that would positively affect either the morality or the political judgement of the current readership.

I should mention here that the exemplary way of justifying historiography is not at all a singularity of so-called Western civilization. Within the Chinese historical tradition, for instance, the *shi*s, who as early as around 1000 BC served as archivists, historiographers and astrologers in many courts, wrote histories to deliver practical orientation to their rulers.[3] This was the case of many histories and annals, most notably Sima Guang's (1019–1086) *Zizhi Tongjian* or, in literal translation, *Comprehensive Mirror to Aid in Government* (1084), a book that would become paradigmatic in many other East Asian cultures as well. As the title indicates, Sima's was a textbook that, drawing on Confucian morality, explicitly aimed to convey historical lessons to the emperor (Shenzong, of the Song dynasty, 1048–1085), as well as to government's bureaucrats.[4] Scholars from several other times and civilizations frequently followed the same path whenever justifying the value of historiography. Early Indian historiographers, for instance, were no strangers to the idea that the past as conveyed by histories 'can and does teach lessons, usually moral lessons'.[5] Furthermore, Ibn Khaldūn (1332–1406), who surely was one of the most extraordinary historical thinkers of all times, testified very clearly to the significance of historical examples within classical Islamic justifications for historiography.[6] In the general introduction to his universal history, which bore the convenient title of *Book of Examples* (*Kitab al-Ibar*), he ascertained that '[history] makes us acquainted with the conditions of past nations as they are reflected in their (national) character. It makes us acquainted with the biographies of the prophets and with the dynasties and policies of rulers. Whoever so desires may thus achieve the useful result of being able to imitate historical examples in religious and worldly matters.'[7]

In any case, throughout the history of Western historical thought, the habit of writing about historians as the providers of models for present agency was usually widespread among ancient, medieval and early modern intellectual elites. Granted, throughout the more than twenty centuries separating the classical Greeks from the intellectuals of the era of the Enlightenment, and within the broad space encompassed by the highly general idea of Western civilization, historical narratives conveyed much more than just exemplars of practical conduct. Even within the much smaller realm of the reflection on the nature and function of historiography, the empirical diversity of the arguments brought about in such a vast period surely hampers any generalizing attempt. In this regard, as Flavius Josephus (37–ca 100) long ago recognized, 'those who essay to write histories are actuated ... not by one and the same aim, but by many different motives'.[8] Still, the continuity and frequency of the exemplary arguments throughout the centuries remains impressive indeed.

Several ancient, medieval and early modern intellectuals agreed (or would agree) with the famous old quote that defines history as 'philosophy teaching by examples'.[9] But in fact, the classical roots of the exemplar theory of history are to be traced within the rhetorical tradition. Isocrates (436–338 BC), a contemporary of Plato (ca 427–ca 347 BC), was a famous Greek rhetorician who saw education's ultimate aim as instructing citizens so that they would be able to properly speak and act within the political arena. According to Isocrates, that aim could be materialized only through practical knowledge that accrued directly from experience, rather than through the theoretical knowledge privileged by the Platonic tradition.[10] Later on, stoic philosophers would have a similar attitude, favouring reflection linked to practical experience instead of philosophical speculation.[11] Throughout classical antiquity, the idea of enhancing human action by direct reference to exemplary models worked out by historiography was relatively opposed to the mainstream of the classical philosophical tradition. The opposition was, however, only relative, since philosophers and rhetoricians (as well as historians) equally recognized the importance of moral education; at the end of the day, their disagreement was only over the didactic means to accomplish the same educative goals.[12]

It is important to point out that ancient rhetoricians developed their exemplar theories of history within the framework of a cyclical notion of time, that is, of a sense that the future was no horizon full of new and unexpected events, but rather a time in which already existing patterns would recur.[13] Nevertheless, it would be a mistake to state that the ancient Greeks generally conceived of time as a circle, or that Jews and Christians, for instance, conceived of it exclusively in linear terms. Shifting the focus from classical philosophers and rhetoricians to classical historians does not necessarily reveal traces of a circular perception of time. Arnaldo Momigliano, who strongly condemned the argument that Greek and early Christian conceptions of time differed radically, affirmed that cyclical time played no crucial role at all in ancient Greek historiography.[14] Momigliano's thesis is largely confirmed by François Hartog's argument that Herodotus and Thucydides (fifth century BC, both) conceived their histories not as exempla, but as perennial accounts (*ktema*) of what they self-confidently experienced as a great and unique present. According to Hartog, both historians were characterized by their efforts to draw a dividing line between epics and what could even then be called 'historiography'. Within this context, they associated the latter with the written and the prose forms, raising 'autopsy' (i.e., seeing for oneself rather than listening to what others have seen) to the rank of a preferred basis for reliable knowledge. Accordingly, their writings referred back to events they were contemporary to (the Persian and the Peloponnesian Wars, respectively) – rather than to the long-ago and often mythical events typical of epic poetry. The kind of relationship with time inaugurated by Herodotus' book actually downplayed the past as barely knowable, focusing instead on the present – that is, on the time one can experience for oneself – and more specifically on the events one could see with one's own eyes. Classical Greek historians thus regarded their present time as superior to all past and at same time cast doubt on the knowledge of past events they could not have witnessed.[15]

As a matter of fact, this attitude did not fit in with the assumption that some segments of the past should be remembered as examples for the present. On the whole, the major works of both Herodotus and Thucydides lack exemplary justifications for writing and reading histories. Hartog argues that the exemplary use of the past only caught on during the fourth century BC, precisely after the Peloponnesian War strongly unsettled the general optimism that had characterized the times of Herodotus and Thucydides. The sense of the superiority of the present vis-à-vis the past was then turned upside down, and historians, following orators and rhetoricians, started to scan the recent past in search of modes of action that could be imitated or avoided. In doing so, they assumed they were elaborating a means for their present to regain its lost dignity.[16]

More than 250 years after Herodotus and Thucydides wrote their famous works, the opening statement of Polybius's (ca 200–ca 120 BC) *Histories* testifies to the consolidation of the practice of ascribing an exemplary function to historiography. Unlike Herodotus and Thucydides, Polybius did not lay out a monograph on a specific war but a universal history dealing with a broader time span, 220–144 BC, and a more complex subject matter, the rise of Rome to a world power. He began his book by holding that there was no longer any need to justify the importance of historiography, since his predecessors had already established that 'the study of history is in the truest sense an education, and a training for political life'. This statement shows that Polybius agreed that the general function of historiography is of a political-didactic nature – that history should be written specifically for the instruction of rulers and political actors.[17] He further agreed that the method his alleged forerunners had used in order to effectively prepare readers to act in the political arena was indeed the most convenient one: the presentation of negative examples. For Polybius, histories teach examples of misdeeds warning the readership against falling into the same errors: 'The most instructive, or rather the only, method of learning to bear with dignity the vicissitudes of fortune is', he concludes, 'to recall the catastrophes of others.'[18] These quotes from the introduction of Polybius's book convey only a statement of intent that his narrative may or may not have fulfilled. But it is significant enough that at least on the intentional level, Polybius clearly ascribed to history the function of extracting, from the past, negative examples that would retain validity for all times.

However, neither Polybius nor any other ancient historian would influence later discourses on the value of history more than Cicero, a Roman rhetorician of the first century BC who never wrote a historical work. The formula most famously associated with the exemplar theory of history shows up in a passage of Cicero's *De oratore,* in which he remarks that history is an important support to speakers. Within this context, he notes some metaphorical definitions for history, including one that ascribes to it the quality of being '*magistra vitae*' (a guide to life, life's teacher).[19] This formulation reaffirms the traditional emphasis on the exemplary function of historical texts, and it is interesting that it situates this function in the general level of morality rather than in the specific level of politics.

This shift towards moral examples can also be traced in the works of important Roman historians. Compared to their Greek counterparts, the Romans wrote history from a much less cosmopolitan perspective, tending to concentrate their narratives in a single scenario, the city of Rome.[20] As Rome's expansionism advanced, Roman intellectuals developed a general self-image of cultural and political superiority that was even stronger than that of classical Greeks'. From the later decades of the Republic onwards, however, historians such as Sallust (86–35 BC), Livy (ca 59 BC–ca 17 AD) and Tacitus (58–116) started to combine this patriotic pride with a strong moral pessimism. They were facing the consequences of Rome's rise to world power, and their appreciation of it was quite negative. For them, the wealth and luxury promoted by the imperial expansion were corrupting traditional Roman virtues.[21] In the preface to his *History of Rome,* Livy addresses his readers by calling attention to what he would like them to focus on while reading his text. He mentions the greatness of the Roman early times, contrasting it to the contemporary 'disintegration of morals' that had led to the then present situation, 'in which we can tolerate neither our own vices nor their remedies'. Having said that, he reaches an important point concerning the use of history in general: 'This is the particularly healthy and productive element of history: to behold object lessons of every kind of model as though they were displayed on a conspicuous moment. From this, you should choose for yourself and for your state what to imitate and what to avoid as abominable in its origin or as abominable in its outcome.'[22]

Livy's definition points to a rather 'pessimistic use of historia magistra', in which exemplary reference to the past serves as a way to reject the present.[23] But during the Middle Ages, the magisterial metaphor's relocation into the context of the Christian world view led to more convoluted adaptations. A case in point is Isidore of Seville's (ca 560–633) acknowledgement that some pagan historiography should still be reckoned as useful, which he justifies by arguing that 'many wise men [pagans] have put past deeds into their histories for the instruction of the present'.[24] A few decades later, Bede (673–735), in the preface to his *Ecclesiastical History,* would confirm the predominance of the exemplary disposition: 'For if history relates good things of good men, the attentive hearer is excited to imitate that which is good; or if it mentions evil things of wicked persons, nevertheless the religious and pious hearer or reader, shunning that which is hurtful and perverse, is the more earnestly excited to perform those things which he knows to be good, and worthy of God.'[25]

In both cases, the notion that histories aim at instructing the present paraphrases Cicero's formula '*magistra vitae*', attesting simultaneously to the arrangements between this classic topos and the Christian world view. Noticeably, historiography then was still taken as a reservoir of examples destined to instruct individuals' practical conduct, but now the lessons to be learned derived from Christian rather than pagan morality. Thus, a new important feature was added to the magisterial metaphor: histories were ascribed the task of delivering examples of God's power.[26] In the twelfth century, the theologian John of Salisbury (1120–1180) articulated this quite clearly by suggesting that history should be written in order to show how 'the invisible things of God may be clearly seen by the things that are done'.[27] This new mode of defining the exemplary function reverberated even after the dawn of the Middle Ages, and also among Protestant thinkers. Martin Luther (1483–1546) held that histories were 'a very precious thing', in which 'one finds both how those who were pious and wise acted, refrained from acting, and lived, how they fared and how they were rewarded, as well as those who were wicked and foolish and how they were repaid for it'.[28] In the same vein, David Chyträus (1530–1600), a Lutheran historian and theologian who had been a pupil of Philipp Melanchthon (1497–1560), argued that everyone could draw from history a beneficial teaching, for histories show examples of how good behaviour is always rewarded while misdeeds are always punished.[29]

Generally speaking, in the intellectual life of the European Middle Ages, theology – in the sense of both the study of the Christian faith and its sacred texts – constituted the most reputable form of human knowledge. It was the field of knowledge to which all others were subordinated; philosophy and the liberal arts were supposed to serve it. That this hierarchy was bound by some tension is illustrated in the theological warnings eventually issued against the dangers of philosophy, which increased especially after the Aristotelian renaissance of the late twelfth century.[30] In any case, to admit that theology was at the top of the medieval tree of knowledge does not automatically imply an assumption that all other forms of knowledge in the Middle Ages had to be entirely and directly related to theological or religious issues. This is mostly the case in historiography, which, incidentally, medieval authors regarded as a subsidiary field of the liberal art of rhetoric. Historians, chroniclers and annalists – the three designations were strongly interrelated all through the Middle Age, and no attempts to specify a differentiation among them actually succeeded[31] – avoided reconciling religious revelation and secular experience, and focused exclusively on the latter. In the prefaces to their texts, they frequently stressed the fragility and the limitations of their accounts, leaving aside the issue of how to connect the events accounted for with the theological issue of the meaning of history.[32] Here they were far from negating the supreme importance of theology, as shown by Orderic Vitalis (1075–ca 1142), who refused to attempt an explanation of some mysterious drownings reported to have happened in the neighbourhood of the abbey he lived in, arguing: 'I am not able to unravel the divine plan by which all things are made and cannot explain the hidden causes of things; I am engaged merely in the writing of historical annals.... Who can penetrate the inscrutable? I make a record of events as I have seen or heard of them, for the benefit of future generations.'[33]

Actually, medieval historiography leaned towards mere narration of past events and tended to sparsity in the explanation of the causal relations that framed them, just as it also usually adopted fairly imprecise chronologies. Apart from the basic intention of recording memorable things, the chroniclers were not bound to try to understand the driving forces operating behind the occurrences' surface. In general, medieval intellectuals referred to worldly events in a way that Erich Auerbach specified as typological (or figural) interpretation. Derived from a procedure developed to support Biblical exegeses, typological interpretation 'explains' an event by referring to the meaning it shares with another event that remains causally and chronologically distant from the former. As examples of a typological interpretation, Auerbach mentions the Christian reading of the sacrifice of Isaac as a figure or prefiguration of the sacrifice of Christ, or Dante's image of the Roman empire of Augustus as a symbol of God's eternal empire. Figural interpretation was ultimately a strategy that the Church fathers fostered in the first centuries of Christianity to manage the strong influences both paganism and Judaism, which, they thought, should be domesticated rather than dismissed. It was open enough to allow the absorption of events and experiences from Jewish and pagan history, but guaranteed that non–Christian experience would be given a Christian meaning. According to Auerbach, this is one of the major tendencies detectable in medieval literary sources, and thus also in medieval historiography.[34]

The avoidance of causal explanation accomplished by typological interpretation had nothing to do with medieval historians' oft-alleged incapacity to conceive of causal relations.[35] It was rather a function of a deep-rooted intellectual humbleness that prevented them from intervening in matters they supposed would be better served by theologians or philosophers. Furthermore, it was the expression of a social order profoundly marked by the ubiquity of the past – a social order in which, as Gabrielle Spiegel noted, 'even innovations in social and legal practices were given the force of custom'.[36] Unsurprisingly, in this context, history turned out to be embedded with a salient political utility that ran parallel to its moral-edificatory function and was supposed to be executed by the same exemplary means. Byzantine medieval historiography was particularly marked by justifications that point to political utility in a way that is directly connected to the Polybean notion of history as a school of politics.[37] Procopius of Caesarea (ca 490–575), Justinian's court historian, justified his *Histories of the Wars* by arguing that he regarded the memory of the wars waged by Justinian as helpful to future generations, 'in case time should ever again place men under a similar stress'. 'For men', he continues, 'who purpose to enter upon a war or are preparing themselves for any kind of struggle may derive some benefit from a narrative of a similar situation in history'.[38]

Early Modern Theories of Historiography

Humanist historiography, with its concern with elegant writing and its increasing connections with source criticism, already evidences a profile distinct from that of medieval chroniclers, especially early-medieval ones.[39] At least regarding the general relationship with time, important differences started to take shape as some fourteenth-century Italian humanists began to cultivate the ideal of a 'renaissance' of classical antiquity. In contrast to medieval chroniclers, many humanists favoured a past that was long discontinued and saw themselves as nurturing its rebirth. This was the core of the historical sense inaugurated by Petrarch (1304–1374), which was marked by general condemnation of the Middle Ages as a barbaric time of darkness and simultaneous praise of classical antiquity as an epoch of radiance and glory. 'What else then is all history, if not the praise of Rome?' is a statement that perfectly synthesizes this view.[40] One can easily follow its unfolding through the sixteenth century and see that it has special resonance in the works of Niccolò Machiavelli (1469–1527), who once remarked: 'But any who, living at the present day in Italy or Greece, has not in Italy become an ultramontane or in Greece a Turk, has reason to complain of his own times, and to commend those others, in which there were many things which made them admirable.'[41]

Despite considerable differences, humanist historiography nonetheless remained as bound to the power of the past as its medieval counterpart, for if it indeed aimed at producing temporal discontinuity vis-à-vis the medieval inheritance, it attempted to do so only by reinvigorating a deceased past. In short, in the general perception of time that predominated in both epochs, there was no accurate sense of the qualitative difference between past and present. Machiavelli, again, testified to this in the preface to the second book of his *Discorsi,* where he crystal-clearly showed himself persuaded that 'the world, remaining continually the same, has in it a constant quality of good and evil'.[42] This was why he could be sure that even the introduction of technical novelties the ancients could not have known, like firearms,[43] would not make the the the military knowledge produced by classical antiquity obsolete but rather intensify its importance.[44]

Thus the continued ubiquity of the past precluded radical discontinuity in the itinerary of the exemplar theory of history as it entered the era of the Renaissance. Nevertheless, an important shift of emphasis to a more decisive political kind of historical exemplarity can be traced in the works of the two Florentine historians whose texts might be taken as the culmination of humanist historiography: Machiavelli himself, and Francesco Guicciardini (1483–1540). The prologues and introductory passages of their books evince an exemplar theory of history that very much resembles the one implicit in the introduction of Polybius's *Histories.* They and many other Italian historical scholars from the early sixteenth century assumed that historians indeed performed a didactic task, defined as equipollent to the instruction of relevant political actors. They thus postulated that histories should teach readers about correct political behaviour, as well as about the laws that govern the functioning of institutions. Ultimately, they perceived history as a means to enrich statecraft and took it as tantamount to state theory.[45]

Machiavelli's *History of Florence,* a book published between 1520 and 1525, holds synthetic evidence of that opinion. Discussing the general vicissitudes of empires, Machiavelli recalls that princes, heads of republics and military commanders, void of own *virtú,* bravery and patriotism, frequently deployed tricks and schemes so as to 'support a reputation they never deserved'. He finishes off the remark by noting that in historically addressing these political farces one might attain a kind of knowledge that 'will not be less useful than a knowledge of ancient history; for, if the latter excites the liberal mind to imitation, the former will show what ought to be avoided and decried.'[46] Noteworthy here is that Machiavelli presupposes a clear criterion for distinguishing the positive from the negative exemplarity associated with historiography: ancient cases are to be imitated, whereas the more contemporary cases he discusses throughout his text indicate what should be avoided. By the mid-sixteenth century, more-over, supporters of Machiavelli's general thesis regarding the political use of historical examples were easily found, even outside Italy. A case in point is the Spanish humanist Pero Mexia (1497–1551), who in 1545 published a history of Rome, justifying it with the argument that histories confront current kings and princes with the deeds of bygone rulers. 'In the histories', he affirmed, 'kings and princes find past monarchs whom they can emulate and with whom they can compete in virtues and excellences, as well as bad monarchs whose practices are avoidable and whose purposes and reputation teach what is not to be done.'[47]

To be sure, not every sixteenth-century humanist shared Machiavelli's enthusiasm for examples drawn from ancient history. Even his friend Guicciardini regarded the issue dubiously. Criticizing precisely the enthusiasm many of his Florentine contemporaries showed for Roman exempla, he remarked: 'What a mistake is theirs who cite on all occasions the example of the Romans! To do as the Romans did, we would need to have a city circumstanced like theirs. To attempt it with means so inferior as ours is to require of the ass the fleetness of the horse.'[48] This plea for caution in importing Roman examples was indeed representative of Guicciardini's more general doubts about the efficacy of historical examples: 'Remember what I said before: these ricordi should not be followed indiscriminately. In some particular case that presents different circumstances, they are of no use. Such cases cannot be covered by any rule, nor is there any book that teaches them.'[49] Here Guicciardini recalls the need for carefulness in deriving patterns of action from historical examples, for the circumstances of action are frequently asymmetrical, and contingency always plays a large role in shaping past and present events. Therefore, he strips the prudential generalizations conveyed in his *Ricordi* of universal validity – in other words, he admits that their exemplarity was not absolute. He nonetheless kept writing a book full of such generalizations, prescribing authorized ways to act derived from his experience as a statesman and historian – even as he remained sceptical as to whether this kind of prescriptive enterprise actually made sense.[50] This paradox surely indicates a significant change in historical exemplarity, but it is probably an insufficient basis for talking about a 'renaissance crisis of exemplarity'.[51] The same is more or less true of an even more radical sixteenth-century critic of exemplarity, Michel de Montaigne (1533–1592), in whose understanding 'every example is lame'.[52] Like Guicciardini, Montaigne had a very ambivalent relationship with exempla, for whereas he argued against the omnipresence of the exemplary tradition in rhetoric and literature, he did not manage to avoid resorting to exempla in his writings. This was probably so because in his day, exempla were still an inescapable cultural device.[53]

The political stream of the exemplar theory of history was still very much alive also in the seventeenth century. It shows up in Samuel Pufendorf's (1632–

1694) reminder that the study of history was particularly useful 'for those who design for employments in the State'.[54] And while Pufendorf related historiography to the instruction of political decision-makers and bureaucrats, Jacques Bossuet (1627–1704) had a much more restricted audience in mind when he expatiated on the use of historical knowledge: 'Even if history were useless to other men, princes should be made to read it. For there is no better way to show them what is wrought by passions and interest, time and circumstance, good and bad advice. Histories deal only with the deeds that concern princes, and everything in them seems to be made for their use. If they need experience to acquire the prudence of a good ruler, nothing is more useful for their instruction than to add the examples of past centuries to the experiences they have every day.'[55]

By early modern times, however, there were two generally differentiable intellectual roles for what is comprised today within the substantive historian. There were, on the one hand, those already mentioned authors who, under the influence of classical historians perceived as masters of rhetoric, composed historical narratives that frequently dealt with issues the audience was already familiar with, and to which they regularly ascribed some kind of edificatory function. On the other hand, there were scholars who, since the fifteenth century in many parts of Europe, specialized in investigating and analysing past sources.[56] The coexistence of these two different roles, and of the conflicts between them, has been a main constitutive tension in the history of historical thought ever since.[57]

In the early modern period, most source researchers were classical philologists or antiquarians. As already described, humanists of the fifteenth and sixteenth centuries played a revitalized image of classical antiquity against the medieval traditions that were temporally closer to them. They tended to despise medieval cultural achievements, preferring to hark back directly to the ancient classics and meanwhile purge them of what they considered to be medieval misinterpretations. This general attitude motivated humanist scholars – first in Italy and later in the North of Europe – to research materials related to the classical cultures and edit, re-edit, translate and comment on classical texts.[58] Other disciplines would soon adapt the methodical mindset developed by classical philologists to their own fields. By the mid-fifteenth century, the emergence of archaeology had prompted the philological method's extension to material remains from ancient times.[59] It did not take long for other disciplines, such as jurisprudence, ecclesiastical history and later on even theology, to incorporate critical principles into the way they dealt with their own canonical texts – respectively, law codes (especially the Roman), the writings of the early church fathers and the Bible.[60] The development of new methods of source research stimulated considerable progress in historical scholarship during the sixteenth and seventeenth centuries. A good deal of it was due to research efforts in the fields of ecclesiastical history and hagiography, and led to the production of annals and collections of documents that would become reputable reference books.[61] Many collections of medieval laws, political documents and literary texts were also published during this period, especially in France and Germany.[62] By the mid-seventeenth century, moreover, almost all the disciplines that modern historical science would take as its auxiliary sciences – such as numismatics, epigraphy, palaeography and diplomatics – either were founded or underwent great developments.

The new critical approach to historical sources and the new informational environment generated by new editions of documents, and in general by the diffusion of book printing, also influenced the kind of historiography written for pragmatic or political purposes. One of the first noticeable impacts the critical method had on traditional historiography was a certain destabilization of the authority of classical historians – something that was already quite evident in Guicciardini. In general, humanist pragmatic historians then and their modern-day counterparts employed very different working methods. Especially those who dealt with ancient history used to write their narratives strongly relying upon earlier stories written by classical authors. For a large branch of humanist historians, then, source criticism was a problem only in so far as they had to decide which of the classical accounts was the most reliable. Once this decision was made, the writing of history was more or less an issue of rephrasing a single author's account.[63] However, this traditional working method became increasingly questionable in light of the new critical attitude towards the sources. The confrontation between traditional historians and source researchers was not intensified until the end of the seventeenth century, but Lorenzo Valla (ca 1407–1457) had already had a hand in it when he demonstrated the existence of factual mistakes in Livy's account of the history of Rome.[64] Critiques like Valla's did not abolish rhetoric's traditional influence over historiography once and for all, but they definitely pushed historians to be more cautious in their use of historiographical sources. From this point on, historians started to relativize especially the classical accounts of the early history of cities and nations.[65]

In general, the new methods and techniques of informational criticism belonged to a different realm from that of the old exemplar theory of history. Antiquarians and archaeologists, for instance, did not directly strive to convey historical examples, and their literary models stemmed from the tradition of ancient geography rather than the historiographical tradition.[66] But in the late sixteenth and early seventeenth centuries, source research and historiography were conflated in the new kind of reflection on history and historiography embodied by the *ars historica* treatises. In the history of historical thought, the *artes historicae* were the first intensive efforts towards both the constitution of a theory of historical writing and clarification of the question of the value and function of histories.[67] It is thus reasonable to regard them as the most important precursors of modern historical theory.[68] Until the mid-sixteenth century, the available systematic meta-historical literature was, in fact, very scarce – especially if one disregards prefaces and introductory parts of historical texts. But after the boom in humanistic historiography and, in the Catholic areas of Europe, the Council of Trent (1545–1563), theory was suddenly in vogue.[69] The clearest evidence of that was the publication of the anthology *The Treasury of Historical Art* (*Artis Historicae Penus*) in 1579.[70]

In their conventional variant, the *ars historica* treatises discussed the principles governing the production of historical texts. They addressed issues such as the specificity of historiography among the literary genres, the authoritative character of classical historiography, the proper way to present history and narrate events, the convenience of employing direct speech, adequate writing style, and so on. However, some of the *artes historicae,* such as those written by François Baudouin (1520–1573), Jean Bodin (1530–1596) and Francesco Patrizi (1529–1597), were marked by both a clear hermeneutical approach and an almost surprising emphasis on the reception of historical texts. The principles they delivered concerned the reading of historical texts rather than the canons of effective writing.[71] Anthony Grafton has recently argued that particularly the *artes historicae* of that second type represented an attempt to conciliate the methodical attitude typical of antiquarian and philological research with pragmatic historiography.[72] He points out that Baudouin, Bodin and Patrizi actually argued for the necessity of combining the reading of classical historians with critical correction and amendment of their texts through complementary research into all kinds of textual and material sources.[73]

But for all that, the way the writers of the *artes historicae* talked about the function of historiography remained circumscribed to the tradition of the exemplar theory of history. For those authors, the historian's major task was neither to extensively conduct source research nor to exhaustively detail the facts being addressed.[74] In their understanding, history's pragmatic effect on moral and political life had much greater importance than objective knowledge of the facts. Take, for instance, the most famous of the treatises on the art of history: Jean Bodin's *Method for the Easy Comprehension of History* (1566). Bodin emphasizes that historical knowledge should derive from critical evaluation and treatment of information accruing from historical texts and material sources. But he nevertheless advises readers to use a kind of 'notebook method' to organize and process historical information: scholars should keep notebooks for themselves in which they write down quotes extracted from the historical texts they read. The events and actions related with these quotes should be further classified into categories such as 'shameful, honourable, useful, and useless'.[75] The headings he suggests show clearly that his idea was that every reader would have a sort of personal book of virtues illustrated by past experience. This is, to be sure, a very exciting idea, but when all is said and done it remains very much within the boundaries of the exemplar theory of history.[76]

Bodin's case indicates that, far from ignoring methodical principles, early modern historical thinkers even seriously attempted to incorporate these principles into their narratives and theoretical reflections. But it also shows that their ultimate priorities were other than the critique of historical examples or the production of factual knowledge.[77] Interestingly enough – as Bodin's *Methodus* again illustrates – a good part of the early modern tradition of both critical research and methodological reflection emerged in strong linkage with exemplary assumptions and purposes.[78] Those humanists working instead to compile historical facts were frequently regarded (and often also regarded themselves) as merely performing a secondary work. Sometimes their final aim was only to provide raw materials to the 'true historians' – other scholars who would be able to transfer the facts established by critical research into the structure of a narrative emulating the classical models and filled with moral and/or political guidance.[79] Additionally, whereas some potential criticism of the pragmatic conception of historiography really arose from scholars oriented towards collecting, verifying and interpreting sources, it must be also recalled that it took a long time for such criticism to be established as general currency.[80]

Actually, the *ars historica* literature represented a first attempt to systematically combine the exemplar sense of history with the research practices inspired by the development of the philological method. In the decades around 1600, it embodied a quite successful attempt that helped awaken a good deal of interest in historical issues and promote a certain institutionalization of the historical discipline at schools and universities.[81] But that wave of interest did not last long, being soon supplanted by a renewed interest in politics.[82] During the seventeenth century, political historiography followed the new fashion, remaining clearly isolated from the heritage of the *ars historica* tradition.[83] Politics replaced rhetorics as the academic field exerting tutelage over historiography. Historians, however, continued to justify their works by resorting to the old exemplary arguments, not least because these were as suitable then as they had been before. All this contributed to enlarging the gap between the intellectual practices of philologists and antiquarians on the one hand, and those of political historians on the other. The division of labour between writers of moralizing (or politicizing) narratives and source researchers was, therefore, strongly reinforced. In his *Ars critica*, published in 1697, Jean Le Clerc (1657–1736) very clearly defined that opposition of intellectual roles: 'Those who have composed histories from ancient sources fall into two categories.... Some try to work out the truth, so far as that is possible, and examine everything diligently, so that, when it is impossible to produce a certain account, they follow the more plausible narrative. Others take little interest in the truth, and choose instead to report the greatest possible marvels, since these are more susceptible of rhetorical adornment, and supply the matter for exercises in the high style.'[84]

The tensions between pragmatists and source researchers intensified once again at the end of the seventeenth century, within the context of the Quarrel of the Ancients and the Moderns.[85] Still, the exemplar theory of history was kept very much alive, at least until the late eighteenth century, and most of the leading figures of the Enlightenment subscribed to it while dealing with history's general issues.[86] In the 'philosophic' or 'conjectural' histories that by then had come into vogue, the superiority of the moderns vis-à-vis the ancients was finally accepted, and the general progress of human societies was held as a strong possibility, if not an inevitability. Nevertheless, since the idea of an essentially constant human nature prevailed in the intellectual landscape of the European eighteenth-century, historians did not have much trouble justifying their intellectual activity by means of the exemplary discourse.[87] Lord Bolingbroke's (1678–1751) *Letters on the Study and Use of History,* published in 1735, is probably the most direct and extensive defence of the exemplar theory of history ever conceived in the era of the Enlightenment.[88] Two of his main adversaries are critical philology and antiquarianism. Against them, Bolingbroke states that human curiosity should be related to knowledge not as an end in itself, but only as a means to an extrinsic purpose. According to him, historiography should serve the practical task of improving private and public virtues; it should 'make us better men and citizens'. Otherwise, even the most cautions investigation into the past would be 'at best but a specious and ingenious sort of idleness … and the knowledge we acquire by it is a creditable kind of ignorance, nothing more.'[89] Bolingbroke furthermore devised a plea for education by examples instead of education by precepts: 'Such is the imperfection of human understanding … that abstract or general propositions, though ever so true, appear obscure or doubtful to us very often, till they are explained by examples: and that the wisest lessons in favour of virtue go but a little way to convince the judgement, and determine the will, unless they are enforced by the same means.'[90]

In his passionate defence of historiography's utility for practical life, Bolingbroke clearly inverted Machiavelli's position, according to which positive examples were to be found in the study of ancient history whereas the histories of more recent events provided models of what not to do. Bolingbroke invites his addressee to put ancient history on hold and turn to the study of 'the more entire as well as more authentic histories of the ages more modern'. For him, only these histories are able to convey to the reader a true sense of how it really was to live in the studied past. Bolingbroke then concludes that only histories of more recent pasts can actually fulfil an exemplary function: 'Thus history', he argues, bearing modern history in mind, 'becomes what she ought to be, and what she has been sometimes called, "magistra vitae", the mistress, like philosophy, of human life. If she is not this, she is at best "nuntia vetustatis", the gazette of antiquity, or a dry register of useless anecdotes.'[91] Among the sub-scribers to this opinion was none other than Voltaire (1694–1778), who prob-ably was influenced by his friend Bolingbroke. Voltaire introduced the subject matter of his *The Age of Louis XIV* (1751) as 'an example for the centuries to come'.[92] Pierre Force has shown that at stake here was actually the consolida-tion of a sense of historical exemplarity based on temporal and geographical proximity, instead of distance. In addition, he argues that Voltaire was also re-shaping historical exemplarity by transferring the subject of imitation from past personalities to an entire century, since for him the example was to be found not so much in Louis XIV as in the entire epoch his name symbolizes. As can be seen, Voltaire's is a kind of presentist exemplar theory of history.[93]

By then, the situation was not much different in Scotland. Despite their sophisticated insights into historical causality, their improved sense of process and their emphasis on universality, the historians of the Scottish Enlighten-ment, too, usually resorted to conventional exemplary justifications. Authors like Adam Ferguson (1723–1816), David Hume (1711–1776) and William Robertson (1721–1793) still felt obliged to educate the political leadership by means of historical examples that would foster virtues and hamper vices. Curiously, by insisting on this edificatory function, they put themselves in broad continuity with the local Calvinist and humanist traditions that many eighteenth-century Scottish historians actually intended to break with.[94] Rob-ert Heron (1764–1807) may be taken as paradigmatic of his contemporaries' widespread attitude with his remark that 'every coffee-house critic can tell you that History is the best school of morality'.[95]

Modernity and Historical Exemplarity

The above-ventured excursion along more than twenty centuries in the history of historiography's justification is not, of course, a specialized account of the issues concerned. Actually, the validity of the overarching kind of story I have decided to develop, with its huge time span, its several complicated time leaps and its sometimes unavoidable superficiality, is easily cast into doubt by spe-cialists on the many issues, epochs and places concerned therein. Yet I believe it was worth the risk, as it enables me to give some historical concreteness to two theses that, more often than not in the meta-historical debate, are merely taken for granted as theoretical assumptions. The first is that the ascription of an exemplary function to historiography is a very important feature of virtually all epochs of Western historical thought. And the second is that in the West, at least up until the late eighteenth century, rather few authors seem to have been concerned with systematically building up justifications that could rebut and replace the exemplar theory of history.[96] I have tried to argue that both theses make sense, and that they are empirically plausible in light of what certain important ancient, medieval and early modern intellectuals stated on the issue of the nature and the significance of historiography. In so doing, I have tried to follow Lord Acton's advice – later reissued by Robin Collingwood – that the historian should 'study problems in preference to periods'.[97]

However, having accepted those two theses as valid, one is automatically led to the following question: Why did a significant number of historians and historical thinkers from the late eighteenth century on start to perceive historical examples as an inadequate vehicle for historical learning? There are reasons to believe that the relative obsolescence of the exemplar theories of history resulted more from a general cultural change than from a shift in the much more particular realm of methodical technologies for dealing with information about the past. I think this change occurred in the age of the Enlightenment and concerned cultural patterns that frame the way individuals experience time. Many historians and sociologists regard this shift as one of the most manifest signals of the dawn of modernity. German scholars frequently refer to it with the term *temporalization* (*Verzeitlichung*).

Variants of the temporalization thesis were developed by the historians Arthur Lovejoy and Friedrich Meinecke, the philosopher Michel Foucault and the sociologists Niklas Luhmann and Wolf Lepenies, among others.[98] But in recent decades, the most prominent advocate of the temporalization thesis has doubtless been Reinhart Koselleck. A good part of Koselleck's work was dedicated to investigating how temporalization affects the way social and political concepts are structured.[99] As the chief editor of the *Geschichtliche Grundbegriffe,* one of the most successful collective enterprises of the German human sciences in the second half of the twentieth century, Koselleck argued that temporalization is a distinctive feature of many of the most significant concepts that formed the modern sociopolitical vocabulary. Before I try to delineate what this temporalization actually means and how it relates to the issue of the justification of historiography, I will note that Koselleck traced the shift towards temporalized (ergo, modern) sociopolitical concepts back to the period 1750–1850, that is, to the period he initially referred to as the '*Sattelzeit*' (saddle period).[100] Koselleck himself later disavowed this expression,[101] but it clearly shows that the kind of conceptual history he projected was not mainly focused on either the periods before the Enlightenment or developments that took place from the late nineteenth century on. It centred instead on a transitional period, more specifically, the period in which modern concepts were taking the approximate shape they display to date – or at least until the time Koselleck was investigating them, the late 1960s. As he would clarify, his choice to shed light on the period 1750–1850 was intimately related to the purpose of understanding his own present; it was, to use the German term he himself employed, *gegenwartsbezogen*.[102]

Koselleck assumes that the key concepts of his contemporary world sprang up in connection with the political, social, economic and technical transformations that took place in the decades around 1800. He argues that all these changes went hand in hand with the genesis of a new perception of time characterized by the experience of radical sociopolitical change, and hence by an heightened sense of the singularity of the present vis-à-vis the past, as well as of temporal acceleration.[103] As Theo Jung recently recalled, Koselleck's notion of *Verzeitlichung* goes beyond the framework of the history of concepts. It is in fact the keystone of a 'theory of modernity' structured upon the diagnosis that, in this period, future expectations were wrenched away from past experience.[104] Koselleck himself addressed this point as follows: 'The burden of our historical thesis is that in the *Neuzeit* the difference between experience and expectation is increasingly enlarged; more precisely, that *Neuzeit* is conceived as a *neue Zeit* only from the point at which eager expectations diverge and remove themselves from all previous experience.'[105]

It is precisely this experience of a gap between past and future, emphasized by Koselleck, that Karl Marx and Friedrich Engels (1820–1895) articulated in their famous remark that, in the 'bourgeois epoch', 'all that is solid melts into air'.[106] Here both were stressing that they saw the acceleration of time and the temporalization of experience as a novelty entirely of their own contemporary age, and at least regarding this point, several other authors affiliated to various political credos would have absolutely agreed. Edmund Burke (1729–1797), who is frequently mentioned as the father of modern political conservatism, saw the French revolution as 'the most astonishing that has hitherto happened in the world'. Its advocates had, he maintained, 'wrought under-ground a mine that will blow up at one grand explosion all examples of antiquity, all precedents, charters, and acts of parliament'.[107] A similar diagnosis of the uniqueness of the modern world as generated by the revolutions of the late eighteenth century is found in the last chapter of the liberal-conservative Alexis de Tocqueville's (1805–1859) *Democracy in America,* where he states: 'Although the ongoing revolution in man's social state, laws, ideas, and sentiments is still far from over, it is already clear that its works cannot be compared with anything the world has ever seen before. Looking back century by century to remotest Antiquity, I see nothing that resembles what I see before me. When the past is no longer capable of shedding light on the future, the mind can only proceed in darkness.'[108]

Of course, in comparison with Marx and Engels, both Tocqueville and Burke were much less certain about whether the abyss that had opened between past and future by the end of the eighteenth century would actually lead to a general enlargement of human freedom.[109] But they all agreed that after the Declaration of Independence of the United States and the materialization of the idea of popular sovereignty it sponsored, something substantially new was going on in world history, something Ranke once cryptically referred to as 'the complete reversal of the principle' (*völlige Umkehr des Prinzips*).[110] Similar evaluations abound also in Droysen's texts on contemporary history, which will be analysed in detail in Chapter 4. Writing in 1843, for instance, he stressed his opinion that he and his contemporaries were living amidst a revolution, initiated some decades before, that had begun to change the general configuration of the whole world. 'Never before', he argued, 'as far as historical memory can reach, there were developments of such an immense amplitude; were there changes that so deeply affected the lowest population strata'.[111]

The origins of the experiences of discontinuity attested by all these statements are, according to Koselleck, traceable to the second half of the eighteenth century. Since then, as he puts it, 'time is no longer simply the medium in which all histories take place; it gains a historical quality. Consequently, history no longer occurs in, but through, time'.[112] Clearly, here Koselleck is incorporating into his general thesis – on the modern world as a world in which experience and concepts underwent a fundamental 'temporalization' – a more specific interpretation of a key concept that is closely related to the modern experience of time: that of history. This history of the concept of history focuses on the development of modern German, starting from the observation that before the mid-eighteenth century, the German equivalents of 'history', *Historie* and *Geschichte,* lacked one of the meanings they currently possess. In their semantic fields one would notice the absence of the ideas of history as a synthesis of 'all past and future experience',[113] and as a general, abstract, dynamic process that leads humankind from the past into an open future – that is, a future not limited by any apocalyptic belief that the end of the world is near. These meanings, Koselleck argues, lends the modern concept of history its most distinguishing trademark.

To understand the specificities that Koselleck identifies in this modern notion of history as a general process, it is helpful to contrast it with a concept of history largely used during the Middle Ages. Curiously, it is the latter that comprises a clearer distinction between past events on the one hand, and accounts of past events on the other.[114] Actually, medieval Latin-writing authors tended to link the idea of history only to the historiographical form of speech on things past, not to the things past themselves. This tendency is documented in the famous distinction between *res gestae* (the things that happened) and *historia rerum gestarum* (the history or narrative of the things happened). The same tendency is perceptible in late-medieval German, for as Koselleck notes, the term *Geschichte,* or rather the plural form *die Geschichte(n),* was frequently used as a reference to 'past events', that is, as equivalent to *res gestae.* At the same time, *Historie* referred to 'accounts of past events', occupying more or less the same semantic field as the expression *historia rerum gestarum.*[115]

According to Koselleck, all these features bespeak of a linguistic horizon on which the modern concept of history – with its reference to a continuous and future-oriented development of the human race – could not have existed. Within this context, expressions that were typical of modern historical thought, such as 'history as such' (*Geschichte schlechthin, Geschichte an sich, Geschichte selbst, Geschichte überhaupt*), or 'the History beyond the histories', would not have made any sense.[116] That horizon, Koselleck argues, changed substantially only within the course of the eighteenth century. Only then would the singular form *die Geschichte* have gained predominance over plural forms like *die Geschichte(n)* or *die Historien,* forms that were associated more with concrete subjects (Charles the Great or France, to mention Koselleck's own examples) than with an abstract 'history as such'.[117] Hence, Koselleck continues, only after 1750 did the notion of history become a truly abstract and temporalized meta-concept, now encompassing not only single accounts of human events but also 'the condition of possibility of all single histories', that is, the historical process in its entirety.[118] At the same time, the term *Geschichte* in particular would have begun to entangle *res gestae* and *historia rerum gestarum* so that the two meanings were no longer differentiable.[119] Between the mid-eighteenth century and the late nineteenth century, philosophy of history, universal history and world history became, Koselleck states, the intellectual fields and narrative models according to which the new concept of history was developed and popularized. By these means, it ended up gaining massive currency within modern social and political discourses.

Koselleck applied a quite ingenious classification to the modern concept of history, whose emergence he intended to clarify. Referring to the fact that in one of its modern meanings, the singular noun *Geschichte* comprises all possible singular histories, he presented this concept as a 'collective singular' (*Kollektivsingular*). However, in recent years, a criticism that cannot be easily dismissed has been levelled against part of the empirical findings and methodical procedures on which Koselleck based his interpretation of the genesis of this collective singular concept of history. Some of the most conspicuous critiques came from Jan Marco Sawilla, who has managed to demonstrate, among other things, that equivalents to the term 'history' were already used in singular form and already referred to both 'past reality' and 'accounts of past reality' well before the German *Sattelzeit*.[120] Relying on French sources from the second half of the seventeenth century, which Koselleck had neglected, Sawilla documents that the French term *histoire* was already invested with many of the meanings displayed by Koselleck's collective singular. Sawilla also criticizes Koselleck's account for having set a general chronology for the emergence of the modern concept of history that focuses almost exclusively on the German word *Geschichte*. As Koselleck did not seriously consider the development of terms such as the Latin *historia* and the French *histoire,* he would have tended to overlook their influence on the history of the German words *Geschichte* and *Historie* – an influence that was actually rather broad in early modern times, as intellectuals in many regions of the *Reich* largely used Latin and then French for written communication. Koselleck's analysis would hence run to a 'story of the triumph of the German lexeme', and Sawilla even suggests that this emphasis on *Geschichte* is actually evidence of Koselleck's proximity to a nationalistic perspective on the history of the German language.[121]

As already indicated, one amazing feature of Koselleck's interpretation of the history of the concept of history is that it manages to set the history of a word and the history of an idea together, under the same chronology and against the backdrop of a social-historical theory of modernization. He argues that the temporalization of the idea of history coincided with a major semantic shift related to the term *Geschichte,* and furthermore that both processes had been set in motion by 1750, reaching a peak more or less while the political, economic, social and technical revolutions that inaugurated modernity were also under way. After refuting substantial sections of Koselleck's history of the words *Geschichte* and *Historie,* Sawilla thus concludes that 'the knots' between the history of the word 'history' (*Geschichte*) and the history of the idea of history 'must be untied'.[122] My explanation of why historical examples became subject to unprecedented criticism as of the end of the eighteenth century follows that proposition. Here I am siding with some recent analysts who have attempted to reassess Koselleck's interpretation after carefully attending to Sawilla's criticism of it. In conclusion, I think the core of Koselleck's temporalization hypothesis holds, even if it requires complemention or further differentiation, and even though the conceptual history he connected to it exhibits the problems mentioned above.[123]

The temporalization of the idea of history that started in the age of the Enlightenment and was reflected in the modern philosophies of history of the late eighteenth and nineteenth centuries was a main cause of the intensification of criticism of historical exemplarity.[124] The spread of a sense of living in a radically new age led philosophers, philologists and historians to adopt an unprecedented attitude of temporalization vis-à-vis past and present. Present and past epochs then came to be seen in terms of their uniqueness, and cultural singularities were brought into focus. Proper historicization of past and present thus actually began. This new sensibility regarding the qualitative difference between past, present and future had no parallel in former conceptions of history. Take, for instance, the case of several early modern humanist historians. Of course, they all knew that their ancient role models and anti-heroes belonged to a different time.[125] Nonetheless, they normally refrained from stressing the difference between their times and those of the classical authors they so much admired. Rather, they idealized classical antiquity as the scene of high cultural and moral standards that should be attained once again in the present. Therefore, they imagined the future not as a time leading to a qualitative novelty but rather as the recurrence of the already lived.[126]

Generally speaking, exemplar theories of history did not combine well with conceptions of history that emphasized the qualitative difference between present, past and future.[127] Indeed, the temporalized notion of history and historiography that, according to Koselleck, emerged in the second half of the eighteenth century did not automatically abolish the old exemplar justifications. Still – at least for those who subscribed to it – it made the past increasingly less immediately relevant to the present.[128] As a result, many historical authors reached the conclusion that past examples were no longer applicable in the way they had been before.

New Arguments on the Use of History

It did not take long for the discontent with historiography's exemplary justification to find some prominent advocates. In 1815, the jurist Friedrich Carl von Savigny (1779–1861) criticized what he labelled as the 'unhistorical school' of law for using history as a mere collection of moral and political examples. As an alternative, he defended a historical approach to law, which for him was 'the only way to a true knowledge of our situation'.[129] In the 1820s, Wilhelm von Humboldt stated that 'history does not primarily serve us by showing us through specific examples, often misleading and rarely enlightening, what to do and what to avoid'.[130] Hegel would stress the same point, arguing that the only thing history could teach was that 'peoples and governments never have learned anything from history'.[131] 'Each period' – he continued – 'is involved in such peculiar circumstances, exhibits a condition of things so strictly idiosyncratic, that its conduct must be regulated by considerations connected with itself, and itself alone'.[132]

For Savigny, Humboldt and Hegel, as well as some other authors throughout the late eighteenth and nineteenth centuries, history was no longer the *magistra vitae*. The temporalized conceptual atmosphere to which they were attached, with its emphasis on the singularity of the present experience vis-à-vis the past, turned the redefinition of historiography's function into an urgent matter. In fact, many of the leading historical thinkers of the period under consideration agreed on that sense of urgency, although the new justifications with which they sought to replace the exemplar theory of history still largely varied. Late eighteenth- and nineteenth-century authors used at least four distinct types of strategies in attempting to deal with the mounting criticism of historical exemplarity. The first gravitates around the argument that historical knowledge is an end in itself and therefore may be called the *autotelic strategy*.

Its most famous representative is Leopold von Ranke. The second was used by authors who saw no reason to question the validity of historical examples and thus subscribed to *traditional historiographical pragmatism*. The third tendency is not even a tendency because it was the preference of only one author, albeit a very influential one, Friedrich Nietzsche, whose arguments ran in a direction that may be called (for lack of a better term) *aesthetical pragmatism*. The final strategy, and the one I associate Droysen with, is characterized by the attempt to conciliate the modern historical perspective with old ideas on the practical value of historiography. It will be referred to as the *neo-pragmatic strategy*.

(1) Maybe the most basic thing one can assert about the exemplary justifications for historiography is that all of them present this intellectual practice as a means to an end located outside it, and not as something that is performed for its own sake.[133] In the nineteenth century, Ranke was probably the most prominent author to try to turn this issue upside down. Curiously, a good departing point for accessing the way he defined the question of the purpose of doing historiography is precisely his most well-known quote. This shows up in the preamble of his *History of the Latin and German Nations between 1494 and 1535,* the book published in 1824 with which the young Ranke established his reputation on the German historiographical scene.[134] It reads as follows: 'To history has been attributed the office to judge the past and to instruct the present to make its future useful. At such high functions this present attempt does not aim – it merely wants to show how things really were.'[135]

The view on the function of historical knowledge expressed in the quote runs through Ranke's entire intellectual biography.[136] In 1854, for instance, after delivering one of several private lectures *On the Epochs of Modern History* to the Bavarian king Maximilian II, Ranke had to deal with a trivial but indeed difficult question. The king wanted to know whether there were more morally developed individuals in the present than in the past. Ranke answered in the affirmative, adding to the king's suggestion the prognosis that, in the future, the ideal of humankind (*Menschheit*) would probably be expanded towards all nations, and concluding that this would be then a real moral progress. But he quickly departed from the role of a substantive philosopher of history, pointing out that historians could neither contradict nor empirically demonstrate the former assumption of the expansion of the idea of humankind. For him, such an assumption should never permeate the work of historians. 'We should be wary to not turn this view into the principle of history', he said, concluding, 'Our task is merely to stick to the object.'[137]

Like Hegel and Humboldt, Ranke advanced the view that the main point of researching and writing history should not be to compile an inventory of perennially valid examples. His positive answer on what was or should be the task of historians was, though, a very peculiar one. In short, he postulates historical knowledge as an end in itself. In the quotes above, he advocates that historians should have no goal other than to produce knowledge about the past, and that they should not attempt to exert direct influence over moral or political life. Thus, he argues in a sense that historical science should be useless – or, better, that it has no pragmatic value. Ranke admitted that history was about the constitution of the present as well as about the past, but he expressly denied that it should somehow be related to practical interests borrowed from the present: 'To incorporate present interests to the historical work normally means to compromise it'.[138] 'True history', he asserts, can succeed in striving after 'visions of the objective' only if it elevates itself above all partisanship. According to him, the task of historians is indeed of a moral and even religious nature, but this does not imply they should take sides and judge the past according to their own moral and religious values – quite the contrary, historians' moral and religious obligation is rather to somehow methodically suspend their own judgement so as to be able to recognize the validity of other moral and religious orders. Only thus is it possible to do justice to the investigated pasts.[139]

To say that Ranke argued for the self-sufficiency of historical knowledge vis-à-vis its older practical applications does not imply the conclusion that he actually succeeded in 'erasing his own self' from his scholarly work, as he himself wished he had.[140] In point of fact, his theoretical plea for historians' objectivity and even neutrality remained in strong tension with political and religious bearings that are implicit in his historiography: his conservative criticism of the French revolution, his commitment to the idea of a German nation, his idealization of Prussia as the saviour of Protestant Germany, his providentialist view of the role of the nation state, and so on.[141] Hence Ranke's historiography is not at all free of ethical or political assumptions, and in this regard I can only agree with Arnaldo Momigliano's observation that 'what history-writing without moral judgments would be is difficult for me to envisage, because I have not yet seen it'.[142] Still, even though Ranke's texts display commitments to specific political, ethical and religious values, on a theoretical level it remains true that he strongly emphasized that history should be researched and written primarily for its own sake.

Ranke's use of such an autotelic strategy against the exemplar theory of history was hardly an isolated case in the context of German nineteenth-century historical thought. Wilhelm Wachsmuth (1784–1866), for instance, in his *Outline of a Theory of History* (*Entwurf einer Theorie der Geschichte,* 1820), purported that 'history, as an image of life ... has its purpose located nowhere else but in itself'.[143] And as early as 1803, Karl Ludwig von Woltmann (1770–1817) had completed the critique against the preponderance of moral and political viewpoints in history by affirming that 'moral and patriotic enthusiasm could only be the cause of one's interest in history, but never its final purpose.'[144] Finally, by the end of the century, the famous methodologist Ernst Bernheim observed that a truly scientific (*wissenschaftlich*) and objective approach to historical issues was a novelty originating in recent times. He then claimed that such an approach came about only after history had acquitted itself of its old 'practical tendencies' and historians had started to conduct research purely for the sake of knowledge.[145]

(2) By criticizing the old 'practical tendencies' in history writing, and by justifying the study of history as something to be done for its own sake, Bernheim, Ranke and others forged a new answer to the problem of the function of historiography that soon became a frequent way for historians to justify their work.[146] However, this relative popularity may end up concealing alternative justifications that also played an important role in the history of modern historical thought. One of them, based on a certain devaluation of the achievements of modern historical research, called for a reawakening of historiography's traditional rhetorical and ethical functions. This attitude had already been anticipated by Bolingbroke, who in 1752 claimed that he would 'rather take the Darius whom Alexander conquered, for the son of Hystaspes, and make as many anachronisms as a Jewish chronologer, than sacrifice half my life to collect all the learned lumber that fills the head of an antiquary'.[147] Some late eighteenth- and early nineteenth-century authors would essentially have agreed with this statement. Blanke, Fleischer and Rüsen, in their extensive investigation of German historical theorists who were active during the period from 1750 to 1900, identified a branch of historians who, like Bolingbroke himself, did not reject the Ciceronian dictum '*historia, magistra vitae*'. Authors and texts belonging in this bracket are, for instance, Siegmund Jakob Baumgarten's *Übersetzung der Allgemeinen Welthistorie* (1744), Georg Andreas Will's *Einleitung in die historische Gelahrtheit* (1766) and Karl von Rotteck's *Allgemeine Geschichte* (1812).[148] An illustrative quote from the latter reasserts that 'history cannot be anything else but a teacher of wisdom, justice and virtue.'[149]

(3) The best known single nineteenth-century text on the value and function of historiography, Friedrich Nietzsche's 'untimely meditation' 'On the Uses and Disadvantages of History for Life' (1874), can give the impression of stemming from the same kind of historiographical pragmatism that underpins Bolingbroke's and Rotteck's statements. In that essay, Nietzsche's attack on what he defines as the contemporary 'fever of history' clearly denotes both a hostility towards factual scholarship and a wish that historiography be practiced not as an end in itself but rather as a means for enhancing the human capacity to act properly in the world. Ultimately, his argument is that the expansion of historical scholarship that his own time and society were experiencing was not a culturally sound tendency. The excess of critical knowledge about the past, he claims, had led to a dangerous mood 'through which the forces of life are paralyzed and at last destroyed'.[150] Excessive historical knowledge has the effect of weakening the individual's personality, for as it extirpates mythological illusions it also extirpates human instincts. Peoples and nations consisting of

individuals tormented by this infinitude of historical facts and cultural perspectives would never be able to reach full maturity. 'All living things', concludes Nietzsche, 'require an atmosphere around them, a mysterious misty vapour; if they are deprived of this envelope, if a religion, an art, a genius is condemned to revolve as a star without an atmosphere, we should no longer be surprised if they quickly wither and grow hard and unfruitful. It is the same with all great things, "which never succeed without some illusion"'.[151]

It is clear that, Nietzsche decisively rejects an autotelic definition for the function of historical knowledge, coming very close to rejecting the whole idea of knowing the past historically. Having done so, he – or more precisely, the Nietzsche of the second *Untimely Meditation,* since he would change his opinion later on – can be regarded as the nineteenth century's most prominent critic of historicism (which here refers to both the general perspective structuring the interpretation of human reality in its temporal dynamics and the scholarly movement that leads to a substantial increase in factual knowledge on the past). According to Nietzsche, the emergence of historicism had contributed significantly to what he perceived as the biggest problem of his contemporary world: the disempowerment of myth. Ultimately, Nietzsche criticizes historiography for enfeebling human artistic capacities and obstructing a reconstruction of mythical consciousness. For him, humankind could only be saved from the deep cultural crisis he perceived it to be in by enforcing an artistic social ethos and a return to a mythical way of making sense of the world. In fact, this aspiration that myth and the arts would again provide culture with a firm foundation is traceable in virtually all his texts.[152]

Nietzsche held that contemporary practitioners of the science of history were entirely unaware that human life is just as much about forgetting as it is about remembering.[153] Nevertheless, he stopped short of intending to totally abolish critical research on past sources. His plea was rather for reallocating it under the 'supreme direction of the ends of life'. Hence, the topmost criterion governing the writing of history should be neither the ideal of showing how things really are, nor the desire to understand the past for the pure sake of it. In reality, according to Nietzsche, that criterion should somehow be brought from the future back into the present. Historians should then see themselves as 'architects of the future', and only as such would they be able to make proper use of the past. The past, for him, lacks a fixed meaning that historians can merely recover by making use of methodical technologies. Instead, it should be approached as an 'oracle' – as a set of symbols that can be moulded into future expectations[154] – so as to empower individuals and nations, and help them build a 'happier and fairer culture and humanity'.[155]

It is easy to admit that the historical theory contained in the second *Untimely Meditation* is an exhortation, both for the revival of an old heroic world view and against the prevalence of the factual in historical culture. Nietzsche made this point explicit by suggesting that one of the proper uses of history is the conveyance of models for present action. History should communicate knowledge on the action of the 'great men'; it should become again a repository of examples suited to offer guidance for life. It should focus on the heroes who will inspire contemporary human beings not only to become properly mature, but also to flee from what he regarded as the 'paralysing upbringing of the present age'. 'Satiate your soul with Plutarch', he proposed, 'and when you believe in his heroes dare at the same time to believe in yourself. With a hundred such men – raised in this unmodern way, that is to say become mature and accustomed to the heroic – the whole noisy sham-culture of our age could now be silenced for ever.'[156] In this way Nietzsche believed himself to be preparing the terrain for an ultimately cultural-critical project: the rejection of the Jewish-Christian linear view of time and its replacement with a putatively neo-pagan notion of eternal recurrence.[157]

However, in the light of most of the statements presented in the last paragraphs, I think it is clear that Nietzsche's argument, overall, does not fit well with traditional historiographical pragmatism. Although his assertions are indeed pragmatic, their pragmatism is quite unconventional in that it is heavily dependent on an aestheticist attitude and an ideal of 'returning to myth' that are typically modern. For this reason, it would probably not be correct to characterize Nietzsche's view as an unmodern or anti-modern alternative to the exemplar theory of history.[158] Labelling it with simple terms may therefore remain an unsolved problem – certainly the term 'aesthetic pragmatism' as used above offers no definitive solution. Moreover, the difficulties of characterizing Nietzsche's attitude towards history and historiography are only deepened by the fact that, shortly after finishing the second 'untimely meditation', he revised several essential aspects of his critique.[159] From 1875 on, he underwent a sort of naturalistic turn, discontinuing his hostility towards the historical approach and scholarship. Praise for the significance of historical scholarship, criticism of philosophers' lack of 'historical sensibility', application of a genuinely historical perspective (such as in *The Genealogy of Morality*, 1887): all these features frequently appeared in the post-1875 works of Nietzsche.[160] Therefore Nietzsche's work, seen as a whole, does not represent a frontal attack on modern historical perspective and methodology, even though several quotes from the second 'untimely meditation' disprove this.[161]

(4) The last group of arguments on the function of historiography I will cover encompasses attempts to tackle the growing gap between critical source analysis and the kind of cultural orientation traditionally provided by historical narratives – a feat, by the way, that the theorists of the *ars historica* tradition had already attempted in the sixteenth and seventeenth centuries. For lack of a better term, this tendency might be called 'neo-pragmatic'. The first advocates of a neo-pragmatic alternative to the exemplar theory of history are found among

the historians of the late German Enlightenment, but many leading figures of nineteenth-century German historiography also subscribed to it. It is within this tendency that Droysen's definitions of the functions of historical studies will finally be located.

Basically, the great novelty introduced by neo-pragmatist historical thinkers was the sense that there could be non-exemplar uses for history – that is, that one could accept the critiques of the validity of historical examples yet continue to affirm history's usefulness. The late eighteenth-century historical thinkers who started developing the neo-pragmatic approach were historians who saw themselves in connection to the *Aufklärung*. In general, they rejected both the exaggerated empiricism of the so-called poly-historians of the seventeenth century and the anti-empirical pragmatism typical of earlier thinkers of the Western Enlightenment. According to Peter Reill, the predominant idea of history among historical *Aufklärers* actually represented an attempt to mediate between empiricism and pragmatism.[162] Authors like Johann David Michaelis (1717–1791), Johann Cristoph Gatterer (1727–1799) and many others even resorted to the term 'pragmatic history' to define their own intellectual endeavours. However, this use of terminology was indicative of much more than a mere attempt to retrieve the old pragmatism, such as that ventured by Bolingbroke. On the one hand, the historians of the German late Enlightenment intended to differentiate their historical approach from that of the poly-historians, scholars whom the former thought intellectually naive, deeming them mere producers of empirical knowledge. The *Aufklärers* supported a much more ambitious conception of historiography that claimed to have assimilated the methods of critical research developed since the beginning of early modern times, and, at the same time, to have subordinated these methods to practical values and purposes. On the other hand, however, the historical *Aufklärers* distinguished themselves from the old exemplar theorists of history, as Reill pointed out, with the complex notion of causality, which the former developed in connection with an increasingly historicized representation of time.[163] Within this context, the *Aufklärers* were able to invest the term *pragmatisch* with a meaning similar to that of words like *philosophisch* and *systematisch*.[164]

That the late eighteenth-century 'pragmatists' indeed offered a relative opposition to the exemplar theory of history can also be confirmed with regard to the author who was probably the most significant of the historians of the German Enlightenment, August Ludwig Schlözer. According to Martin Peters, who published a very extensive survey of Schlözer's life and texts, the latter's relationship to the idea that history is 'life's teacher' varied according to the historical conjecture and the historiographical genre in which he wrote – his oeuvre included historical lectures, critical examinations of sources, universal histories, book reviews, pamphlets and even children's books, among other things. Peters shows that Schlözer's texts on universal history, however, encom-

passed a rejection of the exemplar theory of history.[165] Indeed, while presenting the guidelines of his interpretation of universal history in 1772, Schlözer
consciously avoided a moralizing attitude. He argued that a universal-historical
account should contain no argumentation, no description, no homiletic considerations, but only facts. It was, for him, not the writer, but the reader 'who
alone has to mentally supply [those facts] with judgement'. Schlözer further
claimed that as universal history transfers the act of judging the 'facts' from
the historian to the reader, it stops being pragmatic in the traditional sense in
order to become pragmatic in another way.[166] He thus proposed that historians
should decline the role of supplying society with exemplary instructions on behaviour, and commit themselves to the production of a kind of knowledge that
would only indirectly inspire the reader's practical conduct. By drawing on this
distinction between the task of historical writing and the practical application
of historical knowledge, Schlözer actually became a pioneer of the notion that
history's function is dependent upon the reader's subjective mediation.

   This opinion concerning the function of historical studies was carried on
and adapted by some important German historians and theorists throughout
the nineteenth century. Many of them, like Droysen himself, Georg Gottfried Gervinus (1805–1871), Max Duncker (1811–1886), Heinrich von Sybel
(1817–1895) and Heinrich von Treitschke (1834–1896), among others, derived
from the neo-pragmatist orientation a strictly political notion of history's practical function. They thought that historical knowledge should play an essential
role in shaping political institutions and, above all, in generating and conveying
national consciousness. Most of these politically engaged historians employed
historiography as a means to support and empower the so-called little Germany
solution, in which Prussia would take the lead in German national unification
(among the authors mentioned above, the only exception is Gervinus).[167] Sybel, for instance, was so strongly committed to the German national cause that,
after the foundation of the *Reich* in 1871, he literally confessed to not knowing
what to do with his professional life thenceforth.[168]

   Jacob Burckhardt, for his part, represented a far different case of a nineteenth-century German-speaking historian who subscribed to the neo-pragmatic
strategy while justifying the value of history. Burckhardt ultimately proposed
an aestheticization and a re-mythification of history,[169] so he was somehow
close to Nietzsche – a thinker over whom Burckhardt actually exerted some
influence. Indeed, like Nietzsche, Burckhardt argued for preserving the ties
between history and life. However, quite unlike the Nietzsche of the second
Untimely Meditation, Burckhardt continued to stress the value of critical research and objectivity. Lecturing in 1868–69, he affirmed that 'if history is ever
to help us to solve even an infinitesimal part of the great and grievous riddle of
life, we must quit the regions of personal and temporal foreboding for a sphere
in which our view is not forthwith dimmed by self'.[170] In fact, Burckhardt's

suggestion that historians should locate themselves in a space of objectivity 'not dimmed by self' and his plea that they keep a 'spirit of contemplation'[171] represent even a concession to the autotelic argument.

But essentially, Burckhardt did not subscribe to the autotelic strategy. Actually, he also spoke of a non-exemplary redefinition of historical pragmatism in terms very much akin to Schlözer's. Burckhardt did this precisely while exploring the reasons why the nineteenth century was such a propitious time for the development of historical studies. In his opinion, the depth and speed of the changes experienced since the French Revolution had made historical knowledge absolutely indispensable. Therefore, autotelic justifications of historiography offered, according to him, no acceptable image of the fundaments of historical knowledge. They denied history any direct practical value and ignored the fact that the changes and the changeability of the modern world made historical knowledge on cultural, social and political transformations more important than ever before. Burckhardt then concluded that 'it is an advantage for historical study in our own day that pragmatism is conceived in a much higher and wider sense than it used to be.'[172] To be sure, here he was expressing his perception that a reconstruction or redefinition of historiographical pragmatism was under way in his own times. In his opinion, historiography, as an intellectual practice within the modern world, should convey the results of a practical science. Indeed, one could only keep affirming that historians' task was to induce the development of personal virtues in their readers – somewhat as the old exemplary historiography had done. But Burckhardt saw the new virtues to be inspired as quite different from the old ones. He stated that when historians transform past experience – 'joy and sorrow', in his wording – into knowledge, they simultaneously make available a very special kind of practical orientation, which he presents as different from the provisional cunningness offered by historical examples: 'What was once joy and sorrow must now become knowledge.... Therewith the saying Historia vitae magistra takes on a higher yet humbler sense. We wish experience to make us, not shrewder (for the next time), but wiser (for ever).'[173]

Back to Droysen

The challenging stance sketched above on the exemplar theory of history is also easily traceable in Droysen's historical theory. In general, his criticism follows the same patterns already described with regard to other neo-pragmatists. Droysen never invoked any author but Wilhelm von Humboldt as someone with whom he shared his most essential views on history and historical science. Still, while listing the most important predecessors of his *Historik,* he mentioned that he considered the so-called Göttingen School – which was highly representative of the vanguard of German late Enlightenment in the field of history – as 'really the first historical school.'[174] Granted, Droysen was convinced of the insufficiencies of all historical theories prior to his own, of course including those from the late eighteenth century. But his praise discloses that he shared at least some important assumptions with the mentioned intellectual group. Droysen would not have spoken of the Göttingen School as the first historical school worthy of the name if his own general idea of history and that of the school's representatives had differed qualitatively. It is therefore plausible to infer that, from a general vantage point, Droysen's conception of history emerged precisely as an outcome of a general notion of history already in development at the end of the eighteenth century.

As for the substantial definition of the function of historical studies, Droysen proposed answers that resemble those of Gatterer, Schlözer and Burckhardt. He, too, admitted that history had a pragmatic value that did not correspond to its old exemplary function. In a certain passage of his *Historik,* for instance, he asks whether every schoolboy should copy the example of the great heroes and statesmen that populate history books, and then responds that 'the purpose of history cannot be either to provide examples for imitation or to extract rules for re-application.'[175] In accordance with the neo-pragmatic tendency, however, Droysen's refutation of the exemplar theory of history did not lead him to challenge the general assumption that the study of history must be useful for individuals, societies and humankind. Like several of the historians associated with the Göttingen School, he attempted to dissociate his own view of history from the 'wrongly called pragmatic history'.[176] And like Jacob Burckhardt – an author with whom he would have vehemently disagreed regarding many other important issues – Droysen postulated that history promotes wisdom rather than cleverness: 'If there are sciences which are able to make [one] not merely shrewder but also better, then history is among them.'[177]

In Droysen's opinion, the history of historical thought encompassed a multitude of mistaken attempts to define and redefine the value of writing and learning history. Summarizing the development of theoretical reflection on history and historiography, he complained about how long it had taken scholars to perceive the existence of all those alleged errors. But in lecturing on historical theory in the middle of the nineteenth century, he showed himself aware that things had already started to change.[178] For him, history was indeed a practical knowledge, and the practical task of historians was essentially different from that of jurists, public servants or diplomats.[179] The relationship with the past that these professionals could and should preserve was similar to the one favoured by the exemplar theory of history, for they have to act according to a conventional etiquette that would be ill served by constant reinvention. Droysen saw history, nonetheless, as having already emancipated itself from this kind of pragmatism. As a modern type of knowledge now able to account for qualitative temporal change, it had to reinvent its cultural role, for 'precisely the great and important things, with which history deals the most, do not repeat themselves.'[180]

Droysen, as already laid out, held that historiography comprises not only the study of the past but also, and above all, knowledge of the present's formative process — a knowledge that is hence susceptible to practical application in political and cultural life. Since 'history', as he lectured, 'can by no means be the same once and for all', the value and the meanings attached to every history will also vary according to the features of each epoch. In a fundamental sense, every history is for Droysen a history of the present; it is a means for generating subjective awareness of the historicity of the times one lives in.[181] Accordingly, he assigns to historians in the present the function of interpreting the past; of showing the developmental connection between past, present and future. Droysen's theory of history thus registered a crucial redefinition of historiography's cultural value. In the next chapter, I will show how this redefinition is embodied in the notion of 'historical thinking', a notion Droysen developed in close connection with both his hermeneutic conception of historical method and the idealistic notion of *Bildung*.

Notes

1. Diodorus of Sicily. 1933. *Library of History,* vol. 1: *Books 1–2.34,* Cambridge: Harvard University Press, 7–9.

2. Nadel, 'Philosophy of History before Historicism', 301–302.

3. Piero Corradini. 1994. 'History and Historiography in China', in *The East and the Meaning of History. Proceedings of the International Conference,* November, 1992. Roma: Bardi, 427–428; Ying-shih Yü. 2002. 'Reflections on Chinese Historical Thinking', in Jörn Rüsen (ed.), *Western Historical Thinking: An Intercultural Debate,* New York: Berghahn Books, 158.

4. Jennifer Jay. 1999. 'Sima Guang', in Kelly Bord (ed.), *Encyclopedia of Historians and Historical Writing,* vol. 2, London: Fitzroy Dearborn, 1092–1093.

5. Romila Thapar. 2006. 'The Tradition of Historical Writing in Early India', in Romila Thapar, *Ancient Indian Social History: Some Interpretations,* New Delhi: Orient Blackswan, 253.

6. Georg Iggers and Edward Wang. 2008. *A Global History of Modern Historiography,* Harlow: Pearson, 36.

7. Abū Zayd Ibn Khaldūn. 1967. *The Muqaddimah. An Introduction to History,* vol. 1, Princeton, NJ: Princeton University Press, 15.

8. Flavius Josephus. 1991. 'Jewish Antiquities (Fragment)', in Donald Kelley, *Versions of History: From Antiquity to the Enlightenment,* New Haven, CT: Yale University Press, 132. It is noteworthy that Josephus himself admits to having written his 'Jewish Antiquities' for the public benefit, as a way to counter the 'prevailing ignorance of important affairs of general utility'.

9. This quote has long been erroneously attributed to Dionysius of Halicarnassus (first century BC). The textual corpus where it appears (chapter 9 of the so-called *Art of Rhetoric* attributed to Dionysius) was probably written in the second century AD. See Malcolm Heath. 2003. 'Pseudo-Dionysius Art of Rhetoric 8–11: Figured Speech, Declamation and Criticism', *American Journal of Philology* 124: 81–105.

10. J.F. Dobson. 1919. *The Greek Orators,* London: Methuen, 143.

11. Nadel, 'Philosophy of History before Historicism', 294.

12. Nadel, 'Philosophy of History before Historicism', 294–298.

13. Löwith, *Meaning and History,* 6: 'In the Hebrew and Christian view of history the past is a promise to the future; consequently, the interpretation of the past becomes a prophecy in reverse, demonstrating the past as a meaningful "preparation" for the future. Greek philosophers and historians were convinced that whatever is to happen will be of the same pattern and character as past and present events; they never indulged in the prospective possibilities of the future.'

14. Arnaldo Momigliano. 1966. 'Time in Ancient Historiography', *History and Theory* 6 (supplement 6): 10: 'If one wants to understand something about Greek historians and the real differences between them and Biblical historians, the first precaution is to beware of the cyclical notion of time.'

15. François Hartog. 2003. 'O caso grego: do ktêma ao exemplum, passando pela arqueologia', in François Hartog, *Os antigos, o passado e o presente,* Brasília: Ed. UnB; François Hartog. 2000. 'The Invention of History: The Pre-History of a Concept from Homer to Herodotus', *History and Theory* 39(3): 384–395.

16. Hartog, 'O caso grego', 60–63.

17. Frank Walbank. 1990. *Polybius,* Berkeley: University of California Press, 84–91; John Burrow. 2009. *A History of Histories: Epics, Chronicles, Romances and Inquiries from Herodotus and Thucydides to the Twentieth Century,* New York: Vintage, 66.

18. Polybius. 1889. *Histories,* London: Macmillan, 1: 'Had the praise of History been passed over by former Chroniclers it would perhaps have been incumbent upon me to urge the choice and special study of records of this sort, as the readiest means men can have of correcting their knowledge of the past. But my predecessors have not been sparing in this respect. They have all begun and ended, so to speak, by enlarging on this theme: asserting again and again that the study of History is in the truest sense an education, and a training for political life; and that the most instructive, or rather the only, method of learning to bear with dignity the vicissitudes of fortune is to recall the catastrophes of others. It is evident, therefore, that no one need think it his duty to repeat what has been said by many, and said well. Least of all myself: for the surprising nature of the events which I have undertaken to relate is in itself sufficient to challenge and stimulate the attention of every one, old or young, to the study of my work. Can anyone be so indifferent or idle as not to care to know by what means, and under what kind of polity, almost the whole inhabited world was conquered and brought under the dominion of the single city of Rome, and that too within a period of not quite fifty-three years?'

19. Cicero, *De oratore,* 224: 'Historia vero testis temporum, lux veritatis, vita memoriae, magistra vitae, nuntia vetustatis, qua voce alia, nisi oratoris immortalitati commandatur?' Translation: 'And as History, which bears witness to the passing of ages, sheds light upon reality, gives life to recollection and guidance to human existence, and brings tiding of ancient days, whose voice, but the orator's, can entrust her to immortality?' (225).

20. Christian Meier. 1979. 'Geschichte, Historie. II. Antike', in Otto Brunner et al. (eds), *Geschichtliche Grundbegriffe. Historisches Lexikon zur politisch-sozialen Sprache in Deutschland,* vol. 2, Stuttgart: Klett-Cotta, 606; Fritz-Heiner Mutschler. 2003. 'Zur Sinnhorizont und Funktion griechischer, römischer und altchinesischer Geschichtsschreibung', in Karl-Joachim Hölkeskamp et al. (eds), *Sinn (in) der Antike. Orientierungssysteme, Leitbilder und Wertkonzepte im Altertum,* Mainz: Phillip von Zabern, 40.

21. Burrow, *A History of Historians,* 91–92, 161–162.

22. Livy. 2006. *The History of Rome,* books 1–5, Indianapolis: Hackett, 3–4.

23. François Hartog. 2001. 'Como se escreveu a história na Grécia e em Roma', in François Hartog (ed.), *A história. De Homero a Santo Agostinho: Prefácios de historiadores e textos sobre história reunidos e comentados,* Belo Horizonte: Ed. UFMG, 15.

24. Isidore of Seville. 1912. 'The Etymologies', in Ernest Brehaut (ed.), *An Encyclopedist of the Dark Ages: Isidore of Seville,* New York: Columbia University Press, 103. Isidore's point of

view is perhaps best understood within the context of a more general tendency that originated among Christian apologists such as Clement of Alexandria (ca 150–ca 215) and Basil of Caesarea (ca 330–379), who envisaged the possibility of conciliating Christian faith and pagan legacy. They successfully propagated the argument that the subjective acquisition of the Greek cultural legacy – especially philosophy, science and literature – could be useful in preparing one for the understanding of Holy Scripture and the study of theology. See Edward Grant. 1996. *The Foundations of Modern Science in the Middle Ages: Their Religious, Institutional, and Intellectual Contexts,* Cambridge: Cambridge University Press, 3–4.

25. Bede. 2007. *The Ecclesiastical History of the English Nation,* New York: Cosimo, 1.

26. Felix Gilbert. 1973. *Machiavelli and Guicciardini: Politics and History in Sixteenth Century Florence,* Princeton, NJ: Princeton University Press, 217–218.

27. Quoted by Gabrielle Spiegel. 2007. 'Historical Thought in Medieval Europe', in Lloyd Kramer and Sarah Maza (eds), *A Companion to Western Historical Thought,* Malden, MA: Blackwell, 82.

28. Martin Luther. 1991. 'Preface to Galeatius Capella's History', in Donald Kelley, *Versions of History: From Antiquity to the Enlightenment,* New Haven, CT: Yale University Press, 314–315.

29. Blanke, *Historiographiegeschichte als Historik,* 91.

30. G.R. Evans. 1993. *Philosophy and Theology in the Middle Ages,* London, Routledge, 15–16.

31. On the complex history of the terms history, chronicle and annals from late antiquity to the end of the Middle Ages, see Bernard Guenée. 1973. 'Histoires, annales, chroniques. Essai sur les genres historiques au Moyen Âge', *Annales. Économies, Sociétés, Civilisations,* 28(4): 997–1016. See also Spiegel, 'Historical Thought in Medieval Europe', 80.

32. Carl Watkins. 2007. *History and the Supernatural in Medieval England.* Cambridge: Cambridge University Press, 14–15.

33. Quoted in Watkins, *History and the Supernatural in Medieval England,* 15.

34. Erich Auerbach. 1952. 'Typological Symbolism in Medieval Literature', *Yale French Studies* 9, 5–6. See also Jörn Rüsen. 2003. 'Die Kultur der Zeit. Versuch einer Typologie temporaler Sinnbildungen', in Jörn Rüsen (ed.), *Zeit deuten. Perspektiven – Epochen – Paradigmen,* Bielefeld: Transcript, 36–37; Spiegel, 'Historical Thought in Medieval Europe', 84.

35. Gabrielle Spiegel. 1975. 'Political Utility in Medieval Historiography: A Sketch', *History and Theory* 14(3): 319; Guenée, 'Histoires, annales, chroniques', 1008–1009.

36. Spiegel, 'Historical Thought in Medieval Europe', 85–86.

37. Rommily Jenkins. 1963. 'The Hellenistic Origins of Byzantine Literature', *Dumbarton Oaks Papers* 17: 50.

38. Procopius of Caesarea. 1991. 'History of the Wars (Fragment)', in Donald Kelley, *Versions of History: From Antiquity to the Enlightenment,* New Haven, CT: Yale University Press, 108.

39. Paul Oskar Kristeller. 1961. *Renaissance Thought: The Classic, Scholastic and Humanist Strains,* New York: Harper & Row, 105–106.

40. Quoted and analysed by Theodore Ernst Mommsen. 1942. 'Petrarch's Conception of the "Dark Ages"', *Speculum* 17(2): 236–237.

41. Niccolò Machiavelli. 1893. *Discourses on the First Decade of Titus Livius,* London: Kegan Paul, 189–190.

42. Machiavelli, *Discourses,* 189.

43. Firearms, invented in twelfth-century China, had reached Western Europe by the fourteenth century.

44. Jürgen Huber. 2004. *Guicciardinis Kritik an Machiavelli. Streit um Staat, Gesellschaft und Geschichte im frühneuzeitlichen Italien,* Wiesbaden: DUV, 99–100.

45. Gilbert, *Machiavelli and Guicciardini,* 228; Eduard Fueter. 1936. *Geschichte der neueren Historiographie,* Munich: R. Oldenbourg, 58–59.

46. Niccolò Machiavelli. 1901. *History of Florence,* New York: The Colonial Press, 227: 'And if, in detailing the events which took place in this wasted world, we shall not have to record the bravery of the soldier, the prudence of the general, or the patriotism of the citizen, it will be seen

with what artifice, deceit, and cunning, princes, warriors, and leaders of republics conducted themselves, to support a reputation they never deserved. This, perhaps, will not be less useful than a knowledge of ancient history; for, if the latter excites the liberal mind to imitation, the former will show what ought to be avoided and decried.' See also the interpretation by Quentin Skinner. 2000. *Machiavelli: A Very Short Introduction,* Oxford: Oxford University Press, 92–93.

47. Pero Mexía. 1545. *Historia imperial y cesárea: en la que en suma se contiene las vidas y hechos de todos los césares emperadores de Roma.* Sevilla: Sebastian Trugillo, ii: 'Los reyes y principes hayan en las historias otros a quien imiten y con quienes compitan en virtudes y excellencias, y otros malos de cuyas costumbres huyan, y de cuyos fines y famas escarmienten.' I thank Aaron Bustamante for bringing this quote to my attention.

48. Francesco Guicciardini. 1890. *Counsels and Reflections,* London: Kegan Paul, 50.

49. Quoted by Mark Phillips. 1977. *Francesco Guicciardini: The Historian's Craft,* Toronto: Manchester University Press, 63.

50. Phillips, *Francesco Guicciardini,* 64.

51. I am following here the arguments advanced by Michel Jeanneret. 1998. 'The Vagaries of Exemplarity: Distortion or Dismissal?', *Journal of the History of Ideas* 59(4): 578–579; and Peter von Moos. 1996. *Geschichte als Topik. Das rhetorische Exemplum von der Antike zur Neuzeit und die historiae in <Policraticus> Johanns von Salisbury,* Hildesheim: Olms.

52. Quoted by François Rigolot. 1998. 'The Renaissance Crisis of Exemplarity', *Journal of the History of Ideas* 59(4): 557.

53. Jeanneret, 'The Vagaries of Exemplarity', 573–578.

54. Samuel Pufendorf. 1991. 'An Introduction to the History of the Principal Kingdoms and States of Europe (Fragment), in Donald Kelley, *Versions of History: From Antiquity to the Enlightenment,* New Haven, CT: Yale University Press, 435.

55. Jacques-Benigne Bossuet. 1991. 'Discourse on Universal History (Fragment)', in Donald Kelley, *Versions of History: From Antiquity to the Enlightenment,* New Haven, CT: Yale University Press, 425.

56. George Huppert. 1970. *The Idea of Perfect History: Historical Erudition and Historical Philosophy in Renaissance France,* Urbana: The University of Illinois Press, 5; Muhlack, *Geschichtswissenschaft im Humanismus und in der Aufklärung,* 385.

57. Jörn Rüsen remarked on this with regard to the 'meaning vs. method' opposition. According to him, it constitutes a never-solved problem in the history of historical thought. See Jörn Rüsen. 2002. 'Historische Methode als religiöser Sinn. Dialektische Bewegungen in der Neuzeit', in Jörn Rüsen, *Geschichte im Kulturprozess,* Cologne: Böhlau, 24. The same opposition can alternatively be formulated as rhetoric vs. critique, form vs. content or narrativity vs. objectivity.

58. Muhlack, *Geschichtswissenschaft im Humanismus und in der Aufklärung,* 352–353. Expressions such as historical-critical method, historical-philological method or simply historical method are frequently used to refer to the principles and practices of scholarship then developed.

59. The publication of Flavio Biondo's guide to ancient Roman ruins and topography in the mid-fifteenth century is regarded as the inauguration of archaeology in its modern form.

60. Muhlack, *Geschichtswissenschaft im Humanismus und in der Aufklärung,* 368.

61. Herbert Butterfield. 1974. 'History of Historiography', in Philip Wiener (ed.), *Dictionary of the History of Ideas: Studies of Selected Pivotal Ideas,* vol. 2, New York: Charles Scribner's Sons, 486–487. Some of the most important of these collectively endeavoured works were *The Magdeburg Centuries* (1559–1574), the first Lutheran account of ecclesiastical history ever published, directed by Matthias Flacius Illyricus; the *Ecclesiastical Annals* (1588–1607), a Catholic response to the work of the centuriators of Magdeburg, directed by Cardinal Cesare Baronius; the *Acts of the Saints,* a critical hagiography initiated in 1643 under the coordination of Jean Bolland and finished only in 1940; and the *Acts of the Saints of the Benedictine Order,* organized in 1668 by Jean Mabillon.

62. Bernheim, *Lehrbuch der historischen Methode und der Geschichtsphilosophie,* 217.

63. Gilbert, *Machiavelli and Guicciardini.*

64. E.B. Fryde. 1983. *Humanism and Renaissance Historiography*, London: The Hambledon, 17–18; see also Carlo Ginzburg. 1999. 'LorenzoValla and the "Donation of Constantine"', in Carlo Ginzburg. *History, Rhetoric, and Proof*, Hanover, NH: University Press of New England, 54–70.

65. Butterfield, 'History of Historiography', 484.

66. Daniel Woolf. 2005. 'Historiography', in Maryanne Horowitz (ed.), *New Dictionary of the History of Ideas*, vol. 1, Detroit: Thomson Gale, xlv.

67. Eckhard Kessler. 1971. 'Geschichte: Menschliche Praxis oder kritische Wissenschaft? Zur Theorie der humanistischen Geschichtsschreibung', in Eckhard Kessler (ed.), *Theoretiker humanistischer Geschichtsschreibung. Nachdruck exemplarischer Texte aus dem 16. Jahrhundert*, Munich: Wilhelm Fink, 11.

68. H.-W. Hedinger. 1974. 'Historik, ars historica', 1132.

69. Kessler, 'Geschichte', 8–9, fn. 11.

70. This collective work encompasses sixteen early modern treatises, among them Francesco Patrizi's *Dieci dialoghi della historia* (1560), François Baudouin's *De instituitione historia universae* (1561) and Jean Bodin's *Methodus ad facilem historiarum cognitionem* (1566), as well as two classical texts translated from Greek into Latin, namely, Dionysius of Halicarnassus's essay on Thucydides (first century BC) and Lucian's essay on *How to Write History* (ca 165 AD). For detailed analyses of the treatises related to the *ars-historica* tradition, see Blanke, *Historiographiegeschichte als Historik*, 84–101; Anthony Grafton. 2007. *What Was History? The Art of History in Early Modern Europe*, Cambridge: Cambridge University Press; Kessler, 'Geschichte'; Rüdiger Landfester. 1972. *Historia Magistra Vitae. Untersuchungen zur humanistischen Geschichtstheorie des 14. bis 16. Jahrhunderts*, Geneva: Librairie Droz; Beatrice Reynolds. 1953. 'Shifting Currents in Historical Criticism', *Journal of the History of Ideas* 14(3): 471–492; Astrid Witschi-Bernz. 1972. 'Main Trends in Historical-Method Literature: Sixteenth to Eighteenth Centuries', *History and Theory* 12 (supplement 12, *Bibliography of Works in the Philosophy of History*): 1500–1800.

71. Grafton, *What Was History?* 26, 68; Ulrich Muhlack. 1990. 'Johann Gustav Droysen: "Historik" et Hermeneutique', in André Laks and Ada Neschke (eds), *La naissance du paradigme herméneutique. Schleiermacher, Humboldt, Boeckh, Droysen*, Lille: Presses Universitaires de Lille, 360–361.

72. Grafton, *What Was History?* 231: 'Baudouin, as we saw, called for a union of what had been the largely separate practices of historians and antiquarians, and Bodin envisioned something similar.'

73. Grafton, *What Was History?* 94.

74. Gilbert, *Machiavelli and Guicciardini*, 215–216.

75. Grafton, *What Was History?* 214–217.

76. Nadel, 'Philosophy of History before Historicism', 310. Johann Gerhard Voss's *Ars historica* (1623) also illustrates this same point. Voss criticized the rhetorical tradition of historiography, emphasizing that the most important task of historians is the search for causes of past events. See Horst Günther. 1979. 'Geschichte, Historie. IV. Historisches Denken in der frühen Neuzeit', in Otto Brunner et al. (eds), *Geschichtliche Grundbegriffe. Historisches Lexikon zur politisch-sozialen Sprache in Deutschland*, vol. 2, Stuttgart: Klett-Cotta, 642. Nevertheless, the following quote reveals that Voss's attempt did not exclude a notion of the exemplary function of historiography. Defending the idea that historians, and not only philosophers, should investigate the motivations of human actions, he stated: 'History, as has been said more than once, is philosophy consisting of examples. This conjunction of philosophy with history implies that the philosopher may illustrate his precepts with historical examples, and the historian, in turn, may test certain facts in the light of the philosopher's precepts.' Quoted by Rudolf Unger. 1971. 'The Problem of Historical Objectivity: A Sketch of Its Development to the Time of Hegel', *History and Theory* 11(4): 67. See also Grafton, *What Was History?* 31–32: '… both northern and Italian scholars continued, throughout the sixteenth and seventeenth centuries, to see history as above all a form of rhetoric and a source of exempla – moral and prudential precepts worked out in the concrete form of speeches, trials and battles.'

77. Muhlack, *Geschichtswissenschaft im Humanismus und in der Aufklärung,* 391.

78. Reynolds, 'Shifting Currents in Historical Criticism', 471.

79. Gilbert, *Machiavelli and Guicciardini,* 223–226.

80. Butterfield, 'History of Historiography', 485.

81. Grafton, *What Was History?* 192–193.

82. Grafton, *What Was History?* 231.

83. Reill, *The German Enlightenment and the Rise of Historicism,* 10–11.

84. Quoted by Grafton, *What Was History?* 8–9.

85. The historiographical front of the *Querelle des anciens et des modernes* was the discussion on so-called historical pyrrhonism. The pyrrhonistic argument was that factual knowledge conveyed by classical historiography was generally unreliable. Proceeding on this particular assumption, pyrrhonists also frequently came to the epistemological conclusion that historical knowledge as such is not possible. The best known representatives of historical pyrrhonism were Pierre Bayle, Levesque de Pouilly and Louis de Beaufort. Overall, they radicalized the opinion that classical Roman historians had naively reproduced mythical fables, especially in their accounts of Rome's first centuries. Famous antagonists to such scepticism were Nicolas Fréret, and especially Nicolas Lenglet du Fresnoy. See Bernheim, *Lehrbuch der historischen Methode und der Geschichtsphilosophie,* 220–224.

86. Mark Phillips. 1989. 'Macaulay, Scott, and the Literary Challenge to Historiography', *Journal of the History of Ideas* 50(1): 119–120. See also Johnson Kent Wright. 2007. 'The Historical Thought of the Enlightenment', in Lloyd Kramer and Sarah Maza (eds), *A Companion to Western Historical Thought,* Malden, MA: Blackwell, 123–142.

87. Gerald Aylmer. 1997. 'Introductory Survey: From the Renaissance to the Eighteenth Century', in Michael Bentley (ed.), *Companion to Historiography,* London: Routledge, 259.

88. On the editorial history of this text, see George Nadel. 1962. 'New Light on Bolingbroke's Letters on History', *Journal of the History of Ideas* 23(4): 550–557.

89. Lord Bolingbroke. 1791. *Letters on the Study and Use of History,* Basel: J. J. Tourneisen, 9.

90. Bolingbroke, *Letters on the Study and Use of History,* 10.

91. Bolingbroke, *Letters on the Study of History,* 94–95.

92. Pierre Force. 2009. 'Voltaire and the Necessity of Modern History', *Modern Intellectual History* 6(3): 465.

93. Force, 'Voltaire and the Necessity of History', 466–467.

94. David Allan. 1993. *Virtue, Learning and the Scottish Enlightenment: Ideas of Scholarship in Early Modern History,* Edinburgh: Edinburgh University Press, 169–175.

95. Quoted by Allan, *Virtue, Learning and the Scottish Enlightenment,* 175.

96. Horst Walter Blanke. 1996. 'Aufklärungshistorie und Historismus. Bruch und Kontinuität', in Otto Gerhard Oexle and Jörn Rüsen (eds), *Historismus in den Kulturwissenschaften. Geschichtskonzepte, historische Einschätzungen, Grundlagenprobleme,* Cologne: Böhlau, 73, 86; Koselleck, *Vergangene Zukunft,* 45–46.

97. John Dalberg Acton. 1930. *Lectures on Modern History,* London: Macmillan, 24; Robin G. Collingwood. 1999. *The Principles of History and Other Writings in Philosophy of History,* Oxford: Oxford University Press, 37.

98. Johannes Rohbeck. 2001. 'Verzeitlichung', in Joachim Ritter et al. (ed.), *Historisches Wörterbuch der Philosophie,* vol. 11. Basel: Schwabe, 1026–1027; Theo Jung. 2010/2011. 'Das Neue der Neuzeit ist ihre Zeit. Reinhart Kosellecks Theorie der Verzeitlichung und ihre Kritiker', *Moderne Kulturwissenschaftliches Jahrbuch* 6, 173–174.

99. For a competent introduction to Koselleck's oeuvre, see Niklas Olsen. 2012. *History in the Plural: An Introduction to the Work of Reinhart Koselleck,* New York: Berghahn Books.

100. Daniel Fulda has pointed out that one reason for the positive reception of Koselleck's interpretation of the genesis of the modern world is its resonance with the traditional historicist assumption that 'historical thinking was an achievement of the age of Goethe'. See Daniel Fulda.

2006. 'Rex ex historia. Komödienzeit und verzeitlichte Zeit in "Minna von Barnhelm"', *Das achtzehnte Jahrhundert* 30(2): 180–181.

101. See Javiér Fernández Sebastián and Juan Francisco Fuentes. 2006. 'Conceptual History, Memory, and Identity: An Interview with Reinhart Koselleck', *Contributions to the History of Concepts* 2(1): 120: 'First of all, concerning *Sattelzeit*, I have to tell you that I invented the term and used it for the first time in commercial advertisements created to promote the *GG* – to sell more issues. Although I am happy that succeeded in providing the lexicon with some money, I do not particularly like the term, mainly because it is very ambiguous.'

102. Reinhart Koselleck. 1967. 'Richtlinien für das Lexikon politisch-sozialer Begriffe der Neutzeit', *Archiv für Begriffsgeschichte* 11, 81–82; Reinhart Koselleck. 1972. 'Einleitung', in Otto Brunner et al. (eds), *Geschichtliche Grundbegriffe. Historisches Lexikon zur politisch-sozialen Sprache in Deutschland*, vol. 1, Stuttgart: Klett-Cotta, xiv.

103. Koselleck, *Vergangene Zukunft*, 63–64, 338; Koselleck, *Zeitschichten*, 227–230. Hartmut Rosa has recently provided a very comprehensive sociological analysis of the issue of time-experience in modern societies. His main thesis is that the 'modernization experience is an acceleration experience'. See Hartmut Rosa. 2005. *Beschleunigung. Die Veränderung der Zeitstrukturen in der Moderne*, Frankfurt am Main: Suhrkamp, 51.

104. Jung, 'Das Neue der Neuzeit ist ihre Zeit', 174–175.

105. Koselleck, *Futures Past*, 270.

106. Karl Marx and Friedrich Engels. 2002. *The Communist Manifesto*, London: Penguin Classics, 223.

107. Edmund Burke. 1790. *Reflections on the Revolution in France*, London: J. Dodsley, 11, 85–86.

108. Alexis de Tocqueville. 2004. *Democracy in America*, New York: The Library of America, 831.

109. On Tocqueville's case, see Marcelo Jasmin. 2005. *Alexis de Tocqueville. A historiografia como ciência da política*, Belo Horizonte: Ed. UFMG, 37.

110. Leopold von Ranke. 1971. *Aus Werk und Nachlass*, vol. 2: *Über die Epochen der neuren Geschichte. Historisch-kritische Ausgabe*, Munich: Oldenbourg, 417. Friedrich Jaeger called my attention to this quote, which he analysed in Friedrich Jaeger. 2010. 'Die Neuere Geschichte bei Johann Gustav Droysen', in Horst Walter Blanke (ed.), *Historie und Historik. 200 Jahre Johann Gustav Droysen. Festschrift für Jörn Rüsen zum 70. Geburtstag*, Cologne: Böhlau, 110.

111. Droysen, *Historik 2*: 196 [Die Einleitung in die Vorlesungen über die Geschichte der neuesten Zeit seit 1815, 1843].

112. Koselleck, *Futures Past*, 236.

113. Reinhart Koselleck. 1979. 'Geschichte, Historie. I. Einleitung', in Otto Brunner et al. (eds), *Geschichtliche Grundbegriffe. Historisches Lexikon zur politisch-sozialen Sprache in Deutschland*, vol. 2, Stuttgart: Klett-Cotta, 593.

114. Hans-Werner Goetz. 1989. 'Von der "res gestae" zur "narratio rerum gestarum". Anmerkungen zu Methoden und Hilfswissenschaften des mittelalterlichen Geschichtsschreibers', *Revue belge de philologie et d'histoire* 67(4): 697.

115. Reinhart Koselleck. 1979. 'Geschichte, Historie. V. Die Herausbildung des modernen Geschichtsbegriffs', in Otto Brunner et al. (eds), *Geschichtliche Grundbegriffe. Historisches Lexikon zur politisch-sozialen Sprache in Deutschland*, vol. 2, Stuttgart: Klett-Cotta, 653–654.

116. Koselleck, 'Geschichte, Historie. V', 647–658. Nevertheless, Koselleck also observes that Augustine's (354–430) term *historia ipsa* strongly resembles the German terms *Geschichte schlechthin* and *Geschichte überhaupt*, which he uses as major evidence in his thesis regarding the emergence of the modern concept of history. See Koselleck, *Zeitschichten*, 130–131.

117. Koselleck, 'Geschichte, Historie. V', 649.

118. Koselleck, 'Geschichte, Historie. V', 652: 'Die Geschichte im kollektiven Singular setzte die Bedingung möglicher Einzelgeschichten. Alle Einzelgeschichten standen seitdem in einem komplexen Zusammenhang, der eine nur ihm eigentümliche, selbstständige Wirkungsweise

hat. "Über die Geschichten ist die Geschichte", fasste 1858 Droysen die neue Erfahrungswelt der Geschichte zusammen'; Koselleck, 'Einleitung', xvii: 'Schließlich tauchen Ausdrücke auf, die die geschichtliche Zeit selber artikulieren. Die reflexiv verstandene "Entwicklung", der unendliche "Fortschritt", die "Geschichte schlechthin", die zugleich ihr eigenes Subjekt und Objekt sei, die "Revolution", die aus dem Kreislauf ihres vormaligen Sinnes ausschert und zum allgemeinen Bewegungsbegriff mit gleitender Zielskala aufrückt − all diese neuen Begriffe zeichnen sich durch Zeitbestimmungen aus, die prozessuale Sinngehalte und Erfahrungen bündeln.'

119. Henri-Irénée Marrou recalls some attempts to clearly differentiate the notion of history as a form of knowledge from the idea of history as the reality of the past: Kant's differentiation between *Geschichte* (reality) and *Historie* (knowledge), Croce's distinction between *storia* and *storiografia*, and Henri Corbin's differentiation between *Histoire* and *histoire*. None of them, Marrou claims, actually succeeded. See Henri-Irénée Marrou. n.d. *Do conhecimento histórico*, Lisbon: Aster, 33–34.

120. Jan Marco Sawilla. 2004. '"Geschichte": Ein Produkt der deutschen Aufklärung? Eine Kritik an Reinhart Kosellecks Begriffs des "Kollektivsingulars" Geschichte', *Zeitschrift für historische Forschung* 31: 387. I shall quote only one of Sawila's findings, a passage by the seventeenth-century grammarian Justus Georg Schottel (1612–1672): 'Es ist ein wunderlich Werck/wenn man die Geschichte und das Leben der Menschen durchdenket' (p. 387). Translation: 'To reflect on the history and the life of men is a fantastic achievement.'

121. Sawilla, '"Geschichte": Ein Produkt der deutschen Aufklärung?' 397–399, 411, 413, 428. See also Jan Marco Sawilla. 2011. 'Geschichte und Geschichten zwischen Providenz und Machbarkeit. Überlegungen zu Reinhart Kosellecks Semantik historischer Zeiten', in Hans Joas and Peter Vogt (eds), *Begriffene Geschichte. Beiträge zum Werk Reinhart Kosellecks,* Frankfurt am Main: Suhrkamp, 387–422.

122. Sawilla, '"Geschichte": Ein Produkt der deutschen Aufklärung?' 419.

123. See Fulda, 'Rex ex historia', 182: 'Von Sawillas Kritik betroffen ist nicht die Temporalisierungsthese insgesamt, sondern "nur" ihre Stützung durch Kosellecks "Kollektivsingular Geschichte"'; Stefanie Stockhorst. 2001. 'Novus ordo temporum. Reinhart Kosellecks These von der Verzeitlichung des Geschichtsbewußtseins durch die Aufklärungshistoriographie in methodenkritischer Perspektive', in Hans Joas and Peter Vogt (eds), *Begriffene Geschichte. Beiträge zum Werk Reinhart Kosellecks,* Frankfurt am Main: Suhrkamp, 379: 'Ganz abgesehen von dem etablierten Stellenwert innerhalb der Geschichtswissenschaft sollte, allen berechtigten Einwänden zum Trotz, das Erklärungspotential der Verzeitlichungsthese nicht vorschnell für gänzlich obsolete erklärt warden. Vielmehr scheinen weiterführende Differenzierungen und Ergänzungen des auf das verzeitlichte Geschichtsbewußtsein beschränkten Ansatzes vonnöten.'

124. Koselleck, *Vergangene Zukunft*, 58.

125. Koselleck, *Vergangene Zukunft*, 312–313.

126. Wolfgang Reinhard. 2006. 'The Idea of Early-Modern History', in Michael Bentley (ed.), *A Companion to Historiography*, London: Routledge, 273.

127. Koselleck, *Vergangene Zukunft*, 40; see also Rüsen, *Lebendige Geschichte*, 45–49.

128. Koselleck, *Vergangene Zukunft*, 64–66.

129. Friedrich Carl von Savigny. 1850. *Vermischte Schriften*, vol. 1, Berlin: Veit, 109–111: 'Die Geschichte ist dann nicht mehr blos Beispielsammlung, sondern der einzige Weg zur wahren Erkenntnis unsres eigenen Zustands' (111).

130. Wilhelm von Humboldt. 1967. 'On the Historian's Task', *History and Theory* 6(1): 60–61.

131. Georg Wilhelm Friedrich Hegel. 2001. *The Philosophy of History*, Kitchener, ON: Batoche, 19–20: 'Rulers, Statesmen, Nations, are wont to be emphatically commended to the teaching which experience offers in history. But what experience and history teach is this − that peoples and governments never have learned anything from history, or acted on principles deduced from it'; original text at Hegel, *Die Vernunft in der Geschichte*, 19.

132. Hegel, *The Philosophy of History*, 19–20; original text: Hegel, *Die Vernunft in der Ge-schichte*, 19.

133. On the theoretical distinction between 'history for its own sake' and 'history as a means to an end', see Lemon, *Philosophy of History*, 323–356.

134. Felix Escher. 1989. 'Leopold Ranke', in Michael Erbe (ed.), *Berlinische Lebensbilder*, vol. 4: *Geisteswissenschaftler*, Berlin: Colloquium, 113; Anthony Grafton. 1999. *The Footnote: A Curious History*, Cambridge: Harvard University Press, 38–39.

135. Quoted by Nadel, 'Philosophy of History before Historicism', 315; Ranke, 'Vorwort zu den ‹Geschichten der romanischen und germanischen Völker von 1494 bis 1535›', 45: 'Man hat der Historie das Amt, die Vergangenheit zu richten, die Mitwelt zum Nutzen zukünftiger Jahre zu belehren, beigemessen: so höher Ämter unterwindet sich gegenwärtiger Versuch nicht: er will bloß sagen, wie es eigentlich gewesen.'

136. Leonard Krieger. 1977. *Ranke: The Meaning of History*, Chicago: University of Chicago Press, 5.

137. Ranke, *Aus Werk und Nachlass* 2: 73–75: '– König Max: Ist nicht aber doch jezt eine größere Anzahl von Individuen zu einer höheren moralischen Entwicklung gediehen, als früher? – Ranke: Ich gebe das zu, aber nicht prinzipgemäß; denn die Geschichte lehrt uns, daß manche Völker gar nicht kulturfähig sind, und daß oft frühere Epochen viel moralischer waren, als spätere. (Frankreich in der Mitte des 17. Jahrhunderts z. B. war viel moralischer und gebildeter, als zu Ende des 18. Jahrhunderts). Wie gesagt, eine größere Expansion der moralischen Ideen läßt sich behaupten, aber nur in bestimmten Kreisen. Als Mensch scheint es mir wahrscheinlich, daß die Idee der Menschheit, die nur historisch in den größeren Nationen repräsentiert ist, allmählich die ganze Menschheit umfassen sollte, und dies wäre dann der innere moralische Fortschritt. Die Historie opponiert sich dieser Anschauung nicht, weist sie aber nicht nach. Insbesondere müssen wir uns hütten, diese Anschauungen zum Prinzip der Geschichte zu machen. Unsere Aufgabe ist, uns bloß an das Objekt zu halten'.

138. Leopold von Ranke, 1860. *Englische Geschichte, vornehmlich im 16. und 17. Jahrhundert*, vol. 2, Berlin Duncker und Humblot, xi: 'Flüchtige Ähnlichkeiten mißleiten häufig, wie den Politiker, der auf die Vergangenheit, so den Historiker, der auf die Gegenwart fußen will.… Interessen der Gegenwart in die historische Arbeit hineintragen, hat gewöhnlich die Folge, deren freie Vollziehung zu beeinträchtigen.'

139. Leopold von Ranke. 1975. 'Einleitung zu einer Vorlesung über neure Geschichte', in Leopold von Ranke, *Aus Werk und Nachlass*, vol. 4: *Vorlesungseinleitungen*, Munich: Oldenbourg, 295: 'Die wahre Historie trachtet nach der Anschauung des Objektiven; sie muß sich über diese Parteistandpunkte erheben. Ihrer Natur nach hat sie ein moralisches und ein religiöses Element. Aber das moralische besteht nicht darin, einen jeden nach vorgefaßten Vorstellungen zu beurteilen und zu richten; das religiöse nicht darin, dem besonderen Bekenntnis, dem man angehört, gleichsam allein das Recht dazusein zu vindizieren und die übrigen herabzusetzen, herabzuwürdigen. Sondern darin, jedem moralischen und religiösen Dasein, wenn es auch beschränkt sein sollte, gerecht zu werden.'

140. Leopold von Ranke. 1860. *Englische Geschichte*, 3: 'Ich wünschte mein Selbst gleichsam auszulöschen, und nur die Dinge reden, die mächtigen Kräfte erscheinen zu lassen, die im Laufe der Jahrhunderte mit und durch einander entsprungen und erstarkt, nunmehr gegen einander aufstanden und in einen Kampf geriethen, der, indem er sich in blutigen und schrecklichen Schlägen entlud, zugleich für die wichtigsten Fragen der europäischen Welt eine Entscheidung in sich trug.'

141. Harry Liebersohn. 2007. 'German Historical Writing from Ranke to Weber: The Primacy of Politics', in Lloyd Kramer and Sarah Maza (ed.), *A Companion to Western Historical Thought*, Malden: Blackwell, 166–171; Iggers, Historiography in the Twentieth Century, 25.

142. Arnaldo Momigliano. 1980. 'Historicism Revisited', in Arnaldo Momigliano, *Sesto contributo alla storia degli studi classic e del mondo antico*, Rome: Edizioni di Storia e Letteratura, 29.

143. Quoted by Stefan Jordan, *Geschichtstheorie in der ersten Hälfte des 19. Jahrhunderts. Die Schwellenzeit zwischen Pragmatismus und Klassischem Historismus,* Frankfurt am Main: Campus, 62: 'Bezeichnenderweise enthält der Absatz Wachsmuths über den Nutzen und Zweck von Geschichte den Gedanken, daß "Geschichte als Bild des Lebens … keinen Zweck außer ihr selbst" hat.'

144. Quoted by Jordan, *Geschichtstheorie in der ersten Hälfte des 19. Jahrhunderts,* 63: 'Die Erkenntnis ist das Wesen, und um ihrer selbst willen Zweck, aller Wissenschaft; fremdartige Belehrung irgend einer Art, sittliche oder patriotische Aufregung und dergleichen, kann bloß Ursache eines Interesses an der Geschichte seyn, nicht aber ihr Zweck an sich.'

145. Bernheim, *Lehrbuch der historischen Methode und der Geschichtsphilosophie,* 228–229: 'Von dieser [exemplarischen, pragmatischen] beschränkenden Auffassung musste sich erst die Geschichte losmachen, um allseitig in wissenschaftlicher Weise behandelt werden zu können. Denn diese Auffassung hielt dieselbe in einseitiger Richtung auf das pädagogisch Moralische oder auf das praktisch Hilfswissenschaftliche befangen und verhinderte, dass die historische Erkenntnis als Selbstzweck den Mittelpunkt des Interesses ausmachte. Keine Wissenschaft wird aber zur intensiven Stellung ihrer Probleme und zur Ausbildung ihrer Methoden gelangen, solange sie, in praktischen Nebentendenzen befangen, nicht die Forschung um der reinen Erkenntnis willen betreibt. Daher erklärt sich die sonst fast unerklärliche Erscheinung, dass trotz so vielen theoretischen und praktischen Arbeitens die Methodik unserer Wissenschaft bis ins 18. Jahrhundert so geringe Fortschritte gemacht hat.' Cf. Herman Paul's interpretation of Bernheim's and Ranke's notion of 'self-distanciation' in terms of an epistemic virtue. Herman Paul. 2011. 'Distance and Self-Distanciation: Intellectual Virtue and Historical Method around 1900', *History and Theory* 50(4): 109: 'What does such "elimination" imply? Bernheim was certainly not haunted by a Romantic desire to "extinguish" himself (as Ranke famously put it). Nor did he want the historian to become a disembodied mind…. Bernheim's point is rather that people in the past thought, perceived, and felt differently from people in the present and that such "differences of times" have to be acknowledged.'

146. For a more contemporary version of the autotelic justification, see Paul Veyne. 1984. *Writing History: Essay on Epistemology,* Middletown, CT: Wesleyan University Press, 47–84.

147. Bolingbroke, *Letters on the Study and Use of History,* 6.

148. Blanke, Fleischer and Rüsen, 'Theory of History in Historical Lectures', 335–336.

149. Karl von Rotteck. 1851. *Allgemeine Geschichte: von Anfang der historischen Kenntniß auf unsere Zeiten,* vol. 1, Braunschweig: George Westermann, 45: 'Die Geschichte kann nicht anders, als eine Lehrerin der Klugheit, des Rechtes und der Tugend seyn.'

150. Friedrich Nietzsche, 'On the Uses and Disadvantages of History for Life', in Friedrich Nietzsche, *Untimely Meditations,* Cambridge: Cambridge University Press, 83. For practical reasons, I will directly refer to and quote from the English translation of the text.

151. Nietzsche, 'On the Uses and Disadvantages of History for Life', 97.

152. Alan Megill. 1987. *Prophets of Extremity: Nietzsche, Heidegger, Foucault, Derrida.* Berkeley: University of California Press, 75.

153. Nietzsche, 'On the Uses and Disadvantages of History for Life', 62: 'Forgetting is essential to action of any kind, just as not only light but darkness is essential for the life of everything organic. A man who wanted to feel historically through and through would be like one forcibly deprived of sleep, or an animal that had to live only by rumination and ever repeated rumination.'

154. Nietzsche, 'On the Uses and Disadvantages of History for Life', 94: 'When the past speaks it always speaks as an oracle: only if you are an architect of the future and know the present will you understand it…. Now it would be right to say that only he who constructs the future has a right to judge the past.'

155. Nietzsche, 'On the Uses and Disadvantages of History for Life', 121.

156. Nietzsche, 'On the Uses and Disadvantages of History for Life', 95.

157. Löwith, *Meaning and History,* 214–222.

158. Cf. Annette Wittkau-Horgby. 2005. 'Droysen and Nietzsche: Two Different Answers to the Discovery of Historicity', in Peter Koslowski (ed.), *The Discovery of Historicity in German Idealism and Historism,* Berlin: Springer, 73.

159. Curiously, Nietzsche never returned to using expressions such as 'the supra-historical' and the distinction between monumental, antiquarian and critical history, which later on ended up undergoing a large reception in the context of the debate on historiography. See Thomas Brobjer. 2004. 'Nietzsche's View of the Value of Historical Studies and Methods', *Journal of the History of Ideas* 65(2): 310–311.

160. Thomas Brobjer. 2007. 'Nietzsche's Relation to Historical Methods and Nineteenth Century German Historiography', *History and Theory* 46(2): 178–179; Wolfgang Röd, Heinrich Schmidinger and Rainer Thurnher. 2002. *Die Philosophie des ausgehenden 19. und des 20. Jahrhunderts,* vol. 3: *Lebensphilosophie und Existezphilosophie,* Munich: C.H. Beck, 61.

161. Brobjer, 'Nietzsche's View of the Value of Historical Studies and Methods', 301.

162. Reill, *The German Enlightenment and the Rise of Historicism,* 34–37.

163. Reill, *The German Enlightenment and the Rise of Historicism,* 42: 'In actuality, pragmatic history was for Gatterer the opposite of exemplar history. Pragmatic history placed particulate events into a complex system of acting and interreacting relations. It did not abstract the singular event and attempt to discern some universally valid truth or moral from that isolated occurrence.... The specific meaning Gatterer attached to pragmatic history was one with which the majority of the *Aufklärers* would agree.' Ulrich Muhlack has proposed a very different interpretation of this topic. He affirms that the historians of the German late Enlightenment were still strongly linked to the exemplar theory of history: 'Tatsächlich hängen sie alle der ‹historia magistra vitae› an, mit der eine solche Historisierung zuletzt unvereinbar ist.... Statt um eine Verbindung von historisch-kritischer Quellenforschung und literarischer Darstellung handelt es sich also um eine prekäre Koexistenz zweier gegenläufiger Ansprüche. Dass dabei, wie bei Irenicus oder bei Gatterer, die Quellenforschung vor der literarischen Bemühung überwiegt, ist keine grundsätzliche Lösung, sondern nur ein anderer Ausdruck für einen Widerspruch, der ihm Rahmen humanistischer und aufklärerischer Geschichtswissenschaft nicht aufgehoben werden kann' (Muhlack, *Geschichtswissenschaft im Humanismus und in der Aufklärung,* 403).

164. Daniel Fulda. 1996. *Wissenschaft aus Kunst. Die entstehung der modernen deutschen Geschichtsschreibung, 1760–1860,* Berlin: Walter de Gruyter, 59–61. Much like Muhlack, however, Daniel Fulda argued (167–168) that the pragmatism of the historians of the late Enlightenment still reflected an exemplary strategy of sense generation.

165. Martin Peters. 2003. *Altes Reich und Europa: Der Historiker, Statistiker und Publizist August Ludwig (v.) Schlözer (1735–1809),* Berlin LIT, 183–186.

166. August Ludwig Schlözer. 1997. *Vorstellung seiner Universal-Historie,* Waltrop: Hartmut Spenner, 26: '[Die Universal-Historie besteht] nur [aus] Facta, aber zweckmäßig gewählte, und so neben einander gestellte Facta, daß der Leser von selbst das Urtheil hinzudenken muß. Sie vermeidet die Mine, pragmatisch zu seyn: aber sie instruiert den Leser, es auf eigne Kosten zu werden.'

167. Jaeger and Rüsen, *Geschichte des Historismus,* 86–92; Southard, *Droysen and the Prussian School of History.*

168. Heinrich von Sybel. 1925. 'Brief an Hermann Baumgarten, 27.01.1871', in Julius Heyderhoff (ed.), *Die Sturmjahre der preußisch-deutschen Einigung 1859–1870. Politische Briefe aus dem Nachlaß liberaler Parteiführer,* vol. 1, Bonn: Kurt Schroeder, 494: 'Lieber Freund, ich schreibe von all diesen Quisquilien und meine Augen gehen immer herüber zu dem Extrablatt und die Tränen fließen mir über die Backen. Wodurch hat man die Gnade Gottes verdient, so große und mächtige Dinge erleben zu dürfen? Und wie wird man nachher leben? Was zwanzig Jahre der Inhalt alles Wünschens und Strebens gewesen, das ist nun in so unendlich herrlicher Weise erfüllt! Woher soll man in meinen Lebensjahren noch einen neuen Inhalt für das weitere Leben nehmen?'

169. Jörn Rüsen. 1993. *Konfigurationen des Historismus. Studien zur deutschen Wissenschaftskultur,* Frankfurt am Main: Surhkamp, 325.

170. Jacob Burckhardt. 1979. *Reflections on History,* Indianapolis, IN: Liberty Fund, 41. For practical reasons, I will directly refer to and quote from the English translation of the text.

171. Burckhardt, *Reflections on History,* 38.

172. Burckhardt, *Reflections on History,* 46.

173. Burckhardt, *Reflections on History,* 39.

174. Droysen, *Historik* 1: 50 [Vorlesungstext, 1857]: 'Dem zur Seite [von Kant, Herder, Schiller und Humboldt] gingen dann die großartige historische Tätigkeit der jungen Universität Göttingen, wo Schlözer, Gatterer, Spittler, Michaelis, Heyne, Pütter, bis Hugo hinab, also Theologen, Juristen, Philologen und Staatsrechtler, alle im wesentlichen in derselben Richtung wirkten. Das ist die erste recht eigentlich historische Schule.' On the Göttingen School and the conceptions of world history developed by authors closely connected to it, see André de Melo Araújo. 2012. *Weltgeschichte in Göttingen. Eine Studie über das spätaufklärerische universalhistorische Denken, 1756-1815,* Bielefeld: Transcript.

175. Droysen, *Historik* 1: 251 [Vorlesungstext, 1857]: 'Und soll jeder Schulknabe an den großen Helden und Staatsmännern sich Muster nehmen, ihnen nachzueifern? Weder Muster zur Nachahmung noch Regeln zur Wiederanwendung zu geben kann der Zweck der Historie sein.'

176. Droysen, *Historik* 1: 250 [Vorlesungstext, 1857]: 'Es war der Grundzug der fälschlich pragmatisch genannten Historie, daß man aus der Geschichte lernen solle, wie man sich in ähnlich vorkommenden Fällen benehmen müsse.'

177. Droysen, *Historik* 2: 506 [Über das Geschichtsstudium in Deutschland, 1869]: 'Wenn es Wissenschaften giebt, die nicht bloß klüger, sondern auch besser machen, so gehört die Historie zu diesen.'

178. Droysen, *Historik* 1: 250 [Vorlesungstext, 1857]: 'Aber warum ist es wichtig, sich über das Vergangene zu belehren? Und wieso kann es dienen für das, was im Lauf der menschlichen Dinge sich auf gleiche oder ähnliche Weise ereignen wird? Es ist in der Geschichte unserer Wissenschaft verkehrte Antwort in Menge darauf gegeben worden; denn daß es so sei, empfand man wohl, aber man ist sich spät erst klargeworden, warum es so sei.'

179. Droysen, *Historik* 1: 60 [Vorlesungstext, 1857].

180. Droysen, *Historik* 1: 250 [Vorlesungstext, 1857]: 'Es ist ganz in der Ordnung, wenn in den großen Administrationen sich die Tradition der Geschäfte feststellt, denn davon die meisten wiederholen sich. Aber gerade die großen und wichtigen Dinge, die die Historie am liebsten behandelt, wiederholen sich nicht, sondern nur die gewöhnlichen Dinge.'

181. Droysen, *Historik* 2: 177 [Vorlesung über neure Geschichte, 1842]: 'Sie [die Geschichte] ist keineswegs dieselbe zu aller Zeit, sondern eben wie sie die Betrachtung der Vergangenheiten von der jedesmaligen Gegenwart aus ist, so ist dies ihre fortdauernde Arbeit, mit der fortschreitenden Entwickelung der Gedanken empor zu klimmen und von immer neuen und neuen Höhepunkten aus die Vergangenheit zu überblicken, sie als präsentes Bewußtsein hier und jetzt zu erfassen.'

CHAPTER 2

The Theoretical Design
of a New Justification

Historical Thinking

Despite having rejected the exemplar theory of history, Droysen followed the path formerly described as neo-pragmatic and continued to consider historiography as a didactic enterprise. Ultimately, this means he believed history still had something to teach, even after it was dismissed from its position as *magistra vitae*. However, in reconciling his critique of historiography's exemplary function with his insistence that it should, nevertheless, keep performing a didactic task, he confronted a complicated theoretical problem: Droysen had to explain how historical knowledge could have a non-exemplary impact on human subjectivity and agency. This was, by the way, a problem some of the above-mentioned critics of the exemplary use of historiography deliberately preferred to avoid. Indeed, the majority of them did not comprehensively discuss which arguments and practices would replace the model of historiography they were casting into doubt.

Droysen, contrariwise, did it. In his concept of 'historical thinking', he condensed most of his attempt to re-conceive the function of historiography. That concept basically indicates that what one can reasonably learn from history are not contents and models to be imitated, but rather a formal way of thinking. Historical thinking means the subjective ability to put the present into the perspective of the past, that is, to see the present as a result of past developments. It is hence a tool for perceiving the historicity of a given lifeworld. Moreover, Droysen sees the capacity to think historically about the world one lives in as being not only cognitive but also practical in nature. Accordingly, historical thinking becomes the most important departure point for both realistic and free human agency and decision-making.

Droysen thus discharged a didactics centred on historical examples and replaced it with another focused on the promotion of historical thinking. But what else did he mean by this notion? A good starting point for an answer to that question is to recall that with his *Historik,* Droysen generally attempted to establish a sort of meta-discipline in charge of promoting the self-awareness of historical science. He assumed that historical theory would help historians become more conscious about what is going on when they do their jobs. To accomplish this, historical theory had, among other things, to awaken 'the belief that one thinks and can learn to think historically'.[1]

Historical thinking, or the way of thinking on which the science of history is based, delimits the specificities of the historical approach vis-à-vis other kinds of approaches to reality. In other words, historical thinking is the bedrock of the historical method. As such, it remains in opposition to other basic ways of making sense of reality. It is hence interesting to recall some of the contrasting arguments with which Droysen differentiates historical thinking from other approaches.

First of all, historical thinking is an empirical kind of thinking. It thus is opposed to the non-empirical, purely logical and, finally, 'speculative' way of thinking that Droysen assumes to be typical of metaphysics and theology. Droysen admits that both historical and speculative thinking share the assumption that events and ideas do not occur arbitrarily in human history. Both modes of thinking presuppose that historical events are interconnected within the historical process, and that ultimately this process was put into motion by God. However, according to Droysen, the speculative approach considers historical events as resulting from strictly logical necessities and therefore takes them as predictable. Conversely, the method based on historical thinking is much more open to contingency, and even when it concerns the explanation of causal connexions, it explicitly avoids taking into account either final or absolute causes.[2] It is precisely because it restricts itself to this-worldly causal connections, thus leaving to metaphysics and theology the problem of final and absolute causes, that historical thinking resorts to empirical research and rationale.

Secondly, historical thinking is opposed to what Droysen called the 'mathematical-physical method'. To be sure, he saw both approaches as empirical ways to put reality into perspective, but stated that they differ diametrically in their ways of doing so. Mathematical-physical thinking would predispose one to systematically neglect individual and particular features of the phenomena under consideration, as well as to anchor explanations in general laws.[3] Interestingly enough, however, in contrasting the natural sciences to history, Droysen did not propose to associate the former with knowledge of the general and the latter with knowledge of particulars. For him, historical thinking indeed begins with particular information on events and processes from the past, but it also aims to access a sort of general knowledge. The difference is rather that instead of promoting the establishment of general laws, historical thinking leads to what Droysen called a 'morphological' knowledge, that is, a kind of empirical knowledge centred on 'shaping forces', 'form-giving' (*Formgebung*) and 'anomaly' – in the place of analogy.[4] In Droysen's view, the historical world, unlike nature, is not constituted by 'material substrates made of unchangeable attributes'. Quite the contrary, it is a realm in which the essential units are forms in continuous development and change.[5] Historical thinking therefore brings about a certain general knowledge of the 'shaping forces' (*formende Kräften*) of the historical world. Its cognitive target is these general forces rather than the particular results of their action and interaction – the general forms, rather than the formed stuff itself.[6]

Thirdly, historical thinking differs not only from other scientific methods of human understanding,[7] but also from an aestheticizing way of approaching the past, namely heroic sagas. Droysen defines the saga as a kind of account of a historical event or character that somehow invests it with a mythological aura. He sees sagas as reversed myths: starting with something that happened, a saga blurs at a certain point into something that could not have happened, whereas a myth's point of departure is an event that could not have happened and that is, so to speak, normalized through the account.[8] For Droysen, historical thinking represents a qualitative step beyond sagas and myths, which he regards as 'childish' ways of making sense of the world because they 'arbitrarily beautify the darkness of the past' instead of objectively reconstructing it. Before the emergence of history, Droysen argues, the only resource at the disposal of peoples (*Völker*) wishing to address their pasts was to imagine, by means of myths and sagas, a 'subjective world that was rather a picture of their own interests and gifts than an image of the objective reality.'[9] He recalls that when ancient Greece's classical historians planted the first seeds of historical thinking they put themselves in opposition to myths and sagas. The invention of historiography represented, then, precisely an attempt to 'bring order, coherence, and chronological system into the virgin forest of [mythical] traditions'.[10] Clearly, here Droysen is defining historical thinking as an objective way of addressing the human past, and detaching it from non- or less objective approaches.

In addition, Droysen depicts the type of understanding typical of historical thinking as a step ahead of more immediate types of knowledge of the past. For instance, he distinguishes scientific historical understanding from the kind of knowledge about the past that is directly conveyed by tradition. The latter is a 'knowledge [that] is ours as if it were not', 'owning us more than we own it'. Historical (scientific) understanding, in contrast, stimulates its subjects to attain an awareness of the past in the present, thus helping to overcome the submersion in unreflecting traditions – a cultural condition against which he saw history as the only remedy. We could 'translate' Droysen's point in the following way: with the aid of historical thinking, one becomes able to objectively recognize the circumstances that have interacted to produce one's cultural environment, and to cognitively grasp the traditions one lives in. In short, through historical thinking, one becomes able to properly know and talk about the historicity around and inside oneself.[11]

For Droysen, finally, whenever scholars perform historical thinking, they are pursuing the purpose of finding or telling the truth about the human world. Droysen conceives historical truth as a substance located beneath the surface of history; only by means of historical thinking is one empowered to perceive 'in the appearing things the active forces through which they are and become.'[12] Hence, establishing historical truth equals identifying such forces, mapping their interaction and tracing in their development the genesis of the present. Droysen relates historical truth ultimately to the recognition of the historicity of the human world. True historical knowledge is a valid knowledge of the real cultural, social and economic structures interacting beneath the surface of historical events.[13] These structures, which silently establish the conditions for human life in a certain present, are not immediately accessible and perceivable. According to Droysen, only historical thinking, only historical interpretation, can grant access to them. Historical thinking is again the key to the historicity of the past and the present. It is the competence that enables a historian to see what 'is' from the perspective of what 'became'.[14]

To be sure, Droysen's uses of 'historical thinking' in methodological contexts are highly complex, but they are also dialectically interrelated. All in all, it is plausible to say that he considers historical thinking to be the basic procedure of a special kind of scientific method: the historical method. Knowledge generated with the aid of historical thinking is a praxis-oriented knowledge destined to empirically, morphologically and objectively unveil the historicity of a given present situation.

Hermeneutics

By considering historical thinking as the bedrock of the historical method, Droysen developed a conception of method that can be called 'hermeneutical'. A good indicator of this hermeneutical character of Droysen's historical methodology is his constant emphasis that historical research neither starts nor ends in source criticism. This persuasion thoroughly permeates all Droysen's theoretical texts, and it surely reflects his lack of sympathy for the nineteenth-century champion of factual research, Leopold von Ranke. In fact, by the time Droysen criticized the theoretician Wilhelm Wachsmuth for having professed 'a eunuch-like objectivity',[15] he had already often used similar terms to refer to Ranke, his students, and his followers – and would continue to do so. Particularly in his correspondence, Droysen demonstrates considerable irritation with what he saw as the primacy of the Rankean research program within the then contemporary German historiographical scene. In a letter to his son Gustav, dated only a few months before his death, he criticizes Ranke's research methods and his plea for neutrality in historiography as having exerted a perverse influence on junior historians. Ranke's followers were, Droysen continues, mere composers of 'annals of kings', who specialized in 'adding and subtracting quotes' so as to produce an allegedly objective historical account. They would have rejected the ancient Latin precept (reawakened by Kant's definition of *Aufklärung*) of '*sapere audi*' (dare to know) and hidden themselves behind 'the lazy correctness of trifles'.[16] Indeed, Droysen's considerations of historical method are premised on the irritated assumption that under the influence of the Rankean school, German historians had 'sank into the so-called criticism'.[17] But however strong Droysen's personal and intellectual antipathy towards Ranke might have been, Droysen also had several epistemological and methodological reasons to attack his rival's methodical precepts. The hermeneutical methodology he had worked focused not on the principles behind the historians' factual research, but above all on the linkage of meaning between investigated past and past investigator. Because of that, he moved source criticism into a rather subordinate position.

One notion stands for Droysen's predilection for hermeneutics over factual positivism: understanding or interpretation.[18] Droysen was actually one of the first scholars to resort to the hermeneutical concept of understanding as a way to summarize the typical working method of the human sciences. In his *Historik*, he innovatively related both understanding and interpretation to the production of historical knowledge, condensing this perspective into a formula that is today perhaps his most cited quote: 'the essence of historical method is to understand by means of research'.[19] In the early versions of his lectures, he linked this last sentence to the appositive phrase '[it] is interpretation'.[20] Also noteworthy is that this famous formula first appeared not in theoretical writing, but in the opening statement of the first volume of his *History of Prussian Politics* (1855), where Droysen affirms: 'There are several opinions concerning the nature and the task of the historical studies. Maybe one could sum them up by saying that the essence of the historical studies is to learn how to understand by means of research.'[21]

As probably all analysts of Droysen's methodology have grasped, the formula 'to understand by means of research' (*forschend verstehen*) conveys the quintessence of Droysen's methodology. On the one hand, it acknowledges that history is a science that produces empirical knowledge based on analysis of evidence from the past. But on the other hand, the term understanding indicates that history is not just an empirical but also a practical knowledge. Accordingly, to historically understand is much more than to merely establish facts. For Droysen, understanding presupposes that 'the same ethical and intellectual categories' that are traceable in the phenomenon or expression to be understood are also there in the mind of the observer inside of which the act of understanding takes place.[22] Understanding, to quote another of Droysen's definitions, arises from 'the kinship of our nature with that of the utterances lying before us as historical material'.[23] It is, therefore, a way of cognition that concentrates on the link between the investigated past and the investigator's (and his or her audience's) present.

Droysen developed his hermeneutical notion of method into a threefold scheme of phases of historical research that is structured upon the differentiation between heuristics, criticism and interpretation.[24] The first phase, heuristics, encompasses the finding and selection of the 'historical material', a term Droysen uses to designate the evidence that the historian critically works out and interprets so as to understand a given historical constellation of events or experiences. Droysen's reflections on the phenomenology of historical data are indeed highly interesting, but they can be addressed here only summarily. He starts from the premise that all material to be historically investigated is 'something from the pasts of the human world which has not passed yet'.[25] The material in which historians anchor their accounts refers to the past but is, according to him, actually, present: it is the past as handed down to the present. Correspondingly, Droysen elaborated an ingenious typology of historical materials by which he basically differentiates between sources (*Quellen*) and remains (*Überreste*). On the one hand, sources are a form of evidence produced with the purpose of generating a certain memory of events, as in official documents, memoirs, historical texts and so forth. On the other, remains are characterized as vestiges spontaneously left over from past to present, as for instance, archaeological remains or ongoing traditions, buildings, institutions or languages.[26]

In Droysen's methodological notion of heuristics, however, the finding and selection of the historical material is subordinated to a moment that he defines as the point of departure and the main criterion for every attempt to understand the past. Droysen calls it the 'historical question' (*historische Frage*),[27] which, he explains, arises from a quasi-natural, existential background. As soon as maturity is reached in the life of an individual or a community, he argues, a need emerges to question the contents of traditional representations of the past.[28] As a discursive strategy for correlating past and present, history therefore fulfils the role of a critical alternative to tradition. This existential doubting of the contents of tradition represents a main presupposition for the production of historical knowledge. It is manifested in the fact that historians organize their research with reference to a key question or set of questions they intend to answer. According to Droysen, the historical question thus accommodates cultural demands for orientation, in connection with which it evolves into an insight or a pre-apprehension of what is (or is not) to be empirically captured during the investigation.[29] It is ultimately the crucial mechanism propelling the progress of historical knowledge,[30] as it guides historical researchers along a path that starts in an intuitive form of pre-knowledge and ends up at empirically based knowledge. With this argument, Droysen illustrates how cognitive progress in history has little to do with arbitrary discoveries or uncontrolled curiosity. Research can bring fruitful results only if researchers have an idea of what they want to find. 'One must correctly ask the things,' he maintains – 'only then they can answer.'[31] The methodical wisdom conveyed in this sentence remains as valid today as it was in Droysen's time.

It should be stressed that the idea that the historical question is basic to the development of historical research seems to be an argument pioneered by Droysen. It later turned up in several famous texts on the principles and practice of the human sciences – though without mention of Droysen's name.[32] Max Weber, for instance, would eventually arrive at the idea that what underlies the sciences' working field is 'not the objective interconnections between the "things" but the conceptual interconnections between the problems'.[33] Later on, within the context of the Anglo-Saxon historiographical discussion, Robin Collingwood distinguished himself by juxtaposing his criticism on traditional historiography – which he ironically calls 'scissors-and-paste history' – with the reasoning that genuine historical knowledge ('scientific history') is founded upon the questions a historian addresses to the leftover evidence of the past.[34] Moreover, throughout the twentieth century, the French tradition of historical theory in particular (from Marc Bloch and Lucien Febvre, via Henri-Irénée Marrou, to Paul Veyne and François Furet) very much helped popularize a similar understanding of the centrality of the historical question in historical research and historiography.[35]

The second phase differentiated in Droysen's scheme of historical method is the verification of historical evidence, that is, source criticism (*Kritik*). The task of criticism is to clarify the relationship between the events addressed by the historical question and the evidence at hand that attests to the occurrence of those events. In other words, criticism proves whether and to what extent the information conveyed by the historical materials is reliable. Droysen holds, therefore, that the rightful result of the historian's critical inquiry into the material is not the restitution of an objective or exact fact, but rather 'the placing of the material in such a condition as to render possible a relatively safe and correct view'.[36] Accordingly, he proposes subdividing the phase of criticism into four stages: (1) the criticism of genuineness, by which one ascertains whether the material really is what it claims or is taken to be; (2) the diacritical procedure, by which one investigates the changes and interpolations through which a certain piece of historical material has passed in the process of its transmission up to the present; (3) the criticism of validity, by which one determines to what extent the conveyed information can be held as correct; and (4) the critical arrangement of the verified material, by which one ascertains whether the materials at hand contain all the information needed to answer the research question, and to what extent the available information is incomplete.[37]

But as I have stressed above, the culmination of historical research, for Droysen, was not in the critical verification of the materials but in a third methodical phase, that of interpretation. He often emphasized his opinion that the essence of historical science lay in interpretation rather than criticism: 'Here is the point where I am consciously dissociating myself from the method that has been newly widespread by my discipline colleagues; they use to call this method the critical one, whilst I am pushing the interpretation to the foreground'.[38] Yet in putting interpretation into the methodological spotlight, Droysen does not deny the importance of source criticism; indeed, he keeps recognizing it as a methodical imperative. His emphasis on interpretation rather suggests that the work of historians normally should not have source criticism as its finishing line. For him, the critical treatment of the information conveyed by the historical material only prepares the ground for interpretation, the methodical moment in which information on the past is reconnected with the practical demand for orientation that has already been internalized by the historical question. Droysen assumes that, given the usual complexity of the events historians attempt to understand, historical interpretation can be configured in four different albeit complementary ways: (1) pragmatic interpretation, which reconstructs the course of events through the conflation and synthesis of data obtained from different pieces of historical material – or, in cases where testimonies are scarce, through formulation of analogies and hypotheses; (2) interpretation of the material conditions that framed the events in question – something analogous to what, decades later, would be called structural analysis; (3) psychological interpretation, which focuses on understanding the subjective acts of will behind the emergence of certain events; and (4) interpretation of ideas, which refers the events in question back to the 'ethical powers'.[39]

Furthermore, according to Droysen, historical interpretation is not yet the writing of historical texts – that is, it is not the performance he refers to as 'apodeixis' or 'representation' (*Darstellung*). The space here does not permit a detailed account of Droysen's take on the issue of historical representation, though it is worth mentioning his suggestion that only the historical representation is the final and exclusive measure of the success of the historical question.[40] Besides not taking representation as a synonym for interpretation, Droysen also remains far from naively regarding representation as a mere restitution of facts. Even Hayden White, one of the most prominent critics of nineteenth-century historical thought, recognized this when he remarked that Droysen kept aware that 'the historian's discourse is something quite other than the referent about which it speaks'.[41] In any case, this awareness does not lead Droysen to detach the operation of writing history from that of researching past evidence – something that White's own poetics of historiography indeed does.[42] Quite the contrary, it is this sense of the connectivity between research and representation that ultimately undergirds the methodological significance of Droysen's concept of interpretation. Historical interpretation, as Jörn Rüsen has clearly explained, consists of a sort of meaningful template filled with empirical information that prefigures the historical representation but does not substitute it. As such, interpretation plays a mediatory role between criticism and representation, balancing factuality and fictionality in historiography.[43]

A major consequence of Droysen's emphasis on interpretation and understanding was, finally, a redefinition of the problem of historical truth. Droysen often accused Ranke and other contemporary historical scholars of having reduced the problem of historical truth to that of the accuracy of the facts.[44] In his opinion, the establishment of factual correctness was, in any case, only the first step towards historical truth, and definitely not the last. For this reason he contended that one should 'proceed from correctness to truth'.[45] By elaborating this differentiation, he was proposing a definition that in many ways resembles Giambattista Vico's (1668–1744) consideration that 'philosophy contemplates reason, whence comes knowledge of the true; philology observes the authority of human choice, whence comes consciousness of the certain'.[46]

It is important to mention that, according to Droysen, the historical truth located beyond the realm of source criticism is in no way an absolute truth. It is bounded by the historian's own perspective and context – by what Johann Martin Chladenius (1710–1759), in his pioneering historical hermeneutics, had called 'point of view' (*Sehe-Punkt*).[47] Droysen did believe in a certain form of absolute truth that could be pursued only by means of religious experience, but he emphasized that this was not the sort of truth history was concerned with – and in this respect, at least, his arguments were not Hegelian at all.[48] In Droysen's view, historical truth is equivalent to a relative truth. This means he sees the truth-value invested in historiography as dependent on the historian's own perspective, context, beliefs and opinions: 'I neither want to seem as if I had more nor as if I had less than the relative truth of my standpoint; the truth as bequeathed to me by my fatherland, my religious and political convictions, and by the time I live in.'[49] Droysen thus recognized the epistemological relativity of historical truth in his own historical views over time, admitting that his personal way of seeing history was closely related to his present context. Indeed, as he further acknowledged, in the future one could and probably would see differently what he then saw as being historically true.[50] If we apply this prophecy to Droysen's own passionate *History of Prussian Politics*, we might discover that the theoretician Droysen was terribly right regarding the future of the major work written by the historian Droysen.

Rules of Understanding and Sense of Reality

Despite the above-mentioned divergence over the issue of historical truth, in the main, Droysen's philosophical underpinnings were assimilated from Hegel, whose lectures the student Droysen attended at the University of Berlin with enthusiastic frequency.[51] Droysen's theoretical texts are replete with Hegelian notions – or, better said, with 'Hegelianoid' concepts, for they often resemble but do not simply replicate Hegel's.[52] This is a valid claim, especially if we recall that Droysen shares with Hegel a general, speculative, progressive, teleological conception of history – the idea of a history of humankind that transcends all particular histories, and whose main 'plot' is the realization of the idea of freedom (*Freiheit*). Furthermore, Droysen explicitly elaborated the theory of the 'ethical powers' that features in the second part of his *Historik* from Hegel's ethical theory.[53] The Hegelian notes in Droysen's view of ethics are particularly evident; one could say, for instance, that for Droysen, acquiring an image of past events through historical interpretation only makes sense if the acquired knowledge has the potential to contribute to the ethical (and ultimately religious) task of perceiving, deciphering and building a future that is already encrypted in the process of history.

Nevertheless, whereas Hegel furnished the foundation upon which Droysen built his *Systematik*, that is, his theory of the historical world (where human beings live and which historians strive to cognitively access), Droysen's theory of historical method – or, in his own terms, his *Methodik* – was developed under the strong influence of Wilhelm von Humboldt.[54] Droysen was exceptionally parsimonious with compliments for other past and contemporary historical theorists, but he called Humboldt 'a Bacon of historical science'.[55] Furthermore, he quoted Humboldt's text *On the Historians' Task* at some of the most crucial moments of his own methodological reflections.[56] As a matter of fact, decisive features of Droysen's notions of interpretation and understanding evolved from the intense dialogue he had with some of Wilhelm von Humboldt's texts.

It should be noted first that the forerunner Humboldt had contributed to a significant expansion of the semantic field associated with the concept of understanding. Previously, hermeneutical tradition had regarded understanding as a process related to the philological decoding of texts and text-like artefacts. In the first decades of the nineteenth century, however, Humboldt and others extended the amplitude of the meanings encompassed by the notions of understanding and interpretation by associating them with the general situation of linguistic communication.[57] In so doing, they prepared the terrain for a subsequent differentiation in the semantics of methodological discourse, after which the concept of understanding came into use as a way to sum up the specificity of human science's cognitive performance.

The paradigm on which Humboldt based his hermeneutical considerations is, therefore, that of interpersonal understanding in everyday life. For Humboldt, the general condition of possibility for understanding is that the person who understands possesses in her or himself 'an analogue of that which will be understood later: an original, antecedent congruity between subject and object'. The act of understanding is thus the product of neither a pure subjective projection nor an undistorted specular duplication of the object.[58] Human beings, Humboldt continues, are able to understand other human beings (or what they do, say and write) because the one who is trying to understand something and the other who is delivering something to be understood are never entirely strange to each other. Understanding can take place among them only if they have already come to a situation of a pre-understanding: 'When two beings are completely separated by a chasm, there is no bridge of communication between them; and in order to understand each other, they must, in some other sense, have already understood each other.'[59]

Droysen's historical hermeneutics took over Humboldt's arguments on the condition of possibility for understanding without modifying them substantially.[60] Droysen relates understanding to humans' natural proclivity towards other humans and human products, assuring that animals and plants cannot be understood in the sense that a human being and human utterances can be.[61] Then again, he connects that anthropological assumption with the idea that human beings already possess an immediate subjective (pre-)understanding of human things.[62] Following Humboldt – and the general tendency inaugurated by romantic hermeneutics – Droysen further links understanding to the general assumption that within the process of communication, human beings verbalize something that is already somehow inside them. Understanding is, therefore, someone's understanding of a state of inwardness expressed by someone else; it is the understanding of an 'expression', of an *Ausdruck*. Thus, in order to understand an expression delivered by one person, the second person has to internally re-enact in her or himself the thoughts and feelings that underlie the expression.[63]

Droysen applied these general statements on interpersonal understanding to his characterization of methodical understanding as practised by professional historians.[64] He knew, however, that historical interpretation is far more complicated than mundane interpersonal communication, since dialogue between the historian and human beings from the past, whose 'expressions' the historian attempts to understand, always depends on an intricate chain of transmissions.[65] Droysen observes that frequently, what the historical materials at hand in the present convey 'has already become incomprehensible or almost inaudible'.[66] Past experiences addressed by historical research might have become as strange as a foreign culture, and historians possess only fragments on which to base their views of the whole. According to Droysen, historians can overcome this difficulty only by mutually referring parts to wholes, states to processes, actors to circumstances, past to present and vice versa. To historically understand a particular past phenomenon, historians must, therefore, methodically produce and enter hermeneutic circles.[67]

Droysen's emphasis on historical interpretation or understanding points to the existence of a strong epistemological realm within his *Historik*. In his texts, logical considerations of historical knowledge are particularly predominant in sentences like: 'It does not require deep penetration to see that the human acts which are now historical, at the moment when they happened and in the minds of those through whom and for whom they happened, had only in the rarest instances the purpose or determination to be historical deeds.'[68] 'Deeds', for Droysen, 'turn into history, but they are not history';[69] here he meant, among other things, that the idea of history is indissociable from some sort of subjective interpretation, for instance of a *'forschendes Verstehen'*. This, by the way, was an insight that would significantly impact even neo-Kantian epistemologists by the end of the century.[70] However, it would be hasty to conclude, based on those sentences, that Droysen's notion of interpretation condenses a pure Kantian logic of historical understanding, a sort of critique of historical reason. As Herbert Schnädelbach has pointed out, Droysen worked with conceptions of history and historiography that restrained him from adopting the kind of ahistorical transcendental point of view that characterized Kant's theory of knowledge. In Droysen's theory of history, historical consciousness means both 'consciousness of history' and 'consciousness of itself as a product of history'. Because of this, formal criteria of knowledge and material preconceptions about the process of history (in other words, epistemology and ontology) necessarily interlace.[71]

Droysen's concept of interpretation documents this interconnection, for it is defined as a methodical procedure that presupposes the already mentioned correspondence between *interpretans* and *interpretandum*. In historiography, the 'antecedent congruity between subject and object' (Humboldt) corresponds to the inner connection between the subject of historical knowledge and its object, the historical process. In the cases of Humboldt and Droysen, this connection is established with the aid of the main pillar of modern idealist philosophy, namely, the very notion of 'idea'. Within this framework, ideas are taken as moving forces of a sort that, on the one hand, propel change in the objective world and thus also in the historical process, and on the other, direct human cognitive capacities – among them, in particular, that of historical knowledge. In the philosophical atmosphere of the first half of the German nineteenth century, ideas corresponded – according to Wilhelm Dilthey, one of their earliest and best analysts – to 'a powerful, but not directly visible principle' that lends an initial impulse and a general orientation to historical transformations. Hence, human subjects willing to produce a 'positive historical effect' with their actions must attune their conduct to the general tendency comprised by the idea.[72] It is thus essential that ideas be cognitively apprehended. For Humboldt, historians cannot properly perform their task of 'presenting what actually happened' without resorting to 'ideas' located deep bellow the directly observable surface of events.[73] Droysen's emphasis on the 'interpretation of ideas' as a key part of his theory of method,[74] as well as the centrality of his theory of the ethical powers, which he also calls 'ethical ideas', shows that also in this regard he was continuing on the way paved by Humboldt .

In historiography, ideas link subject and object because they are located on the level of the objects as much as on that of the subjects of knowledge.[75] Droysen's historical hermeneutics is actually a special derivation of this general metaphysics of ideas, according to which 'everything which is active in world history is also moving within the human heart'.[76] For Droysen, everyone who produces or acquires historical knowledge has already been 'produced' by history.[77] History, as an object of knowledge, has always 'flowed' into the subject before he or she starts cognitively to grasp it. History is, finally, always more than an objective process going on outside the boundaries of subjectivity; it represents the temporal continuum within which the subject's lifeworld originates. Droysen's *Historik,* then, presents not only human beings in general, but also the subjects of historical knowledge in particular as points of confluence of historical developments.[78] By connecting historical knowledge with this subjective awareness of historicity, he furthermore delineates a way for historiography to develop into a non-exemplary and genetic channel of cultural orientation.

Evidently, for Droysen, historical interpretation or understanding is not directed merely towards past times, but ultimately towards the effects of the past in the present, that is, towards the present's historicity. 'From every point in the present', he observes, 'a cone of light, energized by our science, shines back into the night of the past (*Nacht des Vergangenseins*).'[79] His insistence on keeping history strongly related to the broad contemporary context within which it is researched and written – in short, his presentism – shows, again, a relative distance from the content of Ranke's most cited formulas. For Droysen, historical understanding neither focuses on merely showing how things really were ('*wie es eigentlich gewesen*') nor assumes each epoch to be immediate to God; rather, it attempts to reveal how the contemporary world emerged and how, within the course of history, one epoch led to another and so on, successively, up to the present.[80] To understand a specific current state of affairs is finally, in his view, to understand the process that generated it: 'There is no doubt that we will completely understand what is, only as soon as we realise how it came into being.'[81]

Despite the semantic overlappings evidenced by Droysen's use of 'historical understanding' and 'historical thinking', there is one important difference between the two terms. It is perceptible in Droysen's insistence on speaking of historical thinking as a mental process that is more than the fundament of the scientific method by which historical scholars can establish truths. According to him, historical thinking not only produces true knowledge but is also, to some extent, itself the goal of all historical knowledge. This means that, for Droysen, historians use, or should use, historical thinking not just to research and write history; they should also convey to others the way of thinking that structures their work. Droysen makes this point clear by stating that 'to think historically is by no means a task that exclusively belongs to historical researchers and writers of history books'. And he continues, mentioning his opinion that all who are theoretically or practically involved with the 'shaping of the ethical powers' should be able to apprehend and understand these powers in their continuity and discontinuity throughout history.[82]

Here Droysen was addressing the issue of conveyance and acquisition of historical thinking, and he would extend his reasoning by highlighting another notion he had borrowed from Wilhelm von Humboldt, namely that of 'sense of reality' (*Sinn für die Wirklichkeiten, Sinn für das Wirkliche*).[83] Every good historian was assumed to possess this skill, which historical texts were supposed to induce also in their readers. It means the capacity to perceive the effective forces that interact under the surface of historical events, or – put another way – the capacity to recognize the deep structures of historical reality. Much like such notions as 'historical thinking', 'understanding' and 'interpretation', that of the sense of reality functions as an alternative description of the procedure that enables historical truths to be reached. But Droysen associates the 'sense of reality' particularly with the historical sciences' social and cultural functions. Humboldt, again, had already established such association, affirming that 'it is the historian who is supposed to awaken and to stimulate a sensibility for reality'.[84] He postulated that the sense of reality that historians should have and help spread is linked with a certain set of basic assumptions. It comprehends the awareness that human existence in time is transient and dependent upon causes that are to be sought in both the past and the present; the recognition that reality is shaped according to an 'inner necessity' – that is, that reason lies behind the world's apparent contingency; and finally the opinion that knowledge of the constitution of the human world by no means contradicts the primacy of human freedom.[85] It is thus no surprise that Droysen found in Humboldt's notion a simple label condensing much of what he himself wanted to express on the issue of the value and function of history.

Droysen also imported from Humboldt's discussion of the sense of reality the idea that historical knowledge's influence on readers and students is a matter of form rather than content. As Humboldt had said, the sense of reality 'occurs more through the form attached to events than through events themselves.'[86] Droysen, of course, agreed. For him, too, histories should be cherished not so much for the content they can convey to their readers, but rather for their potential contribution to development of a form of thinking in the individuals who study them. The differences between Droysen's didactics of historical thinking and previous didactics of historical examples become evident precisely in that point. Unlike the latter, Droysen's theory does not culminate in a fixed canon of pragmatically relevant *contents*, but in a pragmatically relevant *form* of thinking. According to Ulrich Muhlack's interpretation, once Humboldt's notion of the sense of reality was affirmed, the only remaining legitimate historical canon was that of historical method itself: a formal, agreed-upon set of procedures that regulate the historian's approach to past issues.[87]

Droysen, once again, did not think differently. While making the case for the study of history in his theoretical writings, he did not argue for or against the study of certain special experiences and events; his plea was rather for a form of knowledge and not for particular cognitive contents. According to him, one who studies history only to become acquainted with particular occurrences and facts surely misses the point. He repeatedly admits the importance of factual knowledge; however, he argues that it does not touch the essence of historical studies. From a didactic viewpoint, the reconstruction of parts of the human past's factuality is only a secondary issue. What is essential in historical knowledge is its practical effect. Therefore the social value of historiography lies in its capacity to activate its readers' sense of reality.[88]

Historical thinking, then, is a subjective activity linked above all with a formal implication. Accordingly, cultural orientation through historiography becomes a much more mediated affair than was the case within the framework of the exemplar theory of history. Droysen postulates that when historians understand the driving forces located beyond the events under their consideration, they make a non-exemplary form of didactic stuff available. By getting used to the form of such histories – to the way of thinking upon which they are based – readers are stimulated to develop their sense of reality, that is, an enhanced perception of the general features lying beneath the surface of their current life. The readers of such histories do not learn from them any substantial maxim to be applied in action, or concrete instruction on how to behave in particular situations. Instead they learn a form of thinking that enables them to perceive the historicity of their present, and therefore to put the real conditions of their lifeworld into a genuine historical perspective.[89]

Bildung

The notion that history stimulates the individual's sense of reality, introduced by Humboldt and further developed by Droysen, ingeniously redefined the function of historical studies. More precisely, the acknowledgement that the sense of reality is a crucial skill in historiography and practical life alike and the interrelated assumption that the cultural role of historical studies should be to sponsor historical thinking represented two major innovations in the process towards the redefinition of the function of historiography. But in the language Droysen marshalled to argue the thesis that 'the task of historical studies is to stimulate one's learning of historical thinking',[90] another, not yet mentioned concept played a very important role: 'education', or better, *Bildung*. By means of this concept, Droysen reinforced and advanced the points he had made about the notion of 'sense of reality': namely, that historical thinking goes beyond the methodical realm of the work of historians, that it reaches out to the historians' addressees and that these latter are supposed to learn and develop the capacity of thinking historically, with the aid of concrete historical texts and interpretations.

I begin this discussion of Droysen's notion of *Bildung* by endorsing the statement, made by many other scholars of German culture, that the history and the meaning of that term are of a very complex nature. First of all, in languages other than German it is difficult to find single words that cover all the meanings associated with *Bildung*.[91] The English term education, for instance, which takes into account only one aspect of *Bildung,* is closer to *Erziehung* or *Ausbildung*. The best equivalent of *Bildung* would probably be self-formation, a term used by the English philosopher Shaftsbury (1671–1713), who in the eighteenth century exerted one of the key foreign influences over the development of the German concept.[92] *Bildung* refers to a kind of learning that cannot be reduced to schooling or institutional learning – as *Ausbildung,* for instance, can be. Moreover, attempts to associate *Bildung* directly or exclusively with a single science, world view, political mindset, social rank, religious commitment, philosophical preference or aesthetic proclivity render only an insufficient understanding of the meaning of the concept.[93]

In Droysen's time, *Bildung* was already an abstract cross-disciplinary, crossideological meta-concept. The term's origins, however, lie in the mystictheological and natural-philosophical traditions of the German late medieval period. Then, it frequently referred to the theological idea that human beings are passively 'shaped' (*gebildet*) according to God's image and likeness, but it also comprised the notion that all earthly things are products of shaping processes impelled by natural and divine forces.[94] Generally speaking, only in the eighteenth century, as *Bildung* became a central concept in the pedagogy of the Enlightenment, was a new meaning added to the concept. *Bildung* now started to refer mostly to the general development of human spiritual capacities, clearly going beyond religious/mystical experiences. It began to comprise also secular learning processes related to the sciences, the arts and morality, becoming anchored in both an emancipatory ideal of humankind and the general assumption of the humanity and dignity of all human beings.[95] *Bildung*'s importance in the context of modern German social and political discourses derives precisely

from the impact generated by that pedagogical reshaping of the concept.[96]
This was a main source of inspiration for the creation and establishment of the
German modern educational system, a process that, in the states that would
become Germany, is traceable back to the period between 1770 and 1830.[97]

In the course of the nineteenth century, with its increasing attempts to put
the Enlightenment's general and universalistic ideas of education into practice,
Bildung also became an important parameter for social stratification. Educated
persons (*Gebildete*), educated classes (*gebildete Stände*), educated bourgeoisie
(*gebildetes Bürgertum*): these were terms then employed by individuals aiming
to stress their connection with the new educational institutions and thereby
mark their social distinctiveness vis-à-vis the (uneducated) people (*Volk*).[98] *Bildung* was hence a prevailing concept in both the social imaginary and the self-
understanding of the educated middle classes. As such, however, it bore much
more than the obviously hierarchical traits revealed by the distinctions above.
As Reinhart Koselleck pointed out, *Bildung* was first of all characterized by a
large social openness. Throughout the nineteenth century, it also penetrated
the *habitus* of the social strata above and below the educated middle classes:
both aristocrats and workers, for instance, could and did incorporate *Bildung* as
a major concept into their respective world views.[99] Secondly, according to Koselleck, the nineteenth-century discourse on *Bildung* was indispensable to the
constitution of a sphere of human self-reflexivity that not only served social and
self-differentiation, but also fostered self-enhancement and even self-criticism.
Consequently, *Bildung* stood for the development and cultivation of the human individual's understanding, sensibility, aesthetical perception and morality.
Bildung was also regarded as the means for obtaining human freedom. Based on
these assumptions, one spoke of the *Bildung* of collectivities or subjects other
than human beings, such as peoples (*Völker*), nations, societies, humankind,
and so on.[100]

By the mid nineteenth century, therefore, *Bildung* could be used to designate, among other things, general processes of form-taking in nature; special kinds of mystical and religious experience; the general pedagogical project
originating in the philosophy of the Enlightenment; a kind of social lifestyle
opposed to that of the non-educated classes; the individual capacity to enter
into a reflexive (and self-critical) relationship with the world, others and oneself; and the development of human collectivities. In addition – as one could
say *en passant* – it became also a central topos of German national memory.[101]

In Droysen's use of the term *Bildung* throughout his texts, almost all these
meanings are retrievable in different combinations and emphases.[102] In some
noteworthy cases, however, he slightly expanded the concept's semantic field
by relating it to the issue of the function of historical studies. As already mentioned, Droysen saw history as having the didactic task of promoting historical
thinking. Yet as we approach Droysen's passages on the relationship between

history and *Bildung,* we see historical thinking being portrayed in the big picture, and thus showing up as a capacity that is ultimately a means to another end: life. Droysen's general idea of what human life should be about is encapsulated precisely in the notion of *Bildung* to which he subscribed. He argues that two major consequences are to be expected when human individuals undergo the kind of *Bildung* stimulated by historical thinking. First, historical thinking enables its bearer to perceive the historicity of her or his own present, that is, to view the present world as the result of historical processes; and secondly, *Bildung* and historical thinking predispose the human subject to act in favour of the preservation and advancement of the ethical assets accumulated by humankind throughout its history. Historiography's contribution to *Bildung* therefore involves simultaneous improvement of both the subject's cognitive abilities and what could be called her/his 'ethical' capacities.

What 'ethical' means here will shortly be clarified. For now, let me stress that Droysen associates the *Bildung* of the individual human being with the *Bildung* of humankind as a whole. He did not invent this analogical association, which in its modern form can be traced back at least to Gotthold Ephraim Lessing's (1729–1781) *The Education of the Human Race* (1780), a text that Droysen himself counted as one of the founding documents of German modern historical thought.[103] Lessing's text is actually on philosophy of religion; hence, his terminology is predominantly theological. Straight away, in its opening statements, he ascertains that education (*Erziehung*) is to the single individual as revelation (*Offenbarung*) is to the entire human race. According to Lessing, education means revelation coming to the individual, whereas revelation means the education that has come, and is coming, to humankind.[104] Lessing binds the development of the single human being to that of humanity as a whole, though he still does not conceive this connection using concepts such as history and *Bildung.* This was probably first done in the final decades of the eighteenth century by Johann Gottfried Herder (1744–1803), who spoke, for instance, of the 'history of humanity's *Bildung*' (*Bildungsgeschichte der Humanität*) and thereby drew no fundamental distinction between the development of the individual and the development of the human race (*Gattung*).[105] Herder did not actually elaborate a systematic definition of *Bildung,* but all the same, his texts were decisive in expanding the concept far beyond pedagogy and theology.[106]

Droysen's use of *Bildung* follows the way paved by Herder. First of all, Droysen resorts to the concept to designate the formative process that makes human individuals different from all other living beings. Droysen, like many other authors from his intellectual context, located human beings in a special realm within nature, and *Bildung* condenses the explanation of that singularity. Children, for instance, differ qualitatively from adults until they become able to actively 'self-form' themselves in the sense of *Bildung.*[107] Droysen provides no answer to the critical question of when a child enters adulthood, but his remark on children's humanity well illustrates his general argument on human nature. Inspired again by Wilhelm von Humboldt, he regards human nature as a dual nature. Humboldt considered language to possess a spiritual and sensuous nature. Droysen, for his part, generalizes this argument, pointing out that the producers of language – human beings – are also distinguished by the same 'spiritual-sensuous nature' (*geistig-sinnliche Natur*).[108] Like plants and other animals, they, too, are part of nature, but, as he remarks, unlike all other beings, humans are naturally bound to transcend natural history.[109] *Bildung* defines precisely the process human individuals go through beyond nature. Children – as Droysen would say – are still much more sensuous than spiritual; only with the advancement of an individual's *Bildung* does the situation undergo a reversal to reach a proper balance between nature and *Geist*.

As his notion of the dual ('spiritual-sensuous') nature of humans has already signalled, Droysen does not deny the elementary fact that human beings have a natural, creatural side. But his interest is rather in defining what makes human beings special within the panorama of nature. A human being, he states, 'first has to become a human being, in order to be a human being'.[110] One could read this statement in such a way as to press intellectual charges against Droysen for denying humanity to all non-educated people. Such an accusation would nevertheless miss the point. What Droysen stresses here is not that the lack of education transforms someone who should have been a human being into something else, but that human beings are distinguished by a never-ending process of self-formation. Droysen further details this point by stating that 'the essence of the human being is not yet what it still has to become'. Only in the course of this process of 'coming into being' (*Werden*), he continues, does the human being '[become] aware of what she or he must strive to be'.[111]

Humans are thus essentially imperfect beings, and their specificity as a natural 'race' is exactly their imperfection: 'Nature is everywhere perfect; only the human being ... is imperfect'. For Droysen, one properly turns into a human being at the point where one starts being more than only a piece of nature (*ein Stück Natur*).[112] Because humankind has overcome the limits separating nature and history, human individuals are destined to remain imperfect beings. At this juncture, it is important to point out that Droysen did not deduce a negative view of history from the assumption that human nature is imperfect. Contrary to Jean Jacques Rousseau (1712–1778) and his nineteenth-century followers, Droysen neither mourned the loss of the natural state nor dreamed of humankind's return to it. For him, it is precisely the imperfectness of human beings that enables them to break with the 'monotony of creation'.[113] Their imperfection propels them forward towards the transcendence of their natural dispositions. Therefore, Droysen concludes, human beings do not have a natural essence; rather, they are bound to work on the production of their own essence.[114] *Bildung* is the name Droysen gives to this work on the human self. Within the framework of his anthropology, all human beings are imperfect beings, and only through *Bildung* can they partially attempt to overcome this state.

This is an anthropological description of what goes on in *Bildung* as it pertains to the individual. But, as already delineated, Droysen's understanding of *Bildung* is not limited to the individual sphere. Droysen assumes that the *Bildung* of the single individual is embedded in larger formative processes, the largest of those being the self-formation of humankind. This assumption is very clearly outlined in Droysen's reminder that ancient authors termed being human (*Menschsein*) as '*humanitas*'. In this context, Droysen translates *humanitas* as *Bildung*, remarking that '*Bildung* is quintessentially historical' and that 'the content of history is the evolving *humanitas*, the evolving *Bildung*'.[115] Therefore the historical process, in its most general lines, is humankind's autopoiesis. It comprises the accumulation of past cultural goods and the creation of new ones from former developed bases. It leads to the establishment of a human world beyond or inside the natural world. When individual human beings undergo *Bildung*, they assimilate results produced throughout the whole history of humankind; they are, so to speak, updated on the macro process that has generated the extra-natural conditions of the world they live in. For Droysen, the *Bildung* of the individual occurs through a subjective re-enactment of the *Bildung* of humankind. According to him, one really becomes an educated (*gebildet*) human being only after cognitively grasping the general processes that have converged to constitute one's present world.[116]

Droysen illustrated this point by interpreting a famous passage from Johann Wolfgang von Goethe's (1749–1832) *Faust*: 'What thou hast inherited from thy ancestors, earn in order to possess it'.[117] In Droysen's view, Goethe's verses recall that from the moment of birth onwards, the individual involuntarily inherits cultural goods, not only from parents but also from prior human generations. Droysen stresses, however, the existence of a reflexive step beyond this 'natural' transmission of culture. Actually, he holds that 'so long as we have not gained [our cultural inheritance] through our own efforts and have not recognised it as that which it is, [namely] the result of incessant toil on the part of those who were before us, we hold it as if we had it not'.[118] For Droysen, an individual's *Bildung* means precisely the subjective process that enables that individual to benefit fully from the heritage of the past. *Bildung* allows one mentally to live and work through again what generations, nations and humankind have already lived and worked through.[119] A *gebildetes* individual should thus be able to perceive the historical process as the general continuum in which both the formation of humankind and individuals' self-formation take place.

Hence, within the framework of both Droysen's historical anthropology and philosophy of history, *Bildung* represents much more than the egoistic self-cultivation of one's faculties and personality. However, interpreters of German nineteenth-century intellectual history frequently overlook the supra-individ-ualistic traits of the concept of *Bildung* that are quite evident in Droysen's (as well as other contemporary authors') writings. Walter Bruford – who wrote what is probably the most quoted study on the German tradition of *Bildung* in the English-speaking world – argued, for instance, that he considered tradition essentially linked with attitudes such as subjectivism, inwardness, blindness to social reality, obedience to authority, cultivation of private (instead of public) virtues, and so forth.[120] In accordance with this definition, he translates *Bildung* as self-cultivation, illustrating his thesis with a number of worthwhile case studies of German nineteenth-century writers. To a good extent in regard to several of the chosen cases, Bruford's is indeed a plausible interpretation. But his suggestion that it was only during the Weimar Republic that some authors, Thomas Mann (1875–1955) above all, were finally able to break the spell of inwardness and harmonize *Bildung* with a realistic political sense is, honestly speaking, incorrect.[121]

Turning to Droysen's use of the concept of *Bildung* – or stressing the ethi-cal side of Humboldt's or Schleiermacher's individualism, two cases analysed by Bruford[122] – the picture is quite different. For Droysen, *Bildung* is indeed the individual's self-cultivation, but he never implies that this leads individuals to the top of ivory towers. Quite the contrary: *Bildung* only strengthens the link between the individual and society, for it is precisely the process by which the individual digests 'the results of what one's family, people, time, the hu-mankind, have lived through'.[123] So besides representing the process of the self-formation of the individual, *Bildung* is also the process of cultural accumulation that culminates in humankind's present. It is the 'ethical capital emerging from the pasts lived through'.[124] According to Droysen, human beings truly 'become human beings' only after they get in touch with the historical results coagu-lated in the institutions, values, social relationships and languages that they have to live with or within. Ultimately, the more they learn about how to deal with this objective presence of the past in the present, the more they cultivate the humanity in themselves.[125]

Droysen was fairly aware that the concept of historical thinking he elabo-rated with the aid of nineteenth-century *Bildung* theory worked against the exemplar theory of history, as is clearly shown in *Historik*'s section on 'Didactic Representation'. In it, he reiterates that history would not teach one how to behave under circumstances similar to those of the historical events under con-sideration.[126] He recalls that every time historiography aims to provide great models for human action, it enters a competition with literature, a fight the for-mer cannot win. Alexander, he argues, recalling the historical figure on whom he had written a biography, did the right thing when he chose to emulate Homer's Achilles 'rather than some Themistocles or Miltiades'.[127] Interestingly, here Droysen does not reject the heroic sense of history also noticeable in the

exemplar theory of history. In fact, he follows Hegel's theory of world-historical individuals in this regard and assumes that great men like Alexander were
historically necessary,[128] for they ignite, accelerate or accomplish the historical
processes that produce, in every epoch, an 'ethical world'. But if these world-
historical men are better served by literary forms other than historiography,
why, then, is it still important to turn to historians to learn about the past?

This is a question that Droysen formulated himself.[129] In answer, he argues
that history is valuable precisely because it stimulates the individual's *Bildung*.
He clarifies this point by drawing on a special case in which, he assumes,
historiography's formative effect is quite evident: military historiography. For
military officers, he argues, it is highly interesting to peruse the history of war
affairs to find out how great commanders from the past behaved – for instance,
how they led their troops in battles. However, Droysen continues, military
history does not teach young cadets exactly what to do to succeed on the
battlefield. The instruction afforded by histories is of another kind. By reading
histories, mentally reviewing the course of military events and the decisions
and actions that shaped them, a cadet exercises the kind of thinking that is vital
in the risk situations he is preparing for. Droysen's example can be criticized as
militaristic, but again, to do this would be beside the point, for he is talking not
only about military history in particular, but also about history in general. Like
military cadets, ordinary readers of history will not find substantive instructions
on how to live their lives, or which concrete decisions to take, in history books.
According to Droysen, one should not look to history books when seeking
the kind of knowledge that is immediately applicable in practical situations.
For him, historical reading corresponds instead to a complex, mediated mental
exercise through which reflexive competence is attained. It should amount to
a formative experience, namely, *Bildung*.[130]

When Droysen thought about *Bildung* in concrete terms, he related it
mainly to the major careers of public service, thus subdividing the concept into
military, juristic and diplomatic *Bildung*. Here *Bildung*'s universalistic traits are
deformed by Droysen's tendency to over-politicize history, a transformation I
will further explore later.[131] But, still, he saw *Bildung* – at least in theory – as
also related to aims situated outside the sphere of the techniques of governance
and political domination. In his theory of history, he emphasizes historical
reading as a fundamental source for general *Bildung* (*allgemeine Bildung*), that is,
for an educational process whose aim lies beyond any technical purpose. Droysen defines general education (*Bildung*) as the exercise of 'the human qualities
in general'.[132] Such exercise is destined to prepare the individual so that she or
he may not only passively partake in 'the ethical spheres' – the essential social
orders whose genealogy history should deliver – but also actively intervene in
history in a plausible way. In this context *Bildung* and historical thinking are
vital, for they empower individuals with an improved capacity to judge how

they should act in a given case in order to favour the continuity of the histori-cal process. For this empowerment to happen, it is not enough that individuals acquire knowledge of singular models of action from the past: 'What should inspire us and carry us forward are not single examples but history's whole ethical flow.'[133] What Droysen called 'didactic representation' conveys exactly an image of this general flow of history. General *Bildung* means, finally, the competence to identify the constitutive forces of the historical flow, and to act so as to cultivate and enhance them.

Identity

For Droysen, historiography's formative task concerns a simultaneous de-par-ticularization and universalization of human cultural orientation. But before him, Hegel – among others – had already made well-known statements linking *Bildung* and a universalistic framework of action. For instance, Hegel spoke of *Bildung* as the process by which human beings elevate themselves from their particular and physical condition to a general and spiritual mode of existence. As he said of human beings, everyone simultaneously carries a particular and a general determination within oneself, being self-obligated in terms of both one's own physical subsistence and the development of one's 'general nature'.[134]

This claim for the elevation of the human self towards a general nature can also be traced in Droysen's theory of history, the novelty there being Droysen's specific determination of the formative impact generated by historiography. To define the general perspective to be attained by means of historical *Bildung,* he uses the oracular expression 'the self of humankind' (*Ich der Menschheit*), a notion that he opposes to that of the mere 'empirical self' (*empirisches Ich*). Droysen associates the 'empirical self' with *Unbildung* – precisely the opposite of the kind of self-formation that he propagated – as well as with a 'smallish historical perspective' (*kleingeschichtliche Betrachtungsweise*) that 'deems neces-sary to see the big things small and the small things big'.[135] He affirms that historians, among others, while thinking and researching, have to strip their empirical selves of all particularities to attain a general point of view beyond every here and now.[136] For him, this vantage point of the 'self of humankind' is the one from which history should be written, and which historiography should stimulate its readers to arrive at. Droysen also remarks that no par-ticularizing historical examples can help one's elevation to that viewpoint, but only a genetic and all-embracing representation of the course of history.[137] By acquiring the general sense that history is a flow of events leading from the past through the present to the future, history readers are somehow pulled out of their particular life circumstances. Thereby they ignite in themselves the gen-eral dynamics of *Bildung*.

Droysen's plea for historical thinking directly connects to what is, in a broad sense, a philosophy of education. Historical thinking brings about *Bildung* – the self-formation of the individual as a particular process within the macro-process of the self-formation of humankind. To some extent, anyhow, what *Bildung* meant for nineteenth-century German intellectuals partially corresponds to what identity came to be in the Western intellectual discourse from the mid-twentieth century on. Both notions point to human subjectivity, to its development in time as well as to subjective efforts to establish and maintain a sense of unity between individual past and future. Both notions describe such processes and also entail normative implications, since they hold the application of their contents to be desirable – that is, that individuals *should* undergo *Bildung* processes, or cultivate representations of their own identity. Hermann Lübbe has correctly argued that despite the nineteenth-century erosion of the idea that the past teaches the present by means of historiography, the belief that one can still learn something from history lingers. And in part it lingers in the opinion that historians produce an identity-relevant sort of knowledge, a knowledge one can elaborate into one's own sense of self.[138]

But the connection between history and identity per se is no twentieth-century invention. Self-identity, to begin with, was already an important dimension of the nineteenth century's idealistic *Bildung* philosophy, as Droysen's use of terms such as 'empirical self' and 'self of humankind' automatically makes clear. Günther Buck, who sharply explored the connection between *Bildung* and identity, has already shown how the main goal of the nineteenth-century *Bildung* discourse was associated with the production and maintenance of self-identity. According to Buck, most German idealist thinkers would have been close to Jean-Jacques Rousseau in that regard. Both the idealistic notion of self-alienation (*Selbstentfremdung*) and Rosseau's negative philosophy of history would have assumed that as long as history proceeds towards modern times, the human self loses its self-identity – in other words, that subjectivity in the modern world is constantly threatened by its own radical change, fragmentation and discontinuation. But contrary to Rousseau – who repeatedly stressed modern subjectivity as a historical loss – German idealists would have invested in the possibility of somehow regaining self-identity. They resorted to the idea of *Bildung* precisely to define a way of recapturing and reshaping self-identity without intellectually dismissing modernity.[139] Buck, however, retrospectively criticizes the mainstream idealist conception of *Bildung*. It is delusive, he argues, to believe that self-identity would emerge merely as a result of a consciously controlled *Bildung,* for personal identity is not only a matter of deliberated construction but also the result of contingent occurrences and circumstances passively inherited or suffered. In short, for Buck, self-identity encompasses much more than the results of *Bildung*, since it also has much to do with genetic endowments, quasi-natural habits that are learned in childhood and beyond, and, finally, the effects of either repressed or unconscious motifs.[140]

What Buck criticizes with regard to mainstream idealistic *Bildung* discourse is actually the intermingling of the issues of personal identity and individuality. Yet he calls attention to another branch of the *Bildung* discourse where 'identity' was approached in what he argues is a much more fitting way. He mentions authors such as Wilhelm von Humboldt and Johann Friedrich Herbart (1776–1841), who, instead of fixing on the quest for individuality, stressed the connection between the self and the other. As Buck remarks, in the framework of this second tradition, *Bildung* is not connected to the singling out of personal individuality; it does not foster subjectification through singularization, but rather a subjectification of another kind, which evolves from the nourishment of a complex relationship between the general and the particulars.

Buck is praising here the same de-particularization and universalization of the human self that Droysen condensed in the idea of the 'self of the humankind'. Therefore, from Droysen's statements on subjective *Bildung,* one can work out a concept of personal identity. Indeed, this concept stresses both the particularity of every individual self and the contingency implicated in its life, but simultaneously also encompasses a plea for conjoining the individual with the general-human features accumulated throughout humankind's history. The personal self's attainment of a certain level of universality through its *Bildung* does not thereby simply cancel contingency and individuality. In Droysen's view, those who become able to think historically may also represent their own selves in such a way that generality and individuality, universality and particularity are conciliated in complex but historically loaded self-identities.

As the emphasis on the relationship between the individual self and the idea of humankind already indicates, Droysen does not isolate the self-representations of individuals from their representation as members of collectivities big and small. If it is plausible to say that Droysen saw historical thinking as a beacon of human self-identity, then personal identity must be seen as only a link in the chain of identifications activated in daily life by every individual. In this regard, Droysen's notion of 'ethical powers' (*sittlichen Mächte*) might be interpreted precisely as the set of the most relevant collectivities that an individual refers to in constructing and developing representations of belongingness. 'Ethical powers' form the broad sociocultural contexts within which, according to Droysen, every individual life takes place. Unsurprisingly, the philosophical matrix of Droysen's notion of 'ethical powers' is Hegel's ethics. This philosophical platform, in open contrast to Immanuel Kant's moral philosophy, emphasizes the ethical norms already in force within one's social group, rather than the individual morality attainable by one's own rational reflection.[141] In line with Hegel's *Sittlichkeitslehre,* Droysen's system of the ethical powers actually encompasses the attempt to present a sort of communitarian ethics as simultaneously the presupposition and the end of historical thinking. Following his postulate that human nature is a spiritual-sensuous nature, he distinguishes and analyses three types of collectivities: 'natural collectivities' (*Gemeinsamkeiten*), ranging from family, neighbourhood, tribe and clan to nation (*Volk*); the 'ideal collectivities', consisting of languages, the arts (sphere of the beautiful), the sciences (sphere of the true) and the religions (sphere of the sacred); and finally the 'practical collectivities', which, like the spheres of society, economy (*Wohlfahrt*), justice and power, are constituted by both natural and ideal features.[142]

Droysen argues that individuals maintain a dialectical relationship with the 'ethical collectivities' they belong to as both their products and co-producers.[143] Growing up within these ethical spheres, human individuals subjectively incorporate cultural values and social norms, thus amalgamating their natural dispositions with results accumulated throughout the historical process: they become members of a family and a nation, and citizens of a state; they learn languages, adhere to religions and internalize the rules of truth and aesthetic regimes; they occupy, gain and lose spaces within the social and the economic systems, and so on. For Droysen, all these 'ethical spheres' form a cultural web around every individual – a web in which, by the way, the constitutive spheres are often in conflict with one another.[144]

But Droysen is also interested in going a step beyond this primary form of socialization and cultural education, and here *Bildung* again comes into play – the subjective process that can enable one to understand the historical development of the 'ethical collectivities' and hence enter into a reflexive relationship with them. In Droysen's account, though individuals are in a passive relationship with the spheres of the historical world, they can also actively help fashion them. Historical thinking is what empowers the human individuals to do that. The main theme of Droysen's didactics is namely the possibility to rationally appropriate tradition with the aid of historical thinking, so that one can consciously and actively participate in the 'work on history'.

The discriminatory and consequently particularistic traits contained in this metaphor remain to be discussed.[145] For now, it suffices to ascertain that in Droysen's social theory, the individual, who evolves in a dialectical relationship with the spheres of the ethical powers, is obviously supposed to develop representations of her or his belongingness to those spheres: to think of her or his own person as linked to a broader community of persons and values – a family, a state, a language, and so forth. The issue of collective identity is therefore implicit in Droysen's depiction of individuals as surrounded by 'ethical powers'. However, he considers the individual's personal identifications with concrete collectivities to be beyond the scope of the science of history. For instance, he quite sarcastically remarks that the history of his own family, as well as the national histories of countries like Luxembourg or San Marino, is of absolutely no interest vis-à-vis the history of humankind. These histories do possess a 'historical character'; they, too, concern the interaction between individuals and ethical powers that is constitutive of human history. Nonetheless, they can arouse interest only among those directly affected by them.[146] Droysen further illustrates this point by remarking that the thousands of marriages, families and villages found in social life lie far from the general historical consciousness. Despite being the products of historically developed values and customs, they bear only a private historical meaning and cannot concern humankind as a whole.[147] This is why Droysen comes to distinguish special histories from History in a general sense: 'Therefore, we differentiate the history of the development of the ethical powers, the history of the great ethical organisms – so to speak – from the special histories of the particular occurrences taking place within each of those.'[148]

As Droysen tries to show in the last part of his *Systematik* (as developed in the lectures from 1857–58), historiography's primary aim is indeed to produce, enforce and bolster a collective identity, but one of the most universalistic kind. Droysen is quite clear on this point: history, in its proper sense, is exclusively about the human's identity as a human being, as an individual of the human species: 'If there is going to be a history which has more than this or that special and individual meaning, than such history must be shared by all human beings, it must concern the human being as such; it must be everybody's history, it must be the History.'[149]

On a primary level, therefore, history only touches upon the most general sphere of collective identification possible, a sphere actually located beyond what is immediately empirical in the daily world. Droysen knows that 'humankind' is a huge abstraction that can only be perceived with the aid of a great deal of mediation, but still, he thinks of history as precisely the way to give expression to it. By representing the ethical powers' evolution into their present configuration, history demonstrates the long-run connection between present and past human beings. By making this genetic link explicit, it moreover conveys to its audience the sense that human beings all depend on collective achievements that they did not produce but nevertheless must carry further in one way or another. One's identification as a human being hence is possible only when, by means of historical thinking, one's empirical self is elevated to a general self, the 'self of humankind'. It is this general self – a differentiation of the concrete self that emerges in conjunction with consciousness that individuals are bound to a collective work on history – that professional historiography should sponsor.

A logical consequence of Droysen's reflections on understanding, *Bildung* and identity is the claim that historiography has to provide insights into the constitution of the present horizons from which it is pursued. If historical thinking is the understanding of the concrete historicity of the present world – if it is a means to subjective *Bildung* and a sponsor of an elevated form of identity – then it follows that historical research and writing cannot fulfil a purpose in itself. Instead, historiography must retain the pragmatic function of concretely illuminating parts of the process through which the present came about. I suppose that such a presentist view of historiography has become more and more crucial, inasmuch as both the modern idea of history and the modern acceleration of sociocultural change have disseminated the sense that the present is qualitatively different from the past. And I think Droysen's historical hermeneutics was developed precisely as a means for dealing with this modern strangeness or otherness of the past. By resorting to the notion of historical thinking, he was trying to ensure that empirical research in historical science would remain connected to practical demands for orientation emerging from the historians' present. In the next chapter, I will show how he attempted to turn this theoretical assumption into practice through a substantive interpretation of the development of his own world, that is, through a genealogy of the present.

Notes

1. Droysen, *Historik* 1: 64 [Vorlesungstext, 1857]: 'Sie [die Historik] will die Überzeugung wecken, daß man historisch denkt und denken lernen könne; sie will nachweisen, in welchen Formen, in welchem Umfang diese Weise des Denkens zur Anwendung kommt.'
2. Droysen, *Historik* 1: 32–33 [Vorlesungstext, 1857]; Droysen, *Historik* 1: 382 [Vorlesungstext, 1857]: 'Diese Dialektik der historischen Gedanken, das sieht man wohl, hat ihre Ordnung, wenn ich so sagen darf, ihre Logik. Der neue Gedanke tritt nicht willkürlich, nicht zufällig ein, es wird sich erkennen und nachweisen lassen, daß auf solche Gegebenheiten, auf solche Ereignisse dieser Gedanke, und nur dieser folgen konnte. Aber weiter dürfen wir nicht gehen; wir dürfen nicht sagen, dieser Gedanke mußte folgen; wir dürfen nicht beweisen wollen, daß da Luther, da Napoleon eintreten mußte, daß eine geschichtliche Notwendigkeit sie brachte und bestimmte.... Also das ist der Punkt, der uns völlig von der Art scheidet, welche die Spekulation, die theologische wie philosophische, an sich hat. Denn dieselbe Schwäche der Betrachtung, welche die logische Notwendigkeit an sich trägt, hat die dogmatische Antizipation an sich'.
3. In his depiction of the method of the natural sciences, Droysen further traced their success among the scientific community back to their own generality and simplicity, for they were concomitantly suited to explain both 'the organic and the inorganic nature, both the stars and the microscopic world'. See Droysen, *Historik* 1: 19 [Vorlesungstext, 1857]: 'Und die Naturwissenschaften haben ihren staunenswürdigen Fortschritt damit gewonnen, daß sie diese Methode einschlugen, in der sie, das Morphologische zur Seite lassend, die organische und unorganische Natur, die Gestirne und die mikroskopische Welt unter denselben Gesichtspunkten betrachteten.'
Moreover, it must be also recalled that Droysen's image of the natural sciences was based exclusively on the model of Newtonian physics, and that while contrasting them to historiography he did not regard alternative paradigms already existent in his time – for instance that of the life-sciences. Arguing against a monolithic depiction of the Enlightenment as a period characterised essentially by a mechanistic worldview, Peter Reill has pointed out that a general shift from mechanism to vitalism took place in the natural philosophy of the eighteenth century, mostly in consequence of Buffon's (1707–1788) *Histoire Naturelle* (1749), and of the astonishing popularity of this book among intellectual circles of the late century. In the vitalism symbolised by Buffon the genetic model of explanation was employed for the study of nature. Nevertheless, leading

historians from the late century would soon transfer such models from the new life-sciences to their own field. Reill has also mentioned that one of the most important genetic categories that underwent such interdisciplinary transfers was that of 'formative drive' (*Bildungstrieb*), a notion developed mostly by the physiologist Johann Friedrich Blumenbach 1752–1840). Historical thinkers such as August Schlözer, Johann Gottfried Herder, and Wilhelm von Humboldt imported that notion directly from Blumenbach, adjusting it to the study of subjectivity, nations, languages, and the history of humankind. By doing this, they forged one of the most important elements of the language of German nineteenth-century historicism, namely the concept of *Bildung*. See Peter Hanns Reill. 1994. 'Science and the Construction of the Cultural Sciences in Late Enlightenment Germany: The Case of Wilhelm von Humboldt', *History and Theory* 33(3): 347, 357–361; Peter Hanns Reill. 1986. 'Science and the Science of History in the Spätaufklärung', in Hans Erich Bödecker et al. (eds), *Aufklärung und Geschichte. Studien zur deutschen Geschichtswissenschaft im 18. Jahrhundert,* Göttingen:Vanderhoeck & Ruprecht, 440, 445–448.

4. Droysen, *Historik* 1: 20 [Vorlesungstext, 1857]: 'In unserer Disziplin ist [im Vergleich mit den Naturwissenschaften] das Gegenteil der Fall; sie wendet sich durchaus auf das Morphologische, auf die individuellen Formgebungen'; Droysen, *Historik* 1: 21 [Vorlesungstext, 1857]: 'In der geschichtlichen Welt sind nicht die Analogien, sondern, man könnte sagen, die Anomalien das Bewegende.'

5. Droysen, *Historik* 1: 21 [Vorlesungstext, 1857]: 'Auch sie [die historische Methode] sucht analytisch aus den vorliegenden Erscheinungen deren Wesen, aber dies Wesen ist nicht ein stoffliches Substrat mit unveränderlichen Attributionen. Was der historischen Forschung vorliegt, sind Werke, Bildungen, und Umbildungen mannigfachster Art, Charaktere, Taten, in summa: Formgebungen'.

6. Droysen, *Historik* 1: 132 [Vorlesungstext, 1857]: 'Aber da wie überall ist es in unserer Wissenschaft das Wesentliche, nicht in den geformten Stoffen, sondern in den formenden Kräften das Bestimmende nachzuweisen.'

7. Droysen, *Historik* 1: 56 [Vorlesungstext, 1857]: 'Das, was er [der Historiker] erforschen will, lehrt ihn ein Verfahren, wie es dem Zweck angemessen ist, eine Art zu Denken, die weder spekulativ noch mathematisch, sondern eben historisch ist.'

8. Droysen, *Historik* 1: 133 [Vorlesungstext, 1857]: 'Die Sage geht gleichsam den umgekehrten Weg [in Vergleich zu den Mythen]; von einer historischen Tatsachen oder Persönlichkeit erregt, verflüchtigt sie deren Wirklichkeit, formt sie um zu einer Idealvorstellung in dem Maß, daß diese nun in dem sonstigen Ideenkreise der Menschen weiterlebt ohne allen Zusammenhang mit ihrer einstigen Realität.'

9. Droysen, *Historik* 1: 106 [Vorlesungstext, 1857]: 'Und ähnlich wie das lernende Kind verhalten sich die Völker, verhält sich die Menschheit; wie lange sie mit dem subjektiven Sehen, mit Mythen und Sagen beschäftigt, mit denen sie sich das Dunkel der Vergangenheit beliebig ausschmücken und färben. Sie haben eine subjektive Welt, die mehr ein Bild ihrer einen Begabungen und Interessen als ein Abbild der objektiven Wirklichkeit ist.'

10. Droysen, *Historik* 1: 45 [Vorlesungstext, 1857]: 'Mit der Sammlung und Sichtung der Mythen und Sagen hat die früheste Historie, von der wir wissen, die der Griechen, begonnen, – erste Versuche, Ordnung, Zusammenhang, Übereinstimmung, ein chronologisches System in diesen Urwald von Überlieferungen zu bringen, erste Versuche wirklicher Forschung.'

11. Droysen, *Historik* 1: 106–107 [Vorlesungstext, 1857]: 'Unser Wissen, richtiger, der Inhalt unseres Ich ist zunächst Empfangenes, Überkommenes, unser, als wäre es nicht unser. Wir sind damit noch unfrei in diesem unserem Wissen; es hat uns mehr, als daß wir es hätten. Erst mit der Reflexion, in der wir es als vermitteltes erkennen, trennen wir es von uns selbst; die erkannte Tatsache der Vermittlung ist die Erinnerung; und diese Erinnerung trennen wir von uns selbst, geben ihr in unserem geistigen Sein die Stellung, objektiv dem subjektiven Sein gegenüber zu sein.'

12. Droysen, *Historik* 1: 64 [Vorlesungstext, 1857]: 'Und die Begabung des Historikers ist vor allem der Sinn für das Wirkliche, d.h. die Kongenialität, in den erscheinenden Dingen die lebendige, wirkende Kraft, das, wodurch sie sind und werden, ihre Wahrheit zu sehen.'

13. See also Hans-Ulrich Lessing. 2006. 'Das Wahrheitsproblem im Historismus: Droysen und Dilthey', in Markus Enders and Jan Szaif (eds), *Die Geschichte des philosophischen Begriffs der Wahrheit,* Berlin: Walter de Gruyter, 275–286.

14. Droysen, *Historik* 2: 508 [Über das Geschichtsstudium in Deutschland, 1869]: 'Hier lernt [der junge Forscher] historisch zu denken, das heißt[:] er übt an einzelnen Beispielen die Methode der Forschung und Auffassung, die er überall anwenden kann, wo Gestaltungen der sittlichen Welt nach ihrem Gewordensein aufzufassen sind. Er gewöhnt sich, das[,] was ist[,] nach seinem Gewordensein anzusehen'.

15. Droysen, *Historik* 1: 236 [Vorlesungstext, 1857]. For a very insightful critical assessment of the sexist semantics of nineteenth-century historians (and of the role of gender in the academic practices of seminar and archival research), see Bonnie Smith. 1995. 'Gender and the Practices of Scientific History: The Seminar and Archival Research in the Nineteenth Century', *American Historical Review* 100(4): 1150–1176.

16. Johann Gustav Droysen. 1967. *Briefwechsel,* vol. 2: *1851–1884,* Osnabrück: Biblio, 977 [Letter to Gustav Droysen, 8 March 1884]. Interestingly, Droysen begins this letter by praising the recent emergence of the historical economist Gustav von Schmoller (1838–1917) as a leading figure among German academics. For Droysen, Schmoller's then newly acquired intellectual authority represented an important counterpoint to the influence of the Rankean school.

17. Droysen, *Briefwechsel* 2: 442 [Letter to Wilhelm Arndt, 20 March 1857]: 'Wir sind in Deutschland durch die Rankesche Schule und die Pertzischen Arbeiten auf unleidliche Weise in die sogenannte Kritik versunken, deren ganzes Kunststück darin besteht, ob ein armer Teufel von Chronisten aus dem anderen abgeschrieben hat.'

18. Droysen, *Briefwechsel* 2: 442 [Letter to Wilhelm Arndt, 20 March 1857]: 'Es hat schon einiges Kopfschütteln veranlaßt, daß ich feliciter behauptet habe, die Aufgabe des Historikers sei Verstehen oder, wenn man will, Interpretieren. Aber ich hoffe, daß dieser Gedanke ein sehr fruchtbarer ist, wie es denn seit Thucydides jedem ordentlichen Historiker darum und nur darum zu tun war; die höhere, sogar die niedere Kritik ergibt sich auf dem Wege dazu.' In the following discussion, I will mostly use 'understanding' (*Verstehen*) and 'interpretation' (*Interpretation*) more or less interchangeably, as synonyms. Droysen himself proposed using 'interpretation' in regard to historical materials only, and not in regard to the past events the materials refer to; see Droysen, *Historik. Vorlesungen über Enzyklopädie und Methodologie der Geschichte,* 152. However, in several other passages he clearly contradicted that statement of purpose, for instance, in those referring to his types of interpretation, which refer primarily to past reality (conditions, psychological motivations of action, ideas) rather than to the testimonies in the historical material.

19. Droysen, *Outline of the Principles of History,* 12 (translation slightly modified).

20. Droysen, *Historik* 1: 22 [Vorlesungstext, 1857]: 'Das Wesen der geschichtlichen Methode ist forschend zu verstehen, ist die Interpretation.'

21. Droysen, *Geschichte der Preußischen Politik* 1: v: 'Es gibt mancherlei Ansicht über die Art und Aufgabe der historischen Studien. Vielleicht darf man Alles zusammenfassend sagen, ihr Wesen sei forschend verstehen zu lernen.'

22. Droysen, *Historik* 1: 22 [Vorlesungstext, 1857]: 'Die Möglichkeit des Verstehens setzt voraus, daß sich in uns, den Betrachtenden, dieselben ethischen und intellektuellen Kategorien vorfinden, die in den zu Verstehenden ihren Ausdruck haben; und nur soweit dieselben Kategorien hier sich geäußert haben, vermögen wir zu verstehen.'

23. Droysen, *Outline of the Principles of History,* 12–13.

24. Droysen initially considered the 'forms of representation' (*Formen der Darstellung*) to be historical method's fourth operation, but in later versions of *Historik* he dealt with the issue of representation in a separate section. Whereas the 1857 version of the lectures is divided into two basic parts, *Methodik* and *Systematik,* their final version of 1882 consists of three parts, *Methodik, Systematik* and *Topik.* The discussion on the 'forms of representation' was moved to the new part.

25. Droysen, *Historik. Vorlesungen über Enzyklopädie und Methodologie der Geschichte,* 21: 'Das Material also unseres Forschens ist, was aus den Vergangenheiten der sittlichen, der Menschenwelt noch unvergangen ist.'

26. Droysen, *Outline of the Principles of History,* 18: 'Historical material is partly what is still immediately present, hailing from the times which we are seeking to understand (Remains), partly whatever ideas human beings have obtained of those times, and transmitted to be remembered (Sources), partly things wherein both these forms of material are combined (Monuments)'; Droysen, *Briefwechsel* 2: 452 [Letter to Wilhelm Arendt, 8 May 1857]: '[Ich finde das Wesen unsrer Wissenschaft] nicht in dem Verstehen vergangener Zeiten, sondern Verstehen dessen[,] was davon noch übrig und gegenwärtig ist – sei es in Berichten und Darstellungen, sei es in Resten und Zuständen; denn nur Gegenwärtiges können wir menschlicher Weise fassen, und nur[,] was aus dem Vergangenen nicht vergangen ist, läßt uns deutend und verstehend das Bild der Vergangenheiten herstellen.' Also: Droysen, *Historik. Vorlesungen über Enzyklopädie und Methodologie der Geschichte,* 37–38.

27. Droysen, *Historik. Vorlesungen über Enzyklopädie und Methodologie der Geschichte,* 36: 'Die Frage und das Suchen aus der Frage, das ist der erste Schritt der historischen Forschung.'

28. Droysen, *Historik. Vorlesungen über Enzyklopädie und Methodologie der Geschichte,* 32: 'Es muß das erste sein, das, was wir bis dahin gehabt und geglaubt, in Frage zu stellen, um es prüfend und begründend neu und sicher zu erwerben. Das Moment, auf das hier ankommt, tritt mehr oder minder deutlich in der Entwicklung jedes Menschen ein, aber die meisten begnügen sich, es nur auf die ihnen zunächst liegenden, sie persönlich angehenden Verhältnisse anzuwenden und in übrigen in dem guten Glauben weiterzuleben, daß die großen und allgemeinen Gestaltungen der Menschenwelt so sind, wie sie sie gelernt und sie zu sehen sich gewöhnt haben'; Droysen, *Historik* 1: 107 [Vorlesungstext, 1857].

29. Droysen, *Historik. Vorlesungen über Enzyklopädie und Methodologie der Geschichte,* 33: 'Und in meiner Frage umgrenze ich schon ungefähr, was ich, indem ich sie mir zu beantworten suche, zu finden erwarte; ich ahne schon, daß noch anderes und Wichtigeres, als ich bis jetzt weiß, dahintersteckt; meine Frage enthält schon mehr, als ich gelernt habe, eine Ahnung, die mir aus der Gesamtheit dessen, was ich auch sonst bisher innerlich durchlebt und erfahren habe, hervorspringt. Ebendarum kann ich so fragen, frage ich so.'

30. Karl-Heinz Spieler. 1970. *Untersuchungen zu Johann Gustav Droysens ‹Historik›,* Berlin: Duncker & Humblot, 35.

31. Droysen, *Historik. Vorlesungen über Enzyklopädie und Methodologie der Geschichte,* 35–36: 'Denn die Forschung ist nicht auf ein zufälliges Finden gestellt, sondern sie sucht etwas. Sie muß wissen, was sie suchen will; erst dann findet sie etwas. Man muß die Dinge richtig fragen, dann geben sie Antwort.'

32. Alexandre Escudier. 2002. 'Présentation: Refonder les sciences historiques. L'odyssée du monde éthique chez Droysen', in Johann Gustav Droysen, *Précis de theorie de l'histoire,* Paris: Les Éditions du Cerf, 17–18.

33. Max Weber. 1988. *Gesammelte Aufsätze zur Wissenschaftslehre,* Tübingen: J.C.B Mohr, 166.

34. Collingwood, *The Principles of History,* 19–30, 35–37.

35. See Escudier, 'Présentation', 18; Lutz Raphael. 2003. *Geschichtswissenschaft im Zeitalter der Extreme. Theorien, Methoden, Tendenzen von 1900 bis zur Gegenwart,* Munich: C.H. Beck, 102.

36. Droysen, *Outline of the Principles of History,* 27. In his lectures, Droysen also argued that the outcome of criticism was a kind of synthetic factual representation that would organize the perception of complex events by stressing common purposes or effects underlying all of them. In this way, as Droysen illustrates, a war or a revolution is not a simple objective fact but a complex factual synthesis that summarizes the interaction and the results of many 'acts of will' performed by the individuals involved: 'Man sieht, es liegt in dieser Auffassung der Kritik eine bedeutende Unklarheit. Sie ahnt richtig, daß sich unsere historische Forschung an die geschichtlichen Materialien wenden muß, aus denen unsere Kenntnis dessen, was vergangen ist, einzig und allein zu entnehmen ist. Aber mit dem von ihr aufgestellten Begriff der objektiven Tatsache verkennt sie die Natur unserer geschichtlichen Materialien. Was sie als objektive Tatsachen bezeichnet, eine Schlacht, ein Konzil, eine Empörung, – sind diese denn als solche in der Wirklichkeit dagewesen? Sind das nicht vielmehr die Akte vieler, zahlloser Einzelheiten Eines Vorganges, den als solchen

nur die menschliche Vorstellung zusammenfasst nach einem diesen Einzelheiten gemeinsamen Zweck oder Anlaß oder Wirkung usw.? In Wahrheit sind es menschliche Willensakte, ist es Tun und Leiden so vieler einzelner, woraus das, was wir als die Tatsache dieser Schlacht, dieser Empörung bezeichnen, sich der zusammenfassenden menschlichen Vorstellung ergeben hat. Nicht die Schacht, die Empörung war das in jenem Moment Objektive und Reale, sondern die Tausende, die so gegeneinander und durcheinander liefen und lärmten und sich gegenseitig schlugen usw.' Droysen, *Historik. Vorlesungen über Enzyklopädie und Methodologie der Geschichte,* 96–97.

37. Droysen, *Outline of the Principles of History,* 21–26.

38. Droysen, *Historik* 1: 22 [Vorlesungstext, 1857]: 'Hier ist der Punkt, an dem ich mich mit Bewußtsein scheide von der jetzt unter meinen Fachgenossen verbreiteten Methode; sie bezeichnen sie wohl als die kritische, während ich die Interpretation in den Vordergrund stelle'; Droysen, *Briefwechsel* 2: 452 [Letter to Wilhelm Arndt, 4 June 1857]: 'Das andere ist, daß ich das Wesen unsrer Wissenschaft nicht in der Kritik, sondern im Verstehen, in der Interpretation finde'; see also: Rüsen, 'Droysen heute', 181–188; Michael MacLean. 1982. 'Johann Gustav Droysen and the Development of Historical Hermeneutics', *History and Theory* 21(3): 350–352.

39. Droysen, *Outline of the Principles of History,* 26–32. I will return to the issue of Droysen's 'ethical powers' latter in this chapter.

40. Droysen, *Historik. Vorlesungen über Enzyklopädie und Methodologie der Geschichte,* 34: 'Nicht in dem Suchen des Materials zur Beantwortung der Frage, nicht in der Kritik dieser Materialien noch in ihrer Interpretation ... ergibt sich, ob die Frage sachgemäß oder leer und taub war, wohl aber in dem Abschnitt, der die Darstellung behandeln wird.'

41. Hayden White. 1987. 'Droysen's Historik: Historical Writing as a Bourgeois Science', in Hayden White, *The Content of the Form: Narrative Discourse and Historical Representation,* Baltimore: The Johns Hopkins University Press, 90–91.

42. See Lorenz, 'Can Histories Be True?'

43. Rüsen, 'Droysen heute', 186–188.

44. Johann Gustav Droysen. 1967. *Briefwechsel,* vol. 1: *1828–1851,* edited by Rudolf Hübner. Osnabrück: Biblio, 119 [Letter to Friedrich Perthes, 8 February 1837]: 'Rankes Schule am deutlichsten, aber viele mit derselben sehen den Zweck der historischen Studien nur in der Richtigkeit der Tatsachen; diese meinen sie zu erreichen, wenn sie den ersten Quellen nachforschen. Es versteht sich, daß dergleichen wichtig, wesentlich, Grundlage, nur nicht Zweck ist.'

45. Droysen, *Historik* 1: 60 [Vorlesungstext, 1857]: 'Denn in dem historischen Denken ist das Wesentliche nicht bloß, daß man die ihm vorliegenden Objekte kritisch reinigt und interpretierend versteht, sondern daß man das so Verstandene, d. h. die bestimmende Kraft, den Willen, den Geist, die Idee sich vergegenwärtigt und durchdringt, daß man aus den Richtigkeiten zur Wahrheit gelange.'

46. Giambattista Vico. 1948. *The New Science of Giambattista Vico,* Ithaca: Cornell University Press, 56.

47. Koselleck, *Vergangene Zukunft,* 187: 'Seit Chladenius waren die Historiker besser absichert, in der Wahrscheinlichkeit eine eigene, eben eine historische Form der Wahrheit erblicken zu dürfen. Standortgebundenheit ist seitdem kein Einwand mehr, sondern Voraussetzung geschichtlicher Erkenntnis.' See also Escudier, 'Theory and Methodology of History from Chladenius to Droysen'.

48. Jorge Navarro. 1997. 'Fichte, Humboldt y Ranke sobre la idea y las ideas históricas (con un apéndice sobre Hegel y Droysen)', *Anuario Filosófico* 30, 424.

49. Droysen, *Historik* 1: 236 [Vorlesungstext, 1857]: 'Ich will nicht mehr, aber auch nicht weniger zu haben scheinen als die relative Wahrheit meines Standpunktes, wie mein Vaterland, meine religiöse, meine politische Überzeugungen, meine Zeit mir zu haben gestattet.'

50. Droysen, *Historik* 1: 230–231 [Vorlesungstext, 1857]: 'Diese erkannte historische Wahrheit ist freilich nur relativ die Wahrheit; es ist die Wahrheit, wie sie der Erzähler sieht, es ist die Wahrheit von seinem Standpunkt, seiner Einsicht, seiner Bildungsstufe aus; in einer verwandelten Zeit wird sie, kann sie anders erscheinen; man könnte sagen, jede Zeit hat von neuem die Ge-

samtheit der Geschichte durchzuarbeiten, zu begreifen. Und in diesem Begreifen der Vergangenheit wird sich zugleich die fortschreitende und fortgeschrittene Entwicklung jeglicher Gegenwart darstellen. Aber in meiner Gegenwart erscheinen die Dinge so und nicht anders, ihre Wahrheit ist für jetzt diese Auffassung, und nur in dieser Auffassung kann meine Zeit, kann ich sie verstehen, ihre Wahrheit aussprechen.'

51. Between the summer semester of 1827 and the winter semester of 1828–29, Droysen attended six courses taught by Hegel: Logic and Metaphysics, Philosophy of Religion, History of Philosophy, Philosophy of the Spirit (*Geist*), Aesthetics and Philosophy of History. Christiane Hackel. 2008. 'Studium an der Berliner Universität', in Christiane Hackel (ed.), *Philologe – Historiker – Politiker. Johann Gustav Droysen, 1808–1884. Katalog zur Ausstellung des Sonderforschungsbereiches «Transformationen der Antike», Humboldt Universität zu Berlin, 01.07–08.08.2008*, Berlin: G + H, 21.

52. Southard, *Droysen and the Prussian School of History*, 13.

53. Christoph Johannes Bauer. 2001. ⟨*Das Geheimnis aller Bewegung ist ihr Zweck⟩. Geschichtsphilosophie bei Hegel und Droysen*, Hamburg: Meiner, 131, 230.

54. Hermann Blumenthal. 1933. 'Johann Gustav Droysens Auseinandersetzung mit dem Idealismus', *Neue Jahrbücher für Wissenschaft und Jugendbildung* 9: 354; Rüsen, *Begriffene Geschichte*, 117–122.

55. Droysen, *Historik* 1: 419 [Grundriß der Historik, 1882]: 'In den Untersuchungen Wilhelm von Humboldts fand ich diejenigen Gedanken, die, so schien es mir, den Weg erschlossen; er schien mir ein Bacon für die Geschichtswissenschaften.'

56. Droysen also frequently refers to Humboldt's posthumously published book on *The Heterogeneity of Language and its Influence on the Intellectual Development of Mankind* (orig. *Über die Verschiedenheit des menschlichen Sprachbaus und ihren Einfluss auf die geistige Entwicklung des Menschengeschlechts*, 1836). See Droysen, *Historik* 2: 439 [Letter to Gustav Droysen, 31 July 1864]: 'Ungleich wichtiger sind Humboldts Arbeiten, namentlich die "Einleitung zur Kawisprache", weil sie auf die Begründung der historischen Methode oder richtiger darauf ausgehen, zu erörtern, wie es möglich ist, daß wir historisch erkennen.'

57. Hans-Georg Gadamer discussed this transformation in the meaning of *understanding* during the first half of the nineteenth century, focusing rather on Ranke, Droysen and Wilhelm Dilthey – but not especially on Wilhelm von Humboldt. See Gadamer, *Wahrheit und Methode*, 201–207.

58. Humboldt, 'On the Historian's Task', 65: 'All understanding presupposes in the person who understands, as condition of its possibility, an analogue of that which will be understood later: an original, antecedent congruity between subject and object. Understanding is not merely an extension of the subject, nor is it merely a borrowing from the object; it is, rather, both simultaneously'; original text: Wilhelm von Humboldt. 1841. 'Über die Aufgabe des Geschichtsschreibers', in Wilhelm von Humboldt, *Gesammelte Werke*, vol. 1, Berlin: G. Reimer, 14. For a good interpretation of Humboldt's theory of understanding, see Manfred Riedel. 1978. *Verstehen oder Erklären. Zur Theorie und Geschichte der hermeneutischen Wissenschaften*. Stuttgart: Klett-Cotta, 146–150.

59. Humboldt, 'On the Historian's Task', 65; original text: Humboldt, 'Über die Aufgabe des Geschichtsschreibers', 15: 'Wo zwei Wesen durch gänzliche Kluft getrennt sind, führt keine Brücke der Verständigung von einem zum andern, und um sich zu verstehen, muß man sich in einem andern Sinn schon verstanden haben.'

60. Droysen, *Historik* 1: 22 [Vorlesungstext, 1857].

61. Droysen, *Outline of the Principles of History*, 13: 'Animals, plants and the things of the inorganic world are understood by us only in part, only in a certain way, in certain relations, namely those wherein these things seem to correspond to categories of our thinking. Those things have for us no individual, at least no personal, existence. Inasmuch as we seize and understand them only in the relations named, we do not scruple to set them at naught as to their individual existences, to dismember and destroy them, to use and consume them. With human beings ... with

human utterances and creations, we have and feel that we have an essential kinship and reciprocity of nature: every "I" enclosed in itself, yet each in its utterances disclosing itself to others.'

62. Droysen, *Historik* 2: 448 [Antrittsrede bei der Berliner Akademie der Wissenschaften, 1868]: 'Denn allerdings haben wir von menschlichen Dingen, von jedem Ausdruck und Abdruck menschlichen Dichtens und Trachtens, der uns wahrnehmbar wird oder so weit er noch wahrnehmbar ist, unmittelbar und in subjectiver Gewißheit ein Verständniß.'

63. Droysen, *Historik* 1: 24–25 [Vorlesungstext, 1857]: 'In der geistig-sinnlichen Natur des Menschen liegt es, daß sie jeden Vorgang in ihr in sinnliche Äußerung übersetzt: Von der Begierde erglüht das Auge, von der Furcht erzittern die Glieder, dem plötzlichen Schrecken folgt der krampfige Schrei. Jede innerste Seelenbewegung des einen ist sofort dem anderen zu sinnlicher Wahrnehmung zugänglich, auch er würde im Schreck so schreien, in der Furcht so zittern. Aus der gleichen Disposition in sich selbst vermag er, was er wahrnimmt, zurückdeutend zu erfassen; der Schrei der Angst läßt ihn die Angst des Schreienden ermessen usw. In solchen niedrigsten Äußerungen seiner geistig-sinnlichen Natur begegnet der Mensch noch den höchstgearteten Tiere; auch der Hund zittert vor Angst, auch das Pferd schnaubt, wenn es die Trompete hört ... Aber der Mensch bleibt nicht bei diesen kreatürlichen Äußerungen; er schreitet fort zum Vergleichen und Unterscheidungen, zum Urteilen und Schließen, zum Denken und Wollen, zu jener Totalität, die wir besprochen haben, und seiner Natur nach wird jeder dieser inneren Vorgänge in sinnlicher Äußerung, zu sinnlicher Wahrnehmbarkeit hervorbrechen müssen. Das geschieht vor allem in der Sprache ... Unser Sprechen ist nichts anderes als ein Äußerlichmachen unseres Inneren, ein unmittelbares Hervorbrechen jener unserer geistigen Totalitäts ... Und wir werden verstanden, weil durch diese sinnliche Äußerung des Denkens eine ähnliche Totalität in ihrer Sinnlichkeit berührt und zu gleichen Vorstellungen, zu gleichem Denken bestimmt wird'. See also: Joachim Wach. 1984. *Das Verstehen. Grundzüge einer Geschichte der hermeneutischen Theorie im 19. Jahrhundert,* Hildesheim: Georg Olms, vol. 3, 164–166.

64. Once again, it was Wilhelm von Humboldt who had pioneered this trend. Remarkably, Humboldt's general arguments on understanding, mentioned above, came from his text *On the Historian's Task* (1821). The very title of this text is sufficient evidence to conclude that he already regarded understanding from a methodological perspective.

65. Droysen, *Historik. Vorlesungen über Enzyklopädie und Methodologie der Geschichte,* 152–154.

66. Droysen, *Historik* 1: 27 [Vorlesungstext, 1857]: 'Es ist ein Sprechen der vergangenen Zeiten, oft ein halb unverständlich gewordenes, oft ein kaum mehr hörbares, das wir zu verstehen suchen auf ganz ähnliche Weise, wie wir noch heute jeder des anderen Sprache und Seelenausdruck verstehen.'

67. Droysen, *Historik* 1: 162 [Vorlesungstext, 1857]: 'Es ist nur eine Form, eine Ausdrucksweise dieses Verstehens des Gegenwärtigen und Seienden, daß wir es als ein Gewordenes auffassen und darlegen. Und andererseits, dies sein Werden und Gewordensein entwickeln wir uns nur aus dem Seienden, indem wir es so zeitlich auffassen und zerlegen, um es zu verstehen. Wir bewegen uns im Zirkel, aber in einem Zirkel, der uns, wenn auch nicht die Sache, weiterführt'; Droysen, *Historik. Vorlesungen über Enzyklopädie und Methodologie der Geschichte,* 25: 'Das Einzelne wird verstanden in dem Ganzen, aus dem es hervorgeht, und das Ganze aus diesem Einzelnen, in dem es sich ausdrückt. Der Verstehende, wie er selbst ein Ich, eine Totalität in sich ist, wie der, den er zu verstehen hat, ergänzt sich dessen Totalität aus der einzelnen Äußerung und die einzelne Äußerung aus dessen Totalität.'

68. Droysen, *Outline of the Principles of History,* 72 [The Elevation of History to the Rank of a Science, 1863].

69. Droysen, *Historik* 1: 69 [Vorlesungstext, 1857]: 'Aus den Geschäften wird Geschichte, aber sie sind nicht Geschichte'; another example from the same text: 'Also nicht das Geschehene, weder alles Geschehene noch das meiste oder vieles davon ist Geschichte' (8).

70. Erich Rothacker. 1940. 'J.G. Droysens Historik', *Historische Zeitschrift* 161: 89–90.

71. Herbert Schnädelbach. 1974. *Geschichtsphilosophie nach Hegel. Die Probleme des Historismus.* Freiburg: Karl Alber, 91–97.

72. Wilhelm Dilthey. 1981. *Der Aufbau der geschichtlichen Welt in den Geisteswissenschaften*. Frankfurt: Suhrkamp, 133–134.

73. Humboldt, 'On the Historian's Task', 70–71: 'There are two things which the course of this inquiry has attempted to keep firmly in mind: that there is an idea, not itself directly perceptible, in everything that happens, but that this idea can be recognised only in the events themselves. The historian must, therefore, not exclude the power of the idea from his presentation by seeking everything exclusively in his material sources; he must at least leave room for the activity of the idea. Going beyond that, moreover, he must be spiritually receptive to the idea and actively open to perceiving and appropriating it.'

74. Droysen, *Historik* 1: 215.

75. Rüsen, *Konfigurationen des Historismus,* 251.

76. Humboldt, 'On the Historian's Task', 65.

77. Jörn Rüsen has made a similar suggestion, arguing that Droysen depicts historical knowledge as dialectically emerging from both the subjective constructivism inherent to the production of knowledge and the objective constructedness of historical consciousness. Rüsen, 'Droysen heute', 192: 'Droysens Historik gibt einen entscheidenden Hinweis darauf, wie der Zusammenhang zwischen objektiver und subjektiver Geschichte gedacht werden kann. Er läßt sich von seinem Verständnis von der Gegenwart der Vergangenheit her erschließen, von dem Phänomen, das ich (versuchsweise) die gegenwärtige Nachträglichkeit der Vergangenheit im historischen Denken nennen möchte. Im Lebensvollzug des Geschichtsbewußtseins, in seinem praktischen Vollzug als wesentlichem Moment der menschlichen Kultur überschneiden sich Konstruktion und Konstruiertheit.'

78. Droysen, *Historik* 1: 106 [Vorlesungstext, 1857]: 'Das historische Forschen setzt die Reflexion voraus, daß auch der Inhalt unseres Ich ein vielfach vermittelter, ein geschichtliches Resultat ist.'

79. Droysen, *Briefwechsel* 2: 452 [Letter to Wilhelm Arendt, 8 May 1857]: 'Von jedem Punkt der Gegenwart – dem Gewordenen – strahlt durch unsre Wissenschaft erregt ein Lichtkegel rückwärts in die Nacht des Vergangenseins.'

80. Droysen, *Historik* 1: 40 [Vorlesungstext, 1857]: '[Zum Studium der Geschichte aufrufen heißt nicht] … Sondern es heißt durch Beschäftigung mit der gewordenen ethischen Welt, durch die Ergründung ihres Werdens den Sinn für die Wirklichkeit zu entzünden'.

81. Droysen, *Historik* 1: 162 [Vorlesungstext, 1857]: 'Es ist keine Frage, daß wir das, was ist, erst ganz verstehen, wenn wir erkennen, wie es geworden ist.'

82. Droysen, *Historik* 1: 5 [Vorlesungstext, 1857]: 'Historisch zu denken hat mitnichten bloß der historische Forscher oder der Geschichtsschreiber; sondern jeder, der theoretisch oder praktisch mit den Gestaltungen der sittlichen Mächten zu tun hat, muß die Fähigkeit haben und üben, diese Mächte in ihren wechselnden Erscheinungen und ihrer Kontinuität zu fassen und zu erfassen.'

83. Droysen, *Historik* 1: 5 [Vorlesungstext, 1857]: 'Er [jeder, der theoretisch oder praktisch mit den Gestaltungen der sittlichen Mächten zu tun hat] muß, wie W. v. Humboldt sehr treffend sagt, den Sinn für die Wirklichkeiten wecken und nähren'. Droysen perceived Humboldt as the only predecessor of his own approach to the theory of history. The following quote may suffice to illustrate this perception: 'Wenn es uns Deutschen – denn uns wird wohl die Aufgabe zufallen – gelingt, eine Historik, eine Wissenschaftslehre der Geschichte, durchzubilden, so muß Humboldt als deren Gründer genannt werden' (Droysen, *Historik* 1: 53 [Vorlesungstext, 1857]).

84. Humboldt, 'On the Historian's Task', 60. Like Droysen, Humboldt had in mind a tripartite scheme of the ways of scientific knowledge in which history coexisted with 'mathematics' and 'metaphysics'. He argued that each of these intellectual branches had its own 'essential element' or 'activating power', pointing out that in the case of history, the 'sense of reality' was precisely that essential element: 'Every intellectual activity which affects man as a whole possesses something which might be called its essential element, its activating power, the secret of its influence on the mind.… In mathematics this essential element consists in isolating number and

line; in metaphysics it consists in abstracting from all experience.... The element in which history operates is the sense of reality' (60).

85. Humboldt, 'On the Historian's Task', 60: '[The sense of reality] contains the awareness of the transience of existence in time, and of dependence upon past and present causes; at the same time there is the consciousness of spiritual freedom and the recognition of reason, so that reality, despite its seeming contingency, is nevertheless bound by an inner necessity.'

86. Humboldt, 'On the Historian's Task', 60–61: 'History does not primarily serve us by showing us through specific examples, often misleading and rarely enlightening, what to do and what to avoid. History's true and immeasurable usefulness lies rather in its power to enliven and refine our sense of acting on reality, and this occurs more through the form attached to events themselves than through the events themselves.'

87. Muhlack, 'Bildung zwischen Neuhumanismus und Historismus', 93–94.

88. Droysen, *Historik* 1: 40 [Vorlesungstext, 1857]: 'Zum Studium der Geschichte aufrufen heißt da natürlich nicht empfehlen, daß man sich mit soundso vielen einzelnen Vorkommnissen und Tatsachen aus dem Leben der Staaten und Völker bekannt mache, noch weniger, daß man historische Bücher schreibe oder in Regestenarbeit und Quellenkritik den Gipfel wissenschaftlichen Tuns suche, das alles ist an seiner Stelle vortrefflich, unentbehrlich, aber es ist nicht das Wesentliche. Sondern es heißt durch Beschäftigung mit der gewordenen ethischen Welt, durch die Ergründung ihres Werdens den Sinn für die Wirklichkeit entzünden, die Fähigkeit erwecken, in allem menschlichen Seienden die Lebenskraft seines Werdens ... [zu] erkennen und so für den falschen Dualismus, der nur in der Abstraktion entsteht und der von Anfang bis zu Ende unsittlich ist, die Gewißheit der Versöhnung, die die ethische Welt ist, zu gewinnen.'

89. Muhlack, 'Bildung zwischen Neuhumanismus und Historismus', 96.

90. Droysen, *Historik* 1: 5 [Vorlesungstext, 1857].

91. This justifies my preference, in the following, to mostly avoid translating the term *Bildung*. On the singularity of the term, see Georg Bollenbeck. 1996. *Bildung und Kultur. Glanz und Elend eines deutschen Deutungsmusters,* Frankfurt am Main: Suhrkamp, 20–27; Rudolf Vierhaus. 1979. 'Bildung', in Otto Brunner et al. (eds), *Geschichtliche Grundbegriffe: Historisches Lexikon zur politisch-sozialen Sprache in Deutschland,* vol. 1, Stuttgart: Klett-Cotta, 508–509. See also Raymond Geuss. 1996. 'Kultur, Bildung, Geist', *History and Theory* 35(2): 152–164.

92. Reinhart Koselleck. 1990. 'Zur anthropologischen und semantischen Struktur der Bildung', in Reinhart Koselleck (ed.) *Bildungsbürgertum im 19. Jahrhundert,* part 2: *Bildungsgüter und Bildungswissen,* Stuttgart: Klett-Cotta, 13–14.

93. Koselleck, 'Zur anthropologischen und semantischen Struktur der Bildung', 23–24.

94. Ernst Liechtenstein. 1971. 'Bildung', in Joachim Ritter (ed.), *Historisches Wörterbuch der Philosophie,* Basel: Schwabe, 921.

95. Ursula Franke. 2000. 'Bildung/Erziehung, ästhetische', in Karlheinz Barck et al. (eds), *Ästhetische Grundbegriffe,* Stuttgart: J.B. Metzler, 697.

96. A quotation from Montesquieu's *The Spirit of the Laws* clearly illustrates the general assumptions of the 'pedagogy' of the Enlightenment: 'We have said that the laws were the particular and precise institutions of a legislator, and manners and customs the institutions of a nation in general. Hence it follows that when these manners and customs are to be changed, it ought not to be done by laws; this would have too much the air of tyranny.... Nations are in general very tenacious of their customs; to take them away by violence is to render them unhappy: we should not therefore change them, but engage the people to make the change themselves' (quoted by Reill, *The German Enlightenment and the Rise of Historicism,* 71).

97. Liechtenstein, 'Bildung', 921.

98. Bollenbeck, *Bildung und Kultur,* 193–206; Karl-Ernst Jeismann. 1987. 'Zur Bedeutung der "Bildung" im 19. Jahrhundert', in Karl-Ernst Jeismann and Peter Lundgreen (eds), *Handbuch der deutschen Bildungsgeschichte,* Band 3: *1800–1870: Von der Neuordnung Deutschlands bis zur Gründung des Deutschen Reiches,* Munich: C.H. Beck, 3, 20.

99. Koselleck, 'Zur anthropologischen und semantischen Struktur der Bildung', 28.

100. Koselleck, 'Zur anthropologischen und semantischen Struktur der Bildung', 20.

101. On this last issue, see Aleida Assmann. 1993. *Arbeit am nationalen Gedächtnis. Eine kurze Geschichte der deutschen Bildungsidee,* Frankfurt am Main: Campus.

102. On Droysen and the concept of *Bildung,* see also Pedro S. P. Caldas. 2006. 'O limite do historismo: Johann Gustav Droysen e a importância do conceito de Bildung na consciência histórica alemã do século XIX', *Revista Filosófica de Coimbra* 29: 139–160.

103. Droysen, *Historik* 1: 256 [Vorlesungstext, 1857].

104. Gotthold Ephraim Lessing. 1855. 'Die Erziehung des Menschengeschlechtes', in Gotthold E. Lessing, *Gesammelte Werke in 2 Bände,* vol. 2, Leipzig: Göschen, 348, § 1–2: 'Was die Erziehung bei dem einzelnen Menschen ist, ist die Offenbarung bei dem ganzen Menschengeschlechte. Erziehung ist Offenbarung, die dem einzeln Menschen geschieht: und Offenbarung ist Erziehung, die dem Menschengeschlechte geschehen ist, und noch geschieht.'

105. Quoted and commented by Bollenbeck, *Bildung und Kultur,* 125–126.

106. Bollenbeck, *Bildung und Kultur,* 120.

107. Droysen, *Historik* 1: 14 [Vorlesungstext, 1857]: 'Darum sind die Kinder nicht bloß quantitativ von den Erwachsenen unterschieden, ein Kind ist ein qualitativ anderes als der Jüngling, der Mann, der Greis.'

108. Droysen, *Historik* 1: 291 [Vorlesungstext, 1857]; Droysen, *Historik* 1: 419–420 [Grundriß der Historik, 1882]. See also: Navarro, 'Fichte, Humboldt y Ranke sobre la idea y las ideas históricas', 425–426. Silvia Caianiello has also explored the theme of the dual nature of the human being in Droysen's writings, stressing the differences between Droysen's and Wilhelm von Humboldt's anthropologies. See Silvia Caianiello. 1999. *La ‹duplice natura› dell'uomo. La polarità come matrice del mondo storico in Humboldt e in Droysen.* Soveria Mannelli: Rubbettino.

109. Droysen, *Historik* 1: 16 [Vorlesungstext, 1857]: 'Auch der Mensch hat seine kreatürliche Seite, aber dieser sein naturhistorischer Gattungsbegriff füllt nicht sein Wesen aus wie bei Tier und Pflanze.'

110. Droysen, *Historik* 1: 14 [Vorlesungstext, 1857]: 'Er [der Mensch] muß erst ein Mensch werden, um ein Mensch zu sein, und nur in dem Maß ist er es, als er es zu werden und immer mehr zu werden weiß.'

111. Droysen, *Historik* 1: 23 [Vorlesungstext, 1857]: 'Man könnte sich wohl denken, daß das Tier die Summe der Sensationen, die es empfängt, nach einem fertigen Typus aufnimmt und reflektiert; der Mensch, indem er jeden Eindruck zu den früheren sammelt, faßt jeden neuen Eindruck in einen schon reicheren Spiegel auf, er lernt, er ist ein innerlich nicht Fertiges, sondern ein unendlich Werdendes, die typische Grundform seiner Erscheinung ist damit näher bestimmt, daß sein Wesen noch nicht ist, was es zu werden hat, und daß er werdend erst innewird, was er zu sein streben muß.'

112. Droysen, *Historik* 1: 23–24 [Vorlesungstext, 1857]: 'Die Natur ist vollkommen überall, nur der Mensch ist in dem Moment, wo er aufhört, ein Stück Natur zu sein, d. h. wo er Mensch zu sein beginnt, unvollkommen, und richtiger, in der Gefahr, seine Bestimmung zu verfehlen, von seinem Wesen zu verirren. Die Selbsterzeugung seines Wesens ist seine Bestimmung und seine Arbeit.'

113. Droysen, *Historik* 1: 14 [Vorlesungstext, 1857].

114. Droysen, *Historik* 1: 23–24 [Vorlesungstext, 1857]: 'Die Selbsterzeugung seines Wesens ist seine Bestimmung und seine Arbeit.'

115. Droysen, *Historik* 1: 14 [Vorlesungstext, 1857]: 'Mit gutem Grund nennen die Alten das Menschsein die humanitas, Bildung, die Bildung ist durch und durch historischer Natur; und der Inhalt der Geschichte ist die werdende humanitas, die werdende Bildung.'

116. Droysen, *Historik* 2: 455–456 [Denkschrift, die historischen Studien betreffend, 1860]: 'Das [in] den Vergangenheiten [bis] daher Erarbeitete, dessen Ergebnisse die Gegenwart erfüllen und adeln, im Geist durchlebt und nachgelebt, es in seinen großen Typen innerlich neu durch-

arbeitet und so erarbeitet haben, in diesem Sinn in dem Niveau seiner Zeit stehen, das und nur das heißt gebildet zu sein'; Droysen, *Historik* 1: 14 [Vorlesungstext, 1857]: 'Er [der Mensch] lernt sich erst hinein oder hinauf zu diesem lebendigen Inhalt seiner Gegenwart, welche die Summe und das Ergebnis unendlicher historischer Durchlebungen ist, diese hat er zu erleben und nachzuleben, d. h. nachzulernen.'

117. Johann Wolfgang Goethe. 1986. 'Faust. Eine Tragödie', in *Goethes Werke. Hamburger Ausgabe,* vol. 3, Munich: C.H. Beck, 29.

118. Droysen, *Outline of the Principles of History,* 74 [The Elevation of History to the Rank of a Science, 1863].

119. Droysen, *Historik* 1: 459–460 [Die Erhebung der Geschichte zum Rang einer Wissenschaft, 1863].

120. Walter Horace Bruford. 1975. *The German Tradition of Self-Cultivation: Bildung from Humboldt to Thomas Mann,* Cambridge: Cambridge University Press.

121. The point of departure of Bruford's argument is a quote from Thomas Mann's speech *Geist und Wesen der deutschen Republik,* which was delivered in 1923, hence in the aftermath of what Bruford considered to be Mann's conversion from apoliticism. Mann's text – as quoted and translated by Bruford, *The German Tradition of Self-Cultivation,* vii – reads as follows: 'The inwardness, the culture [*Bildung*] of a German implies introspectiveness; an individualistic cultural conscience; consideration for the careful tending, the shaping, deepening and perfecting of one's own personality or, in religious terms, for the salvation and justification of one's own life; subjectivism in the things of the mind, therefore a type of culture that might be called pietistic, given to autobiographical confession and deeply personal, one in which the world of objective, the political world, is felt to be profane and is thrust aside with indifference, "because", as Luther says, "this external order is of no consequence". What I mean by all this is that the idea of a republic meets with resistance in Germany chiefly because the ordinary middle-class man here, if he ever thought about culture, never considered politics to be part of it, and still does not do so today. To ask him to transfer his allegiance from inwardness to the objective, to politics, to what the peoples of Europe call *freedom,* would seem to him to amount to a demand that he should do violence to his own nature, and in fact give up his sense of national identity.'

122. Bruford, *The German Tradition of Self-Cultivation,* 22: 'Humboldt was in fact, as we have seen, an individualist of the type so common in the age of German Idealism, self-centred from what seemed to him the highest motives'; (84–86): 'Schleiermacher's unlimited sympathy with others and his trust in life are attractive youthful features in the Soliloquies, but looked at historically, the belief in and pursuit of individuality, especially in its political applications, may well be regarded as the starting-point of dangerous tendencies, as well as of intoxicating new hopes…. Schleiermacher was a great and a good man, in public and in private life, but looking back after a century and a half and remembering the calamities that have resulted for the world from the excesses of German nationalism, one cannot help questioning some of the views he put forward in all innocence.'

123. Droysen, *Historik* 1: 14 [Vorlesungstext, 1857]: 'Dadurch, daß jeder sich in die Resultate des von seiner Familie, seinem Volk, seiner Zeit, von der Menschheit durchlebte hineinstellt, sich in dies Niveau der gewordenen Gegenwart hinaufarbeitet, dadurch also, dass er in der Geschichte und die Geschichte in ihm ist, eben dadurch erhebt er sich über die bloß kreatürliche zu der geistigen Existenz, die den Menschen über die Monotonie der übrigen Schöpfung stellt, ihn aus dem bloßen peripherischen Dasein zu einem neuen Mittelpunkt macht.'

124. Droysen, *Historik* 1: 252 [Vorlesungstext, 1857]: '… ethisches Kapital der durchlebten Vergangenheiten.'

125. Droysen, *Historik* 1: 14 [Vorlesungstext, 1857]: 'Er [jeder einzelne] wird hineingeboren in die ganze historische Gegebenheit seines Volkes, seiner Sprache, seiner Religion, seines Staates usw.; und erst dadurch, dass er das so Vorgefundene, Unendliches lernend, ohne es selbst zu wissen, in sich nimmt und verinnerlicht, es so mit seinem eigensten Wesen verschmilzt, dass er damit, wie leiblich mit seinen Organen und Gliedern, unmittelbar schaltet, erst dadurch hat er mehr als tierisches, ein menschliches Leben.'

126. Droysen, *Historik* 1: 250 [Vorlesungstext, 1857]: 'Es war der Grundzug der fälschlich pragmatisch genannten Historie, daß man aus der Geschichte lernen solle, wie man sich in ähnlich vorkommenden Fällen benehmen müsse.'

127. Droysen, *Historik* 1: 251 [Vorlesungstext, 1857]: 'Aber will man Muster, Paradigmen für die Nacheiferung, so hat wohl Alexander sich besser den Homerischen Achill gewählt, als er irgendeinen Themistokles oder Miltiades hätte wählen können. Denn die Poesie, sagt sein Lehrer Aristoteles, ist philosophischer und idealistischer als die Geschichte.'

128. Bauer, ‹*Das Geheimnis aller Bewegung ist ihr Zweck*›, 133.

129. Droysen, *Historik* 1: 250 [Vorlesungstext, 1857]: 'Aber warum ist es wichtig, sich über das Vergangene zu belehren?'

130. Droysen, *Historik* 1: 250–251 [Vorlesungstext, 1857]: 'Wenn jemand auch noch so viele Schlachten beschrieben gelesen, im gegebenen Fall würde er darum noch keine Schlacht führen können…. Aber es wird für einen Offizier das größte Interesse haben, in der Kriegsgeschichte zu sehen, wie große Feldherren sich in bestimmten Fällen benommen, wie sie ihre Schlacht geliefert haben; er hat die verschiedenen Möglichkeiten, dann den Moment der Gefahr in sich kurz mit zu durchdenken, die Mittel mit zu kombinieren, er fühlt sich wie inmitten des Vorgangs, geistig durchlebt er ihn. Der Gewinn, den er davon hat, ist nicht, dass er nun weiß, nach welcher Regel er sich einmal seinerseits zu benehmen hat, sondern das Verständnis des im Geist durchlebten, die durchgemachte geistige Übung.'

131. See Chapter 4.

132. Droysen, *Outline of the Principles of History*, 54; Droysen, *Historik* 1: 251 [Vorlesungstext, 1857]: 'Und diese geistig durchgemachte Übung ist Bildung, militärische, juristische, diplomatische, wenn sie für diesen technischen Zweck angestellt ist, allgemeine Bildung wenn nicht dies oder jenes einzelne, sondern das allgemein Menschliche zu üben der Zweck ist.'

133. Droysen, *Historik* 1: 251 [Vorlesungstext, 1857]: 'Nicht die einzelnen Vorbilder, sondern der ganze hohe ethische Zug der Geschichte soll uns durchwehen und uns mitreißen'.

134. Georg Wilhelm Friedrich Hegel. 1986. 'Rechts-, Pflichten-, und Religionslehre für die Unterklasse', in Georg Hegel, *Werke in 20 Bänden*, vol. 4: *Nürnberger und Heidelberger Schriften, 1808–1817*, Frankfurt am Main: Suhrkamp, 252: 'Der Mensch als Individuum verhält sich zu sich selbst. Er hat die gedoppelte Seite seiner Einzelheit und seines allgemeinen Wesens. Seine Pflicht gegen sich ist insofern teils seine physische Erhaltung, teils [dies], sein Einzelwesen zu seiner allgemeinen Natur zu erheben, sich zu bilden.'

135. Droysen, *Historik* 1: 370 [Vorlesungstext, 1857]: 'Wir würden etwas Falsches sagen, wenn wir jene Betrachtungsweise von dem jedesmaligen empirischen Anlaß aus ungeschichtlich nennen wollten; aber kleingeschichtlich sie es; es ist die Mikrologie, welche die großen Dinge klein und die kleinen Dinge groß zu sehen das Bedürfnis hat; es ist die Unbildung, welche es erträgt, das, was sie beschäftigt, ohne Zusammenhang mit dem Hohen und Höchsten zu fassen, es für wichtig zu halten, weil es sie beschäftigt.'

136. Droysen, *Historik* 1: 365 [Vorlesungstext, 1857]: 'In diesem allgemeinen Ich denkt und forscht auch der Historiker. Und indem dies mein empirisches Ich im Forschen und Denken sich seiner Besonderheiten entkleidet, sich generalisiert, sich als das wesentlich typische und allgemeine Ich gesetzt hat, erhebt es sich zugleich über die Schränke des Hier und Jetzt hinaus, es hört auf, nur mein Ich zu sein, es ist das allgemeine Ich …'

137. Droysen, *Historik* 1: 251–252 [Vorlesungstext, 1857]: 'Dieser Typus des Wesentlichen, Entscheidenden, Gewaltigen, diese Macht der großen Gesichtspunkte, der großen Motive und Kräfte, das ist es, was die Geschichte der Seele bildend zuführt. Sie erhebt sich damit über ihre kleine und kleinliche Besonderheit, sie lernt groß zu fühlen und aus dem Ich der Menschheit zu denken.'

138. Hermann Lübbe. 1977. *Geschichtsbegriff und Geschichtsinteresse. Analytik und Pragmatik der Historie*, Basel: Schwabe, 204–224.

139. Günther Buck. 1981. *Hermeneutik und Bildung. Elemente einer verstehenden Bildungslehre*, Munich: Wilhelm Fink, 123–129.

140. Buck, *Hermeneutik und Bildung*, 134–137.

141. Michael Inwood. 1992. *A Hegel Dictionary*, Oxford: Blackwell, 92; Wolfgang Kersting. 1995. 'Sittlichkeit; Sittenlehre', in Joachim Ritter and Karlfried Gründer (eds), *Historisches Wörterbuch der Philosophie*, vol. 9, Basel: Schwabe, 910–914.

142. Droysen, *Historik* 1: 438–441 [Grundriß der Historik, 1882].

143. Droysen, *Historik* 1: 290 [Vorlesungstext, 1857]: 'Es ist ein irregeleiteter Stolz des menschlichen Geistes, wenn er verkennt, daß die Persönlichkeit nicht der Anfang, sondern der Schluß, nicht, wie man es ausgedrückt hat, der erste sittliche Organismus, sondern ein Ergebnis aller sittlichen Sphären ist, aber freilich so ist, daß sie in jeder derselben wieder die Bedingung und Voraussetzung ist. Es ist die Dialektik, welche durch alle Verhältnisse des endlichen Geistes hindurchgeht.'

144. Droysen, *Historik* 1: 363–364 [Vorlesungstext, 1857]: 'Aber diese sittlichen Gemeinsamkeiten sind untereinander keineswegs in gleicher Bewegung, sie rivalisieren untereinander, sie schließen sich bis zu einem gewissen Grade aus.… Wir durften sagen, in jeder Persönlichkeit sei für ihre Spanne Leben mikrokosmisch die sittliche Welt; es liegt in der Natur der menschlichen Persönlichkeit, daß sie ein Gewebe aus allen Fäden sittlicher Gestaltungen um sich her habe, wie fein oder roh es denn sei.'

145. See Chapter 4.

146. Droysen, *Historik* 1: 362 [Vorlesungstext, 1857]: 'Es kann mir einfallen, meine Familiengeschichte zu erforschen, die wenige außer mir interessieren wird, aber an sich ist sie ebenso geschichtlicher Natur und mit derselben geschichtlichen Methoden zu behandeln wie die des Hauses Habsburg oder Howard. Wer will leugnen, daß auch das Ländchen Vaduz oder der kleine Staat San Marino seine Geschichte hat; sie wird nur nicht eben andere interessieren, als die sie unmittelbar angeht; sie hat eben kein höheres, kein allgemeines Interesse.' Droysen explains the reasons for that lack of general interest as follows: 'Nur wo wir einen Beitrag für die fortschreitende Bewegung der Menschheit finden, haben wir das Interesse, zu sehen, wie sie sich da einleitete, formte, vollzog, was sie ergab; in diesem Zusammenhang und für denselben erscheint uns alles bedeutsam und der Erforschung wert' (Droysen, *Historik* 1: 368 [Vorlesungstext, 1857]).

147. Droysen, *Historik* 1: 366–367 [Vorlesungstext, 1857]: 'Und wenn schon die tausendfache Wiederholung der Ehe, der Familie, der Dorfgemeinde usw. dem allgemeinen geschichtlichen Bewußtsein durchaus fern liegt, so sind wir nach allem, was wir bisher besprochen und erkannt haben, doch nicht berechtigt, diesen Verhältnissen es abzusprechen, daß jedes von ihnen geschichtlicher Art sei. Und doch haben wir instinktiv die Gewißheit, daß diese Dinge gleichsam nur privatim einen geschichtlichen Charakter haben.'

148. Droysen, *Historik* 1: 367 [Vorlesungstext, 1857]: 'Wir unterscheiden also einmal die Geschichte der Entwicklung der sittlichen Mächte, gleichsam die Geschichte der großen sittlichen Organe, sodann die spezialgeschichtliche Betrachtung der einzelnen Erscheinungen in jeder Reihe.'

149. Droysen, *Historik* 1: 367 [Vorlesungstext, 1857]: 'Wenn es nun eine Geschichte geben soll, die mehr als diese besondere und individuelle Bedeutung hat, so muß es eine solche sein, bei der alle Menschen, bei der der Mensch als solcher, beteiligt sind, es muß die Geschichte aller, es muß die Geschichte sein.'

CHAPTER 3

Historical Thinking and the Genealogy of the Present

The Premodern History of Freedom

An important factor that led Droysen to theorize an alternative to the exemplar theory of history was, as already laid out, the dynamization of the sense of time and temporalization of human experience set in motion in the second half of the eighteenth century. Droysen elaborated his didactics of historical thinking precisely as a means to deal with a general historicization of lifeworld and world view. He associated historical thinking with a basic subjective competence that would help one to make sense of the world's formative process, as well as to act and interact under conditions generated by it.

Yet to properly understand what is involved in Droysen's theory of historical thinking, it is necessary to consider how this theory relates to his own general sense of history. In fact, save for a few exceptions, analysts of Droysen's historical theory have leaned towards dissociating his concrete historical interpretations from his epistemological or methodological arguments. As a result, Droysen's substantive views on history have been left rather understudied.[1] However, it is inevitably worth asking what concrete perceptions of historicity were connected to Droysen's own theoretical efforts. If Droysen regards historical thinking as the best of what historical science can teach, then how did he himself historically think? If historical thinking summarizes the mental act through which one is able to interpret the world one lives in, then how did Droysen interpret his? In other words, what concrete perceptions of historicity lay behind or beyond his historical didactics? These questions will guide the discussion below.

In general lines, the process of history, as Droysen presupposed and interpreted it, equals a long-ranging teleological movement, initiated in classical

---

antiquity and further advanced through the Middle Ages and early modern times up until his own days. Droysen's genesis of the present thus enfolds what he deemed the formative process of Western culture – the very same process that, since the late eighteenth century in German-speaking spaces, many world and universal histories have attempted to intellectually grasp and represent. Since Droysen's genetic interpretation of the present sprang out of a teleological conception of temporal change, it presents the macro-process of history as the process through which humankind gradually accomplishes a general goal. In this instance, the goal is the same as the one formerly defined by Droysen's philosophical teacher, Hegel, namely, the materialization of the idea of freedom. For Droysen, interpreting the genesis of the present means applying historical thinking in order to understand the objective developments the idea of freedom has undergone, from its inception to the present.

While putting historical thinking into practice, Droysen thus sought linkages between the present world and the macro-process by which freedom evolves. He saw 'freedom', considered history's *telos,* as the main interpretative guideline by which past facts, experiences and processes are selected (or dismissed), described and evaluated. Although Droysen never wrote a comprehensive history of the idea of freedom, he always had in mind an overarching conception of that historical process, which can be reconstructed in its general lines. In his view, the history of the idea of freedom was a process to which classic Greek civilization, Hellenism, Christianity, the Protestant Reformation and finally the revolutions of modern times made the most important contributions. In the following, I will discuss Droysen's macro-interpretation of universal history as the evolving of the idea of freedom, that is, his substantial historical thoughts. I will attempt to underscore that for Droysen, to think historically meant to be able to mentally connect the experienced present and the expected future to the cognizable past of universal history.

Like Droysen, many nineteenth-century German historical thinkers regarded universal history as a process characterized by a main guiding line: the origins, changes, and diffusion of the idea of freedom. A widespread agreement that prevailed among them was, in fact, that the idea of freedom first emerged within the context of ancient Greek civilization. In his lectures on *Philosophy of History,* Hegel delivered what is today the most famous expression of that general point of view, by remarking that 'the consciousness of freedom first arose among the Greeks, and therefore they were free'. Hegel also contrasted the novelty brought about by the Greeks with the situation elsewhere: 'The Orientals' – he continues – 'have not attained the knowledge that the Spirit is free; and because they do not know this, they are not free. They only know that one is free'.[2] Leaving aside the Eurocentrism charges that many readers will be likely to press on this last quote, it is unquestionable that Hegel's view is representative of the central role played by the reference to ancient Greek culture in nineteenth-century historical thinking. Greece was then projected as the historical scenario where freedom was born; where, for the first time ever, human beings became aware of their real condition as free beings. Contrarily to the 'Orientals', the Greeks would have produced a social order within which freedom became a norm applicable not only to the political ruler, but also to all those held as direct participants in the national community. This, of course, excluded non-nationals – as well as women – from the sphere of liberty, and caused Hegel to conclude that Greeks and Romans, although having attained the consciousness of freedom, did not move beyond the idea that freedom was only for some and not for everybody. Ancient Greek freedom, he states, was restricted and accidental, for 'it was implicated with the institution of slavery'. Even though, it was in ancient Greece that he saw the deepest root and the main predecessor of modern liberty.[3]

In general, Droysen's view on the origins of the idea of freedom does not differ from Hegel's. Droysen was actually one of the few nineteenth-century historians who did not ostensibly repudiate the Hegelian philosophy of history, and who effectively acted as a mediator between it and the German human sciences.[4] Droysen, too, believed that 'the great achievement of Athens was to have attained and set in motion the consciousness of freedom'.[5] Still following Hegel, he connects the motif of the attainment of the consciousness of freedom in ancient Greece to that of the breakthrough from myth into history.[6] This breakthrough is for him a notorious case of the general situation in which a collectivity is exposed to a cultural drive that forces it out of its immediate traditions. The first setting in which such a situation came about would have been precisely classical Athens, when traditional sociopolitical determinations were undermined by the establishment of democracy, and by the resulting dethronement of birth as the sole criterion for both social status and participation in the political community. In one of his first published texts, Droysen stresses the significance of the break with tradition inaugurated by democracy's emergence, stating that the sort of 'historical life' that had started to take place among the Greeks was 'an enemy of all natural and given conditions'.[7] The situation of a fragile relationship prevailing between a given present order and the traditions that previously regulated collective life is, according to Droysen, paradigmatic for the general importance of historical knowledge. This is, furthermore, the structural experience behind not only the classical breakthrough from myth into history, but also the modern transition from the exemplar justification of historiography to a didactics of historical thinking.

Based on the reasoning described above, Droysen acknowledges that ancient Greek culture (particularly after the establishment of the Athenian democracy) was the first really historical culture. 'Historical' here indicates his ascertainment that the Greeks were the first who were able to actually put tradition into question. Droysen argues that the emergence of history took place within the scenario of an emergent 'rationalism', a scenario that he also calls the Hellenic Enlightenment. He associates the rise of such rationalism with tendencies such as the sense of the insufficiencies of poetical representation the notion that the causes for natural and historical events are to be searched in this-worldly processes; and the spread of prose as a cultural resource.[8] That rationalism would have nourished the sources of Greek drama, historiography and philosophy altogether.

All in all, Droysen regarded drama, historiography and philosophy as components of a new way of making sense of the world, which was fundamentally opposed to that of myth and poetry. Interestingly enough, however, he does not simply (retrospectively) greet the Hellenic Enlightenment. In fact, he criticizes it for not having supported a dialectical way out of the tensions between old and new, poetry and prose, myth and rationalism.[9] Meanwhile, the parallels between this criticism, voiced in the 1930s, and the criticism he would cultivate later on modern Enlightenment are intriguing. The cultural failure in mediating between tradition and consciousness of freedom was, according to Droysen, a constant experience in classical and post-classical Greek history. Even Aristotle, whom Droysen identified as 'Antiquity's greatest spirit', stood under the spell of the incapacity to deal constructively with tradition. For Droysen, Aristotle's philosophy, though 'appearing to be once again blown by the breeze of the idea', was no longer able to connect with the 'older poetic forces of Greek culture', since after the break with myth 'the ancient Gods were mopped away, [and] dialectical forms and natural laws now rule the once beautiful world'.[10] Because of its incompatibility with tradition, the freedom of the ancients – as interpreted by Droysen – seems here to have reached what could be called an aporia.

But however intense his view of classical Greece was, the Hellenistic period was the premodern epoch that Droysen most researched and wrote about. His largely positive appraisal of that historical period contrasted strongly with traditional interpretations that regarded the Macedonian dominance over Greece as having initiated the downfall of Greek classical freedom. Informed by what was then the modern scholarship on Alexandrian literature,[11] Droysen's *History of Alexander the Great* (1833) and the subsequent *History of Hellenism* (1836, 1843) comprised arguments counter to that traditional understanding. In fact, they emphasized that Phillip's and especially Alexander's conquests furthered rather than sabotaged the evolution of freedom. The concept of Hellenism conveyed in those texts was probably the most decisive step towards a positive re-evaluation of that historical epoch. Today's common reference to Hellenism as a historical period between the decay of the classical polis and Rome's rise to world power is largely a result of the posthumous influence of Droysen's concept.[12]

Droysen's positive view of Hellenism also underscores one very significant difference between his and Hegel's macro-interpretations of universal history.

This difference regarding the value of Hellenism was significant enough to have a major impact on their explanations for the emergence of Christianity. Hegel operated, in this regard, with two interrelated premises: that 'spirit' (*Geist*) and 'freedom' were transmitted from the Greeks to the civilization of the Roman Empire; and that the latter augmented its Greek legacy with a new universalism that somehow prefigured and prepared the universalism of the Christian era.[13] He paid no especial attention to the period that Droysen understood as Hellenistic, so the issue of how classical Greek culture was conveyed to the Romans is ultimately left untouched in his philosophy of history. Hegel explained the transition from classical Greece to the Roman Empire as a 'purely metaphysical operation'.[14] It was exactly this gap in Hegel's interpretation of the genesis of Christianity that Droysen intended to fill with his research and writings on 'Hellenism'. In addition, as Droysen – unlike Hegel – held Greek culture to have been the ancient culture par excellence, he was able to downplay Roman cultural achievements, and even to consider Roman history to be within the scope of Hellenism.[15]

In Droysen's view, the world's preparation for the emergence of Christianity was achieved by the Greeks, or more precisely by the fusion of the Hellenic and Oriental cultural and religious elements that he called Hellenism. However, Droysen never carried his account of the rise of Christianity up to the times he had once expected to reach. After publishing three volumes on the political history from Alexander to the year 221 BC (the *History of Alexander the Great* and the two volumes of the *History of Hellenism*), he never finished the two other volumes he once had planned: one accounting for Hellenistic political history from 221 BC until the first century AD, the time of Augustus and Jesus Christ; and the other covering cultural history from the time of Alexander until the Arab invasion of Egypt and Syria in the seventh century AD.[16] The *History of Hellenism* would therefore remain restricted to political history, despite its comprehensive cultural and religious-historical programme. In practice, the issue of Christianity's emergence would remain marginal within the text's narrative flow.

In light of these facts, it comes as no surprise that the key to Droysen's positive appraisal of Hellenism is an argument related to the history of the idea of freedom, and hence to philosophy of history in the substantive sense. For him, Hellenism represented the period or the civilization that universalized classical freedom. Previously, freedom would have been merely a particularistic idea; it was produced as the sociopolitical norm of a specific community, the polis, and was not meant to go beyond its borders. Yet Macedonian expansionism, in Droysen's account, led to the overcoming of Greek traditional particularism. This expansionism spread the Greek cultural heritage throughout a huge number of cultures and territories, thus helping to forge 'the unity of the historical world'.[17] Accordingly, universal history's inaugural gesture was Alexander's propagation of Greek freedom and culture across the Middle East, Southern Asia, Northern Africa and Southern Europe.

Interestingly enough, however, Droysen points out that the beginnings of universal history were characterized by processes of cultural change and learning that not only influenced the subjugated societies but also reverberated back into Greek culture. He remarks that as a result of Alexander's conquests, the Greeks adopted an intercultural attitude that superseded the rigid distinctions between the we-identity and the they-identity that had been typical of the classical era.[18] Within the context of Alexander's world empire, Droysen states, differences that had hitherto been inherent to history, such as those between Occident and Orient, Hellenes and barbarians, 'now had to die out for the benefit of the unity of a world monarchy'.[19] Greeks would finally have learned that Egyptians, Babylonians, Persians, Bactrians and Indians were definitely not 'barbarians' as postulated by Hellenic traditions, but representatives of highly respectable civilizations. Not only would Greek culture be exported to them, but their own cultural elements were also learned and appropriated by the Greeks.[20] As additional evidence, Droysen also mentions that, in an attitude openly incongruent with the Greeks' former sense of superiority, Alexander started to offer sacrifices to foreign gods, to take part in foreign festivities and to observe Asian protocols while receiving Asian chiefs, even wearing Asian gowns.[21]

For Droysen, Hellenism hence represents the period in which the first world-scale civilization emerged. It was the astonishing product of an intercultural experiment never tried before: the fusion of elements of eastern and western cultures. Within the Hellenistic world, he argues, the particularism that marked the classical idea of freedom was overcome in favour of an ethnic universalism. Nevertheless, Droysen does not conclude that the universalism of the Hellenistic age resolved the main aporia of the classical idea of freedom, namely, its radical incompatibility with tradition. All positive appraisals aside, he ultimately assumes that the Hellenistic reconciliation between Orient and Occident only 'prepared a future in which both of them would lose themselves'.[22] In a sense, the Hellenistic Age paved the way to a solution to the estrangement between freedom and tradition, but that solution would be reached only after Hellenism had come to an end. The universalization of human freedom that Droysen stresses as Hellenism's central contribution to world history ultimately corresponded to the universalization of the aporiae of freedom. The freedom of the ancient Greeks (whether classical or Hellenistic), according to him, never went beyond the personal sphere, never reached the public realm. Therefore, 'it atomised itself, and was lost in the sporadic infinity of personal caprices and interests'. The main internal contradiction of ancient freedom was that the radical break with tradition that supported the possibility of personal freedom 'undermined the substantial basis of public life'.[23]

For Droysen, the limitations of both the classical and the Hellenistic conceptions of freedom accrued from the same circumstance, which he once defined as 'Antiquity's heathen character' (*der heidnische Charakter des Altertums*).[24] Droysen deemed ancient freedom to have been essentially pagan freedom, and in paganism he saw no possible solution to the aporiae inaugurated by the classical Greeks. Therefore, in the end he could posthumously attribute only subordinate historical significance to the cultural universalism he identified within Hellenistic civilization (as well as to what he regarded as the merely formal freedom of the Romans).[25] In his view, the importance of Hellenism (a term that, in Droysen's use, sometimes included even the Romans)[26] was due much less to its own achievements than to the fact that it prepared the world-historical setting where one specific achievement would take place, namely, the emergence of Christianity:[27] 'The greatest thing that the ancient world could have accomplished under its own steam', Droysen concludes, 'was the disempowerment of paganism'.[28] The historical significance of Hellenism was thus that it multiplied and intensified the contradictions of pagan freedom.

According to Droysen, the rise of the idea of freedom set in motion a historical dynamics that, for paganism, represented the beginning of an autophagic process. In his view, the ancient awareness of freedom, having acquired its Hellenistic reformulation, led 'the human spirit' to sever itself from 'the natural soil to which it used to be attached'. Hereby, 'the spirit' was 'wrested from its positive content and stance' as it put itself 'alone and away from the Gods'. In this situation, Droysen concludes, 'the human spirit became full of terror and hopelessness'.[29] These strong metaphors convey a picture that can be translated as follows: the consciousness of freedom pushed the ancients away from the collective narratives that had formerly supported their pagan world views, yet did not offer them new, positive contents with which to somehow reconcile old and new, past and present, individuality and collectivity.

It was Christianity's task to accomplish this reconciliation, which for Droysen marked a new turning point in history – indeed, the most important one. According to him, the *telos* of virtually the entirety of ancient history was the emergence of Christianity. The history of humankind was ultimately 'a search for God', and the pagan cultures of antiquity were heavily engaged in that search.[30] Again, Droysen stresses, they never succeeded in it because they tried to find God by relying exclusively on the forces inherent in free human beings. With the expansion of the Greek search for God into the Hellenistic space, and consequently its multiple amalgamations with many different non-Greek religious traditions, cultural exhaustion would have taken place, in turn making Christianity into a historical necessity. Droysen argues that around the beginning of the Roman Empire, a 'sense of tiredness and inadequacy' arose in relation to the endeavours of classical freedom. As a result, 'the perky and joyful confidence in the inherent human forces gave way to a longing for a higher assistance, a force that would infinitely surpass all human force'. Droysen maintains that the Christian revelation took place exactly within that context. Thereafter, 'the once so proud and now broken force of the finite spirit bowed in silent humility to the magnificence of the eternal father.'[31]

The aporiae of ancient freedom, sharpened by Hellenism, were definitively solved 'when the fullness of time came' and God sent his son to ransom an exhausted humanity. At this juncture, Droysen introduces the doctrine of the 'new alliance' as the vehicle by which the transition from ancient history into the new Christian era became possible. As a result of Hellenism, 'Jews, pagans, peoples from all over the world' were 'broken in their ethnic force and got deadly tired'. By sealing a 'new alliance' with God, Droysen concludes, they finally found 'consolation and peace', and in exchange for the 'lost home (*Heimat*) here below' they were offered another, 'a higher and spiritual home to be found in the kingdom of God'.[32] In this kingdom, 'which is not from this world', Droysen moreover sees the realization of a conception of humankind that largely surpasses the universalism of the Hellenistic era. For him, the latter was a mere beginning of universalism, since it never attained an idea of humankind suited to really encompassing all peoples and individuals in the same way a non-ethnic religion could.[33]

It is worth mentioning that in his interpretations of the history of the Christian era, Droysen keeps an eye on developments that took place all over the historical world established within the context of Hellenism. In the foreword to his *Lectures on Medieval History* (1840), he mentions, for instance, that in the Oriental world the Christian doctrine was unable to fully overcome paganism and thus degenerated. Islam took advantage of that spiritual vacuum in the seventh century and, sponsored by a much worldlier understanding of political power than Christianity's, expanded into the Middle East, Northern Africa and parts of the Iberian Peninsula.[34] On the other hand, Droysen also calls attention to the Byzantine Empire, criticizing it for its peculiar form of merging temporal and spiritual power, which in his view rendered the Orthodox Church highly dependent on political ups and downs. Additionally, he indicates that the Byzantine Empire cultivated its Greek cultural heritage in a rather external, dogmatic, spiritless way, so that no trace of the old idea of freedom could any longer be sensed there.[35]

But as expected, neither the Byzantine nor the Arab Empires were spaces where, according to Droysen, the history of the idea of freedom would continue. This would instead take place in the territories of the Romanic-Germanic peoples, a cultural space established during a series of Germanic migrations into areas ruled by the Roman Empire (ca. 300–ca. 700). Droysen particularly emphasizes the German peoples, who had only just appeared on the historical scene, as a 'fresh field' for the newly established Christian church. As the Ger-

manic invasions put an end to the Roman Empire, he remarks, 'the Christian
church, the heiress of Antiquity's spiritual accomplishments, starts her silent
conquest over the conquerors'. Militarily conquerors but spiritually conquered
by Christianity's conversion effort, the Germanic tribes exchanged their sagas
for the Christian history of salvation and mixed their languages with the Latin
of the priests.[36] Thereby, another cultural merging process started to take shape
and was also deemed world-historically relevant by Droysen. By its end, the
Germans had taken the lead in the historical process via the establishment of
the Holy Roman Empire in the tenth century and the emergence of the Protestant Reformation in the sixteenth. In the meantime the descendants of the
Germanic tribes had had to properly assimilate the results of history, the formative process of the humankind in which they hitherto had not taken part.[37]
Droysen saw their conversion to Christianity as having this deep world-historical
and *Bildung*-theoretical meaning. For him, the signature of the Treaty of Verdun
(843), which divided the Carolingian Empire and prepared the ground for the
foundation of the Holy Roman Empire (962), was the main indicator of the
Germans' bounce into history. The history of the German state, argued Droysen, was set into motion by that very event.[38]

Robert Southard cleverly mentioned that, for Droysen, history had begun
and was bound to end with a close association between God and the world.
Yet, Southard added, Droysen hardly saw the intervening period from classical Greece to modernity as a waste of time.[39] History, properly speaking, was
for Droysen the maturing time of the idea of freedom, and the reconciling of
freedom and tradition, personal liberties and public life, is the main distinguishing feature of the modern re-approximation between God and the world. According to Droysen, the Protestant Reformation was precisely the event that
prepared this reconciliation.[40]

As already described, Droysen saw the coming of Christ and the establishment of the Christian church as forming the framework within which
the idea of freedom could be restored, humankind redeemed, and God and
the world reconciled. But after Christianity's early years, the history of the
church would have increasingly kept its distance from that original historical
task. Pagan antiquity had detached 'this world' (*Diesseits*) from the 'afterworld'
(*Jenseits*). As it emerged, Christianity was bound to re-establish the balance
between 'this world' and the 'afterworld', and consequently to preserve and
surpass the ancient idea of freedom. Yet Droysen interpreted the history of the
Catholic Church as the escalation of an attitude of repudiation of this world
and an increasingly one-sided concentration on the afterworld. The history of
the Catholic Church hence becomes a process of degeneration that culminates
with the mere inversion of the aporiae of ancient freedom.[41] In this connection, Droysen recalls that the ancient religions had long represented failed at-

tempts to merge the divine and the worldly, having led only to 'de-godizing the world' (*Weltentgötterung*) – that is, detaching God and the supernatural from this world. Conversely, throughout the Middle Ages the Catholic Church (as well as Islam) had led to 'de-worldizing God' (*Gotentweltlichung*) – to rejection of this world and a completely afterworldly idea of God.[42]

To be sure, Droysen's general characterizations of both ancient and Christian religions are indefensible in the light of today's scholarship on these matters.[43] Still, they very well suit his explanation of the Protestant Reformation as the starting point of the process of establishment of a new agreement between God and the world. According to him, Martin Luther's (1483–1546) doctrines of justification by faith alone and the priesthood of all believers had brought finitude back into a lively relationship with eternity. This, in his view, was what permitted the overcoming of questionable practices nested in the Catholic Church, such as the sacerdotal blessing, the magical techniques intended to elicit divine interventions in worldly affairs, the legends of saints and miracles, the cults of the Mother of God, and so on.[44] For Droysen, then, the Reformation represents a fundamental rejection of the Middle Ages. But it simultaneously also represents a return to the ancient classical models and its ethical, legal and aesthetic ideals, as well as to what he held to be the unadulterated standards of early Christian communal life. By recombining ancient freedom and the early Christian spirit, the Reformation abrogated the corrupted outcomes of the Catholic Church's history. With the Reformation, Droysen states, 'the work of an entirely new time started', a time whose goal was the production of a 'positive mediation' (*Vermittlung*) in which the rigid opposition between this world and the afterworld would fade. Droysen argues that such a reconciliation induces 'the re-conduction of the creation to God' (*Rückleitung der Schöpfung zu Gott*), a process he identifies as being the 'great vocation of Protestantism' (*große Beruf des protestantischen Lebens*).[45]

For Droysen, the Protestant Reformation also marked the first genuinely German input into world history. In his commemorative speech for the thousandth jubilee of the Treaty of Verdun, he spoke of the Reformation as having spread out of the '*deutsches Gemüt*', the totality of the German temper and sensibility.[46] That formulation expresses his opinion that with the Reformation, the Germans, having assimilated the results of other peoples' historical experience, finally started to make their own contribution to the evolving humankind. But he was also pointing out that after the Reformation, the main stage of world history, where the idea of freedom would continue its historical evolution, was no longer the area embraced by the territories of the Romanic-Germanic peoples. Almost all positive developments of the idea of freedom in modern history would thenceforth take place in an abridged scenario: the German cultural space.

The Outset of the Present

Droysen regarded the Protestant Reformation as having laid the spiritual groundwork that made the 're-conduction of the creation to God' a thinkable idea and a plausible civilizational project. However, from Droysen's present perspective the work of the project, though already initiated, was still far from being accomplished. The final reconciliation between God and the world was for him an event not yet experienced, but to be expected. Within the spiritual field, the Reformation had indeed re-equilibrated the relationship between humankind and God, but in other fields, such as political and social life, Droysen felt that the right balance had yet to be produced. The first step for that was, anyhow, the rise and affirmation of the territorial national states throughout the sixteenth, seventeenth and eighteenth centuries, a process Droysen defined as 'the apprenticeship of the modern State'.[47]

Droysen discusses the world-historical significance of the modern state in the first chapters of his *Lectures on the Wars of Freedom*.[48] Here he recalls that in the European late Middle Ages, the *Ständestaat* had established itself as the most important form of political and social organization. *Ständestaat,* or estates of the realm, defined a caste-like division of society into large groups (*Ständen*) like the clergy, the nobility and the commoners (burghers and peasants). Droysen claims that the *Ständestaat* was based exclusively on private law – private rights and duties that mutually supported and controlled each other. Yet he states that by the end of the fifteenth century, some European royal dynasties started to centralize power, universalize their own private rights and increasingly dissolve the privileges of the *Ständen*.[49] In this way, he continues, 'the idea of state arose, no longer as an aggregate of private rights, liberties, and arrangements, but as the complete power of the majesty, the general, the essential, the rational'.[50] Droysen saw the origins of the modern state in connection with the set of major events that historians traditionally credit as the starting points of modern times: the European maritime expansion, the discovery and colonization of America, humanism and Renaissance, the dismissal of scholasticism and, of course, the Protestant Reformation. However, among all those 'tremendous forces' set 'in fermentation' at this time, the modern state had been the most effective contributor to the dissolution of the medieval world.[51]

Nevertheless, the sympathy Droysen cultivated for the real states of early modern times was hardly unconditional. He indeed thought the centralization of state authority and the enfeeblement of particularisms was a necessary step forward within the historical process, but he also regarded the modern state as actually unable to fulfil its historical task. Throughout the sixteenth, seventeenth and eighteenth centuries, Europe had been, in his view, an arena in which states increasingly distanced themselves from their ethical mandate.

Droysen summarizes this in a retrospective reproach of the national monarchies that aimed 'first of all at becoming power rather than state'.[52] The modern absolutist states against which revolutions would arise in the late eighteenth and early nineteenth centuries had long since converted themselves into raw power; they had become 'vicious, monstrous, beyond all remedy'.[53]

Actually, considering Droysen's macro-interpretation of world history in its entirety, the degeneration of the modern state into absolutism was merely the prelude to the time frame that he himself perceived as the present. In 1858, whilst introducing his lectures on the era of the revolution, Droysen delimited his subject matter as comprising 'the fifty years that broke down the old times, and gave birth to the new time, to our present'.[54] In the mid nineteenth century, he and several other European intellectuals assumed that their contemporary times had begun with the political revolutions of the late 1700s. For Droysen, such events had 'shaped our present and are still directing it'.[55] He perceived the present as a time that took shape only after those revolutions had transformed 'all presuppositions and conditions of the European life, all social and political forces, all spiritual and material factors.'[56]

Although Droysen addressed the formative phase of his present time in numerous lectures delivered throughout his lifetime, his only extensive publication dedicated to this theme was the *Lectures on the Wars of Freedom*. Published in 1846, after the lectures given in the winter semester of 1842–43, the book takes into account several political events that occurred between 1776 and 1815, mostly in Europe and the Americas. Droysen treats three 'wars of freedom' in detail, namely, the American Revolutionary War, the French Revolution and the Prusso-German uprising against Napoleonic domination. In what follows, I will summarize his interpretations of these three political-military events because they are crucial for assessing his own sense of the present, and thus the way he concretely articulated his own historical thinking.

'Modernity's first great war of freedom' was, according to Droysen, the colonial war of independence in North America (1775–1783).[57] For him, this event represented the most precise inauguration mark of his contemporary epoch, for as he puts it: 'a new era in world history knocked on the door as America broke free from its mother country.'[58] Droysen's account of the American Revolution is extremely positive. He frequently emphasizes the morality of the founding fathers,[59] who in his opinion had managed to realize radical political change without damage to personal and property rights – unlike other revolutionary leaders of the time.[60] In addition, Droysen vigorously praises the new political institutions of the emerging country, and the new type of legitimacy that originated with them. The U.S.-American state is seen as having sprung from long-running European historical developments; as such, it would have preserved in the new world the best of the old continent's political traditions.[61] For Droysen, it also lacked much of the 'irrational' forces that worked against the advancement of a modern political order in Europe. In fact, no monarchy, no feudal classes or rights, no state religion, no people's tutelage – indeed, only slavery – would burden the U.S.-American state.[62] He saw the emergent state as the first example of a 'state that does not want to be power',[63] or of what could be called an 'ethical state'. To be sure, this was an excessively optimistic view of the history of the United States, especially because Droysen's image of the North American 'ethical state' would be largely contradicted by its increasingly imperialistic foreign policies in the first half of the nineteenth century. Furthermore, by treating the persistence of slavery as a mere bad appendix, Droysen deceptively minimized its influence over the core of North American social and political life.

However, it is still noticeable that he thought of the independence of the United States as a 'war of freedom' whose world-historical significance was due not only to its general contribution to the expansion of the idea of freedom, but also to the essential role it played in terms of dislocating the geographical scenario of world history. According to Droysen, world history had been distinguished by the Occident-Orient polarity ever since antiquity, but the North American Revolution wrought a major redefinition of this polarity. After it took place, the main historical opposition became that between the ancient and the new worlds.[64] In addition, in Droysen's world-historical scheme, as the Old World encompassed not only Europe but also the whole Mediterranean space and beyond, the New World comprised not only the United States, but all the states that would emerge in North, Central and South America in the first half of the nineteenth century. Droysen argues that the independence of the United States was the first step and the main source of inspiration for the establishment of a system of states across the American hemisphere. Consequently, he also regards later cases of national emancipation elsewhere on the American continents as 'wars of freedom' and moreover stresses that it was independence from European motherlands that empowered American countries to actively participate in the historical process.[65] This argument is not suited to be empirically tested – as it frequently happens with historical-philosophical ideas – but it is anyhow interesting to see how he approaches the political and cultural history of the Americas from a perspective that was not yet dominated by the Latin vs. Anglo America dichotomy.

Droysen was clearly less sympathetic towards the second of the major 'wars of freedom', the French Revolution, which he generally regarded as warning of the threats to the continuity of history rather than constituting a positive solution to the modern dilemmas posed by the idea of freedom.[66] Throughout the *Lectures on the Wars of Freedom*, he reiterates his opinion that the revolution annihilated historical traditions by replacing them with models of state and society extracted from abstract theories and utopias. Yet his criticism is levelled not against the change in the old European order that the revolution ignited, but against what he reckons to be rational, abstract, anti-historical solutions instituted by the French revolutionaries. Indeed, though he posthumously applauds the legal fundaments of the new state that were prepared by the National Assembly in the summer of 1779 – the *Declaration of the Rights of Man and the Citizens,* the dismantlement of feudal institutions and rights, and the affirmation of the principles of popular sovereignty and communal autonomy, among other measures – he nonetheless censures the National Assembly's attempt to 'found an entirely new state in a rationalistic manner',[67] stressing the differences between those attempts and the U.S.-American recent accomplishments. In the United States, a modern political order had resulted from the exercise of an already existing civil freedom, whereas in France it was originating from 'an *anticipatio naturae,* according to which all social relations, and – what was even riskier and more complicated – every person should be completely altered'.[68]

Droysen becomes decidedly hypercritical where Jacobinism is concerned. He condemns, above all, what he calls 'the system of terror', the set of values and practices that predominated under Jacobin rule in 1793–94. For Droysen, that system was an extremely radicalized version of essential features of the French Revolution as a whole. Terror's supporters were fanatics who enthusiastically agreed to be 'nothing more than citizens',[69] to sacrifice all particularities – even personal and religious commitments – for the cause of the revolutionary state.[70] For Droysen, it was especially (but not at all exclusively) the Jacobin attempt to substitute a sort of civic cult for religion that represented a major threat to the very idea of history. Its success, he maintained, would undo Christianity's historical accomplishments and replace them with a new form of paganism in which nationality would prevail as the ultimate fundament of social and individual life.[71]

But for him, the most dangerous jeopardy to history, freedom and Christianity was epitomized by Napoleon Bonaparte. According to Droysen, Napoleon's ultimate intention was the construction of a type of rule that would resemble 'that *mécanique céleste* that even a major investigator could ransack "without finding God in there"'.[72] Napoleon aimed to establish 'a state without historical basis',[73] which would be shaped in accordance with 'scientific-mathematical' principles. For Droysen, the materialization of Napoleon's rational state necessarily entailed an 'annihilation of history', that is, a major disintegration of the chain of generations that linked contemporary Europeans to ancient Greeks. 'Never before', Droysen retrospectively assessed, had humankind's 'most precious goods [been] so endangered'.[74] He saw the Napoleonic state as symbolizing all possible perversions that could follow the process of human emancipation. In the name of freedom, Napoleon would have built a hypertrophied state that grievously interfered with individual liberties and rights. Such a state was, therefore, close kin to the absolutist practices that the revolution had proclaimed to be abolished. Actually, Droysen defined the early modern absolutist state as an institution whose final purpose was to produce and exercise power – an institution that claimed 'the omnipotence to dispose of anyone and anything, at any time'.[75] Backed by this definition, he presented the Napoleonic system as the fulfilment of absolutism rather than as a step towards emancipation. Napoleon would have been the ruler of 'a *l'état c'est moi* more complete and energetic' than that of Louis XIV.[76] Napoleonic rule was held to encompass a highly perverse type of despotism far removed from Droysen's ideal of the ethical state. It was, in fact, the perfect example of the 'despotism of the idea of state'.[77]

Regarding his third major war of freedom, the Prusso-German uprising against Napoleonic France, Droysen was unsurprisingly positive. Since the beginnings of the Napoleonic wars in 1792, France had either annexed or occupied German-speaking territories. Between 1813 and 1815, however, the German states, led by Prussia, and their allies managed to break the French domination, finally provoking Napoleon's withdrawal. Shortly thereafter, these events came to be known as the 'wars of freedom' (*Freiheitskriege*) or, more often, 'wars of liberation' (*Befreiungskriege*). The evocation of such wars became a commonplace in nineteenth-century German politics and historiography, though different and somewhat opposing patterns of recollection can be discerned. Droysen himself reckoned them as a sort of myth of national rebirth. He speaks about the 'three unforgettable years in which the German nation fought and triumphed, impelled by the delightful feeling of its unity'.[78] Unlike interpretations from farther left, however, he stresses both the popular character of the uprising and the role played by the Prussian monarch.[79]

Even the general arrangement of the lectures published in 1846 reflects the centrality of the German liberation wars and correlated events in Droysen's image of contemporary history. His use of unconventional terminology to summarize the historical meaning of the events he addresses is striking. At least in the *Lectures on the Wars of Freedom,* he explicitly avoids the more common expression 'Age of the Revolution' (*Zeitalter der Revolution*).[80] He justifies this by saying that he aimed to stress 'the positive content of the transformative movements that occurred in those fifty years'.[81] In a letter of 1845, Droysen confessed his weariness with the negative accounts of those recent years, which insisted on interpreting the then recent history 'as if it were a history of revolution and destruction, whereas it was indeed a history of liberation'.[82] He supposed the term Age of the Revolution to be linked with a reactionary tendency he did not subscribe to and resorted to more positive expressions such as wars of liberation or wars of freedom in its place.

Two additional reasons underscored his adoption of this terminology. First, by turning to *Freiheitskriege,* Droysen performed a semantic manoeuvre that metonymically dislocated a concept of particular import in recent German history to the entirety of world history. Thus he managed to uphold the German war of liberation as the climax of all other contemporary movements that also rallied under the banner of freedom.[83] Second, Droysen preferred to link present and future to the old Germanic principle of freedom rather than to 'revolution', a practice he considered anti-historical and socially disruptive. He sensed that a long continuity marked the history of the idea of freedom and indeed admitted that 1776 had inaugurated a new epoch in world history. Nevertheless, he saw what had transpired then as no radical novelty, but rather an expansion of the field of that idea's application. In his opinion, a revolution of the French type was actually dispensable in the German-speaking area, since the Protestant Reformation had long ago already fulfilled a good part of the revolutionary aims.[84] For Droysen, as for most German liberals of the first half of the nineteenth century, freedom was not to be achieved via revolutionary transformation but only through the extension of the reform principle from the sphere of religion into political and social life.

Droysen clearly exposed his creed on reforms as a means for political and social enhancement while addressing a set of events prior to the German war of liberation but very much intermingled with it: the Prussian reforms (1807–1815), initiated in the aftermath of the Prussian defeat against France in the battles of Jena and Auerstedt in October 1806. Like the liberation war later on, in Droysen's opinion, the reforms represented a momentum of national awakening and moral rebuild. They embraced major changes in the agrarian structure, as well as in taxes and customs policies; reorganization of bureaucracy, the army, and the municipalities; emancipation of Jews; and reform of the educational system (mostly conceived by Wilhelm von Humboldt). Speaking of the reforms, Droysen commented that 'as Prussia was annihilated as a power, it started to re-establish itself as a state'.[85] He contrasts 'power' and 'state' to stress the point of view that the reforms worked a sort of moral purification in Prussia. The Prussian state of the age of the reforms preserved the positive features of both the English and the French models: it 'positively combined the civil liberty of old England with the state energy that the [French] revolution produced'. At the same time, it was far from reproducing their most deplorable vices, namely, English colonialism and the mechanism of the French state.[86] In Droysen's view, the reforms' general orientation – both against the feudal heritage and for the strengthening of civil society – fostered an unprecedented mutuality between state and society (*Volk*). The result was the emergence of a new political model deemed appropriate to promote the reconciliation between politics and society, since in it 'the state belongs to the people; the people belongs to the state'.[87]

The Aftermath of the Revolutions

Droysen's identification with the time of the German wars of liberation was not only a matter of academic and political interest. Born in 1808 as a son of a military chaplain, he related his earliest personal recollections to the war he experienced, and to the military environment in which he grew up. It is reasonable to suppose that this environment and those war events exerted a decisive influence over the shaping of his personality, and thus also over the main traits of his historical interpretation of the age of the revolution.[88] Providing sufficient evidence to support this argument is no easy task, however. Anyway, as already mentioned, Droysen not only cherished personal memories from certain late events he connected to the 'wars of freedom', but also regarded these wars as a turning point in both the history and the collective memory of his time. For him, the age of the revolution precisely marked the outset of the temporal order he recognized as his present: it had triggered the historical dynamics that, in his perception, was still characterizing his own contemporary epoch.[89] Granted, Droysen was aware that both the post-1814 restoration and the waves of political reaction that spread throughout Western Europe thereafter had reversed most of the revolutions' achievements. But he was firmly convinced that these were just minor incidents taking place on the surface of history, for the age of the revolution had introduced an un-resettable modification in the core of historical life. 'Historical development's will' – as he put it in 1847 – was not on the conservative side. Droysen was therefore confident that 'false alternatives' like 'either revolution or reaction', or 'either popular sovereignty or legitimacy', would still be overcome.[90]

Actually, for Droysen the most effective heritage bequeathed by the 'wars of freedom' was an extension of the scope of application of the idea of freedom. As I am attempting to show, in Droysen's account, the idea of freedom is a Western cultural asset with a long history. It emerged among the classical Greek civilization and underwent further major developments, especially within the contexts of Hellenism, Christianization and the Protestant Reformation. Droysen supposed, however, that the 'wars of freedom' had led to a qualitative change in the history of freedom, and therefore, following Hegel, he opposed the ancient to the modern notion of freedom. For Droysen, European medieval and early modern social orders constituted either a reversal or, at best, a continuation of the already limited freedom standards set by the ancient Greeks. He would concede that the Protestant Reformation had been a step towards advancing these standards, but it was circumscribed to the religious realm. Consequently, the crucial turn to modern freedom remained, according to him, in the 'wars of freedom'.

This explains why Droysen could consider the revolutions as a world-historical leap forward, whilst simultaneously despising most of the 'awful agitations' that he perceived as characteristic of the revolutionary years. In a deep sense, the American Revolutionary War, the French Revolution and the refoundation of the Prussian state had resulted in an irreversible change in the ways political power was exerted. This sense is conveyed in his remark that after those 'revolutions', 'people after people learned how to recognise itself, its vocation and its rights. What else has [so strongly] determined the meaning of the present – of our present inclusively?'[91] As a matter of fact, here Droysen is suggesting that the 'wars of freedom' taught the peoples (*Völker*) – that is, social subjects located clearly beneath the political elites – how to attain self-consciousness, to claim their own rights and to become aware of the possibility of freedom. Citizens thus became less and less prone to sacrifice their own liberties in favour of a state confined to the mere wielding of power.[92]

As already mentioned, in Droysen's reading, liberty was a matter of historical necessity, and his views on the consequences of the 'wars of freedom' show it very clearly. According to him, freedom provided the telos of the historical process; that is, freedom was the state towards which history could be shown to be running. Within this context, it is interesting that Droysen attempts to differentiate his idea of historical necessity from the one that characterizes Hegel's general scheme of the course of history. One very important reason for this attempt is of a religious nature. As early as the 1830s, influenced by pietism – a tendency rejected by Hegel[93] – Droysen, in two private letters to the famous publisher Friedrich Perthes (1772–1843), criticized the Hegelian idea that philosophy should strive for absolute knowledge of the world. In one of them, Droysen remarks that Hegel only managed to find 'an absolute that is not God', but rather 'a clock pointer that shows at which moment the human knowledge of God is'.[94] Droysen indeed was an advocate of historical necessity: he believed that God governed the universe, and even that 'no hair falls from the head without his will'. But unlike Hegel, he argued that no human being, whether philosopher or historian, was able to entirely understand such 'wonderful mystery', or to fully conceive in detail the 'necessity of what happens'.[95] Droysen's critique of the Hegelian philosophy of history moreover holds a political rationale that he made explicit in many of his writings. In 1857, for instance, arguing against Hegel, Droysen stresses that the modern revolutions had not come close to accomplishing the materialization of the idea of freedom. He further accuses Hegel of having justified the primacy of the past over the present, and of having been a friend of restoration and reaction.[96] In light of contemporary scholarship on Hegel, Droysen's accusations can surely be declared unfair.[97] But exaggerated though they were, they undoubtedly buttressed Droysen's claim that his general view of the dynamics of the historical process was different from Hegel's.

In any case, even though he had incorporated from Hegel the general notion that freedom was a historical necessity, Droysen, much more than his teacher, stressed that the materialization of the idea of freedom was a process permeated by serious threats – such as (the already discussed) 'despotism of the idea of state', as well as uncontrolled capitalism and 'materialism'.[98] According to Droysen, freedom was not to be brought about spontaneously, and one would better not underestimate the power of its adversaries. He saw freedom's recent advancements during the revolutionary era as a beginning rather than an end.[99] Hence, he would stress that the present signified neither the end of history nor the fulfilment of all promises of liberty. What history had successfully carried out till then were only the preconditions for expansion of the realm of human freedom. However, the materialization of such possibilities was, for Droysen, a mission to be still accomplished in the future. During the 'wars of freedom' and up until the present, as he remarked, 'the peoples were still not mature' for fully tapping all potentials developed in conjunction with the modern idea of freedom.[100]

It is correct, therefore, to relate Droysen's general considerations on history and liberty to a sort of democratic postulate: 'A simple glimpse at history teaches that as the realm of historical life ... has been expanded over lands, continents, and, finally, over the whole surface of the Earth; it has simultaneously been disseminated down to the masses, vitalising and ennobling them.'[101] As already mentioned, Droysen deduced the universal-historical significance of the 'wars of freedom' from the argument that, within their course, the 'peoples' (*Völker*) finally seized the idea of freedom. In his view, modern freedom was the freedom of all, and by the same token modern history turned into the history of the geographical and social expansion of the idea of freedom. Nevertheless, Droysen consciously avoided terms such as 'democracy' and 'democratization' when addressing the modern encounter between the *Völker* and freedom. This option was coherent with his monarchism and his record as a delegate to the Frankfurt National Assembly (1848–49), where he belonged to a faction frankly opposed to radical-democratic and egalitarian tendencies.[102] Like most major figures of the German national-liberal intelligentsia in the nineteenth-century, Droysen fought against the introduction of the principle of universal suffrage in the political system.[103] Therefore, the emphasis on the lower classes' inclusion in the realm of freedom that he placed within his interpretation of the constitution of the present did not lead him to advocate for egalitarian forms of concrete political participation.

A similar critique might also be levelled against Droysen's remarks on the emancipation of women. Indeed, on the one hand, he censured societies that linked women's value solely with the capacity of bearing children and suggested that those societies were ethically underdeveloped.[104] But on the other hand, his statements on nature and history of the family were very much framed within a patriarchal scheme of thought. In the *Lectures on the Wars of Freedom*, for instance, while comparing national economy with a household, he traces an analogy between the role of the king in the former, and the role of the father in the latter. Thereby, he depicts women as free but simultaneously subordinate beings. For him, the man remains the centre of opinion and the source of decision and action in the household: women, children and servants are to rally around him, respecting his patriarchal authority and benefiting from it.[105] All in all, Droysen's historical thought is profoundly marked by a masculine bias that finds expression in what is held today to be a sexist rhetorics, as well as in an exclusion of women from the field of the legitimate subjects historians might be interested in.[106]

In contrast, Droysen's critique of European colonialism shows a more inclusive dimension of his liberalism. Despite admitting the cultural superiority of European civilization – as virtually every nineteenth-century intellectual did – in the *Lectures on the Wars of Freedom,* he condemns the colonial system as one the many persisting absurdities of 'old Europe'.[107] In the same text, he also tends to depict colonial uprisings in positive terms. According to him, not only the independence of the United States but also other national emancipations in the Americas contributed to the geographical dispersion of the idea of freedom. For Droysen, even the radical case of Haiti, where independence from France was obtained through an insurrection of slaves, represented a 'war of freedom'.[108] It is also noteworthy that he retrospectively praised the edict of 1812's extension of citizenship rights to the Jews residing in Prussia's territory.[109]

The Capitalist Threat

It is already clear that Droysen was unashamed to reprove the many events and developments that he saw as out of order in the then contemporary world. Indeed, he once compared the present to a disease that everyone tries to heal without having actually understood the causes behind the symptoms.[110] This shows, among other things, that he did not take the modern expansion of the scope of freedom for granted. Actually, by mid-century – especially during the period ranging from the failure of the Frankfurt National Assembly's project for German unification in 1849, to the (practical) end of Friedrich Wilhelm IV's rule in Prussia in 1858 – he very much feared that the idea of freedom could derail within the process of its own realization. This feeling was especially acute in several of his political writings, such as the 1854 article 'On the Characteristics of the European Crisis', in which he articulated a very critical perspective on the problems that marked his contemporary times:[111] 'Our present is as follows: everything is shaken; everything is undergoing immensurable disruptions, agitations, brutalisation. All the old things are worn out and falsified; they are all consumed by worms and are impossible to recover. And the new things are all still without form and end; for now they remain solely chaotic and destructive.'[112] Therefore, he concludes, 'we are within one of those big crises in the world history that lead from one epoch to another.'[113]

At this particular moment, Droysen felt especially apprehensive about a possible 'repetition of what had happened between 1792 and 1815.'[114] His concerns related to the tensions that culminated in the Crimean War (1853–1856), but the argument in which he expressed them was not at all restricted to this particular event. For him, the new historical dynamics inaugurated by the 'wars of freedom' comprised not only emancipatory potentials but also several risks. Droysen was alarmed by the Crimean conflict because he feared it would highlight the fundamental contradictions of the new European order, contradictions that had been dormant since 1815. He actually feared that this conflict could ignite modernity's pathological structures to explode into political and social chaos.

One of the pathologies he then identified as a major cause of the present's 'crisis' was capitalist economy. Interestingly enough – for an author whose theory of history represents what one of its analysts qualified as 'the most advanced form of the bourgeoisie's self-understanding'[115] – a sharp critique of capitalism is traceable in Droysen's genesis of the present. The framework of modern capitalist economy, he argued, had replaced moral and symbolic values traditionally associated with the means and structures of material production. According to him, what was learned and professed in modern times was that the soil of a rural estate had nothing but monetary value; that people could be considered as mere workforce; that property and savings could be turned into credit. Within the context of capitalism, hence, 'money develops an expansion force similar to water vapour',[116] which led to a commoditization of human beings and their material assets.

Droysen held that capitalism was a common feature of modern Western societies, but its pathologies were nowhere more visible than in the country that had pioneered the industrial revolution. In England, the modernization of agriculture had led to an expansion of the leasehold system and the destruction of traditional rural forms of life. In addition, Droysen continued, 'the peasants became day labourers; they stopped being sedentary, and started to continuously move from county to county in search of work'.[117] In the cities, furthermore, the working life of the lower classes would change radically following the introduction of the factory system by the mid-eighteenth century. Droysen observed that the factories subverted the work rhythm that was typical of both agriculture and domestic work. Later on (by the late eighteenth century), the incorporation of 'the unresting machine' into the structure of the factory would further enforce the new working discipline. As a result of these processes, Droysen indicated, 'the masses became proletarians', remarking ironically that, given the circumstances, they should consider themselves satisfied 'if only they could manage to survive, if commercial crises did not force the factory into stoppages, if overproduction did not generate price cuts'. Ultimately, as he saw it, English industrial capitalism induced a degeneration in the realm of human work. Its most regrettable consequence was the emergence of 'a new type of slavery', which this time was 'a thousand times more sordid, degrading, and acrimonious than ever before'.[118] For Droysen, by the time of the 'wars of freedom', while France was distinguished by the 'sovereignty of power' (*Machtsouveränität*), England was living under the 'sovereignty of money' (*Geldsouveränität*).[119] In his view, both situations represented different ways along which modern freedom could be perverted.

The outlines of Droysen's critique of capitalism are also interestingly discernible in his ironies concerning the wave of material prosperity and consumption that took place in France after the Directory was empowered (1795). He asserts that after the silencing of the guillotine, 'bar money obtained a tremendous preponderance', thus deeply changing the character of society. Further, he points out that this change was also reflected in people's new manners and costume: 'Soon one decayed into a distasteful mix of tunic and plume. Mad. Tallien and Mad. Beauharnais turned Greek fashion into convention; one loved the enchantments of the nude; one exercised ostentation in banquets and orgies, exhibited showy artefacts, sneering at the much vaunted equality; one rushed back to the once abandoned atmosphere of private life; in fact, one avidly searched everywhere for profits and pleasures.'[120] Droysen condemns all these concrete changes, lampooning them as the 'delights of materialism', pointing out that such changes not only bred an increasing licentiousness among youth but also diminished the public attractiveness of politics.[121] His view of this short period of the French revolution is illustrative of his general interpretation of economical modernity and of what he saw as the products of its pathological structure.

It must be recalled that the ideas above were reconstructed mostly from Droysen's *Lectures on the Wars of Freedom* and the article 'On the Characteristics of the European Crisis'. Yet a change of focus to the *Historik* lectures can reveal an interpretation of the nature and development of modern capitalism that strongly deviates from the arguments discussed above. Friedrich Jaeger seems to be the only author who has attempted to explain Droysen's contradictory views of modern capitalism. Critically commenting on Rüsen's interpretation, Jaeger agrees that one of the factors that motivated Droysen to systematize a theory of history (in the late 1850s) was indeed his perception that the world was then experiencing a deep crisis. Jaeger further acknowledges that Droysen conceived the *Historik* as a therapeutic resource to counter such a crisis, but he argues that in this regard Droysen missed his target.[122] Hence, whereas a very critical tone vis-à-vis the problems generated by modern economy is easily perceived in Droysen's texts on contemporary history and politics, his systematic analysis of the 'ethical powers' does not even mention such problems. The best example of how Droysen overlooked his own critique of capitalism in the context of his theory of history is found in his philosophical remarks on work (*Arbeit*) as the basic activity of economic life. Here Droysen starts from the anthropological premise that only human beings are able to work, in the proper sense of the word. 'Work' presupposes the capacity to 'master and overcome one's own natural drives and to subordinate them to a purpose' and, Droysen holds, other animals do not possess this capacity. He then concludes that there is a strong correspondence between human work and human freedom: 'One might say that the history of work is the history of freedom and of its progression'[123] In this philosophical reasoning – which quite well summarizes Droysen's theoretical considerations on economics and welfare –[124] he clearly elides the bad side of economical modernity that he addressed in other texts.[125] Here, he does not account for the fact that industrialization triggered what he himself had defined as 'a new type of slavery' – that is, the opposite of freedom.

The Decomposition of the *Geist* and the Urgency of Historical Thinking

The more contemporary segments of Droysen's genealogy of the present basically address two sets of ideologies frankly opposed to his own general conceptions of history and freedom. The first was embodied in the kind of political conservatism that aimed to return Europe to its pre-revolutionary status quo. Albeit agreeing with the conservative critique of what he deemed revolutionary attempts to implode the continuity of the historical process, Droysen was, after all, an advocate of political and social modernity.[126] His political opinions and beliefs emerged from the context of German post-restoration national liberalism – a political programme combining an aversion to revolutionary ideals with a general quest for political change, especially concerning the issue of the German national state.[127] Droysen recognized that conservatives had indeed made a valid diagnosis of the problems of the contemporary (European) world, but he strongly condemned the therapeutics they prescribed.[128] He contrasted the conservative topos of 'historical rights' to the metaphor of the 'right of history' and thereby highlighted his distance from a reactionary position. In fact, he argued that the conservative appeal to the authority of 'historical rights' was thoughtless, since it negated the 'right of history' (ergo, the possibility of historical transformations) by automatically evaluating sociopolitical change as historical loss.[129]

The second group of ideas that Droysen situated in opposition to his historical world view was, as he called it, the 'materialistic', and I will focus on his criticism of 'materialism' in what follows. Briefly defined, materialistic ideas are those that consider all entities and processes are reducible to matter or material forces.[130] However, Droysen's use of the term throughout his texts was much more ambiguous and less systematic than the usual definitions in philosophical dictionaries. Droysen basically regarded materialism as a threat to freedom, for he assumed that if human life is reducible to mere material or physical processes, then human individuals cannot be free. He thus interpreted materialism as a radical attempt to sweep transcendence away from both the natural and the human world. This conflicted with one of the most fundamental notions structuring his world view, namely *Geist* (spirit, mind).[131] Within the tradition of German idealism – and to a good extent the historiographical historicism practised by Droysen was a continuation of idealist philosophy – *Geist* was a very complex notion.[132] It was related to Christian religiosity, philosophy of history, aesthetics and individual psychology, among other fields. No serious attempt to define the general meaning of this difficult notion will actually be made here.[133] It suffices to say, however, that in Droysen's usage the term *Geist* refers to an extra-natural and semi-secularized realm produced by human beings throughout the chain of generations. It points to the historical evolution of humanity and to humankind's partial emancipation from nature.

But above all, *Geist* does not point to materiality.[134] Hence, in Droysen's perception, materialistic attempts to naturalize *Geist* would necessarily lead to its dissolution. Considered from a materialistic perspective, the human self becomes a mere 'contingent manifestation inside nature's general metabolism', and as such is deprived of its most essential qualities – in short, of its *Geist*. Consequently, according to Droysen, someone who looks at human beings and sees mere physical phenomena ignores the sources of the human feelings of self-worth and responsibility, and disregards all the presuppositions that enable human willpower, freedom, opinion and belief to flourish,[135] finally eradicating the basis for either religious faith or secular ethics.

For Droysen, 'materialism' condensed in a single conceptual label almost all the modern pathological tendencies that he attempted to diagnose in his genealogy of the present. It embraced the 'despotism of the idea of state' in the field of politics and the 'sovereignty of money' in the realm of economics, as well as intellectual tendencies such as Enlightenment, rationalism, scientism and positivism. Droysen held all these blanket concepts in a partial but sizeable semantic superposition, because ultimately he could trace in all of them a frontal antagonism to the idea of history at the core of his own convictions. He once referred to his own world view as the 'ethical-ideal or historical-philosophical mode of culture' (*Bildungsweise*) and was, of course, persuaded of its superiority vis-à-vis all others, including its materialistic adversary. But in the middle of the century, Droysen clearly felt that his historical world view was threatened by the mounting popularity of 'materialism' among the educated classes.[136] In 1854, he noted that 'the level of our spiritual (*geistigen*) life is sinking wrenchingly fast; the highness, the ideality, the potency of thought (*Gedankenmächtigkeit*), which have characterised it, are just disappearing'.[137] Droysen's diagnosis might have been overstated, but it allows a very good insight into how he defined his own perspective in contraposition to what he called materialism. What really matters within the framework of his historical perspective cannot be quantified or formalized in general laws. It is hence irreducible to the method of the natural sciences. As he concludes, this is the reason why the 'historical-philosophical culture is always linked with something exclusive, indescribable, and difficult'.[138]

Droysen's methodological objections to 'materialism' were furthered and developed within the context of a debate triggered in 1857 by the publication of Henry Thomas Buckle's (1821–1862) *History of Civilization in England*. The son of a rich English merchant, Buckle was an amateur historical scholar without institutional ties.[139] His work was one of several mammoth research and literary projects that came out of nineteenth-century Western historiography. Its two published volumes (1857, 1861) comprised no more than an unfinished general introduction, where he imparted his method and his conception of history. Not being a professional scholar, Buckle was in a position to attack mainstream historians with vigour. The beginning of his text describes his contempt of historiography's cognitive achievements, qualifying them as inferior to those of the physical sciences. At this juncture, he also observes that 'the most celebrated historians are manifestly inferior to the most successful cultivators of physical science: no one having devoted himself to history who in point of intellect is at all to be compared with Kepler, Newton, or many others'.[140]

What particularly bothered Buckle about the members of the 'guild of historians'[141] was their exclusive focus on the particularities of the past, and therefore their neglect of what should be their real task, namely, elaboration of the universal laws that moved and move humankind's history in past and present, and towards the future. In his *History of Civilization in England,* Buckle assured his readers that he would demonstrate how this methodological 'inferiority' would be overcome by relating concrete historical events to general regularities similar to those characteristic of the natural sciences.[142] He subscribed, therefore, to a positivistic epistemology that conceived scientific knowledge as nomological knowledge[143] – and he did not conceal the extent to which August Comte's positive philosophy had inspired him.

In general, European professional historians did not welcome Buckle's attempt to reshape historical method by adjusting it to the Comtean conception of scientific knowledge. Still, the (rather extra-academic) popularity of his book ended up sensitizing many historians to the epistemological and methodological issues at the core of their discipline. Particularly after the left-Hegelian Arnold Ruge (1802–1880) translated the book into German in 1860–61, it unleashed a discussion that culminated in supporters of history and the human sciences resorting to the concept of understanding (*Verstehen*) to radically stress their theoretical and methodological differences vis-à-vis the positivistic model of science.[144]

Droysen had already developed both his cultural criticism of materialism and his historical theory when the German edition of Buckle's book came out.

Droysen reacted to the latter with a critical review published under the ironic title 'The Elevation of History to the Rank of a Science' (1863). This text, which represents the starting point of the positivism controversy in the German-speaking world,[145] begins precisely by locating the issue of positivistic scientism within the broader context of the modern materialistic world view. The popularity enjoyed by Buckle and many other supporters of scientism, Droysen argued, accrued not only from the astonishing cognitive and practical results then exhibited by the physical sciences; it also lay 'in the mode of culture (*Bildungsweise*) that prevails in our age'.[146] In Droysen's perception, the present world was intellectually dominated by materialism. He thus saw Buckle's attempt to reshape history according to a scientistic conception of knowledge as an invidious attack on the most important of the intellectual counter-forces that could offer resistance to such domination.

Though Droysen was far from sharing Buckle's radical disdain for the entirety of historical thought, he had his own critiques of what he perceived as the mainstream historians of his age. From this perspective, he could even state that 'a work like Buckle's is well adapted to remind us how very unclear, contradictory and beset with arbitrary opinions the foundations of our science are'.[147] But Droysen obviously did not think Buckle had achieved what the latter himself had proposed to do. For him, Buckle's method did not raise history to the rank of an autonomous science but merely placed it among the natural sciences.[148] Droysen called for a methodological pluralism to counter Buckle's monism fixed on the model of the physical sciences. According to Droysen, in science (*Wissenschaft*), the choice of method should actually be guided by the nature of the objects investigated rather than by a priori conceptions about what scientific knowledge should look like. It was precisely the specific attributes of the historical phenomena that would necessitate the autonomy of the historical science: 'If there is to be a "science of history" (*Wissenschaft der Geschichte*), in which we too believe, this means that there exists a circle of phenomena for which neither the theological, the philosophical, the mathematical nor the physical manner of consideration is adapted'.[149]

Within this argumentative context, Droysen reintroduced his (posthumously famous) distinction between explanation (*Erklären*) and understanding (*Verstehen*), meanwhile imparting to it a new meaning. Previously, Droysen had emphasized the notions of understanding and interpretation in his critiques of the Rankean school, which he accused of an obsession with source criticism.[150] Furthermore, at least in the first version of the *Historik* lectures, the distinction between explanation and understanding served Droysen's intention to differentiate history not from science but from the Hegelian philosophy of history.[151] But as the nineteenth century advanced, the main counter-field against which theoretically minded historians delimited their own field shifted from philosophy to the natural sciences.[152] Droysen's review of Buckle's book provides some of the clearest evidence of that shift. Here, in a casual remark, Droysen employs the distinction between explanation and understanding exclusively against the positivistic attempt to rehabilitate historical necessity by translating it into non-religious scientific laws of history. 'Fortunately', he states, 'there are between heaven and earth things ... which demand not to be "developed" or "explained" but understood'.[153] Basically, his argument is that the excellent results rendered by induction and deduction in other scientific fields did not automatically imply that history should resort to those methods. Droysen does not deny that historians could profitably make use of even quantitative methods. But he stresses that quantitative methods have at best an auxiliary value for historical research, for they alone cannot unveil the historicity of the phenomena under investigation.[154]

Droysen is sometimes criticized for having contributed to a radical polarization between the human and the natural sciences, as well as for having discouraged methodical exchanges between history and the then emerging social sciences.[155] This criticism has surely a point, but generally it tends to disregard one very important underlying factor in Droysen's aversion to positivism: his insistence on stressing both historical science's hermeneutical constitution and its fundamental differences vis-à-vis the nomological natural sciences relates to reasons that are not purely methodological. By refusing to theoretically ground historical knowledge upon quantitative and nomological proceedings, he was rejecting not only a methodological conception, but also both the (materialistic) world view and the political ethos that he perceived as associated with that conception.[156] In fact, as Michael MacLean has noted, within the German intellectual context of the second half of the nineteenth century, methodological divergences were normally related to opinions on the political use of history. On the one hand, established historians like Droysen were frequently moderate liberals who, always fearing the chaos of political revolutions, tended to lean towards the right side of the political spectrum.[157] As a result, they conceived historiography as a didactic means destined to propagate the opinion that political and cultural changes would follow the course of progressive reforms. Adherents of scientism, on the other hand, tended towards the political left. Most of them espoused different sorts of radicalism, and many, like Buckle, were also supporters of democratic principles. Accordingly, they assumed that historical knowledge should not support moderate social reforms but more radical attempts to change the structures of society.[158]

Droysen himself was probably concerned less about the enforcement of a positivistic methodological programme per se than about the general political and ideological consequences that he anticipated as possible outcomes of positivism's success in academia. Late-century methodological positivism – unlike its Comtean matrix in this regard – encompassed an emancipatory political programme that maintained that scientific knowledge would ultimately liberate human beings from all norms and constraints transmitted by the past. In line with this, historiography was regarded as a critical means to disempower tradition and help prepare for an entirely new kind of social practice. The emancipatory utopia behind positivist methodology was, therefore, the ideal of a 'liberation from history'.[159]

Droysen's general conception of history was also – as already stressed – closely related to the purpose of emancipation, but in a very different way. Like many other German historical thinkers of the time, Droysen vehemently rejected the emancipatory ideal associated with the materialistic world view because he did not accept that freedom would result from a sudden, radical break with historical continuity. He rather envisaged the realization of the idea of freedom as an outcome of the historical process's prolongation. What Droysen's emancipatory ideal therefore corresponded to was not a 'liberation from history' but a 'liberation *to* history'.[160] His resistance to attempts to shape history as a positive science was guided by the feeling that the eventual triumph of such attempts would culminate in historiography being put into the service of what, in his estimation, were the wrong political and cultural causes. In reaction to that feeling, he claimed that historians should instead sponsor the learning of historical thinking, so that human subjects would possess the means to perceive the genetic link connecting past, present and future. And in doing so, he also believed that conveying the capacity to think historically would be one way to ensure the preservation of that very link.

It now becomes clear how Droysen's historical hermeneutics and its correlated didactics of historical thinking were strongly embedded in his interpretation of the genesis of the present. As discussed above, Droysen saw bygone history as a process driven by the telos of the idea of freedom's fulfilment. In several texts, he followed the dialectical evolution of this idea from classical Greece through the Hellenistic Age, the Middle Ages, early modern times and the age of revolution, up until his own present. But Droysen's sense of historical necessity was, as already shown, not as rigid as, for instance, Hegel's. Droysen assumed that God ruled the course of history, but he did not think human knowledge could possibly come to understand God's purposes in their entirety. This disjunction between historical necessity and the possibility of understanding history's final purpose opened some space for uncertainty, whereupon doubt arose: would the future take shape as a continuation of past and present, or would it lead to a break with history?

In Droysen's view, the present was – as Robert Southard stated – characterized by a promise of historical success, as well as by a threat to it.[161] Droysen, of course, wanted the threat countered and the promise carried out, and thought historical studies could contribute significantly to this end. Ultimately, by highlighting the centrality of notions such as 'historical thinking', 'understanding' and '*Bildung*', Droysen was not only developing original didactic and methodological concepts but also elaborating potential intellectual safeguards against a scientistic world view whose increasing influence on nineteenth-century society he regarded as a cultural threat.

Especially during the 1850s and the 1860s, Droysen frequently expressed the thought that the world had come to a moment of truth where two mutually exclusive choices introduced themselves. As he saw it, his age could either follow the path of continuity indicated by historical thinking and thus succeed, since this option would effectively support the advance of human freedom and reconciliation between humankind and God; or it could choose to replace historical culture with materialism and its correlates (for instance: scientism, positivism, democracy, atheism), and then everything would derange as the future would be lost.[162] In any case, Droysen regarded the arena of politics as the main stage where this issue was to be resolved. On this stage, his theory of historical knowledge and his substantive philosophy of history blended into political ideals, the most prominent of which, during the better part of Droysen's lifetime, was that of German unification under a Prussian lead. The following chapter will concentrate on Droysen's political standings and expectations, and their impact on his political historiography. It will investigate Droysen's concrete uses and applications of the notion of 'historical thinking', pointing to significant tensions between theory and practice in his writings. The analysis of these tensions will also reveal some limits of Droysen's way of justifying the value and function of historiography.

Notes

1. This criticism was voiced by Jörn Rüsen as early as the 1960s, but I think it is still partially valid today. See Rüsen, *Begriffene Geschichte,* 13: 'Um sie [Droysens Geschichtstheorie] unter die legitimen Vorläufer der Geschichtstheorie rechnen zu können, die in Diltheys Philosophie der Geisteswissenschaften und in der philosophischen Hermeneutik menschlicher Geschichtlichkeit als Grundlage historischer Erkenntnis kulminiert, mußte von ihrer Verankerung in der konkreten Geschichte abgesehen werden, der sich Droysen historiographisch und politisch zugewandt hatte.' There are, however, some very significant exceptions to the picture painted above, e.g., Bauer, ‹*Das Geheimnis aller Bewegung ist ihr Zweck*›; Benedetto Bravo. 1966. 'Hégélianisme et recherche historique dans l'oeuvre de J.G. Droysen', in Jan Burian and Ladislav Vidman (eds), *Antiquitas graeco-romana ac tempora nostra. Acta congressus internationalis habiti Brunae diebus 12–16 mensis Aprilis,* Prague: Academia; Rüsen, *Begriffene Geschichte;* Southard, 'Theology in Droysen's Early Political Historiography'; Southard, *Droysen and the Prussian School of History.*

2. Hegel, *The Philosophy of History,* 31–32.

3. Hegel, *The Philosophy of History,* 32: 'But they [the Greeks], and the Romans likewise, knew only that some are free – not man as such. Even Plato and Aristotle did not know this. The Greeks, therefore, had slaves; and their whole life and the maintenance of their splendid liberty, was implicated with the institution of slavery: a fact moreover, which made that liberty on the one hand only an accidental, transient and limited growth; on the other hand, constituted it a rigorous thraldom of our common nature – of the Human'.

4. Bauer, ‹*Das Geheimnis aller Bewegung ist ihr Zweck*›, 4.

5. Johann Gustav Droysen, *Des Aischylos Werkes,* vol. 1, Berlin: G Finke, 163–164 [Erläuterung des Übersetzers, 1832]: 'Ich glaube die Tat Athens ist das Bewusstsein der Freiheit errungen und betätigt zu haben.' Quote translated by James McGlew. 1984. 'J. G. Droysen and the Aeschylean Hero', *Classical Philology* 79(1): 4.

6. Stefan Jordan. 1995. 'G. W. F. Hegels Einfluss auf das philologische und altertumswissenschaftliche Schaffen Johann Gustav Droysens', in Helmut Schneider (ed.), *Jahrbuch für Hegelforschung.* Sankt Augustin: Academia, 145–146.

7. Droysen, *Des Aischylos Werkes* 1: 163 [Erläuterung des Übersetzers, 1832]: 'Denn es ist das natürliche Verhältnis des menschlichen Beieinanderseins, dass dies Gehorchen und Gebieten sich nach Unterschieden der Geburt bestimmt … dass Adel und Volk sich kastenhaft gegenüberstehen, ohne dass die Einen den Anderen ihr Recht bestreiten, ihren Druck lindern mögen. Aber das geschichtliche Leben, der Geist, wie er im Volke Gestalt gewinnt, ist dem Natürlichen und Gegebenen feind; und sobald einmal an jenem natürlichen Unterschiede und den durch die Gewohnheit der Jahrhunderte eingewurzelten Zuständen zu zweifeln und zu modeln begonnen ist, wird der erwachte Geist nicht müde, gegen jedes Bestehende sein furchtbares Warum geltend zu machen.' For Droysen, historical life is actually surrounded by nature. The emergence of the spirit (*Geist*) compels natural societies to jump into history, but that does not cancel natural determinations: 'Wer will das erste Erwachen des Geistes beschreiben? Mit dem ersten Wort schon ist er da; in geheimnisvoller Ähnlichkeit ist ihm des Wortes Klang für das, was es bedeutet; er bildet sich her seine eigene Daseinssphere. So beginnt er diese Natur, wie sie um ihn und an ihm ist, für sich zu erwerben. Aber sie allein noch ist es, woher es erwirbt, wohin er wirkt.… Sie [die Natur] ist der Boden, auf dem der Geist emporwächst, der mütterliche Schoß, von dem er sich loszuringen trachtet.' Johann Gustav Droysen. 1980. *Geschichte des Hellenismus,* vol. 3: *Geschichte der Epigonen,* Darmstadt: Wissenschaftliche Buchgesellschaft, 6 [2nd ed., 1877–78].

8. Johann Gustav Droysen. 1894. *Kleine Schriften zur alten Geschichte,* vol. 2, Leipzig: Veit, 65 [Zur griechischen Literatur, 1838]: 'Um die Zeit als das athenische Volk an die Spitze des griechischen Lebens trat … der Geist began zum Bewusstsein seiner selbst zu gelangen … man empfand die Unzulänglichkeit dichterischer Vorstellungen, man suchte in den Dingen selbst ihre Bestimmung.… Es begann die prosaische Darstellung zugleich mit der prosaischen Auffassung.'

9. Droysen, *Kleine Schriften zur alten Geschichte,* 65 [Zur griechischen Literatur, 1838]: 'Das attische Leben war bestimmt den Kampf des Alten und Neuen, der Poesie und des Rationalismus in sich durchzukämpfen. In diesem Gegensatze hat sich die vollendete Herrlichkeit der attischen Tragödie entwickelt, deren Geschichte selbst das immer steigende Übergewicht des prosaisch Rationellen dokumentiert.… Die begonnene rationelle Entwicklung des Geistes musste zu unwiderstehlichen Konsequenzen treiben. Nach dem Zusammenhange und den Gründen der Erscheinung forschend war die Philosophie tief und tiefer in Zweifel und Verneinungen hineingekommen.' See also Rüsen, *Begriffene Geschichte,* 25.

10. Droysen, *Kleine Schriften zur alten Geschichte,* 68 [Zur griechischen Literatur, 1838]: 'Sie [Aristoteles' Philosophie] erscheint wieder begeistert und von dem lebendigen Hauche des Gedankens durchweht. Aber freilich die so nachgewiesene Geistigkeit ist nicht mehr die altpoetische des Griechentums; die alten Gottheiten sind gewichen, dialektische Formeln und natürliche Gesetze beherrschen die einst so schöne Welt. Die Prosa in ihrer ganzen Strenge und Kälte hat den vollkommensten Sieg nachdem sie in letztem Kampfe den schönen Traum einer Ideenwelt überwunden hat.'

11. Arnaldo Momigliano. 1970. 'J. G. Droysen between Greeks and Jews', *History and Theory* 9(1): 141.

12. The historian Hans-Joachim Gehrke, for instance, opened his *Geschichte des Hellenismus* by stating that 'wenn wir heute von Hellenismus als eine historische Epoche sprechen, dann stehen wir in einer von Johann Gustav Droysen begründeten Tradition.' See Hans-Joachim Gehrke. 2003. *Geschichte des Hellenismus,* Munich: Oldenbourg, 1.

13. Arnaldo Momigliano. 2000. 'Die Geschichte der Entstehung und die heutige Funktion des Begriffs des Hellenismus', in Arnaldo Momigliano. *Ausgewählte Schriften zur Geschichte und*

Geschichtsschreibung, vol. 3: *Die moderne Geschichtsschreibung der alten Welt,* Stuttgart: J.B. Metzler, 129.

14. Bravo, 'Hégélianisme et recherche historique dans l'oeuvre de J.G. Droysen', 155–157.

15. Momigliano, 'Die Geschichte der Entstehung und die heutige Funktion des Begriffs des Hellenismus', 136–137.

16. Droysen, *Historik* 2: 445 [Antrittsrede bei der Berliner Akademie, 1867]; Momigliano, 'J. G. Droysen between Greeks and Jews', 143; Nippel, *Johann Gustav Droysen,* 39–40, 308.

17. Johann Gustav Droysen. 1980. *Geschichte des Hellenismus,* vol. 2: *Geschichte der Diadochen,* Munich: DTV, 443 [2nd ed., 1877/78]: 'Bestehen und in rastlos weiter wachsenden Wellenkreisen sich steigernd bleibt nur das, was er [Alexander], mit rücksichtslosem Idealismus wagend und schaffend, als Mittel und Stütze seines Werkes gewollt hat, die Verschmelzung des hellenischen Wesens mit dem der Völker Asiens, die Schaffung eines neuen west-östlichen Kulturlebens, die Einheit der geschichtlichen Welt in der hellenistischen Bildung.'

18. Theodor Schieder. 1959. 'Johann Gustav Bernhard Droysen', in *Neue Deutsche Biographie,* vol. 4, Berlin: Duncker & Humblot, 135.

19. Johann Gustav Droysen. 1980. *Geschichte des Hellenismus,* vol. 1: *Geschichte Alexander des Großen,* Munich: DTV, 223 [2nd ed., 1877/78]: 'So gewann er [Alexander] die Völker für sich, indem er sie sich selbst und ihrem volkstümlichen Leben wiedergab; so machte er sie fähig, auf tätige und unmittelbare Weise in den Zusammenhang des Reiches, das er zu gründen im Sinne trug, einzutreten, eines Reiches, in dem die Unterschiede von Abend und Morgen, von Hellenen und Barbaren, wie sie bis dahin die Geschichte beherrscht hatten, untergehen sollten zu der Einheit einer Weltmonarchie.'

20. Droysen, *Geschichte des Hellenismus* 1: 434 [2nd ed., 1877/78]: 'Die Erinnerungen und die Kultur Ägyptens rechneten nach Jahrtausenden; welche Fülle polytechnischer Meisterschaft, astronomischer Beobachtungen, alter Literaturen bot die syrisch-babylonische Welt; und erschloss sich nicht in der lauteren Parsenlehre der Iranier und Baktrier, in der Religion und Philosophie des Wunderlandes Indien eine Welt ungeahnter Entwicklungen, vor denen der noch so selbstgefällige hellenistische Bildungsstolz staunen mochte? In der Tat, diese Asiaten waren nicht Barbaren wie die Illyrier, Triballer, Geten, nicht Wilde und Halbwilde, wie sich der hellenische Nativismus gern dachte, was nicht griechisch sprach; ihnen gegenüber hatten die Eroberer nicht bloß zu geben, sondern auch zu empfangen; es galt zu lernen und umzulernen.'

21. Johann Gustav Droysen. 1932. *Geschichte Alexanders des Großen,* Leipzig: Alfred Kröner, 268 [1st ed., 1833]: 'Alexander war zunächst und allein die Einheit des weiten Reiches, der Kernpunkt, um den sich die neue Kristallisation bilden sollte. Wie er ihren Göttern [die der Asiaten] geopfert und Feste gefeiert hatte, so wollte er auch in seiner Umgebung, in den Festen seines Hoflagers zeigen, daß er den Asiaten angehöre. Seit dem Ende des Dareios begann er, die Asiaten, die zu ihm kamen, im asiatischen Kleide und mit asiatischem Zeremoniell zu empfangen, die nüchterne Alltäglichkeit des makedonischen Feldlagers mit dem blendenden Pomp des morgenländischen Hoflebens abwechseln zu lassen.'

22. Droysen, *Geschichte des Hellenismus* 1: 221 [2nd ed., 1877/78]: 'So begann sich Alexanders Heer in das asiatische Leben hineinzuleben und sich mit denen, die das Vorurteil von Jahrhunderten gehaßt, verachtet, Barbaren genannt hatte, zu versöhnen und zu verschmelzen; es begann sich Morgen- und Abendland zu durchgären und eine Zukunft vorzubereiten, in der beide sich selbst verlieren sollten.'

23. Droysen, *Historik* 2: 157 [Altgeschichte-Vorlesung, 1846]: 'Aber das Volk der Griechen, sich aus der naturgegebenen Bestimmtheit zur freien Persönlichkeit, zur Bewußtheit derselben heraus entwickelnd, geht unter in den Consequenzen der nur persönlichen Freiheit, die sich in eine sporadische Endlosigkeit persönlicher Willkür und persönlicher Interessen atomisirt und verliert, die die substantielle Basis des öffentlichen Lebens untergräbt und an die Stelle der Bürgertugend den Kosmopolitismus, an die Stelle der Religion die Philosophie treten läßt.'

24. Droysen, *Geschichte des Hellenismus* 3: 5 [2nd ed., 1877/78].

25. Droysen, *Historik* 2: 168–169 [Vorlesung über die Geschichte des Mittelalters, 1840].

26. Droysen, *Historik* 2: 244 [Privatvorrede, 1843]: 'Ich habe den Hellenismus bezeichnet als die moderne Zeit des Alterthums, ich denke, man wird diese Bezeichnung in ihrem ganzen Umfang, in gewissen Betracht auch für die Entwicklung Roms, geltend machen dürfen.'

27. Droysen, *Kleine Schriften zur alten Geschichte,* 63 [Zur griechischen Literatur, 1838]: 'Das Griechentum ist berufen gewesen, den Übergang aus der heidnischen in die christliche Welt zu erarbeiten; es hat das schwierigste und fruchtreichste Tagewerk in der Geschichte der Menschheit vollgebracht.'

28. Droysen, *Geschichte des Hellenismus* 3: 6 [2nd ed., 1877/78]: 'Das Höchste, was das Altertum aus eigener Kraft zu erreichen vermocht hat, ist der Untergang des Heidentums.' See the same formulation also in Droysen, *Historik* 2: 249 [Verdun Jubileumsrede, 1843].

29. Droysen, *Kleine Schriften zur alten Geschichte,* 72 [Zur griechischen Literatur, 1838]: 'Hier war der wahrhafte Untergang des Heidentums, der Menschengeist löste sich von der Erde, an die er gebunden, und von der er hervorgegangen war. Aber es wurde ihm hiermit sein positiver Inhalt und seine Haltung entrissen, er war ohne Götter, einsam bei sich, er war voll Grausen und Verzagen.'

30. Droysen, *Kleine Schriften zur alten Geschichte,* 64 [Zur griechischen Literatur, 1838]: 'Sehr schön hat man die Geschichte der Menschheit ein "Suchen Gottes" genannt. Durch die eigene, freie Menschenkraft sucht ihn das Heidentum.'

31. Droysen, *Kleine Schriften zur alten Geschichte,* 64 [Zur griechischen Literatur, 1838]: 'Die eigene treibende Unruhe zwingt den Geist weiter und weiter zu ringen, er ist unermüdlich in diesem Üben der eigenen Kraft, und immer neue Völker führt er an die Arbeit, die ermüdeten abzulösen und ihr Werk weite zu fördern. Erst wenn alle seine Mittel und Kräfte entwickelt sind und in höchster Anstrengung und Vollendung gearbeitet haben, wenn das lebendigste Gefühl ihrer Erschöpfung und Unzulänglichkeit wach geworden ist, wenn das kecke und freudige Vertrauen auf die eigene menschliche Kraft der Sehnsucht nach einem höheren Beistande, nach einer unendlich über alles Menschliche hinausreichende Kraft weicht, erst da kommt der trostbedürftigen Menschheit die Gnade der göttlichen Offenbarung entgegen, und die einst so stolze, nun in sich gebrochene Kraft des endlichen Geistes beugt sich in stiller Demut vor der Herrlichkeit des ewigen Vaters.'

32. Droysen, *Geschichte des Hellenismus* 3: 424 [2nd ed., 1877/78]: 'Nun endlich tritt dieser letzte und tiefste Gegensatz der Alten Geschichte Stirn an Stirn widereinander; es beginnt die letzte, die entscheidende Arbeit des sich erfüllenden Altertums; es vollendet sich, "als die Zeit erfüllet war", in der Erscheinung des menschgewordenen Gottes, in der Lehre des Neuen Bundes, in dem jener letzte und tiefste Gegensatz überwunden sein, in dem Juden und Heiden, die Völker aller Welt, in ihrer ethnischen Kraft gebrochen und auf den Tod erschöpft, endlich, wie die Propheten verhießen, die Weisen geahnt, die Sibyllen, der Völker Mund, laut und lauter gerufen, Trost und Ruhe und für die verlorene Heimat hienieden eine höhere, geistige, die in dem Reiche Gottes, finden sollten.'

33. Droysen, *Geschichte des Hellenismus* 3: 6 [2nd ed., 1877/78]: 'Wie weit entfernt sind diese Anfänge von der Vorstellung der einen Menschheit, die alle Völker umfaßt, des einen Reiches, das nicht von dieser Welt ist, – jener Vorstellung, die ihren vollendeten Ausdruck in der Erscheinung des Heillandes gewinnt! Das ist der Punkt, zu dem hin die Entwicklung der alten, der heidnischen Welt strebt, von dem aus ihre Geschichte begriffen werden muss…. Es gilt, jene Sonderungen zu überwinden, über jene lokalen, natürlichen Bestimmungen sich hinauszuarbeiten, an die Stelle der nationalen Entwicklung die persönliche und damit die allgemein menschliche zu gewinnen.'

34. Droysen, *Historik* 2: 170 [Vorlesung über die Geschichte des Mittelalters, 1840].

35. Droysen, *Historik* 2: 170 [Vorlesung über die Geschichte des Mittelalters, 1840].

36. Droysen, *Historik* 2: 250 [Verdun-Rede, 1843]: 'Das ohnmächtige Reich erliegt wehrlos; neue Herrschaften entstehen auf romanischem Boden. Aber die höhere Bildung ist bei den Bewältigten; die christliche Kirche, die Erbin und Trägerin aller geistigen Errungenschaft des Alterthums, beginnt ihre stillen Siege über jene Sieger; sie beugen sich der Zucht der Kirche; über deren Legenden und die heilige Geschichte des Testamentes vergessen sie ihre Stammsagen, ihre

Heldenlieder; ihre Sprache durchmischt sich mit der gebildeteren ihrer Priester, ihrer Unterthanen. Jahrhunderte währt dies Durchgähren; Italien, Gallien, Hispanien ist voll dieser romanischen Durchdringung.'

37. Droysen, *Historik* 2: 249–250 [Verdun-Rede, 1843]: 'Es folgt der Kampf Roms mit den Germanen; wie ganz zeigen sie in ihrer strengen Sprödigkeit, in ihrer sporadischen Sonderung jenen ethnischen Charakter. Sollen sie das Werk der Geschichte weiter zu führen übernehmen, so müssen sie sich nacharbeiten, das schon Errungene auf sich nehmen, müssen hinaus aus ihrer natürlichen Weise.'

38. Droysen, *Historik* 2: 252 [Verdun-Rede, 1843]: 'So beginnt doch mit dem Tage von Verdun die nationale Entwicklung des deutschen Staats. Nicht mehr national in dem Sinn der alten ethnischen Weise; der Lehnstaat, das Christentum ist hinzugekommen; unendlich bereichert beginnt die deutsche Nation ihr geschichtliches Leben.'

39. Southard, *Droysen and the Prussian School of History*, 40.

40. Droysen, *Historik* 2: 254 [Verdun-Rede, 1843]: 'Ich spreche von der Reformation. Sie hat, nicht außer, sondern in ihrer religiösen Bedeutung eine tiefere, allgemeiner. Aus dem eigensten Wesen des deutschen Gemüts erwachsen[,] gibt sie jenem großen Zwiespalt des Kaisertums und Papsttums, der weltlichen und geistlichen Ordnung eine Lösung oder doch das Prinzip der Lösung.'

41. Droysen, *Historik* 2: 254 [Verdun-Rede, 1843]: 'So einseitig das heidnische Alterthum, wurzelnd auf dem Boden des natürlichen Daseins, dem Diesseits zugehört hatte, eben so einseitig wurde, seit die römische Kirche das frische Leben der abendländischen Barbaren ergriffen hatte, in immer steigender Ausschließlichkeit das Jenseits geltend gemacht, wurde der Herrschaftstitel einer Hierarchie, die sich bis in das tiefste Geäder des Volkslebens hinab verzweigte. Ihre furchtbare Entartung zeugte endlich laut wider sie und ihr todtes Gesetz.'

42. Droysen, *Historik* 2: 255 [Verdun-Rede, 1843]: 'Hatte das Heidentum begonnen mit der Verschlungenheit Gottes und der Welt, war es seine Entwickelung gewesen, sich zu lösen und zum völligen Dualismus zu zerreißen, war nach der Weltentgötterung des sinkenden Altertums das Mittelalter, Islam wie Katholizismus, gleichsam die Gottentweltlichung, die eben so starre Außerweltlichkeit Gottes, die ebenso blinde Verachtung und Verstoßung des Irdischen, das sich eben darum nur desto wüster und losgebundener in seiner Natürlichkeit verwilderte, – so begann mit dem Jahrhundert der Reformation eine Bewegung, welche die abendländische Welt in ihren tiefsten Gründen umgestalten sollte.' The translations of the terms are borrowed from Southard, *Droysen and the Prussian School of History*, 39.

43. Southard, *Droysen and the Prussian School of History*, 39.

44. Droysen, *Historik* 2: 254–255 [Verdun-Rede, 1843]: 'Nicht in der mechanischen Fortpflanzung priesterlicher Weihe, nicht in der magischen Einwirkung des Jenseits auf das Menschliche und Irdische sollte ferner die Macht und die Wahrheit des Christenthums gefunden sein, sie sollte gesucht werden in der stets lebendigen und gegenwärtigen Durchdringung des Endlichen mit dem Ewigen, in dem allgemeinen Priesterthum aller Christenmenschen, in der innerlichsten und persönlichsten Betheiligung jedes Einzelnen bei seiner Rechtfertigung.'

45. Droysen, *Historik* 2: 255 [Verdun-Rede, 1843]: 'Mit der Rückkehr zu den großen Mustern des classischen Alterthums in seiner irdischen Gesundheit, Schönheit und Zuversicht, seiner verständig sichtenden, ordnend beherrschenden Auffassung der Wirklichkeiten, den künstlerischen und sittlichen, rechtlichen und staatlichen Idealen, die es ausgeprägt hatte – mit der Rückkehr zu den ersten ungetrübten Vorbildern christlichen Gemeindelebens, zu der einfachen evangelischen Geschichte, die ein Wust von Legenden, Wunderthätereien, Muttergottesculten überwuchert hatte, zu dem unverfälschten Wort Gottes und seiner Beglaubigung in dem innerlichsten Erlebniß neu gegründeter Lebensgemeinschaft mit Gott, – mit der freien Aufnahme beider in den mündig gewordenen, durch die Jahrhunderte harter Gesetzeszucht erstarkten Geist, der die Fesseln der Hierarchie zu durchbrechen ging in dem Bewußtsein, Träger der lebendigen und undurchrissenen Fortbildung der wahren Kirche zu sein, – in diesen allseits mächtigen, erweckenden, durchgährenden Impulsen begann die Arbeit einer völlig neuen Zeit, die positive

Vermittelung jenes starren Gegensatzes des Diesseits und Jenseits, ein kühneres, freieres Ringen des Geistes mit der Natur, "daß er ein Priester der Schöpfung werde, durch den sie als ein reines Opfer emporsteige an den Thron Gottes", ein Durchgeistigen der stummen Endlichkeit, daß die Welt in Wahrheit eine Gotteswelt werde. Diese Versöhnung und Verklärung der Welt – ein altes mystisches Wort nennt es die Rückleitung der Schöpfung zu Gott – ist der große Beruf des protestantischen Lebens.'

46. Droysen, *Historik* 2: 254 [Verdun-Rede, 1843].

47. Droysen, *Historik* 2: 260 [Verdun-Rede, 1843]: 'Recht eigentlich das waren die Lehrjahre des modernen Staates.' Translation borrowed from Southard, 'Theology in Droysen's Early Political Historiography', 388.

48. This translation of *Freiheitskriege* as 'wars of freedom' follows the pattern established by Southard, *Droysen and the Prussian School of History,* 32.

49. Droysen, *Freiheitskriege* 1: 19–20: 'Hatte bisher die weltliche Ordnung, der ständische Staat, wenn man ihn Staat nennen will, aus einer Summe von vertragsmäßigen Rechten und Pflichten, von Privatrechtlichkeiten bestanden, die sich gegenseitig hemmten und stützen, so begann nun die fürstliche Gewalt überzugreifen, ihr Recht aus dem bisherigen Zusammenhang von Begründungen und Verpflichtungen herauszulösen, ihre Befugnisse zu verallgemeinern, aus sich selber zu entnehmen.'

50. Droysen, *Freiheitskriege* 1: 21: 'Denn zunächst in dieser rohesten Gestalt war es, daß die Idee des Staates auftrat, des Staates nicht mehr als einer Gemeinsamkeit vieler privaten Rechte, Freiheiten, Vereinbarungen, sondern als einer Machtvollkommenheit der Majestät, des Allgemeinen, Wesentlichen, Vernünftigen; – in so abstrakter Fassung erscheint dies moderne Prinzip, rechtfertigt es sich.'

51. Droysen, *Freiheitskriege* 1: 18–19: 'Eine Fülle großer weltumgestaltender Momente bezeichnete den Ausgang des fünfzehnten Jahrhunderts. Man umsegelt den Erdkreis; eine neue Welt erschließt sich dem Verkehr der Menschen, dem geschichtlichen Leben. Aus mehr als tausendjähriger Vergessenheit taucht die Herrlichkeit des klassischen Altertums wieder auf; ihr nachringend gewinnt die Kunst neue Vollendungen; and an der Hand des Alten tritt die Wissenschaft aus den Nebeln scholastischer Spekulation, gewinnt den festen Boden der Wirklichkeiten. Und schon vollendet sich der Bruch in dem kirchlichen Leben der abendländischen Christenheit; der Ruf der christlichen Freiheit durchdringt die Massen bis in die tiefsten Kreise hinab. Ungeheure Kräfte sind in Gärung; aus der Überfülle reichsten Lebens, trotzigster Kraft, blühenden Wohlstandes will sich ein neues Weltalter emporringen. Das ist die Zeit, wo der moderne Staat seinen Anfang nimmt, unter allen großen Umwandlungen jenes großen Jahrhunderts zunächst die folgenreichste. An diesem Neuen erstarrt und erstirbt die blühende Welt des Mittelalters; mit ehernem Tritt, allzerstörend, erbarmungslos schreitet es durch die Länder dahin.'

52. Droysen, *Freiheitskriege* 1: 180: 'Eben dieß Moment der nationalen Einheit hoch über den ständischen und localen Besonderungen gab der beginnenden Monarchie ihre Kraft; aber indem sie weder im Innern noch nach Außen die Consequenzen ihres Principes zu machen oder zu dulden wagte, verlor sie ihre territoriale Bestimmtheit und ihre nationale Allgewalt. Ihr erstes Ziel war nicht Staat, sondern Macht zu sein.'

53. Droysen, *Freiheitskriege* 1: 180.

54. Droysen, *Historik* 2: 376 [Vorlesung über das Zeitalter der Revolution, 1858]: 'Ich werde in diesen Vorles[ungen] das Zeitalter der Revolution, wie man es wohl nennt, die fünfzig Jahre, welche die alte gute Zeit zerbrochen und die neue Zeit, unsere Gegenwart geboren haben, darzustellen versuchen.'

55. Droysen, *Freiheitskriege* 1: 5: 'Und nun schauen wir hin, wie das, was unsere Gegenwart gestaltet hat und noch bewegt, in einem weiten Zusammenhang stetigen Fortschreitens angebahnt und vorbereitet worden [ist].'

56. Johann Gustav Droysen. 1933. *Politische Schriften,* Munich: R. Oldenburg, 322 [Zur Charakteristik der europäischen Krisis, 1854]: 'Wer im Stande ist, ruhig zu beobachten und klar zu denken, muss die Überzeugung gewinnen, dass sich seit zwei Menschenaltern alle Vorrau-

setzungen und Bedingungen des europäischen Lebens, alle sozialen und staatlichen Kräfte, alle geistigen und materiellen Faktoren verwandelt haben.'

57. Droysen, *Freiheitskriege* 1: 270: 'Wir haben diesen amerikanischen Krieg als den ersten großen Freiheitskrieg der neuen Zeit bezeichnet.'

58. Droysen, *Politische Schriften,* 329 [Zur Charakteristik der europäischen Krisis, 1854]: 'Die neue Weltepoche hat an die Tür gepocht, als sich Amerika vom Mutterlande losriss.'

59. Droysen, *Freiheitskriege* 1: 283: 'Man mag es einen besonderen Segen des Himmels nennen, daß Männer wie Washington, John Adams, Samuel Adams, Jefferson, Madison, Franklin den Anfängen dieses Freistaates gegeben waren.... So weit man in der Geschichte umherschauen mag, nicht noch einmal wird man einen solchen Verein von Selbstverleugnung, Gerechtigkeit, Wahrhaftigkeit und wahrem Bürgersinn, eine solchen Verein von Tugend finden; und wenn andere Staaten von großen Helden, Eroberern, Herrschaftstalenten gegründet sind, so sind Amerikas Gründer Männer von wahrer moralischer Größe.'

60. Droysen, *Freiheitskriege* 1: 255: 'Will man, was hier vor sich ging, eine Revolution nennen, so war sie von der Art, dass keins der wesentlichen inneren Verhältnisse verrückt, die Kontinuität des inneren Rechtslebens an keinem Punkte unterbrochen, der Zustand der Personen und des Eigentums nicht weiter, als es der dauernde Krieg notwendig machte, verändert wurde.'

61. Droysen, *Freiheitskriege* 1: 273: 'Vielmehr ging er [der U.S.-amerikanische Staat] hervor aus der ganzen Vergangenheit europäischer Entwicklungen, war eins ihrer Resultate, gleichsam ein lebendiger Trieb, den man aus dem überwuchernden und absterbenden Gestrüpp der geschichtlichen Bildungen Europas rettete, um ihn in den jungfräulichen Boden der neuen Welt einzusenken.'

62. Droysen, *Freiheitskriege* 1: 281: 'Wie ist er [der U.S.-amerikanische Staat] in jeder Weise allen europäischen Staaten entgegengesetzt. In Europa Monarchien, feudale Stände, Staatsreligionen, Polizei, Fiskalität, Bevormundung des Volkes, ein Wust von Vergewaltigungen und Hemmungen, – hier Freiheit, Toleranz, Selbstregierung, Selbstbesteurung, Selbständigkeit, kein Adel, keine Staatskirche, keine Feudalrechte, keine Beamtenhierarchie, – nur die traurige Anomalie der Negersklaven in einzelnen Staaten.'

63. Droysen, *Freiheitskriege* 1: 284: 'Hier zum ersten Male ist ein Staat, der nicht Macht sein will, und so mächtiger wird, je mehr er nur Staat ist und bleibt, – mächtig nicht zur Verknechtung und Gewalttat, sondern zur Abwehr, zur Entwilderung weiter Gebiete, zur Entwicklung nie geahnter sozialer Kräfte.'

64. Droysen, *Freiheitskriege* 1: 286: 'Die Schwerpunkte des geschichtlichen Lebens sind nun verwandelt; es beginnt sich eine völlig neue Polarität in der Geschichte zu bilden; der Gegensatz des Abend- und Morgenlandes, der seit den glorreichen Tagen des alten Hellas in immer neuen Gestaltungen das Leben der Menschheit beherrscht hat ... beginnt nun ersetzt zu werden durch den der alten und neuen Welt.'

65. Droysen, *Freiheitskriege* 1: 286: 'Und auch hier erkennen wir die hohe Bedeutsamkeit des ersten großen Freiheitskrieges, mit dem sich die neue Zeit einleitet. Mit ihm beginnt ein neuer Weltteil, der seit drei Jahrhundert nur leidend an den Bewegungen der Geschichte Teil genommen, als mitarbeitend in die Geschichte einzutreten, nicht in Kraft seiner autochthonischen Bevölkerung, sondern erfüllt mit den Lebenskeimen der Bildung, Gesittung, ja der Volkstümlichkeiten, die sich die alte Welt in tausendjähriger Geschichte erarbeitet hat.'

66. Southard, 'Theology in Droysen's Early Political Historiography', 389.

67. Droysen, *Freiheitskriege* 1: 368: 'Die Nationalversammlung fühlte die Pflicht, Ordnung zu schaffen.... Es war die Nacht des 4. August; es folgten jene enthusiastischen Auftritte, mit denen man das ganze Gebäude feudaler Pflichten und Rechte, der Privilegien, Exemtionen, Ungleichheiten, Pensionen, Zünfte, die Summe irrationaler Verhältnisse über den Hausen stürzte. Theoretisch war nun tabula rasa, war Raum da, aus der Theorie, auf dem Wege des Rationalismus einen völlig neuen Staat zu gründen.'

68. Droysen, *Freiheitskriege* 1: 368: 'Seine Grundlage [des neuen französischen Staats] wurde die Erklärung der Rechte des Menschen und Bürgers, das Prinzip der Volkssoveränität, der Auto-

nomie der Gemeinden, – nur dass sie hier nicht wie in Nordamerika das Resultat einer bürgerlichen Freiheit, sondern ein Postulat, eine anticipatio naturae war, nach der sich erst die Verhältnisse und – was schwerer und gefährlicher war – die Personen völlig umwandeln sollten.'

69. Droysen, *Freiheitskriege* 1: 459: '… man soll nichts sein als Bürger, als ein völlig selbstloses Teilchen dieses Allgemeinen, das allein herrschen und da sein soll; das nackte, prädikatslose Dasein der Individuen ist die Grundlage dieser fanatischen Existenz.'

70. Droysen, *Freiheitskriege* 1: 458: 'Das ist das grausig großartige System des Schreckens. Mit blutigster Konsequenz war es hindurchgeführt. Dieser Fanatismus, diese eisige Kälte, im Dienst des Allgemeinen alles Besondere, Private, Persönliche hinzugeben, jedes andere Empfinden zu ertödten, das ist die Tugend, deren schöner Name immer wieder die Verhandlungen jener dunklen Zeit durchtönt.'

71. Droysen, *Freiheitskriege* 1: 459: '… man gelangte rückwärts zum rein heidnischen Wesen der ausschließlichen Berechtigung des Nationalen; man hatte die Geschichte vertilgt und behielt nichts als die natürliche Gegebenheit des ethnischen Daseins.'

72. Droysen, *Freiheitskriege* 2: 491–492: 'Die Spitze seiner [Napoleons] Aufgabe ist es, ein Herrschaftssystem zu gründen, das sich selber trägt und regelt, gleich jener *mécanique céleste* der Gestirne, die ja auch ein großer Forscher durchsuchte "ohne Gott zu finden".'

73. Droysen, *Freiheitskriege* 2: 125: 'Nie in der Geschichte hat sich menschlicher Verstand in umfassenderer und durchgreifenderer Weise ordnend und formend gezeigt. Denn hier galt es, eine völlig neue Ordnung der Dinge zu schaffen … einen Staat ohne historische Basierung, ganz dem Hier und Jetzt zugehörend, wenn nicht die nivellierende Revolution selbst seine Voraussetzung gewesen wäre.'

74. Droysen, *Freiheitskriege* 2: 492: 'Nur dreißig Jahre hat er sich gewünscht – die Zeit einer Generation; das heranwachsende Geschlecht wird keine Geschichte kennen als die seines Ruhmes, keine Tugend als Ergebenheit gegen ihn, keine Religion als an seinen Stern zu glauben. In Wahrheit, nie ist die Gefahr größer gewesen für die edelsten Güter des Menschen, für den Beruf der Menschheit.'

75. Droysen, *Politische Schriften,* 323 [Zur Charakteristik der europäischen Krisis, 1854]: 'Wie die große Maschinenindustrie das kleine Handwerk fort und fort absorbiert, so zehrt der Staat, aus einem Inbegriff von gegebenen und in sich ruhenden sozialen und Rechtszuständen verwandelt in eine Institution, Macht zu erzeugen und zu üben, die Autonomie aller untern Kreise auf, braucht und fordert die Omnipotenz, Jeden und Jedes in jedem Augenblick nach diesem höchsten Zwecke zu verwenden, anders und anders zu bestimmen, zu mobilisieren.'

76. Droysen, *Freiheitskriege* 2: 127: 'Mit einem Wort, hier ist die Vollendung der Monarchie, wie sie seit dem Zeitalter der Reformation sich zu erheben versucht hat, – ein *l'état c'est moi,* vollständiger und energischer als es je Ludwig XIV. möglich gehalten haben mochte. Die Nation mit allen ihren alten Unterschieden und Gliederungen war ja absorbiert worden in jene Republik der Einheit, Freiheit und Gleichheit, die nun eben so vollkommen der neue Monarch absorbierte, beginnend in der Form eines kollegialischen Konsulates, bald als einziger lebenslänglicher Konsul, endlich als Kaiser – ein Cäsar im vollsten Sinne des Wortes.'

77. Droysen, *Freiheitskriege* 2: 128.

78. Droysen, *Freiheitskriege* 1: 3: 'Mit dem Namen der Freiheitskriege pflegen wir in Deutschland jene drei unvergeßlichen Jahre zu bezeichnen, in denen, zum ersten Mal nach Jahrhunderten, das deutsche Volk gemeinsam und in dem Hochgefühl seiner Einheit gekämpft und gesiegt hat.'

79. Christopher Clark. 1996. 'The Wars of Liberation in Prussian Memory: Reflections on the Memorialization of War in Early Nineteenth-Century Germany', *The Journal of Modern History,* 68(3): 553–554.

80. However, later on, for instance in 1858, he would call his lectures on European contemporary history *Vorlesungen über das Zeitalter der Revolution* ['Lectures on the Era of the Revolution'].

81. Droysen, *Freiheitskriege* 1: 1: 'Es ist üblich, die Zeit, welche sie besprechen [die Vorlesungen über die Freiheitskriege] als das Zeitalter der Revolution zu bezeichnen. Es schien mir

unbedenklich statt dieser Bezeichnung eine andere zu wählen, welche den positiven Inhalt der umgestaltenden Bewegungen jener fünfzig Jahre andeutet.'

82. Droysen, *Briefwechsel* 1: 321 [Letter to Albert Heydemann, 26 December 1845]: 'Ich langweile mich an der ewig negativen Fassung der neuesten Zeit, als sei sie die Geschichte der Revolution, der Zerstörung, wo sie doch die der Befreiung ist.'

83. Droysen, *Freiheitskriege* 1: 4: 'Denn jene [die deutschen] Freiheitskriege sind doch nur der Schluß einer ganzen Reihe von Völkerkämpfen um die Freiheit, von Kämpfen, die durch einen weiten Kreis umbildender Entwicklungen vorbereitet, endlich hervorbrachen, um in fünfzig Jahren ungeheuerster Wechsel alle staatlichen und sozialen Verhältnisse, die gesamte Weltlage umzugestalten.'

84. Reinhart Koselleck. 1984. '"Revolution" und ihre Gegenbegriffe in geschichtsphilosophischer Perspektive', in Otto Brunner et al. (eds), *Geschichtliche Grundbegriffe. Historisches Lexikon zur politisch-sozialen Sprache in Deutschland*, vol. 5, Stuttgart: Klett-Cotta, 745–746: "Die in Deutschland ausgebliebene Revolution wird durch die vorangegangene Reformation teils erübrigt, teils kompensiert. Jedenfalls spielte das so genannte germanische Freiheitsprinzip in der Folgezeit eine gewichtige Rolle, um Deutschland in der Reihe der tatsächlichen und der erwarteten Revolutionen einzuordnen. Deshalb verzichtete Droysen bewusst auf die Bezeichnung das "Zeitalter der Revolution", als er 1843/46 seine Vorlesung über "Das Zeitalter der Freiheitskriege" veröffentlichte. Der neue Epochenname enthielt ein politisches Programm. "Freiheitskrieg" rückte in eine semantische Opposition zu "Revolution", weil jener Begriff den positiven Inhalt der umgestaltenden Bewegungen herausstreichen sollte.'

85. Droysen, *Freiheitskriege* 2: 404: 'In solcher Tugend höchster Selbstverleugnung und Hingabe an das Vaterland war das neue Preußen auferbaut.... Als Macht vernichtet, begann es sich als Staat neu zu gründen.'

86. Droysen, *Freiheitskriege* 2: 408: 'Es galt, sagten wir, die bürgerliche Freiheit Altenglands und die staatliche Energie, die die Revolution hervorgebracht, auf positive Weise zu vereinen. Von den Völker des Britischen Reiches wie wenige hatten an der Staatlichkeit desselben Anteil, ja wie war in demselben "in beklagenswerter Disharmonie" Untertanen von Aktiengesellschaften, Unterdrückte ihres Glaubens wegen, Sklaven. Und wieder die Revolution hatte freilich den Unterschied der Stände tot gesprochen, das Volk in eine uniforme Masse umgeschmolzen, seine Souveränität proklamiert; aber indem man mechanisch in der Trennung der Gewalten das Wesen des Staates und die Garantien seiner inneren Gesundheit zu finden glaubte, war Frankreich aus der Autokratie der gesetzgebenden in die der ausführenden Gewalt hinübergeschwankt, in der einen wie anderen ohne bürgerliche Freiheit, ohne anderer sittliche Existenz als die des Staates zu sein.'

87. Droysen, *Freiheitskriege* 2: 410–411: 'Die Vielen und die Einheit, Volk und Staat, das ist der alte Gegensatz; aber nun nicht mehr äußerlich nebeneinander, noch wider einander, noch das Eine statt des Andern, sondern der Staat ist des Volkes, das Volk des Staates in wesentlichster Gegenseitigkeit, wie Leib und Seele des Menschen, nur unendlich reicher als ein nur organisches Leben.'

88. Gustav Droysen, *Johann Gustav Droysen*, 14–15.

89. Droysen, *Freiheitskriege* 2: 726: 'Jene große Gegensatz, der in seinem ersten Stadium eine neue freie Staatenwelt jenseits des Ozeans schuf, der dann Frankreich und das alte Europa zu furchtbarstem Kampf gegen einander führte, fortan wiederholte er sich in jedem einzelnen Lande, und die heilige Allianz diente nur dazu, ihn auszuprägen und zum Bewusstsein zu bringen.'

90. Droysen, *Politische Schriften*, 103 [Preußen und Deutschland, 1847]: 'Wer will es verkennen, dass in dem Wollen "historischer Entwicklung" eine Wendung des staatlichen Wesens liegt, die mehr gewährt als 1789 auch nur geahndet, 1815 auch nur gefürchtet ist, – ein endliches und allversöhnendes Ueberholen der falschen Alternativen von Volkssouveränität und Legitimität, von Revolution und Reaktion, an denen das alte Europa zu immer neuen Fehlgeburten krankt.'

91. Droysen, *Freiheitskriege* 2: 727: 'Volk auf Volk lernte sich selbst, seinen Beruf und sein Recht erkennen. Ist es nicht das, was der Gegenwart, auch der unsrigen, ihre Bedeutung gibt?'

92. Droysen, *Freiheitskriege* 1: 16: 'Vor Allem [ist das Resultat von den revolutionären Erschütterungen], daß jenes große Prinzip [das Prinzip der Freiheit], dessen Momente nacheinander der Abfall Nordamerikas, die Revolution Frankreichs, die Neugründung jenes protestantisch deutschen Staates dargestellt hatten, das Bewusstsein der Völker zu erfüllen, die Summe ihres Strebens zu bestimmen begann; ein Princip, mit dem die alte Weise der Staaten, nur Mächte zu sein, auf gegenseitige Hemmung und Ueberwältigung hinzuarbeiten, den Staatangehörigen nur ein passives Verhältnis zu dem Staat und seinen Bestimmungen zu gestatten, Alles nur für das Volk, nichts durch das Volk zu wollen, überholt und überwunden war.'

93. Bauer, ‹*Das Geheimnis aller Bewegung ist ihr Zweck*›, 56.

94. Droysen, *Briefwechsel* 1: 118 [Letter to Friedrich Perthes, 8 February 1837]: 'Man kann allerdings keine erhabenere Auffassung menschlicher Geistigkeit und Entwicklung sehen als diese Hegelsch; aber welcher Irrtum! Hier ist jenes Absolute, was nicht Gott ist, nicht der Ewige, Alleinige, den uns Christus geoffenbart hat, sondern – der Zeiger einer Uhr, anzuzeigen, auf welcher Stunde die Erkenntnis des Menschen von Gott steht.' The idea of an 'absolute that is not God' was actually first used by Perthes in an earlier letter to Droysen.

95. Droysen, *Briefwechsel* 1: 118 [Letter to Friedrich Perthes, 30 October 1836]: 'Ich habe mich Ihnen schon als einen streng Glaubenden bekannt und ich hoffe, Sie erkennen diese Ansicht wieder in dem, was Sie von mir lesen. So durchdrungen bin ich von der allmächtigen Regierung Gottes, daß ich meine, es kann auch kein Haar vom Haupte fallen ohne seinen Willen; aber die Endlichkeit unserer Einsicht hemmt uns, dies wunderbare Mysterium zu durchschauen; und die erhabene Aufgabe wissenschaftlichen Strebens ist, von dem endlichen und menschlichen Standpunkt aus uns dem zu nähern, was uns die Lehre Christi als Wahrheit geoffenbart hat. Und näher: der Historiker ist nicht imstande, bis ins einzelne hinein die Notwendigkeit des Geschehens zu begreifen, so wenig wie der einzelne noch alle alltäglichen Vorfälle des Lebens; aber wir glauben, daß in allem bis auf das Kleinste hin die ewige Führung Gottes mächtig und sorglich ist.' On the differences between Droysen's and Hegel's ideas of historical necessity, see also Erich Rothacker. 1972. *Einleitung in die Geisteswissenschaften,* Darmstadt: Wissenschaftliche Buchgesellschaft, 171–174.

96. Droysen, *Historik* 1: 161–162 [Vorlesungstext, 1857]: 'So hat Hegel die Geschichte in seiner Philosophie derselben immer erklärt – eine Betrachtungsweise, die, in das Praktische und Politische übersetzt einfach die Macht des Gewesenen über das Gegenwärtige, die falsche historische Doktrin, die Restauration und Reaktion proklamiert.'

97. Christoph Bauer has argued that straightforward association of Hegel's philosophy of history with the Prussian political restoration is an old and common misinterpretation of Hegel's statements. See Bauer, ‹*Das Geheimnis aller Bewegung ist ihr Zweck*›, 46–56. Droysen not only subscribed to this opinion but, according to Bauer, also actively contributed to popularizing it.

98. These two last historical tendencies are about to be discussed in this chapter.

99. Rüsen, *Begriffene Geschichte,* 16–21.

100. Droysen, *Freiheitskriege* 2: 726–727: 'Als der Friede kam, ohne zu bringen, was sie [die Völker] noch unklar hofften, wie verwirrten sich da die Gedanken, wie trat da noch einmal verkommenes Recht und neuer Anspruch, provinzielles Vorurteil und nationales Verlangen, die Masse und die Bildung, der Adel und das Volk wider einander; wie leicht täuschte sie bald die eitle Vorspiegelung des Liberalismus und die Fantasterei heimlicher Umtriebe, bald die Huld fürstlicher Verheißungen und das sichere Gängelband bürokratischen Besserwissens. In Wahrheit, man möchte sagen, die Völker seien noch nicht reif.'

101. Droysen, *Historik* 2: 257 [Verdun-Rede, 1843]: 'Ein Blick auf die Geschichte lehrt, dass der Bereich des geschichtlichen Lebens in demselben Maße, wie es sich, von einzelnen sporadischen Punkten beginnend, über Länder, über Weltteile, endlich über die gesamte Erdoberfläche ausgedehnt hat, in gleichen Pulsen sich mehr und mehr in die tieferen Schichten, in die Masse der Bevölkerung hinab belebend und adelnd verbreitet hat.'

102. Thomas Nipperdey. 1998. *Deutsche Geschichte 1800–1866. Bürgerwelt und starker Staat,* Munich: C.H. Beck, 611.

103. Nippel, *Johann Gustav Droysen,* 125–126.

104. Droysen, *Historik* 1: 296 [Vorlesungstext, 1857]: 'Wie kann, wo der Wert des Weibes nur im Gebären der Kinder gesehen wird – so in Israel, wo die Unfruchtbare heimgesandt wird –, die ganze Kraft der Gegenseitigkeit sich sittlich ausprägen? Je höher die sittliche Entwicklung, desto inniger wird die monogamische Ehe …'

105. Droysen, *Freiheitskriege* 1: 97: 'Denn der König ist in der großen Volkswirtschaft, was der Familienvater an der Spitze seines Hauswesens: wie sich Weib und Kind und Gesinde um den Hausherrn schart, seinen Meinungen folgt, ihm die Sorge des Ganzen überlässt, so patriarchalisch, frei über Freie, aber willig Gehorchende gebietet der König.'

106. See Falko Schnicke. 2010. *Prinzipien der Entindividualisierung. Theorie und Praxis biographischer Studien bei Johann Gustav Droysen,* Cologne: Böhlau, 82–94.

107. Droysen, *Freiheitskriege* 1: 214: 'Nicht die moralische Seite des Colonialwesens ist es, die wir zu betrachten haben. Schmachvoll genug, daß es dazu hat führen können, den Menschenhandel bis zu der empörendsten Vollendung zu steigern; daß der Name des Christenthums hat entweiht werden müssen, maaßlose Verknechtungen und Ausrottungen friedlicher Indianerstämme, die Herrschsucht und Habgier forderte, zu beschönigen; daß den überlebten Culturvölkern Asiens und den rohen Naturvölkern Afrika's das reich entwickelte geschichtliche Leben des Abendlandes bei weitem nicht in seinen edleren Gestaltungen, sondern in seinen verzerrtesten Entartungen entgegengetreten und mit hinterlist, Treuelosigkeit und Frevellust gleichbedeutende geworden ist.'

108. Droysen, *Freiheitskriege* 2: 201–202: 'Es begann der furchtbarste Sklavenkrieg – auch ein Kampf um die Freiheit, auch eine Lösung scheußlich irrationaler Verhältnisse, wie sie deren das alte Europa unzählige gegründet hatte und für gutes Recht ausgab.'

109. Droysen, *Freiheitskriege* 2: 418: 'In eben diesem Geist war den Juden "eine neue, der allgemeinen Wohlfahrt angemessene Verfassung" erteilt; denn dem Wesen des Staates ist es unmöglich, in seinem Bereich unorganische Massen zu haben, wie nach der rohen mittelalterlichen Herkömmlichkeit die Judengemeinden bisher gewesen waren, und mehr noch widerstreitet es dem Wesen des rechten Staates, religiöse Ansichten zum Maßstab politischer Befugnisse zu machen.'

110. Droysen, *Historik* 2: 373 [Vorlesungen über neuere Geschichte, 1856]: 'Unsere Zeit ist wie eine Krankheit, in der her und hin curirt wird, ohne daß man ihre Diagnose hat, und jedes versuchte Mittel verschlimmert das Uebel, steigert die Gefahr und das Elend, das materielle wie moralische.'

111. According to Rüsen, before the failure of the attempt to build a unified Germany in 1849, Droysen did not use the concept of 'crisis' in characterizing his present horizon. See Rüsen, *Begriffene Geschichte,* 90, fn. 5. The introduction of this concept and the central role credited to it in several writings Droysen produced at the time of the Prussian reaction (1849–1858) and beyond thus attests to a newly intensified criticism of the contemporary world.

112. Droysen, *Politische Schriften,* 328 [Zur Charakteristik der europäischen Krisis, 1854]: 'So ist die Gegenwart; Alles in Wanken, in unermesslicher Zerrüttung, Gärung, Verwilderung. Alles Alte verbraucht, gefälscht, wurmstichig, rettungslos. Und das Neue noch formlos, ziellos, chaotisch, nur zerstörend.'

113. Droysen, *Politische Schriften,* 328 [Zur Charakteristik der europäischen Krisis, 1854]: 'Wir stehen in einer jener großen Krisen, welche von einer Weltepoche zu einer neuen hinüberleiten.'

114. Droysen, *Briefwechsel* 2: 241 [Letter to Wilhelm Arendt, 3 April 1854]: 'Die Dinge im Orient oder richtiger in Europa sind in einer Lage, gegen die 1848 nur Kinderspiel ist. Die Situation ist unermesslich ernsthaft, und ich bin gefasst auf eine Wiederholung der Zeiten von 1792–1815.'

115. Irene Kohlstrunk. 1980. *Logik und Historie in Droysens Geschichtstheorie. Eine Analyse von Genese und Konstitutionsprinzipien seiner ‹Historik›,* Wiesbaden: Franz Steiner, 4: '[Droysens] historische Hermeneutik ist das abstrakte Konzentrat jenes realen Bewußtseins, das die moderne

"bürgerliche Gesellschaft" von sich besitzt. Sie erscheint als die avancierstete Form "bürgerlichen" Selbstverständnisses, auch in dem Sinn, daß sie in der Verpflichtung auf die historische Zeit Elemente produziert, die über sie hinausweisen.' A similar argument had already been introduced in Herbert Marcuse. 1937. 'Rezension von J. G. Droysens "Historik", Hrsg. v. R. Hübner', *Zeitschrift für Sozialforschung* 6: 421–422.

116. Droysen, *Politische Schriften*, 323–324 [Zur Charakteristik der europäischen Krisis, 1854]: 'Mit den staatlichen Umgestaltungen hielten die Wirkungen der Geldwirthschaft gleichen Schritt. Sie wirkten da, wohin die politische Zersetzung nicht zu dringen vermochte, um so ungestörter und zu dem gleichen Ziel. In dem Maße, als der moderne Staatszweck Alles in fungible Sachen verwandelt, lehrt und lernt man in Grund und Boden nur die Rente zu sehen, an den Personen nur die Arbeitskraft zu kalkulieren, die Ersparnisse (das Vermögen) in Kredit aufzulösen, die – denn in dieser Verwandlung entwickelt das Geld eine Expansivkraft wie Wasserdampf – dann Zins bringen von fiktiven Werten, von Kapitalien, die weder vorhanden waren, noch erworben werden.'

117. Droysen, *Freiheitskriege* 2: 525: 'In der Agricultur überholten große Pachtungen die kleine Arbeit, es schwand der Bauernstand völlig, die Feldarbeiter wurden Tagelöhner, hörten auf seßhaft zu sein, zogen Arbeit suchend von Graffschaft zu Graffschaft.'

118. Droysen, *Freiheitskriege* 2: 525: 'Der lockende Verdienst trieb die kleinen Leute in die Fabriken; schnell war die Hausarbeit durch die ermattende Arbeit in den Fabriksälen verdrängt, bald der Arbeiter durch die Maschine ersetzt, der Arbeiter der Sklave der rastlosen Maschine.... Die Masse des Volkes wurde Proletarier, glücklich genug, wenn sie das Leben fristeten, wenn Handelskrisen nicht die Fabriken zum Stillstand zwangen, zu großer Erntesegen nicht die Preise drückte. In eben der Zeit, da des wackeren Wilberforce Bemühungen für die Negersklaven Erfolge gewannen, entstand hier angesichts des prunkendsten Überflusses, des stolzesten Nationalgefühls, des höchsten Freiheitsgenusses eine neue Art Sklaverei, nur tausendfach elender, entwürdigender, erbitternder.'

119. Droysen, *Freiheitskriege* 2: 528: 'Wie in Frankreich die Revolution zur Machtsouveränität, so führte die innere Umgestaltung Englands zur Geldsouveränetät.'

120. Droysen, *Freiheitskriege* 2: 15–16: '[Nach dem] Stillstehen der Guillotine ... gewann das bare Geld ein ungeheures Übergewicht, mit Geld konnte man Alles ... Der Charakter der Gesellschaft wandelte sich in gleichem Maaß ... bald gefiel man sich in geschmacklosen Gemenge von Tunica und Plume. Mad. Tallien und Mad. Beauharnais brachten griechische Moden in Gang, man liebte den Reiz des Nackten; Gastmähler, Schwelgereien, prunkendes Gerät als Schaugepränge des Reichtums bot der vielgerühmten Gleichheit Hohn; man stürzte sich in die langentbehrte Luft des Privatlebens; mit wahrer Gier suchte man überall Gewinn und Genuß.'

121. Droysen, *Freiheitskriege* 2: 16: 'Was bot das Dasein Besseres als die Freuden des "Materialismus"? Und man genoss sie ohne Gram und Schäm; zu dem widrigen Zerrbilde jener Zeit gehört die maaßlos wachsende Ausschweifung und die Schämlossigkeit, mit der sie getrieben wird; "die Jugend", sagt ein Erlass an die Polizeibeamten von Paris, "die Jugend schweift aus, eher sie noch die Jahre dazu hat, und selbst die Kindheit wird schon verdorben". Das Politische verlor seinen Reiz bis auf den einen, immer neue Gelegenheit zu Gelderwerb zu geben.'

122. Friedrich Jaeger. 1994. *Bürgerliche Modernisierungskrise und historische Sinnbildung. Kulturgeschichte bei Droysen, Burckhardt und Max Weber*, Göttingen: Vandenhoeck & Ruprecht, 279, fn. 28; cf. Rüsen, *Begriffene Geschichte*, 81, 89–93.

123. Droysen, *Historik* 1: 344 [Vorlesungstext, 1857]: 'Man kann sagen, die Geschichte der Arbeit ist die der Freiheit und ihres Fortschreitens. Sie umfaßt alle die Stadien zwischen unendlichen Arbeitsteilung in der Zivilisation und der fast tierähnlichen Selbstgenügsamkeit, der Trägheit und Stumpfheit, wie sie noch jetzt in den rohesten Völker zu sehen ist; sie zeigt den unendlichen Fortschritt von dem bornierten Vorrecht des Nichtarbeitens in der antiken Welt zur sittlichen Anerkennung der Arbeit im Christentum, auch da hat es erst der tiefgreifenden Reformation bedurft, um die Arbeit zu ihrer Ehre zu erheben, sie zu emanzipieren; die freie Arbeit ist das glänzende Ergebnis der großen Bewegung der Aufklärung im 18. Jahrhundert geworden.'

124. Droysen, *Historik* 1: 342–351 [Vorlesungstext, 1857].

125. Kohlstrunk, *Logik und Historie in Droysens Geschichtstheorie,* 87–94.

126. Droysen, *Briefwechsel* 1: 66–67 [Letter to Friedrich Gottlieb Welcker, 1 September 1834]: 'Sie wissen schon, daß ich Verehrer der Bewegung und des Vorwärts bin; Cäsar, nicht Cato, Alexander und nicht Demosthenes ist meine Passion. Alle Tugend und Moralität und Privattrefflichkeit gebe ich gern den Männer der Hemmung hin, die Gedanken der Zeit aber sind nicht bei ihnen.'

127. Nipperdey, *Deutsche Geschichte 1800–1866,* 400–402.

128. Droysen, *Politische Schriften,* 339 [Zur Charakteristik der europäischen Krisis, 1854]: 'Man wird sagen dürfen, daß diese Partei [die Partei der Reaktion] deren Diagnose der Gegenwart durchaus richtig war, sich in den Mitteln für die Heilung vergriff; sie hat sich die Aufgabe falsch gestellt.… Leugnen, dass in der historisch herangewachsenen Umwandlung aller Verhältnisse und Anschauungen auch Berechtigtes, auch ein Recht und eine Macht ist, heißt darauf zu verzichten, dass die göttliche Weltordnung noch jetzt wie immer in den Geschicken der Menschen waltet. Es gilt, wie wüst auch noch die Gärung, wie verworren die Vorstellung sind, das Lebensvolle und Wahrhafte, was in ihnen ist, zu erkennen, zu erfassen, zur Gestaltung zu bringen. Man muss eben durch!'

129. Droysen, *Historik* 2: 241 [Privatvorrede, 1843]: 'Hat die sogenannte historische Ansicht kein höheres Criterium, als das des *fait accompli,* als das einer durchgesetzten factische Geltung, so kann sie consequenter Weise keine Art von Instanz gegen die Phase von Entwicklungen geltend machen, welche sie verdammt. Es ist eine Gedankenlosigkeit, sich auf die Autorität historischen Rechtes zu berufen, ohne zugleich das Recht der Geschichte anerkennen zu wollen.'

130. George Stack. 1998. 'Materialism', in Edward Craig (ed.), *Routledge Encyclopaedia of Philosophy,* London: Routledge, 171.

131. Droysen, *Politische Schriften,* 325 [Zur Charakteristik der europäischen Krisis, 1854]: 'Bei den evidenten Erfolgen dieser [mathematisch-physikalischen] Methode in der Erforschung der Erscheinungswelt liegt es nahe, mit ihr und von den gewonnenen Resultaten aus auch die Brücke zu schlagen nach denjenigen Gebieten, welche man bis dahin die des Geistes nannte. Schon dringt man auch in das innere seelische Leben des Menschen und der Menschheit ein. Man verfolgt in den Verletzungen dieser, jener Theile des Gehirns die unmittelbar folgenden Störungen bestimmter seelenthätigkeiten, die sich somit als eben diesen Gehirntheilen zugehörig schluß, die Willenskraft zeigt sich als Function bestimmter Stücke des Gehirns; schon ist die Muthmaßung geäußert, daß das Gewissen, ich glaube, die Zusammenwirkung gewisser Frictionen oder Ausschwitzungen sei.'

132. On the relationship between the Hegelian variant of idealism and the so-called 'historical school', see Rothacker, *Einleitung in die Geisteswissenschaften,* 82–107.

133. For further clarifications, see Friedrich Fulda. 1974. 'Der Begriff des Geistes bei Hegel und seine Wirkungsgeschichte', in Joachim Ritter (ed.), *Historisches Wörterbuch der Philosophie,* vol. 3, Basel: Schwabe, 192.

134. Orrin Summerell. 1996. 'Geist', in Peter Prechtl and Franz-Peter Burkard (eds), *Metzler Philosophie Lexikon.* Stuttgart: J.B. Metzler, 180.

135. Droysen, *Politische Schriften,* 326 [Zur Charakteristik der europäischen Krisis, 1854]: 'Freilich bei dieser [materialistischen] Anschauungsweise verliert das Ich jenen Zusammenhang seines Ursprungs und seines Berufs, jenes starke Gefühl seines Werts, seiner Verantwortlichkeit und seiner Rechtfertigung, in der sonst die Willenskraft, der Stolz der Freiheit, der Adel der Gesinnung, die Macht des Glaubens erwuchs; es wird auf eine völlig andere Basis verpflanzt, eine Basis, auf der ihm nichts bleibt, als in dem allgemeinen Stoffwechsel eine zufällige Erscheinungsform zu sein.'

136. Droysen, *Politische Schriften,* 326 [Zur Charakteristik der europäischen Krisis, 1854]: 'Diese materialistische Betrachtungsweise, von den Naturwissenschaften, die das Recht haben, sich auf dieselbe zu gründen … ist in unermeßlichen Umsichgreifen, beherrscht schon das gebildete Bewußtsein.'

137. Droysen, *Politische Schriften,* 327 [Zur Charakteristik der europäischen Krisis, 1854]: 'Das Niveau unseres geistigen Lebens sinkt reißend schnell; es schwindet die Hoheit, die Idealität, die Gedankenmächtigkeit, in der es sich bewegte.'

138. Droysen, *Politische Schriften,* 326 [Zur Charakteristik der europäischen Krisis, 1854]: '… und während die frühere ethisch-ideale oder, wenn man will, historisch-philosophische Bildungsweise immer etwas Unanschauliches, in sich Schwieriges, Ausschließliches an sich hatte, das den Vielen nur eben in der Form des Positiv-Religiösen zugänglich wurde, vermag das Neue, wie es denn ohne alle Mystik, dem Verstand leicht fasslich und den praktischen Interessen förderlich ist, einem unermesslich größeren Kreise von Menschen zugänglich zu werden.'

139. Lucian Boia. 1991. 'Henry Thomas Buckle', in Lucian Boia (ed.), *Great Historians of the Modern Age: An International Dictionary,* Westport, CT: Greenwood, 188.

140. Henry Thomas Buckle. 1866. *The History of Civilization in England,* vol. 1, New York: Appleton, 5.

141. It is worth noting that English equivalents to *Zunft der Historiker* – a term that was also ironically quoted by Droysen (*Historik* 1: 452 [Erhebung der Geschichte zum Rang einer Wissenschaft, 1863]) – do not show up in Buckle's original text, but only in the German translation.

142. Buckle, *The History of Civilization in England* 1: 4–5.

143. Thomas Burger. 1977. 'Droysen's Defense of Historiography: A Note', *History and Theory* 16(2): 168–169.

144. On what might be called the first *Methodenstreit* (quarrel of the methods) within German historical culture, see Michael MacLean. 1988. 'History in a Two-Cultures World: The Case of the German Historians', *Journal of the History of Ideas* 49(3): 474–478.

145. Eckhardt Fuchs. 1997. 'Positivistischer Szientismus in vergleichender Perspektive: Zum nomothetischen Wissenschaftsverständnis in der englischen, amerikanischen und deutschen Geschichtsschreibung', in Wolfgang Küttler et al. (eds), *Geschichtsdiskurs,* vol. 3: *Die Epoche der Historisierung,* Frankfurt am Main: Fischer, 403.

146. Droysen, *Outline of the Principles of History,* 62 [The Elevation of History to the Rank of a Science, 1863]; for the original quote, see Droysen, *Historik* 1: 452 [Erhebung der Geschichte zum Rang einer Wissenschaft, 1863].

147. Droysen, *Outline of the Principles of History,* 66 [The Elevation of History to the Rank of a Science, 1863]; for the original quote, see Droysen, *Historik* 1: 454 [Erhebung der Geschichte zum Rang einer Wissenschaft, 1863].

148. Droysen, *Historik* 1: 456 [Erhebung der Geschichte zum Rang einer Wissenschaft, 1863].

149. Droysen, *Outline of the Principles of History,* 69 [The Elevation of History to the Rank of a Science, 1863]; for the original quote, see Droysen, *Historik* 1: 456 [Erhebung der Geschichte zum Rang einer Wissenschaft, 1863].

150. Droysen, *Briefwechsel* 2: 424 [Letter to Wilhelm Arendt, 29 July 1856]: 'Die Parole [des in Jena von Droysen begründeten Forschungsseminars] ist: der Historiker hat nicht bloß Kritik zu treiben, wie Ranke in seiner Schule voranstellt, sondern ist Interpret, muß verstehen lernen und lehren.'

151. In the first version of the *Grundriß der Historik,* when he first stated that 'the historical investigation does not propose to explain … but to understand', his primary adversary was neither Buckle nor Comte, but Hegel: 'Die historische Forschung will nicht erklären, d.h. in der Form des Schlusses ableiten, sondern verstehen.' See Droysen, *Historik* 1: 403 [Grundriß der Historik, 1857–58]. In the corresponding passage of the *Historik* lectures, Droysen criticizes Hegel for having attempted to 'explain' the historical process. Thereby, Droysen clarifies that 'to explain' means to conceive historical phenomena as necessary results of conditions pre-established in the past. 'Explanation', in Droysen's initial definition, is thus linked to a critique of historical-philosophical pre-formism, that is, the assumption that each and every historical event happens in a certain way, time and place because of historical necessity – a necessity that was ultimately traceable back to God's will or plans, and could furthermore be used as a legitimatizing tool by the political

conservatives. See Droysen, *Historik* 1: 161–162 [Vorlesungstext, 1857]: 'Die Gewohnheit der erzählenden Darstellung, der genetischen Entwicklung hat die Meinung hervorgebracht, daß man das Gewordene geschichtlich erklären könne und müsse, daß man die Notwendigkeit des Gewordenen, daß es da und da und gerade so werden mußte, geschichtlich darlegen könne.... So hat Hegel die Geschichte in seiner Philosophie derselben immer erklärt. Eine Betrachtungsweise, die, in das Praktische und Politische übersetzt, einfach die Macht des Gewesenen über das Gegenwärtige, die falsche historische Doktrin, die Restauration und Reaktion proklamiert.'

152. Friedrich Jaeger. 1997. 'Geschichtsphilosophie, Hermeneutik und Kontingenz in der Geschichte des Historismus', in Wolfgang Küttler et al. (eds), *Geschichtsdiskurs*, vol. 3: *Die Epoche der Historisierung*, Frankfurt am Main: Fischer, 45.

153. Droysen, *Outline of the Principles of History*, 76 [The Elevation of History to the Rank of a Science, 1863]; for the original quote, see Droysen, *Historik* 1: 461 [Erhebung der Geschichte zum Rang einer Wissenschaft, 1863].

154. Droysen, *Historik* 1: 462 [Erhebung der Geschichte zum Rang einer Wissenschaft, 1863].

155. Fuchs, 'Positivistischer Szientismus in vergleichender Perspektive', 409–410; Jörn Rüsen. 1973. 'Johann Gustav Droysen', in Hans-Ulrich Wehler (ed.), *Deutsche Historiker*, Göttingen: Vandenhoeck & Ruprecht, 127.

156. Droysen, *Briefwechsel* 2: 48 [Letter to Theodor von Schön, 1 February 1852]: 'Der krasse Positivismus findet in dem Gang der deutschen Wissenschaften selbst leider große Unterstützung. Die glänzenden Resultate, welche die physikalische Methode, die der Wage und des Mikroskopes, die mit ihrem Recht materialistische, in den ihr zukommenden Bereichen gewonnen hat, versuchten mit größtem Erfolg die anderen Disziplinen. Ich bin erstaunt und betroffen zu sehen, daß hier in Mitteldeutschland diese induktive Methode bereits den höheren Schulunterricht, nicht bloß den der polytechnischen Anstalten, beherrscht, daß man das heranwachsende Geschlecht auch die alten Sprachen, womöglich auch die Geschichte, nach dieser Art "stets selbst suchend und beobachtend" lernen läßt. Schon merkt man wie daraus ein aberwitziges und altkluges, ein intellektuell überreiztes und an Willensstärke, Pflichtgefühl und höherer Geisteszucht verkommenes Geschlecht wird, voll Eitelkeit, Selbstsucht und Lüsternheit, ohne Strenge, ohne Idee und Ideal. Dazu kommt, daß die derzeitig übliche "Gesinnungstüchtigkeit" die freie Bewegung der Geister möglichst ausschließt.'

157. Nipperdey, *Deutsche Geschichte 1800–1866*, 400–402.

158. MacLean, 'History in a Two-Cultures World', 486–488.

159. MacLean, 'History in a Two-Cultures World', 487–488.

160. Kohlstrunk, *Logik und Historie in Droysens Geschichtstheorie*, 15: 'Dem aufgeklärten Rationalismus lastet Droysen es an, dass er den Menschen von der Geschichte befreit hat, indem er ihn aus ihr hinauskatapultierte, statt ihn zur Geschichte zu befreien, sich zum geschichtsfähigen Subjekt zu läutern.'

161. Southard, 'Theology in Droysen's Early Political Historiography', 378.

162. Droysen, *Historik* 2: 242 [Privat-Vorrede, 1843]: 'Denn allein eine wahrhaft historische Ansicht der Gegenwart, ihrer Aufgabe, ihrer Mittel, ihrer Schranken wird imstande sein, die traurige Zerrüttung unserer staatlichen und socialen Verhältnisse auszuheilen und die rechten Wege zu einer froheren Zukunft anzubahnen.' See also Rüsen, *Begriffene Geschichte*, 60: 'Das entscheidende Motiv zur Ausbildung einer "Historik" als Wissenschaftstheorie der Geschichte ist also für Droysen die drohende Geschichtslosigkeit der Gegenwart, ihre Emanzipation aus geschichtlich vorgegebenen Ordnungen.'

CHAPTER 4

The Politics of Historical Thinking and the Limits of the New Function

The Primacy of Power

As Droysen's career advanced, neither historical theory nor ancient history occupied the bulk of his intellectual energies. At least in terms of research and historiographical activity, what mattered most to him from the 1840s onwards was the politically motivated history of a political entity: the Prussian state. Droysen had never been an apolitical historian, even when writing on ancient history. But as he undertook to write the most important texts of the last phase of his career, the *Life of York von Wartenburg* (1851–1852)[1] and the *History of Prussian Politics* (1855–1886), the boundaries between historiography and politics tended to blur. These intellectual products were motivated by the explicit wish to see the German countries politically reunited under the lead of Prussia.

Committing himself to the cause of Germany's unification, Droysen put the universals of historical thinking into the service of a particular politics of history. A striking feeling thus emerges when the focus changes from his theory of historical knowledge and his macro-interpretations of the historical process to his political thought and activism. It is the feeling that the formal universalism that features in Droysen's theoretical reflections on historical thinking was not something Droysen was especially concerned with conveying to the realm of real politics. In fact, traces of the kind of universalism that abound in his theoretical reflections are quite elusive in both his late historiographical production and his post-1848 political activism. The type and the intensity of Droysen's political engagement in promoting the German national cause hence conflicted with his own notion that historiography is generally about sponsoring historical thinking, and that it concerns the general *Bildung* of the human being as such.

Notes for this section begin on page 170.

To provide this thesis with sufficient evidence, it is advisable to begin with a short characterization of Droysen's political stance. A good key to it is a statement he made on a very curious occasion in early 1867, when he was running for representative in elections held in the newly established North German Confederation. It was Droysen's second – and last – stint as a candidate for a political mandate, and he was attempting to rally support with a letter addressed to the voters of his electoral district of Kolberg (today, the Polish Kołobrzeg), in Pomerania. In it he conveyed the following political self-portrait: 'You and my voters ask me what I am and how I shall vote. Then let me tell you: neither liberal nor conservative, but Prussian, that means German; German, that means Prussian.'[2]

Droysen's claim that he was not a liberal shows first of all how far he saw himself from the mainstream of European political liberalism. Indeed, even though his texts, and particularly those on historical theory, are full of positive and central references to the idea of freedom, he would be better characterized as a supporter of what was, within the framework of German nineteenth-century politics, called national-liberalism.[3] And in fact he did subscribe to some of liberalism's basic assumptions. He agreed, for instance, with the liberal demand that political power be regulated by a constitutional law, and accordingly concurred that the German state-to-be should be a constitutional one. But he did not accept the premise that such a constitution should represent a kind of social contract by which private individuals would be granted protection against the state and its rulers,[4] and he vehemently disagreed with the classical-liberal tendency to ground general norms on the doctrine of natural rights.[5] As a matter of fact, Droysen made the case for a way of justifying norms and laws that frontally opposed the jusnaturalistic approach. He saw history as the fundament of law, both constitutional and ordinary, and hence thought a nation's juridical norms should not be artificially derived from abstract ideas such as reason or natural rights, but come from its own historical mode of life, uses and customs. In this regard, he sided with Friedrich Carl von Savigny and the German historical school of law, albeit remaining critical of their residual traditionalism.[6]

Furthermore, unlike many thinkers of classical liberalism, Droysen did not postulate a fundamental incongruence between state power and individual liberty. In this he was definitely not alone in his time and place. German political thought had, since the Protestant Reformation, distinguished itself by taking a rather positive view of the role of the state. Save for certain notable exceptions like Immanuel Kant, most of its representatives tended to assume that the state operates as a precondition to human freedom, not as an obstacle to it.[7] So did Droysen, who neither conceived of the state as a necessary evil nor saw individual liberty as liberty from the state. He argued that throughout history, one could observe a progressive movement towards what he conceived as the 'ethicization' of the state. Indeed, according to him, 'the essence of the state is to be power, inwards and outwards',[8] but interestingly enough, power here does not necessarily mean raw power. He conceded that in more distant times, primordial forms of state were marked by the arbitrary use of violence, but he firmly believed also that the later development of political life, at least in some areas of the world, had led to more advanced forms of state. The state had undergone a process of 'ethicization', so that in the present it was no longer a threat to freedom but its guarantee, and a means to its expansion.[9] Because of this perception, Droysen had no problem considering the state as one of the 'ethical powers' (*sittliche Mächte*) introduced in his *Systematik*.

Nonetheless, the long-range historical perspective in which he saw the development of the forms of state as a progressive movement towards the 'ethical state' did not blind him to the 'un-ethical' character of modern absolutism. It was precisely to guard against the arbitrariness of the absolutist system that Droysen agreed with the introduction of constitutional limitations on the exercise of state power. In light of this, it is tempting to designate him a liberal thinker. This might be correct, albeit in a very weak sense: he was a liberal only to the extent that he did not wish for a despotic mode of state. His liberalism, however, was not strong enough to push him towards either sympathy for parliamentarianism – a system of government he saw as 'nothing less than a panacea'[10] – or the idea of separating the state's powers into spheres of mutual control and balance, something he reckoned as 'an unfortunate error'.[11]

Droysen was also not a republican. He always contended that Germany, once unified, should be a hereditary monarchy with state power strongly concentrated in the hands of the monarch. The monarch would embody the entirety of the state in his own person, acting as a guarantor of political stability. According to Droysen, the parliament should be too weak to threaten the monarch's power or that of his ministers; concretely, it should not be allowed to interfere in either military or foreign affairs.[12] Droysen also thought Germany should consist of a federative state, and should in any case avoid the centralism followed by France. In more specific terms, he was convinced that the position of German kaiser should be occupied by the king of Prussia, who would transmit it through his dynasty. Accordingly, it was Prussia that should extend its state institutions into other German states and absorb them. Regarding the issue of which areas should be integrated to the German state, it suffices to say that from 1848 on, Droysen supported the so-called little-German solution (*kleindeutsche Lösung*), that is, the proposal to exclude the German areas of the Austrian Empire from the state to-be.[13] He initially thought that such a unification could be achieved by peaceful means, as a result of the individual states' spontaneous endorsements of a federative constitution. However, after this attempt failed – when Prussia's King Friedrich Wilhelm IV rejected the crown of German kaiser offered to him by the National Assembly in 1849 – Droysen radicalized his view. Later on, when Otto von Bismarck (1815–1898) drove Prussia to war against Austria in 1866, Droysen saw him as Prussia's and Germany's saviour – despite having previously faced Bismarck's government with criticism and reservations.[14]

Droysen took for granted that a German Empire thus configured would have at its disposal the necessary preconditions to materialize his ideal of the 'ethical state', that is, a form of state that was opposed to the mere power-state. But the exact stages in which such an ethical state would come about was a question he did not come to grips with. Instead, especially after 1848, he clearly privileged issues related to the state's shape and strategies for consolidating its power in the domestic and European contexts. Clearly, Droysen's wish to see a strong, unified, Prussia-led Germany triumph over the forces pressing for political fragmentation led him to prioritize power issues over all others. In the previously mentioned 1867 letter to the electoral committee of Kolberg, for instance, he explained his political platform by repeating that furthering the unification process was the national priority. In light of the importance of this task, all other questions were secondary. They could 'be postponed to the time when we will have our house under one roof'. And he continued: 'Then I will become a liberal, as liberal as required by our national life in its current stage, and as the duty of maintaining our protective roof permits.'[15]

In the meantime, however, he saw liberal issues such as basic civil rights as not only impertinent but also dangerous. Commenting on the constitutional debates at the Frankfurt National Assembly in 1848, he already had made his position clear: 'All our basic civil rights and constitutional forms', he argued, 'will be for nothing, if we do not understand that we have to raise our "Reich" to the rank of a power [*Macht*]. And, indeed, such empowerment of the state is so crucial that without it even freedom would be valueless.'[16] If one believed – as Droysen very much did – that the unification of Germany would automatically lead to an 'ethical state', then one would naturally agree that the issue of basic civil rights (*Grundrechte*) was of lesser importance. Droysen's strategic disregard for civil rights is a perfectly logical consequence of his general political ideas: he probably held as self-evident that in the 'ethical state' no one would need to be protected from the state's eventual abuses of power, because there would be no place for such a thing there.[17] Conversely, if such a state did not come about (that is, if Prussia did not decidedly command the German unification), then all civil liberties would face a devastating threat. This was why, in 1867, he asked the voters of the Kolberg electoral district not to vote for him if they wanted the liberal Constitution of 1849 restored. Someone like him, he argued, who had actively followed and shaped the events at the National Assembly two decades before, would have only distrust, pity or disdain for those who yearned for the failed constitution. After the Austro-Prussian War and the founding of the North German Confederation – that is, after Prussia finally

started to fulfil what Droysen saw as its unification task – support for the introduction of a constitution that stressed liberal rights rather than issues of power
was tantamount to 'putting a spoke in Germany's wheel'.[18]

Droysen's political ideas, while far from classical Western European political liberalism, were even farther from democracy. Not once in his life did he
show sympathy for the political groups that identified themselves as democrats.
His newspaper articles commenting on the activities of the Frankfurt Parliament came down particularly hard on his leftist colleagues. For instance, he
once said that he refused to regard them as real representatives of the *Volk*. One
would have no reason to fear the democrats, he maintained, 'if the sycophancy
of the *Volk*'s bootlickers [the democrats] were not corrupting its current "sov-
ereign" [the *Volk*] in a much more certain and bad way than the adulators of
the princes ever did before.'[19]

By mid-century, almost all reputable history professors in the German-
speaking space shared the disposition behind these harsh statements, the most
notable exception being Georg Gottfried Gervinus, who after 1849 adhered
to democratic values.[20] Anyhow, Droysen's dislike of democracy was not just
a matter of personal choice or inclination but also a theoretical bent. In his
genealogy of the idea of freedom,[21] he stressed that the most important sign of
modern times was the beginning of popular participation in politics, a general
tendency that he tried to depict in his analysis of the 'wars of freedom'. In
the final chapter of the book, Droysen easily allows that throughout human
history, the most effective and long-lasting forms of 'political energies' were
those emanating from the '*Volk*'.[22] This acknowledgement may have brought
him closer to democratic ideas, but his sense was that the differences between
his world view and that of then contemporary democrats far outweighed any
possible similarity.

The main difference he perceived was that German democrats' appreciation of the historical process was diametrically opposed to his own. He saw in
their outlook the same anti-historical feature that, in his opinion, was embodied by both the French revolution and what he termed 'materialism'.[23] This
would have led democrats to positive appraisals of natural and semi-natural
kinds of social organization, like the one embraced by the German notion of
Volk. Droysen accused the democrats of elevating nature and naturalness to
the position of a main political criterion. He asserted that the philosophical
doctrine holding that all naturally grown entities are per se 'the highest and the
best' only resulted in 'the worst form of popular sovereignty possible'.[24] This
was simultaneously an attack on a central tenet of the world view commonly
shared by democrats at that time, and an explanation of what Droysen did not
mean when he accorded a leading role to the *Volk* in his history of the idea of
freedom. Instead of 'popular sovereignty' (*Volkssouveränität*), Droysen would

adopt the formula 'sovereignty of the nation' (*Souveränität der Nation*), popularized by the national-liberal politician Heinrich von Gagern (1799–1880).[25] Droysen's critique of the glorification of the people (*Volk*) as a quasi-natural and therefore good principle of political organization is consistent with his reckoning of popular sovereignty as a 'monstrous idea'.[26] In the same vein, at the National Assembly in 1849 he strongly opposed a proposal to introduce universal suffrage – or in his words, 'the absurdity of the unrestricted vote'.[27] He did not see popular elections as a means for political participation and the exercise of citizenship rights, but rather as occasion for political instability.

In the end, however, it is important to recall that Droysen's main adversaries were neither the left-liberals nor the democrats. As indicated above, his national-liberal views did frequently clash with left-liberals' emphasis on basic rights and the principle of popular sovereignty cherished by democrats. But in hindsight, the conflict between national-liberals, left-liberals, and democrats in mid nineteenth-century Germany (during the National Assembly debates of 1848–49) was about means more than ends. Though with different emphases, all three groups pursued the same general aims: establishment of the German national state and expansion of human freedom. By this token, their common enemies comprised the Austrians and other local patriots, who were never persuaded that German political fragmentation was a problem worth tackling (by setting up a strong unified state). Confronted by opponents of the very idea of political unification, even Droysen could come to relativize his normally acid opinion of liberals and democrats – and at least once he admitted that it had been a mistake not to join forces with them.[28]

Of course, Droysen's political ideas were – as ideas always are – inextricably bound to his own time, to the experiences and expectations in play during the last two thirds of the nineteenth century in the German political arena. The extent to which they should be understood in connection with the future history of German nationalism, particularly the Third Reich and the Holocaust, is a matter that not only merits cautious treatment but also serves investigative purposes different from those I am pursuing here. Still, it is worth mentioning that Droysen never suggested that Germany should follow the path of territorial expansionism.[29] Moreover, he positioned himself as decidedly opposed to discrimination against Jews during the *Antisemitismus-Streit* triggered in 1879 (by the publication of a text written by Heinrich von Treitschke, which asserted for instance that 'the Jews are our misfortune').[30] What is indeed easier to ascertain is that Droysen, a historian with strong theoretical and idealistic bindings, did not lack political realism. When German national unification finally materialized (through 1864 and 1866) with the foundation of the German Reich in 1871, the general shape of the new state was in many important points coincident with his former projects.[31]

Theory versus Practice

If Droysen's theory and didactics of historical knowledge are abstracted from their concrete political and religious contents, then it is uncomplicated to posit that the notion of historical thinking – which I have been considering as an innovative answer to the problem of the justification of historiography – is universalist in its potential applications. Historical thinking, thus understood, can relate to any kind of history, any level of historical learning and any type of historical 'learner'. This would support the conclusion that, at least in principle, historical thinking is a general form of thinking that anyone can apply to any kind of subject matter. This conclusion is what leads me to associate Droysen's didactics of historical thinking with universalism, which of course I count as a positive feature here.

Nevertheless, Droysen's political thought and opinions are also linked to a particularistic horizon of expectations centred on the ideal of German national unification by a robust power. It is unsurprising, then, that significant tensions emerge if the postulates of his historical theory are compared with the politics of history by which he attempted to apply them. As a matter of fact, even Droysen's theoretical texts hold evidence of certain obstacles to the universalization of historical thinking. In the *Historik* lectures, for instance, he connects to the notion of historical thinking the very significant idea that human beings partake in the 'work of history' (*geschichtliche Arbeit*). This metaphor has an undeniable Hegelian flavour, pointing to history as a progressive, endless work that human beings join in, each time against the backdrop of a specific arrangement of 'ethical powers'. In line with that metaphor, Droysen designates human individuals as 'history's workers' (*Arbeiter der Geschichte*), further classifying them into 'handymen' (*Handlager*) on the one hand, and 'artificers' (*Werkmeister*) on the other. The former are constrained by a smallish perspective that prevents them from perceiving the historical nature of human things. They merely pursue their petty life aims, unconscious of the 'historical work' they are performing thereby.[32] Only the 'artificers', Droysen postulates, 'know what is going on in the day-to-day activity; only they know that it goes beyond the ephemeral day's work, and that the smallest things are also knots in the great fabric of history'. According to Droysen, they know it because they have learned to think historically. For the same reason, it is up to them to guarantee the continuity of the historical process. Only they can properly perceive humankind's historical development, so only they are actually responsible for the preservation of history's precious outputs and for the proper continuation of the historical movement. Hence, strictly speaking, only the actions conducted by 'artificers' really matter, for only they can make or unmake history. 'Filled with the great connections of historical things, the artificer recognises the past in its direction, realising and shaping the future with a creative intuition.'[33]

Interestingly, by connecting history's 'artificers' to the ability to think historically, Droysen introduces a major transformation to Hegel's famous theory of 'world-historical individuals'. For Hegel, these were distinguished as the instruments through which the 'cunning of reason' operates, whereas Droysen, with his softer approach to the issue of historical necessity, places much more emphasis on (at least some) individuals' capacities and freedom to shape the historical world.[34] But the most important point in this discussion of 'historical work' and 'historical workers' is that upon asking who, for Droysen, should undergo the learning of historical thinking, we find an answer that definitely is not socially all-embracing. Right after delivering his decisive statement on historical thinking,[35] Droysen remarks that the bearers of historical thinking should not be only historians but 'anyone who, theoretically or practically, had to do with the shaping of the ethical powers'.[36] Here he connects historical thinking to the lifeworld situated beyond academic practice. In so doing, he ensures that historiography will remain a practical knowledge that delivers the main frame of reference for all who are able to influence the course of history. But the answer he gives to the question of *who* can be a subject of historical thinking is nonetheless restrictive. For him, the shapers of the ethical powers can only be statesmen, military officers and university professors. In any case, they would not be 'ordinary' men, and probably not women.

These practical exclusions clearly show some of the limits and internal contradictions of the universalism of historical thinking. But also perceivable are certain rather 'external' contradictions between theory and practice (that is, theory of historical knowledge and learning on the one hand, and the practice of historical inquiry and writing on the other). Lying midway between political thought and historical theory, Droysen's political historiography is the main field in which limits to his groundbreaking didactics of historical thinking can be sought.

From the beginnings of his career as a classical philologist onwards, Droysen forcefully amalgamated his political hopes and activism with his scholarly work. Even his very first major work, the *History of Alexander the Great,* holds plenty of evidence of that. Indeed, the German Question – as Otto Hintze argued – was meaningfully situated in the background of that text.[37] In the course of Droysen's narrative, analogies with the then current German political fragmentation abound. Droysen interpreted ancient Greek history as the history of a struggle for political unification. Before Macedonian rule, he argued, ancient Greeks – exactly like modern Germans – formed a politically disintegrated nation, a cultural and linguistic community divided into mini-states. Only after Philip II (382–336 BC) and especially his son, Alexander, did that situation change. Droysen notes that in face of war against the Persians, Philip managed to promote a unification of the Greek states.[38] Supported by the new political institutions founded by his father, Alexander then massively expanded the area under Greek cultural and political dominance, hence paving the way connecting ancient and modern freedom.

Droysen's *History of Alexander the Great* is clearly more than an inquiry into Alexander's political trajectory and its impact on the ancient world. It is also a historical-philosophical and political-educational case study of how to tackle political fragmentation. As such, it clearly projects a contemporary problem into the past. For Droysen, ancient Greeks faced the same political difficulty that contemporary Germans were facing, and by showing how the former dealt with it, he surely aimed to inspire the latter to think and act so as to encourage the unification of Germany. Droysen's message here is clear: just as only political unification under Macedonian rule could have saved Greece, only unification under Prussian leadership could save contemporary Germany. The Hellenistic system, founded after Alexander defeated the Persians, was a product of the same kind of audacity that, in Droysen's view, had to be pursued if Germany was to become a unified national state. It becomes evident here that the book subliminally conveyed a political message coded in a language that Droysen himself rejected as obsolete in his theoretical texts: the language of historical examples.

Nevertheless, only after he shifted his attention from antiquity to modern political history did he abandon a discreet approach to the German Question in favour of a more direct one. In the *Lectures on the Wars of Freedom,* which he read and published in Kiel during the final years of the pre-March period (*Vormärz,* 1830–1848), that shift is automatically sensed in the choice of subject. But Droysen did not mind declaring his intentions. He introduced the text by affirming that it was an expression of his love for the fatherland and a justification of his creed on it.[39] The general outlines of the *Lectures* have already been discussed,[40] so it suffices to mention that even though the book narrates, explains and evaluates events across the Western world between 1776 and 1815, it very much remains a book written by a German scholar for the German public. It is safe to say that its aim was to provide a historical foundation for the political programme that Droysen thought Prussia and other German countries should pursue.[41] Its main thesis is that what the revolution had been to France was equivalent to what the Prussian state reforms conducted between 1807 and 1819 by Karl Freiherr vom Stein (1757–1831) and Karl August Fürst von Hardenberg (1750–1822) had been to Germany. Both events emblematized two different ways of modernizing politics, and Droysen was adamant that the German countries had no option but to follow the second path. He regarded the time of the political, administrative, economic and social reforms initiated shortly after the Prussian defeat of Napoleon in 1807 as modern Germany's golden era. However, the anti-liberal Carlsbad decrees of 1819 had finally buried that glorious age, and ever since, Droysen held, Germany's political development had been characterized by its incompleteness.[42] The absence he felt most deeply was the lack of a unified German national state. With his book, he thus intended to convince his readership of the unsatisfactoriness of the then existing state of affairs. For him, following the pause imposed in 1819, Germany's historical development should finally proceed forwards, though in a 'calm way' more suited to its 'historical fundaments'.[43]

It is thus apparent that Droysen interpreted the era of the Prussian reforms as a historical example and the men who had led it as role models for contemporary Prussia and its major political actors. This exemplary function was embedded in his interpretation of Prusso-German history and, as I will show in the following, would only be more distinct later on in the *Life of Count York von Wartenburg* and the *History of Prussian Politics*. For Droysen, the Prussian reforms had a paradigmatic value: they symbolized the kind of political action he would have liked the Prussian political elite of his own time to adopt. In a sense, Droysen researched and wrote contemporary history to demonstrate the historical necessity and feasibility of the reform programme by which he intended to link the present he perceived with the future he desired.[44] In the end he highlights the Prussian reforms as historical examples, but in any case he was neither merely calling for a return to good old times nor claiming the superiority of that epoch in comparison to his present. He actually wanted his historical example to inspire a continuation of the developmental work initiated in the times of Stein and Hardenberg: 'We should not overestimate the successes of those years: their merits are not in what was then achieved, but rather in what was deemed achievable'.[45]

In numerous passages above, I have suggested that the genetic sense of history developed from the late eighteenth century on does not harmonize well with the traditional argument that histories convey models of action to be imitated. Droysen's case shows, however, that complex arrangements between the old exemplarity and the modern focus on singularity, development and historicity could still persist. By the same token, it also shows how complicated it was to conciliate methodology, didactics, historiography and political activism in nineteenth-century Germany.

Political Historiography as Opinion-Making

Two years after the publication of the *Lectures on the Wars of Freedom,* Germany seemed to be moving in the direction Droysen had anticipated and wished for. As the 1848 Revolution culminated in the formation of a National Assembly invested with the task of deliberating on a pan-German constitution, he thought that the time was ripe for national rebuilding and decided to take an active part in it. He had been engaged in the Schleswig-Holstein Question since his move to Kiel in 1840. This conflict over the sovereignty over the two duchies, which pitted Denmark against certain German states, was one of the most complex struggles in Europe's entire diplomatic history. In fact, it was so intricate that the British statesman Lord Palmerston (1774–1865) is quoted as saying in the 1860s that only three people were really able to understand it fully: Prince Albert, who was already dead by then; a German professor who had gone mad; and Palmerston himself, who unfortunately had since forgotten all about it.[46] Anyway, Droysen's engagement opposing the Danish territorial claims in the 1840s brought him close to local political networks in Holstein, a decisive circumstance in his election as representative to the Frankfurt Parliament in 1848. Subsequent events, however, took a very different direction from the one he desired. Particularly after the Prussian king Friedrich Wilhelm IV refused the kaiser's crown, the expectations the National Assembly had raised for German unification were definitively frustrated.

Nonetheless, the Frankfurt Parliament remained the most crucial stage for those of Droysen's generation who strove for the cause of the German national state. In general, a considerable change of emphasis marked Droysen's political ideas from 1848 onwards. They became not only more realistic and bellicose, but also more centred on Prusso-German interests, as well as more supportive of the notion of a strong state – all qualities that were already latent in several of his pre-1848 texts.[47] Droysen himself was quite aware of this change of emphasis, declaring in 1857 that if there was any lesson to be learned from the experience of the revolution and from the National Assembly, it was that 'one must look at the concept of state more closely than has hitherto been the case'.[48] However, the radicalization of these qualities led to tension in the increasingly conservative atmosphere that followed the National Assembly's disintegration, especially after November 1850, when Prussia and Austria signed the Agreement of Olmütz, under which the former gave up every residual claim it had to leadership of the German states.

It was within this unfavourable context that Droysen shifted from politics back to historiography. Self-reflecting on his post-1848 situation, he once called himself a 'Prussian *in partibus*', a Prussian in a land of unbelievers. Vis-à-vis 'Prussia's misery', he reasoned that he could do nothing but stick to his Prusso-German ideals and propagate them through his writing and teaching.[49] His use of the term 'propagate' (*propagandieren*) indicates that he was hardly burying his activism for the cause of a national state led by Prussia. Instead, after his somewhat failed parliamentary experience, he let his political energies flow into his historical work with unprecedentedly great intensity. From then on, he researched and wrote on political history more than ever, so as to deliver political instruction and influence strategic sectors of the public opinion.[50]

Droysen's shift to a form of historiography designed to directly serve political purposes is documented by his two last major books, both published after 1848, the *Life of York* and the *History of Prussian Politics*. Though I will discuss some important general features of these books here, I am unable to analyse them extensively. In any case, the importance of these books probably lies, as Robert Handy claimed, 'less in their contents than in their concepts',[51] so a summary interpretation of their general interpretative architecture may suffice for my purposes.

The Life of Field Marshal Count York von Wartenburg is, to begin with, the biography of a military commander who became notable during the Prusso-German war of liberation (1813–1815). Droysen's intention was to honour and 'renew' (*erneuern*) the memory of a great man who, for him, embodied old Prussian virtues like strength and loyalty, and had contributed significantly to rebuilding Prussia after the catastrophic defeat of 1807.[52] In fact, Yorck's status as a Prussian national hero was due to his signing the agreement known as the Convention of Tauroggen (now Tauragė, in Lithuania) with Russia in December 1812. Some months earlier, Napoleon's France had invaded Russia, helped by troops from allied and subjected countries. The invasion was turning into a fiasco, so Yorck, who was stationed with his troops in East Prussia trying to block the advance of the Russians, decided to let them pass. In doing so, he disobeyed superior orders and opened himself to a charge of treason that could have cost his life. But Yorck's insubordination ended up sparking popular mobilizations against French domination in many German areas and finally moved the Prussian king, Friedrich Wilhelm III (1770–1840), towards reversing his policy of collaboration with Napoleon.[53] That move became the starting point of the Prusso-German war of liberation to which Droysen, as already seen,[54] ascribed considerable world-historical meaning.

Marshal Yorck clearly lacked the historical rank of the other political leader whose biography Droysen wrote, namely, Alexander. Yet, contrary to what has been recently argued, the obvious difference in reputation between the generally known Alexander and the less renowned Yorck does not correspond to Droysen's differentiation between history's artificers and handymen.[55] Indeed, Droysen's value system divides human beings past and present into those who are no more than pawns in the game of universal history and great men with an active share in historical development. But one need not be an Alexander to fall into the second category. Actually, had Droysen thought otherwise, then he would have had no reason to plead for the learning of historical thinking, which ultimately would have been possible for only some dozen people in all of world history. As already mentioned, Droysen's politics of historical thinking targeted not only political leaders but also public officials, intellectuals and military officers. According to him, individuals performing those social functions should have a good sense of history precisely because their actions were supposed to impact the historical process. This means that Droysen saw them, too, as artificers. As regards the specific case of Yorck, I have already shown that the wars of liberation were a rather central event in Droysen's general view of the historical process, where they surely were of a magnitude comparable to that of the wars of Alexander. And certainly Yorck's momentous decision in Tauroggen was crucial for the deflagration of the German upheaval against France: without his actions, things might have turned out very differently. Therefore it would be mistaken to see him as an interchangeable historical actor or to assume that Droysen came close to seeing him this way.

Droysen started the research for the *Life of York* some years before 1848. His main sources were Yorck's personal documents – which the family of the deceased marshal made available to him – as well as talks with contemporary witnesses of the narrated events.[56] The biography of Yorck was re-edited eight times in Droysen's lifetime, and it was probably Droysen's most read book. A fifth of its contents are dedicated to Yorck's life prior to 1813, whereas its remaining pages concentrate on Yorck's actions during the liberation wars.[57] When the book was first published, in 1851–52 (originally in three volumes), it surely served as a foil whereby readers could contrast their eventual disappointment in the present with what Droysen regarded as the most significant segment of Prussia's past. Yorck's Prussia had commanded a pan-German upheaval against a foreign occupation, and Droysen implicitly suggested that it was this kind of leadership attitude that was wanting in the Prussia of Friedrich Wilhelm IV.

It is, moreover, interesting that the book on Marshal Yorck and Droysen's previous books were not addressed to the same audiences. The earlier works were intended for the educated public in general, whereas the *Life of York* speaks primarily to Prussian army officials. Retrospectively explaining his motivations for writing the book, Droysen confessed that he had not been interested in Yorck as a single individual but only as a type. He focused on Yorck's actions during the wars of liberation as a way of showing 'what is essential to the Prussian army, and what it cannot lose'.[58] Friedrich Meinecke argued that in the *Life of York,* Droysen confused the task of historical biography with that of general history.[59] This was why Droysen consciously avoided mentioning several issues, chiefly concerning private life, that had potential to sully Yorck's reputation. What the historical Yorck did, apart from his historical role in the Prussian army, did not really matter to Droysen:[60] 'it did not belong to history', as he told one of his former students in 1884.[61]

Obviously, Droysen deliberately selected, omitted and interpreted facts according to the patriotic sense of history he espoused. His main character, Yorck, was little more than a pretext for talking about the military history of Prussia during those years that he so cherished. As a result, Droysen ended up with a seemingly paradoxical type of biography marked by what may be called a 'de-individualizing' approach, that is, an approach to the life trajectory of past individuals in which individuality is at best secondary.[62] As a matter of fact, in the *Life of York,* Droysen employed scholarly research and historical representation as political instruments. He wrote less about the historical Yorck than about the Yorck he thought could inspire the Prussian military to make history; that is, he worked out a model to be imitated in the present. Even more than in his books on Hellenism and the *Freiheitskriege,* here Droysen invested his historiography with an exemplary function.

He did the same in his *History of Prussian Politics.* Droysen worked for some thirty years on this unfinished project, which ultimately comprised around 7,600 pages distributed among fourteen volumes. The books tell the history of the Prussian state from the early fifteenth century until 1756 (the beginning of the Seven Years' War). They were accompanied by more than twenty other publications, such as complementary investigations and compilations of primary sources.[63] Droysen's original plan was, again, to focus on the period from 1780 to 1813 (and probably beyond). He intended to elaborate an account of Prussia's contemporary political history based on official sources, an enterprise that the inaccessibility of the Prussian state archive had hitherto deterred. In the end, he too was unable to obtain access to the files, but in compensation he was authorized to use documents from former periods. Ultimately, this is why he expanded his time frame back into the fifteenth century.[64]

The premise of the *History of Prussian Politics* was that ever since Emperor Sigismund (1368–1437) granted the House of Hohenzollern hereditary control over the Margravate of Brandenburg, in 1411, Prussia had been entrusted with the historical mission of accomplishing German unification. 'What founded this [Prussian] state', Droysen affirmed right in the preface, 'what sustains and drives it, is a historical necessity, if I may so express myself.'[65] The historical necessity he was referring to was, of course, Germany's political unification. According to Droysen, of all the German states, only Prussia was invested with a 'calling for the whole'—a German vocation. Droysen presented Prussian history as the history of the policies that either embraced or neglected this supreme mission. Every time Prussia embraced it, it acted according to its own essence and historical necessity; every time it did not, it became 'weak, declining, close to collapse'.[66] Here Droysen clearly projected into the past what he wished Prussia's unifying performance to be in his present. Having assumed that the whole of Prussian history since the early fifteenth century was about the struggle to fulfil that historical task, Droysen narrated the ups and downs of Prussia's 'German mission' accordingly, in fourteen volumes. In the present, Prussia was dormant in regard to its greatness and the historical task such greatness entailed. Therefore, Prussia needed to be awakened. Droysen's interpretation of the history of the Prussian state was clearly based on a teleological scheme. He postulated that the ultimate goal governing the existence of the Prussian state was Germany's unification, and consequently he saw German-national history as a continuation of Brandenburg-Prussian history. Having presupposed this sense of continuity, he was able to assume that Germany's and Prussia's interests were one and the same, which led him to consider every diplomatic and military action of the Prussian state as something that moved the German cause forward or backwards.[67]

Indeed, the *History of Prussian Politics* was, as Nippel put it, 'a stillborn scientific enterprise'. It enthused neither the general public nor even those historians whose political inclinations were the same as Droysen's. Meanwhile, over the book's thirty years of editorial history and especially after German unification really began, Droysen's general concept, his obsession with the idea of Prussia's historical vocation, his arguments on the ethical traits of the Prussian state and his fixation on foreign policy increasingly seemed outdated.[68] In addition, further factual research – most of it conducted by Droysen's ex-students – would soon definitively refute Droysen's assertions that Prussian rulers such as the Great Elector, Friedrich I, and Friedrich II, the Great, acted out of a sense of German national patriotism.[69]

Although he based his account on very extensive historical research, Droysen made no attempt to disguise the political message he wanted his *History of Prussian Politics* to transmit. By arguing that Prussia had always been committed to the German cause, he was trying to favourably sensitize Prussian rulers and political elites to the little-German project of nation-building.[70] At the same time, he was attempting to convey to them historical images from glorious segments of the Prussian past, and expecting those images to be taken as guides to a reawakening of the German national cause. The political bias and one-sidedness of his book's general perspective were widely taken for granted among its analysts. What has not yet been sufficiently stressed is that the book epitomizes a return to the same old exemplary function that Droysen criticized in his theoretical texts.

Historical Thinking and the State

Droysen's political commitment to the Prusso-German national cause formed the cornerstone of his political thought and permeated his political historiography decisively. But he went beyond writing books, academic articles and newspaper texts on past and present political issues connected to his utopia of a strong national state led by Prussia. In 1859, after he had spent nearly two decades teaching at the regional universities of Kiel and Jena, he was granted a history professorship at the prestigious University of Berlin. The new position linked him to the centre of Prussia's political power, and from then on he tried to influence state affairs directly through personal contacts with the Prussian royal family and high-ranking politicians.

The best testimonies of these attempts are private memoranda that he wrote throughout the 1860s on the political use of historical knowledge. These memoranda very clearly convey both Droysen's view of state and his under-standing of the practical roles that historians and historical scholars should play with regard to the state and the national community. In one of these texts – written in 1860 and probably addressed to the then minister of cultural af-fairs, Moritz August von Bethmann-Hollweg (1795–1877)[71] – Droysen articu-lates his opinion that Prussia should not ignore the important contribution that historical studies could offer to the management of state affairs. He warns that Prussia's neighbours, Austria, Belgium, France, and Bavaria, were already conscious of the mounting strategic importance of historical studies, and insists that Prussia should follow the same trend.[72] According to him, the obvious fact that the state was not new meant Prussia needed historical studies to properly instruct its politicians and bureaucrats. The state, he argues, 'is rooted in the past'; therefore it is important that state agents develop an understanding of things past.[73] Bearing this circumstance in mind, Droysen recalls the old topos that the 'statesman is the historian in practice', explaining that statesmen, who can adequately perform their duties only if they are able to understand how the state came into its current shape, need a genuine sense of history to be able to think and act in favour of historical development, not against it. For him, historical thinking – the way of thinking that modern historical studies exercise and convey – is thus a matter of strategic importance in the conduct of state affairs.

In the 1860 memorandum (as in others that followed), Droysen not only expresses his view of historical studies' contribution to the management of the state, but also details some concrete proposals for accomplishing this contribu-tion. For instance, he calls for a reform of the Prussian archive system, suggest-ing that the latter should become much more than a simple storehouse for old documents of no use in day-to-day political business. Droysen held that Prus-sian archives should rather be part of a 'historical office' (*historische Büreau*), an institution set up to provide public officers with valuable historical information that could be applicable in several realms of state administration.[74]

Certainly Droysen was aware that history, as researched and taught at the universities, exerted its main influence on the state and on national issues through its intersections with the school system. In the German university landscape, history chairs had since long existed at faculties of arts (*Philoso-phische Fakultäten*), which traditionally prepared students for the higher, career-oriented faculties of medicine, law and theology. However, since the 1810s faculties of arts had gained importance, not least because they had started to replace faculties of theology as the main institutions where secondary teachers were trained.[75] The secularization of education was opening up career paths traditionally reserved for theologians to philologists, mathematicians and histo-rians, and in this context Droysen maintained that history education at schools should remain closely connected to professional historical research and writing. This link between the history taught in schools and the history produced by university-trained historians meant, for him, primarily that history classes should not aim mainly to convey 'names, numbers and facts from political history' to the students.[76] The aim of history education in schools should instead be attuned to the circumstance that historical science's greatest achievement was not the immense repository of factual knowledge it pushed forward, but rather the establishment of a 'method' for understanding facts[77] – in other words, a way of thinking about them and onwards from them. History education should thus promote the subjective development of historical thinking. It should be a process of general *Bildung*. No doubt, this definition comprises a universalistic and inclusive but also abstract idea of humankind, evidenced on this particular point by Droysen's lack of differentiation between, for instance, the humanistic *Gymnasium* and the other school types ranked below it. Here Droysen was, again, following a broad path paved by Wilhelm von Humboldt. As the head of the Prussian office for educational affairs between 1809 and 1810, Humboldt had initiated reforms in Prussia's education system that aimed, among other things, to issue a general school curriculum that would sponsor individual *Bildung* without regard to social or estates-based differences.[78]

In practice, however, general *Bildung* was not the only goal Droysen linked to historical education. In many of his political writings, *Bildung* coexists with another important task that he describes as 'popular' or 'national education' (*Volkserziehung*).[79] In discussing the education of the *Volk* or the nation, Droysen presented a special form of historical learning as an indispensable requirement for the realization of the Prusso-German national project he endorsed. For him, history classes and the reading of historical texts could and should function as tools to improve the sense of national allegiance he held as necessary for the consolidation of a unified German state. They constitute a key dimension of the education that Droysen connected to the aim of transforming 'human beings into a *Volk,* the citizens of a state into a nation'.[80] The Prussian state, according to him, had frequently neglected this dimension, thus giving rise to a deplorable situation. This tendency should be countered, for, as Droysen avows, when a people 'holds such a glorious past as that of the Prussian state', there is no better means to stimulate patriotic devotion than teaching national history in schools.[81]

Droysen's arguments on the aims of historical education echo ideals developed earlier, at the beginning of the nineteenth century, by a generation of educational reformers who reshaped German learning and scholarly institutions after 1806. These ideals emerged from the sense that Prussia's defeat against Napoleonic France had spawned a 'crisis of social cohesion' that clamoured for innovative solutions. By then, certain philosophers, pedagogues and politicians had concluded that the many different parts and levels of Prussian society should be brought into a unified whole by means of 'national education'. This idea of using education to strengthen bonds between individuals and the national community incorporated the humanistic ideal of general *Bildung*. *Bildung* and national education were actually complementary, since the former was also supposed to reinforce the cohesion of the social fabric. *Bildung* was intended to be a form of education that stimulated the overcoming of egotism – that is, the personal inclinations perceived as a main source of conflict between the individual and the state.[82] It would do so by connecting the individual with the most significant cultural results of human general history – by elevating the 'empirical self' (*empirisches Ich*) onto the 'self of humankind' (*Selbst der Menschheit*), to recall Droysen's own terms.[83] Nevertheless, during the nineteenth century within the German space, a clear distinction unarguably arose between a national-oriented 'education for citizenship' and a cosmopolitan and universalistic 'education for humanity'. And clearly, the former type of education tended to gain ever more importance.[84]

A very important document related to the ideal of national education is Johann Gottlieb Fichte's (1762–1814) *Addresses to the German Nation*. Delivered in 1808, exactly at the time of the Napoleonic rule over Prussia, Fichte's *Addresses* established the combination of universalistic anthropology and German patriotism that by mid-century would so strongly influence Droysen and the Prussian school of historians.[85] Inspired by Johann Heinrich Pestalozzi's (1746–1827) pedagogical approach, Fichte devised guidelines for a renewal of the educational system in German-speaking countries. His paramount aim was to stimulate Germany's reawakening as a political and cultural force. He held that this could be accomplished by conveying patriotic values in schools, which should bind German society together, enable political unification and, finally, help shield the German territories from prospective foreign invasions.[86] Fichte's proposals combine philosophical idealism with national and democratic aspirations, and it is plausible to say that they, too, aimed to minimize social differences, especially between the educated middle class and the working class. His proposed national education was intended to beget a community of patriotic values beyond and against all social differences. This is why he explicitly avoided defining his project in such terms as 'popular education' (*Völkererziehung*), which traditionally referred to the education of the lower classes.[87]

But Fichte's project for 'national education' (*National-Erziehung*) was also rooted in the sense that Germany had a cultural mission vis-à-vis the world.[88] 'If you sink', he warns in his last address to the German-speaking community, 'then all of humankind will sink as well, and there will be no hope of recovery'.[89] This sense of a German mission that Fichte expressed in his *Addresses* is fundamental to understanding Droysen's proclivity for turning historical knowledge into an instrument in the service of the Prusso-German cause. In line with this sense, Droysen justified historical studies' contribution to Prussian state and war affairs not with strategic reasoning, but with an argument emanating directly from his most intimate historical-philosophical assumptions and historical-religious creeds – his conviction that Prussia was invested with the historical task of unifying the German states.[90] Additionally, he believed that the emergence of a unified German state would have an important ethical impact on the then existing European system of states.[91] Ultimately, Droysen was convinced that Prussia had a historical mission to unify Germany, and that Germany in turn had the historical mission of ensuring the continuity of the historical process, thus saving the rest of the world from 'materialism', scientism and modern despotism.

This fervent belief in the historical role of a someday unified Germany, especially after 1849, contributed to Droysen's near embrace of a Machiavellian conception of state. In 1850, shortly before his move from Kiel to Jena, his lectures on 'practical politics' developed a theory of state featuring a new emphasis on power issues, as well as a devaluation of liberalism. These lectures were grounded in a scholarly tradition of lectures on political theory based on Aristotelian notions that had existed in German universities since at least the late fourteenth century.[92] By the mid-nineteenth century, Friedrich Christoph Dahlmann's (1785–1860) political theory was the most well-known exemplar of that tradition.[93] During the pre-March period, Dahlmann's political theory provided the framework for those who attempted to combine the ideal of national unification with the liberal aspiration to a constitution that would protect basic individual rights from state intervention. After the failure of the National Assembly's project, many German intellectuals started to keep an increasing distance from the national-liberalism espoused by Dahlmann, embracing instead what they regarded as a more 'realistic' view of state affairs. The term 'practical', which Droysen used to qualify his own reflections on politics, already points to that tendency towards realism or political pragmatism.[94]

Unlike Dahlmann's *Politics,* whose main issue, in line with the enduring Aristotelian heritage, was the ideal constitution, Droysen's political theory takes the leitmotif of power. Accordingly, the science of politics would comprise knowledge of means, relations and disruptions of state power.[95] Power is hence, for Droysen, the state's main feature, and the essence of politics is conveyed by the following tautology: 'The state – no matter how it is shaped or in whose hands it may be – rules because it has power, and it is ruler in order to have power.'[96] According to Droysen, the highest purpose served by the state is that of 'its own internal and external self-preservation'.[97] Here he distances himself somewhat from German political thought's traditional emphasis on the state as an 'ethical' agent that facilitates the advancement of human freedom, and hence also from the perspective he himself had adopted in the 1830s and 1840s. As an intellectual heir of Kant and Hegel, Droysen was aware of the shift, but he nonetheless justified his new view by recalling that his was not a theory of how the state should look, but rather a purely descriptive theory of state.

He stressed that he was not recommending that states should hold the end of self-preservation above all other possible ends and means, but rather simply establishing facts that could not be unmade by mere denunciations.[98] In any case, Droysen's focus on power, his emphasis on a strong state and his choice of a Machiavellian political theory undeniably remain in tension with the humanism and universalism that informed other segments of his thought.

Downplaying Universalism

In light of that general conception of state, Droysen's attempt to enlist historical thinking in the service of a political cause is less surprising. In Droysen's entire opus, perhaps the strongest statement concerning historiography's political instrumentalization is a passage in which he refers to historical studies as 'undoubtedly belong[ing] to the realm of [the states'] intellectual readiness for war (*intellektuelle Kriegsbereitschaft*)'.[99] No doubt, the practical function for historical knowledge that Droysen is proposing here is difficult to harmonize with the universalistic anthropology underlying his own theoretical notion of historical thinking. This tension between theory and practice even led him once to partially critique the very notion of general education (*allgemeine Bildung*). In his memoranda from the 1860s (all of which, it seems, were addressed to high-ranking Prussian office holders), he repeatedly complains that Prussian historical scholars disregarded the history of the Prussian state in their research and teachings. One of the reasons for that, he explains, was that the prevailing understanding of education was only minimally centred on national issues. Here Droysen does not entirely reject the universalism embedded in the idea of *Bildung,* but rather regrets what had to be faced as one of its collateral effects, which he describes as the German propensity to devalue its own cultural heritage and idealize the cultural accomplishments of other times and nations.[100] Prussia, he claims, had stimulated general education more than any other state, and this was indeed a valuable effort. However, he deplores the outcome of this effort as the diffusion of a 'cosmopolitan way of emptiness' instead of a desirable increase of popular loyalty to the Prusso–German national cause.[101]

In Droysen's time and place, many other historical authors shared the problem of choosing between, on the one hand, a universalism linked to the idea of humankind developed in the era of the Enlightenment and, on the other, the rising particularism spreading out of feelings of national belongingness. To be true, some of them believed they had already solved it. The late Ranke, for instance, introduced his last major work with the remark that 'world history would dwindle into fantasies and philosophemes if it broke away from the firm ground of national histories.... The history of humankind emerges within the nations.'[102] Ranke reasons that there is no contradiction between the history of humankind and national histories because there is no history of humankind as such. He claims, therefore, that 'the nations' are not particularistic communities but, to the contrary, would rather work as privileged bearers of the ideal of humankind. National communities would then correspond to the highest practicable form of universalism.

In the 1830s, Dahlmann, who was closer to the Enlightenment tradition than the late Ranke, had developed a more optimistic approach to the problem. He believed that particular nation-states, while undergoing their historical development, were doing the groundwork for the 'great collective work of humankind'.[103] Evidently, Dahlmann sees no contradiction whatsoever between nation states and humankind. The nationalism noticeable in his conception of state is unproblematically articulated with a universalistic idea of humankind as a community formed by all nations and human beings.

Droysen dealt with the same issue, but his writings, taken as a whole, reveal a heightened tension between anthropological universalism and the particularism of his Prusso-German patriotism. In fact, he forcefully repudiates universalism in its pure and abstract form, as his deprecation of Enlightenment ideals such as 'humanity', 'philanthropy', 'fraternity' and 'human rights' very clearly shows.[104] By doing so, he actually reinforced a tendency that originated in the first decade of the nineteenth century, just after Prussia's defeat against France, when many historical authors started to reproach the cosmopolitan values and feelings emphasized in Enlightenment pedagogy for failing to provide adequate spiritual support to the German military reaction.[105] But Droysen, regarding what he once called a nation's 'world-historical disposition', clearly indicates that certain national communities – the German above all – were not, in his view, 'unilaterally national'. These communities embodied universal values, and therefore could not be said to be merely particularistic.[106] He saw German nationalism as indeed automatically filled with universal content, and he corroborated this belief by arguing that the German countries had been the vanguard of humankind's cultural development ever since the Protestant Reformation.[107]

Even so, despite Droysen's attempts to theoretically reconcile humankind and nation state, after 1849 the former clearly tended to fade away in both his political thought and historiography. It is, then, plausible to conclude that when faced with the dilemma of choosing between his theoretical-anthropological universalism and his national-political ideals, Droysen many times stuck to the latter, sometimes even to the detriment of the former. Even though Droysen considered historiography and politics to be intermingled, he often put politics above knowledge and used knowledge as an instrument of politics to boot. As a consequence, in these cases he ended up abandoning the universalism that characterizes his didactic theory of historical thinking. This conclusion is not new. Friedrich Meinecke, who had attended Droysen's lectures and once held them in high esteem, long ago stated: 'In the single-minded determination of his [Droysen's] Prusso-German wishes and thoughts, the universal-historical range that had previously characterized his interests narrowed – albeit only with regard to his practical work and not to his spirit.'[108]

Droysen's practical downplaying of universalism and his (already discussed) tendency to resort to historical examples in his political historiography illustrate the extent to which his politics of historical thinking remains in tension with notions he himself had developed in the methodological, didactic and anthropological passages of his texts. It is a very difficult task to account for the considerable difference between Droysen the theorist of a universalistic historical thinking and Droysen the political historian who sacrificed some of his own theoretical premises to a political cause. Yet some scholars have recently attempted to carry it out. Droysen's biographer Wilfried Nippel has suggested that Droysen's historical theory was both a rationalization of the politically motivated choices that shaped his historiographical oeuvre and the product of a strategy of self-dramatization designed to sell the impression that he occupied a special place within the historians' guild and thus support his own professional ambitions.[109] According to Nippel, Droysen's theoretical reflections are thus merely sublimated politics, if not a refined form of careerism. More recently, Andreas Greiert, who indeed took Droysen's historical theory much more seriously than Nippel, has followed a similar path. Greiert criticizes Droysen for having provided legitimacy to the social and political order of his time and place, and for having rejected classical liberalism and democracy. In this regard, Greiert concludes, there is no double Droysen (the revolutionary theoretician and the reactionary politician), but only one.[110] However, as in Nippel's interpretation, that one Droysen would be the post-1849 political historian. Accordingly, Droysen's reflections on historical method, his insights into the historicity of the human world, his phenomenology of historical materials and his didactics centred on the learning of historical thinking (instead of the accumulation of facts) were no more than instruments of a strategy of sociopolitical domination.

I believe that Nippel's and Greiert's tendency to portray Droysen's theory of history as a spin-off of his practical and political agenda is reductionist, even though I also concede that they are correct to stress the significance of politics in the *Historik* lectures. In my opinion, a more convincing explanation of the tensions between theory and practice in Droysen's writings was formulated by Thomas Welskopp, who has argued that Droysen's wide-ranging theory of history can be understood as compensating for his narrow-minded historiographical practice. In this view, Droysen formulated theoretical standards that not only were incompatible with the possibilities of then contemporary historiography but also proved unattainable in his own historical works.[111] This explains why many who still regard his historical theory as containing pathbreaking and inspiring theoretical reflections seem much less enthused by his political historiography.

To a good extent, Droysen's historical theory – and here I am complementing Welskopp's interpretation with a key idea developed recently by Herman Paul – can be read as a catalogue of 'epistemic virtues'. Especially its more methodological and didactic aspects can be seen as attempting to define an ideal set of values, personal attitudes and modes of professional conduct that historians should strive to observe. In general, as Paul notes, reference to such virtues is not limited to methodological textbooks, for they are an irreducible means of orientation in the practice of professional historians. However, whether and to what extent such theorized (or idealized) virtues are really put into practice is another matter.[112] It is thus reasonable to conclude that in part, the tension between theory and practice that Droysen's works evince is in no way anomalous. Indeed, an important feature of all theories of historical method seems to be precisely that methodological precepts are never fully accomplished by historians in their research, writing and communicative practices.

This conclusion does not erase the late Droysen's fixation on the history of the Prussian state, which points to the over-politicization of his historical research and writing, as well as to a rejection of many methodological possibilities that, curiously enough, he theorized in exactly the same decades in which he wrote his *History of Prussian Politics*. But it also favours a cautious look back at the *Historik* lectures, whereupon there emerge some surprising theoretical arguments against the centrality of politics in historiography.[113] The strongest evidence here is the simple fact that Droysen speaks of the state as one 'ethical power' among many others. For Droysen, as one may recall, the 'ethical powers' correspond to the particular 'spheres' of the human world – family, religion, language, arts, science, economy and society, among others – which altogether comprise the historical method's field of application.[114] In the 1857–58 *Systematik,* having discussed all the spheres of 'ethical powers', Droysen concludes: 'We cannot deny that every [concrete] formation in such spheres has a historical nature, and hence is suited to be taken as subject of historical investigation.'[115] In the end, if 'the historical world is actually the ethical world'[116] and the ethical world comprises many other 'spheres' beyond the state, then historiography must not be necessarily about political events. In theory, historians may investigate the other realms of the ethical world as well, provided that their subjects of study relate to the development of the human mind (*Geist*) and freedom.[117] 'The domain of the historical' – to add a final confirmatory statement – 'has no borders', for 'every human relationship can be considered in a historical way and is worth remembering.'[118]

In another part of the *Historik,* Droysen complains that historians had traditionally reported on only 'a tiny part of history'. They were only interested in source materials related to political events concerning war and peace, or conflicts between church and state. But that is not enough for Droysen, who proposes that historiography 'must take the great step that will lead it to conceiving its task in a different and deeper way'. This new way comprises a new historical sensibility for social, legal, intellectual, aesthetic, religious and technical developments and phenomena – that is, towards the other 'ethical spheres'. It also includes a new kind of relationship towards historical material that differs greatly from the one that characterizes traditional political history. For Droysen, historians do not necessarily need to focus on a source's referential content. They need not always ask whether what the source 'says' is true or false, accurate or inaccurate. They can also investigate a source as an unconscious bearer of meanings generated in an even more distant past than the one that 'produced' the source. For a text may contain evidence of a deeper past, as in the case of Mother Hulda's fairy tales or Snow White, in which linger 'mythologems pertaining to another time, a time when the German tribes still had not severed themselves from the Indic Aryans'.[119] As can be seen, Droysen's theoretical reflections do not quite match the popular stereotype of the positivist scholar obsessed with establishing political facts from official sources. And the same is true of many other nineteenth-century historians who bucked the trend of common designations such as 'histoire-batailles', 'histoire événementielle' or 'histoire historisante'.[120]

At this point, it goes without saying that in the *Wars of Freedom,* the *Life of York,* and the *History of Prussian Politics,* Droysen's emphasis on only one of the 'ethical powers', namely the state, does not represent the realization of an epistemological postulate. Once again, his historical theory and his historiographical practice reveal their differences. Sebastian Manhart is probably right in arguing that Droysen actually concentrated his research and writing on state issues because he thought that in a place like the German-speaking areas of the nineteenth century –especially after the failure of 1848 – politics was the main arena for the battle among the historical forces of the time. Droysen saw the making of the German national state led by Prussia as a goal whose importance surpassed all else; hence, the other 'ethical spheres' could temporarily remain backstage. This does not imply, however, that Droysen did not accord to past or future historians the right to concentrate on spheres other than the political.[121]

This chapter has provided abundant evidence that Droysen not infrequently reduced historical thinking to an instrument of Prusso-German politics. In fact, the main concrete use of historical thinking that he developed meets few of the theoretical standards that he himself set while justifying the study of history. But there is also plenty of evidence that Droysen ascribed to historical thinking other uses and applications that went far beyond that particular one. For this reason, it is plausible to hold that he devised historical thinking not only as an instrument to be used by Prussian statesmen willing to intervene in German politics, but also as a general tool of understanding – a tool that remains open to all who intend to grasp the historicity of the world they live in.

Notes

1. The most common spelling of the name of the field marshal is 'Yorck'. I will make use of this spelling while referring to him, and reserve the spelling '*York*' (in italic) to direct references to Droysen's book on Yorck.

2. Droysen, *Briefwechsel* 2: 881 [Letter to the Electoral Committee of Kolberg, January 1867]: 'Fragen Sie und meine Wähler mich, was ich bin, wie ich stimmen werde, so sage ich: weder liberal noch konservativ, sondern preußisch, das ist deutsch, deutsch, das ist preußisch.' Droysen sent the letter to the electoral committee, but its message is addressed to both the committee and the voters of the electoral district of Kolberg.

3. Thomas Nipperdey. 1998. *Deutsche Geschichte 1866–1918*, vol. 2: *Machtstaat vor der Demokratie*, Munich: C.H. Beck, 314–317.

4. Chris Thornhill. 2007. *German Political Philosophy: The Metaphysics of Law*, London: Routledge, 140.

5. See Norberto Bobbio. 2005. *Liberalism and Democracy*, London: Verso, 12.

6. Jaeger, *Bürgerliche Modernisierungskrise und historische Sinnbildung*, 58–61.

7. Thornhill, *German Political Philosophy*, 4; James Sheehan. 1983. *German Liberalism in the Nineteenth Century*, Chicago: The University of Chicago Press, 43.

8. Droysen, *Historik* 2: 322 [Politik-Vorlesung, 1850]: 'Das Wesentliche des Staats ist[,] Macht zu sein[,] Macht nach innen und außen. Denn der höchste Zweck des Staates ist seine innere und äußere Selbsterhaltung.'

9. Droysen, *Historik* 1: 356 [Vorlesungstext, 1857]: 'Der Staat, in welcher Form, in wessen Hand er denn sei, herrscht, weil er die Macht hat, und ist Herr, um die Macht zu haben. Das ist die Summe aller Politik. Wird damit etwa die Herrschaft der rohen Gewalt proklamiert? Allerdings in niedrigen Entwicklungsstufen hat der Staat wenig oder nichts als das Attribut der Gewalt und Willkür. Aber sein Fortschreiten ist, daß er das Wesen der Macht tiefer, wahrer, sittlicher zu fassen lernt, daß er endlich in dem freien Willen des Menschen, in ihrer Freiheit, Hingebung und Begeisterung, in der höchsten Entwicklung alles Guten, Edlen, Geistigen die wahre Macht erkennt und zu organisieren lernt. So wenig ist der Begriff der Macht niedrig, roh, unsittlich, daß er vielmehr in allem wahrhaft sittlichen Funktion seine Nahrung, seine Bedingung findet.'

10. Droysen, *Briefwechsel* 2: 906 [Letter to Gustav Droysen, 29 December 1872]: 'Ist denn wirklich die Volksrepräsentation so ohne weiteres die höchste Instanz und die Autorität, nach der sich alles richten muß, damit es gut gehe? Ich dächte, die Erfahrungen in England und mehr noch in Frankreich lehren, daß die parlamentarishe Regierung nichts weniger als ein panacée ist.'

11. Droysen, *Historik* 2: 266 [Verdun-Rede, 1843]: 'Aber es ist ein unseliger Irrthum, diese drei Gewalten für trennbar zu halten in der Art, daß sie zur gegenseitigen Bewachung geeignet, ihre Trennung eine Garantie der Verfassung wäre.' For an in-depth analysis of Droysen's relative opposition to liberalism, see Robert Henry Handy. 1966. *J.G. Droysen: The Historian and German Politics in the Nineteenth Century*, Ph.D. Thesis: Georgetown University, Washington, D.C., 87–99.

12. Sybille Lewark. 1975. *Das politische Denken Johann Gustav Droysens*, Ph.D. Thesis: Eberhard-Karls-Universität zu Tübingen, 159.

13. At the time of his activity in the Frankfurt Parliament, Droysen still thought that the new German state could comprise the German-speaking parts of the Austrian empire. He moved to consistently back the lesser-German idea only in the autumn of 1848. See Lewark, *Das politische Denken Johann Gustav Droysens*, 94.

14. Handy, *J.G. Droysen*, 318–326.

15. Droysen, *Briefwechsel* 2: 881 [Letter to the Electoral Committee of Kolberg, January 1867]: 'Der Feldzug von 1866 hat es möglich gemacht, daß es endlich einmal ein Anfang praktischer deutscher Politik, der Anfang einer wahrhaft nationalen Machtbildung gemacht werden kann. Die seit den Hohenstaufen politisch tot gelegte deutsche Nation hat endlich einmal die Möglichkeit, sich zu einigen, auf ihre eigenen Füße zu stellen.... Die Waffen unseres Heeres, die Energie unserer Staatslenkung hat Norddeutschland zusammengeführt, und den Süden auf den Punkt gebracht, hinzutreten. Es gilt nur noch, dies große Ergebnis ankerfest zu machen. Das und nur das ist die Aufgabe. Ihr gegenüber scheint mir jede andere Frage untergeordnet; sie kann vertagt bleiben, bis auf die Zeit, wo wir unser Haus unter Dach haben. Dann werde ich liberal sein, so liberal, wie das entwickelte Bedürfnis unseres Volksleben fordert, und die Erhaltung des schützenden Daches gestattet, ohne irgendwelchen Servilismus gegen die Macht oben wie und das Volk unter.'

16. Droysen, *Politische Schriften*, 184 [Die Spitze des Reiches, 1848]: 'Mit allen unsern Grundrechten und Verfassungsformen ist es nichts, wenn wir nicht verstehen, unser ‹Reich› zu einer Macht zu erheben. Ja, so sehr kommt es auf Macht und nur auf Macht an, daß selbst die Freiheit werthlos ist ohne sie.' For a chronological account of Droysen's participation at the Frankfurt Parliament, and of the opinions he supported and defended in the context of parliamentary discussions, see Walter Fenske. 1930. *Johann Gustav Droysen und das deutsche Nationalstaatsproblem. Ein Beitrag zur Geschichte der Frankfurter Nationalversammlung von 1848/49*, Erlangen: Palm & Enke.

17. Lewark, *Das politische Denken Johann Gustav Droysens*, 68–71.

18. Droysen, *Briefwechsel* 2: 881 [Letter to the Electoral Committee of Kolberg, January 1867]: 'Wollen Sie einen Vertreter haben, der opponiert, der mit blendenden Einwürfen und kühnen Förderungen der Regierung Verlegenheiten bereitet, der noch einige Grundrechte und sonstige Freiheiten gelegentlich herauszuschlagen sucht, wenn auch auf die Gefahr, daß das jetzt möglich Werk darüber in Stücke geht, so wählen Sie mich nicht. Noch weniger wenn Sie die Reichsverfassung von 1849 restituiert haben wollen. Ich kenne sie, ich habe ihren ersten Entwurf mit meiner Hand geschrieben und im Verfassungsausschuß zu Frankfurt die Beratungen über dieselbe Schritt vor Schritt mitgemacht.... Wer wie ich die Vorgänge kennt, kann nicht anders als mit Mißtrauen, Mitleid oder Verachtung auf diejenigen sehen, die jetzt diese Reichsverfassung herbeisehnen, um sie den zu endlich gedeihlichem Abschluß fortschreitenden Deutschland wie einen Knüttel zwischen die Beinen zu werfen.' The constitution deliberated in Frankfurt never really came into effect. The sections on basic civil rights, though, either migrated to or served as a model for articles of both the Weimar Constitution (1917) and the current German constitution, the *Basic Law for the Federal Republic of Germany* (1949).

19. Droysen, *Politische Schriften*, 173–174 [Die ‹Frage an Österreich›, 1848]: 'Freilich es giebt eine glückliche Bornirtheit, die mit irgend welchem Princip – wie früher Legitimität, so jetzt etwa Demokratie – das verworrene Knäul der Politik lösen zu können meint. Mögen sie «von ihrem Standpunkt aus» sich für wahre Volksmänner halten, man wird sie weder beneiden noch bedauern, auch fürchten würde man sie nicht, wenn nicht das Speichellecken der Volksschranzen den derzeitigen "Souverain" noch viel gewisser, wie verderblicher verdürbe, als es je die Schmeichler der Fürsten gethan.'

20. Gangolf Hübinger. 1984. *Georg Gottfried Gervinus. Historisches Urteil und politische Kritik*, Göttingen: Vandenhoeck & Ruprecht, 187–197.

21. See Chapter 3.

22. Droysen, *Freiheitskriege* 2: 642.

23. See Chapter 3.

24. Droysen, *Freiheitskriege* 2: 642–643: 'Die Erfahrung unbeschreiblicher Niederlagen und Erhebungen muß endlich gelehrt haben, dass unter allen geschichtlichen Gründungen die dauerndsten unter allen politischen Energien die nachhaltigsten die Volkstümlichkeiten sind, denn in ihnen durchdringen sich die Elemente des menschheitlichen Daseins, Natur und Geschichte. Nicht als wäre dies «Naturwüchsige» schon an sich das Höchste und Beste und, wie es eben ist,

das allein Berechtige; die Lehre, welche sich so entscheidet, vergisst, dass ihre Definition die schlechteste Art von Volkssouveränität ergibt.'

25. Nippel, *Johann Gustav Droysen,* 94–95.

26. Droysen, *Historik* 2: 264 [Verdun-Rede, 1843]: 'Die deutsche Verfassung will nicht ruhen auf einem Vertrage zwischen Fürst und Volk, ein Gegensatz so verkehrt wie Kopf und Körper, hergebracht aus den traurigsten Zeiten des Feudalismus – sie will nicht die monströse Vorstellung der Volkssouverainität zur Grundlage haben, noch die monströsere, der Souverain, der jedesmalige, einzelne, sei der alleinige Träger und Inhaber der staatlichen Vernunft ...'

27. Droysen, *Briefwechsel* 1: 527 [Letter to Wilhelm Arendt, 10 March 1849]: 'Die Koalision der Österreicher, Baiern und Linken versuchte in vier Anläufen während letzter Woche das Wahlgesetz zweite Lesung vorher einzuschieben, die Linken in der Hoffnung, daß jene ihnen den Unsinn der unbeschränkten Wahl mit durchholen würden.'

28. Droysen, *Politische Schriften,* 181 [Die Spitze des Reiches, 1848]: 'Und wir haben vielfach geirrt; wir alle wie jeder einzelne. Wir alle vielleicht am meisten darin, daß wir uns nach dem Unterschiede von Monarchie und Republik geschieden glaubten, statt in dem Particularismus unsern gemeinsamen Feind zu erkennen.'

29. Handy, *J.G. Droysen,* 332.

30. Heinrich von Treitschke. 1879. 'Unsere Aussichten', *Preussische Jahrbücher* 44, 575. For Droysen's opinion on the *Antisemitismusstreit,* see Droysen, *Briefwechsel* 2: 938 [Letter to Heinrich von Treitschke, 16 November 1880]; Nippel, *Johann Gustav Droysen,* 289–290.

31. Handy, *J.G. Droysen,* 328.

32. Droysen, *Historik* 1: 386–387 [Vorlesungstext, 1857].

33. Droysen, *Historik* 1: 388 [Vorlesungstext, 1857]: 'Diesen Arbeitern an der Geschichte, man kann wohl sagen, den Tagelöhner und Handlangern, stehen die Werkmeister gegenüber, ich meine die, welche wissen, um was es sich auch in dem tagtäglichen Tun handelt, daß es nicht bloß Tageswerk und ephemeres Geschäft ist, sondern jedes, auch das Kleinste, eine Masche in dem großen Gewebe der Geschichte. Wie gar anders erscheinen den so Wissenden die menschlichen Dinge; wie bedeutsam und in seinem Zusammenhang verständlich auch das Kleine und scheinbar Flüchtige. Erfüllt von dem großen Zusammenhang der geschichlichen Dinge, werden sie das Vergangene in seiner Richtung erkennen und das Künftige mit schöpferischer Ahnung erfassen und gestalten. Sie werden mit Bewußtsein und frei wollend in jener Dialektik der historischen Gedanken stehen, durch sie wird sich dieselbe vollziehen.'

34. Rothacker, 'J.G. Droysens Historik', 86–87.

35. Droysen, *Historik* 1: 5 [Vorlesungstext, 1857].

36. Droysen, *Historik* 1: 5 [Vorlesungstext, 1857]: 'Historisch zu denken hat mitnichten bloß der historische Forscher oder der Geschichtsschreiber; sondern jeder, der theoretisch oder praktisch mit der Gestaltung der sittlichen Mächte zu tun hat, muß die Fähigkeit haben und üben, diese Mächte in ihren wechselnden Erscheinungen und ihrer Kontinuität zu fassen und zu erfassen.'

37. Otto Hintze. 1942. 'Johann Gustav Droysen', in Otto Hintze, *Zur Theorie der Geschichte. Gesammelte Abhandlungen,* Leipzig: Koehler & Amelang, 157. See also Hagen Schulze. 1998. *Gibt es überhaupt eine deutsche Geschichte?* Stuttgart: Reclam, 32.

38. Droysen, *Geschichte Alexander des Großen,* 13–14: 'Tiefer blickende Geister erkannten, daß das Leben des hellenischen Volkes, schon zu reich und beweglich für den engen Raum der Heimat, erst dann Einheit und Ruhe gewinnen könne, wenn es nach außen hin die hochentwikkelte Kraft versuche, und Isokrates rief mit lauten Worten die Staaten von Hellas auf, sich zum letzten Kampf gegen Asien zu vereinen. Da übernahm es König Philipp von Makedonien, und begann das große Werk, die Staaten Griechenlands zum Kriege gegen Persien zu vereinen; und man muß gestehen, daß er mit bewundrungswürdiger Gewandtheit diese mehr als herkulische Arbeit vollbracht hat'; Droysen, *Geschichte Alexander des Großen,* 18: 'So stand Phillip an der Spitze des freien Griechenlands, das, in sich zu vielbewegtem Einzelleben atomistisch aufgelöst, und, solange alle Kraft nur nach innen gewandt war, in furchtbaren Kämpfen zerrissen, doch eine

Beweglichkeit und Überfülle individuellen Lebens entwickelt hatte, die allein imstande war, die abgestorbenen Völkermassen Asiens mit einem neuen Leben zu durchgären.'

39. Droysen, *Freiheitskriege* 1: vi: 'Und noch einmal, möge die Liebe zum Vaterlande und, was mehr ist, der Glaube an dasselbe, – und sie sind es, die in diesen Vorlesungen sich auszusprechen und zu rechtfertigen versucht haben, – ihnen die Nachsicht erwerben, deren auch das beste Wollen bedarf.'

40. See Chapter 3.

41. Hintze, 'Johann Gustav Droysen', 162.

42. Günter Birtsch. 1964. *Die Nation als sittliche Idee. Der Nationalstaatsbegriff in Geschichtsschreibung und politischer Gedankenwelt Johann Gustav Droysens*, Cologne: Böhlau, 237–238.

43. Droysen, *Freiheitskriege* 1: v: 'Man mahnt die deutschen Völker, sich historisch, ihren geschichtlichen Grundlage gemäß, in ruhiger Maaßhaltung weiter zu entwickeln…. Wieder erwacht trotz aller Zersplitterung und Verwitterung ist den deutschen Völkern das tiefe Gefühl der alten Gemeinsamkeit zu Einem Reich und Einem Recht; wieder erwacht ist ihnen die Einsicht, daß nur das treue Zueinanderhalten sie vor neuen Schäden wahren, die alten ausheilen, uns eine Zukunft bereiten kann, wie sie der deutschen Art gerecht ist.'

44. Droysen, *Freiheitskriege* 1: 17: 'Bis dann endlich das Alte und Neue sich auf dem neutralen Gebiet der Reform zu begegnen begann, die Einsicht zu siegen begann, daß das wahre historische Recht nicht die Herstellung der Vergangenheit, sondern die lebendige Fortbildung ihres großen Resultates, der Gegenwart ist, – daß das wahre Vernunftrecht nichts gemein hat mit jenem faden Radikalismus, der in jedem Augenblick den Staat und das Recht von Neuem anfangen und aus utopischer Abstraction ableiten zu können meint, sondern daß in dem Gewordenen selbst und in dem Wege, wie es geworden, dem forschenden Auge sich die ewige Vernunft jenes Werdens offenbart, das zu begreifen Trost und Erhebung, das mitwirkend weiter zu führen des tätigen Mannes höchster Beruf ist.'

45. Droysen, *Freiheitskriege* 2: 446: 'Überschätzen wir die Arbeit jener Jahre nicht; ihr Wert ist bei weitem nicht in dem, was sie erreichte, sondern in dem, was sie erreichbar glaubte.'

46. Mary Fulbrook. 2010. *A Concise History of Germany*, Cambridge: Cambridge University Press, 127.

47. Handy, *J.G. Droysen*, 41–44.

48. Droysen, *Historik* 1: 360 [*Vorlesungstext,* 1857]: 'Wenn die Bewegung von 1848 irgendeine Lehre enthalten und in die Welt gebrachten hat, so ist es die, daß man sich den Begriff des Staates schärfer ansehen muß, als bisher geschehen.'

49. Droysen, *Briefwechsel* 2: 185 [Letter to Georg Beseler, 20 March 1853]: 'Nebenbei freilich hat es das Gute, daß ich, ungestört durch die preußische Misère im Innern als Preuße in partibus wirken, die Idee Preußens festhalten, lehrend und schreibend sie, wenn man sie drinnen auch verkümmert und schändet, propagandieren kann.'

50. Friedrich Meinecke. 1930. 'Johann Gustav Droysen. Sein Briefwechsel und seine Geschichtsschreibung', *Historische Zeitschrift* 141: 271; Southard, *Droysen and the Prussian School of History,* 196.

51. Handy, *J.G. Droysen,* iv. Here I am amplifying the meaning of the quote, since Handy referred only to the *History of Prussian Politics.*

52. Johann Gustav Droysen. 1851. *Das Leben des Feldmarschalls Grafen York von Wartenburg,* vol. 1, Berlin: Veit, 3: 'Nie hat sich ein Staat aus tieferem Sturz schneller und stolzer erhoben als Preußen nach dem Tage von Jena. Auch fernliegende Verhältnisse, die Wechsel der allgemeinen Weltlage haben mitgewirkt. Aber das Wesentliche war, daß man sich innerlich aufrasste, daß sich, der alten Kraft und Treue des Preußenthums neue Formen und Ziele zu schaffen, ein Kreis von Männern um den Thron schaarte, wie die Zeit ihrer bedürfte, – mächtige Charactere, Talente seltenster Art. Einer aus diesem Kreis ist es, dessen Gedächtniß die folgende Darstellung erneuern will.'

53. Christopher Clark. 2008. *Iron Kingdom: The Rise and Downfall of Prussia, 1600–1947,* Cambridge: Harvard University Press, 358–364.

54. See Chapter 3.

55. Cf. Falko Schnicke. 2010. *Prinzipien der Entindividualisierung. Theorie und Praxis biographischer Studien bei Johann Gustav Droysen,* Cologne: Böhlau, 140, 145. Even though I disagree with Schnicke's interpretation on this particular point, I have – as will be evident later – benefited from his insightful analysis of Droysen's theory and practice of biography as governed by 'principles of de-individualization'.

56. Droysen, *Briefwechsel* 2: 931 [Letter to Alfred Dove, 16 July 1878].

57. Nippel, *Johann Gustav Droysen,* 179.

58. Droysen, *Briefwechsel* 2: 931 [Letter to Alfred Dove, 16 July 1878]: 'Über den Ursprung des York waren Sie nicht gut unterrichtet. Ich hatte im Verkehr mit militärischen Freunden in Berlin 1845/46 oft Gelegenheit, von den bedenklichen Symptomen in der Armee unter den gestreichen Einflüssen vom Thron her zu hören; ich faßte den Plan, in der typischen Gestalt Yorks das, was die preußische Armee Wesentliches habe und nicht verlieren dürfe, darzustellen.'

59. Meinecke, 'Johann Gustav Droysen', 271.

60. Droysen, *Briefwechsel* 2: 968 [Letter to Gustav Droysen, 8 September 1883]: 'Ich habe schon bei dem York diese Bedenken gehabt, mir damit geholfen, daß ich sagte, nur was von seiner Persönlichkeit zur Erklärung seiner geschichtlichen Leistung gehört, gehört in die Biographie; ob er nebenbei sich Mätressen gehalten, ob er seinen zweiten Sohn fast mißachtet und verstoßen, ob er gelegentlich in Gütern geschachert hat, ist mir gleichgültig.'

61. Quoted by Nippel, *Johann Gustav Droysen,* 178. The former student was Bernhard Erdmannsdörffer.

62. Schnicke, *Prinzipien der Entindividualisierung,* 170–171.

63. Nippel, *Johann Gustav Droysen,* 295.

64. Nippel, *Johann Gustav Droysen,* 216–219.

65. Droysen, *Geschichte der Preußischen Politik* 1: 3: 'Was diesen Staat gegründet hat, was ihn trägt und leitet, ist, wenn ich so sagen darf, eine geschichtliche Nothwendigkeit. In ihm hat oder sucht die eine Seite unsres nationalen Leben ihren Ausdruck, ihre Vertretung, ihr Maaß.'

66. Droysen, *Geschichte der Preußischen Politik* 1: 4: 'Auch Preußen umfaßt nur Bruchtheile deutschen Volkes und Landes. Aber zum Wesen und Bestand dieses Staates gehört jener Beruf für das Ganze, dessen er fort und fort weitere Theile sich angegliedert hat. In diesem Beruf hat er seine Rechtfertigung und seine Stärke. Er würde aufhören nothwendig zu sein, wenn er ihn vergessen könnte; wenn er ihn zeitweise vergaß, war er schwach, verfallend, mehr als einmal dem Untergange nah.'

67. Birtsch, *Die Nation als sittliche Idee,* 244.

68. Nippel, *Johann Gustav Droysen,* 295, 301–307.

69. Hintze, 'Johann Gustav Droysen', 184.

70. Droysen, *Briefwechsel* 2: 126–127 [Letter to General Gustav von Below, 25 August 1852]: 'Schon lange beschäftigt mich der Gedanke einer *histoire de la diplomatie Prussienne.* Nichts scheint mir beklagenswert, als der Mangel an Einsicht und Kontinuität der Einsicht in die durch die Natur und Geschichte dieses Staates bedingten auswärtigen Verhältnisse. Faßt man die Aufgabe hoch genug, so ist die Geschichte der auswärtigen Beziehungen Preußens die einzige, aber auch beste Instruktion für den praktischen Gebrauch.'

71. Nippel, *Johann Gustav Droysen,* 273.

72. Droysen, *Historik* 2: 454–455 [Denkschrift, die historischen Studien betreffend, 1860].

73. Droysen, *Historik* 2: 458 [Denkschrift, die historischen Studien betreffend, 1860]: 'Der Staat ist nicht von heut; mit allen seinen Lebensbedingungen, mit allen seinen Functionen wurzelt er in den Vergangenheiten; sie bedingen ihn. In jedem seiner einzelnen Momente ist er das, was er ist, geworden; und dies Gewordensein bietet und ist die Deutung dessen, was er ist.'

74. Droysen, *Historik* 2: 459–460 [Denkschrift, die historischen Studien betreffend, 1860]. Droysen reissued and detailed this proposal for archive reform in another memorandum in 1866: Droysen, *Historik* 2: 467–478 [Denkschrift, das preußische Archivwesen betreffend, 1866].

75. Friedrich Paulsen. 1885. *Geschichte des gelehrten Unterichts auf den deutschen Schulen und Universitäten. Vom Ausgang des Mittelalters bis zur Gegenwart,* Leipzig: Veit, 570.

76. Droysen, *Historik* 2: 456 [Denkschrift, die historischen Studien betreffend, 1860]: 'Man wird unzweifelhaft mehr und mehr zu der Erkenntniß kommen, daß die Lehrer der Jugend, namentlich die der höheren Lehranstalten, ihr Verhältniß zum historischen Unterricht nicht richtig fassen, wenn sie denselben auf Namen, Zahlen und Tatsachen aus der politischen Geschichte stellen.'

77. Droysen, *Historik* 2: 455 [Denkschrift, die historischen Studien betreffend, 1860].

78. Wilhelm von Humboldt. 1964. 'Der königsberger Schulplan' [1810], in Wilhelm von Humboldt, *Bildung des Menschen in Schule und Universität*, Heidelberg: Quelle & Meyer, 11–22. See also: Herwig Blankertz. 1992. *Die Geschichte der Pädagogik. Von der Aufklärung bis zur Gegenwart*, Wetzlar: Büchse der Pandora, 120. Remarkably, the prestige of Humboldt's universalistic concept of a generally undifferentiated school system did not prevent the emergence, as early as the 1820s and 1830s, of different types of secondary schools that in fact crucially influenced the dynamics of social differentiation in German-speaking countries in the nineteenth century and beyond. At the top of this pyramid of schools was the humanistic Gymnasium. See Fritz Ringer. 1990. *The Decline of the German Mandarins: The German Academic Community, 1890–1933*, Cambridge: Harvard University Press, 25–27.

79. Droysen, *Historik* 2: 455–457 [Denkschrift, die historischen Studien betreffend, 1860].

80. Droysen, *Historik* 2: 456 [Denkschrift, die historischen Studien betreffend, 1860]: 'Die gemeinsame Geschichte, nicht bloß das Erlebte und Gethane, sondern das Wissen davon als einem Gemeinsamen und als einem Fideikommiß macht die Menschen zu einem Volk, die Angehörigen eines Staates zu einer Nation.'

81. Droysen, *Historik* 2: 456 [Denkschrift, die historischen Studien betreffend, 1860]: 'Wo ein Volk eine so stolze[,] so beredte Geschichte hat wie im preußischen Staat, da giebt es kein edleres Mittel[,] ein ächtes Selbstgefühl und die freudige Hingebung an das Vaterland zu nähren[,] als seine Geschichte. Schon in den Schulen kann und muß in diesem Sinne gewirkt werden.'

82. Matthew Levinger. 2000. *Enlightened Nationalism: The Transformation of Prussian Political Culture, 1806–1848*, New York: Oxford University Press, 198–201.

83. See Chapter 2.

84. Pandel, *Historik und Didaktik*, 265. Pandel imported the distinction between 'Bildung zum Bürger' und 'Bildung zum Menschen' from one of his nineteenth-century sources, the historian Karl Ludwig Pölitz (1772–1838).

85. In the *Lectures on the Wars of Freedom*, Droysen positively remarks that Fichte's speeches 'ignited the German nation' ('Wie zündeten Fichtes Reden an die deutsche Nation'). Droysen, *Freiheitskriege* 2: 496.

86. Johann Gottlieb Fichte. 1808. *Reden an die deutsche Nation*, Berlin: In der Realschulbuchhandlung, 37: 'Mit Einem Worte, eine gänzliche Veränderung des bisherigen Erziehungswesens ist es, was ich, als das einzige Mittel die deutsche Nation im Daseyn zu erhalten, in Vorschlag bringe.' See also Pandel, *Historik und Didaktik*, 258–259.

87. Fichte, *Reden an die deutsche Nation*, 41–42: 'Es bleibt sonach uns nichts übrig, als schlechthin an alles ohne Ausnahme, was deutsch ist, die neue Bildung zu bringen, so daß dieselbe nicht Bildung eines besonderen Standes, sondern daß sie Bildung der Nation schlechthin als solcher, und ohne alle Ausnahme einzelner Glieder derselben, werde, in welcher, in der Bildung zum innigen Wohlgefallen am Rechten nämlich, aller Unterschied der Stände. Der in anderen Zweigen der Entwickelung auch fernerhin stattfinden mag, völlig aufgehoben sey und verschwinde; und dass auf diese Weise unter uns keinesweges Volkserziehung, sondern eigenthümliche deutsche National-Erziehung entstehe.'

88. Frederick Copleston. 1985. *A History of Philosophy*, vol. 7: *Fichte to Nietzsche*, New York: Image, 74–75.

89. Fichte, *Reden an die deutsche Nation*, 488–490: 'Ist in dem, was in diesen Reden dargelegt worden, Wahrheit, so seyd unter allen neueren Völkern ihr es, in denen der Keim der menschlichen Vervollkommnung am entschiedensten liegt, und denen der Vorschritt in der Entwickelung derselben aufgetragen ist. Gehet ihr in dieser eurer Wesenheit zu Grunde, so geht mit euch

zugleich alle Hoffnung, des gesamten Menschengeschlechtes auf Rettung aus der Tiefe seiner Uebel zu Grunde.... Auch uns ist die gesammte Oberfläche der Erde recht wohl bekannt, und alle die Volker, die auf derselben leben. Kennen wir denn nun ein solches, dem Stammvolke der neuen Welt ähnliches Volk, von welchem die gleichen Erwartungen sich fassen ließen? Ich denke, jeder, der nur nicht bloß schwärmerisch meint und hofft, sondern gründlich untersuchend denkt, werde diese Frage mit Nein beantworten müssen. Es ist daher kein Ausweg: wenn ihr versinkt, so versinkt die ganze Menschheit mit, ohne Hoffnung einer einstigen Wiederherstellung.'

90. Droysen, *Politische Schriften,* 228–229 [Preußen und das System der Großmächte, 1849]: 'Preußen darf sich nicht mehr dabei beruhigen wollen, doch nur die zweite Macht in Deutschland zu sein. Die deutsche Macht zu sein ist seine geschichtliche Aufgabe'; Droysen, *Politische Schriften,* 212 [Preußen und das System der Großmächte, 1849]: 'Die preußische Monarchie steht vor einer jener großen Krisen, wie sie ihrer Entwicklung eigenthümlich sind. Sie hat weder die Nothwendigkeit einer geschlossenen Nationalität, noch die natürlicher Umgrenzungen; ihre Notwendigkeit ist eine geschichtliche und ihre Existenz der Ausdruck einer Aufgabe.'

91. Droysen, *Politische Schriften,* 228 [Preußen und das System der Großmächte, 1849]: 'Überall das Bedürfniß, aus der oligarchischen Gebundenheit, die die lebensvolle Entwickelung der einzelnen Staaten hemmte, hinauszutreten und ein System der Freiheit und Gerechtigkeit statt dessen der Willkühr und Gewalt zu gewinnen. Nur durch die Neugestaltung Deutschlands ist es zu gewinnen; es ist da, so wie Preußen in dem begonnenen Wege fortschreitend erfüllt, was Friedrich II. mit dem Fürstenbunde einzuleiten gedachte.'

92. Wilhelm Bleek. 2001. *Geschichte der Politikwissenschaft in Deutschland.* Munich: C.H. Beck, 44; Manfred Riedel. 1973. 'Aristotelismus und Humanismus: Der Einfluß der humanistishen Aristotelesrezeption auf die politische Sprache der neuzeitlichen Philosophie', *Zeitschrift für philosophische Forschung* 27(3): 370; Gangolf Hübinger. 2006. *Gelehrte, Politik und Öffentlichkeit. Eine Intellektuellengeschichte,* Göttingen: Vandenhoeck & Ruprecht, 46–65.

93. Friedrich Christoph Dahlmann. 1968. *Die Politik,* Frankfurt am Main: Suhrkamp. The first edition of the text is from 1835; a second edition came out in 1847.

94. Droysen, *Historik* 2: 324 [Politik-Vorlesung, 1850]: 'Schon aus dieser summarischen Eintheilung ist ersichtlich, daß es die Politik in unserm Sinn am allerwenigsten mit dem Auffinden letzter allgemeiner Principien zu thun hat, aus denen sie sich als ein normatives System entwickeln müßte. Sie ist durch und durch voller individueller Erscheinungen, sie ist der Pragmatismus einer unendlichen Mannigfaltigkeit von Wechselwirkungen, deren Verlauf die Geschichte ist. Sie ist selbst nichts anderes als die Gegenwart der Geschichte, aber nicht unter dem Gesichtspunkt der Zuständlichkeit wie die Statistik, sondern unter dem der bewegenden Kräfte, der maaßgebenden Bedingungen, der indicirten Richtungen.' On Droysen's lectures on politics, see Rudolph Hübner. 1917. 'Johann Gustav Droysens Vorlesungen über die Politik', *Zeitschrift für Politik* 10, 325–376.

95. Droysen, *Historik* 2: 323 [Politik-Vorlesung, 1850]: 'Die Politik ist die Wissenschaft von den Machtmitteln und Machtstörungen, von den Machtverhältnissen und Machtverwickelungen der Staaten.'

96. Droysen, *Historik* 1: 356 [Vorlesungstext, 1857]: 'Der Staat, in welcher Formen, in wessen Hand er denn sei, herrscht, weil er die Macht hat, und ist Herr, um die Macht zu haben. Das ist die Summe aller Politik.'

97. Droysen, *Historik* 2: 322 [Politik-Vorlesung, 1850]: 'Denn der höchste Zweck des Staates ist seine innere und äußere Selbsterhaltung.'

98. Droysen, *Historik* 2: 330–331 [Politik-Vorlesung, 1850]: 'Ich bitte zu beachten, daß dies nicht Lehren und Maximen sind, die ich empfehle, sondern Thatsachen, die *toto die* in der Politik vorkommen und die man nicht damit beseitigt, daß man sie verdammt.'

99. Droysen, *Historik* 2: 455 [Denkschrift, die historischen Studien betreffend, 1860]: 'Es dürfte an der Zeit sein, daß auch Preußen die Frage der historischen Studien schärfer ins Auge faßte; das um so mehr, da dieselben unzweifelhaft in den Bereich der geistigen Kriegsbereitschaft gehören, welche für diesen Staat von nicht geringerer Wichtigkeit ist als diejenige der – mit voll-

stem Recht – unablässig die größten finanziellen Opfer gebracht werden'; furthermore, Droysen, *Historik* 2: 494 [Gutachten betreffend die Förderung des Studiums der preußischen Geschichte, 1866]: "Oesterreich hat seit 1849 außenordentliche Summen für sein ‹Archiv zur Kunde österreichischer Geschichte›, für die Publikation der *fontes* hist. Austr. u.s.w. verwandt.... Es dürfte an der Zeit sein, daß man diese Dinge, die wesentlich in den Bereich der geistigen Kriegsbereitschaft dieses Staates gehören, mehr im großen Styl und vom Staatsinteresse aus zu behandeln anfinge.'

100. Droysen, *Historik* 2: 479–480 [Gutachten betreffend die Förderung des Studiums der preußischen Geschichte, 1866].

101. Droysen, *Historik* 2: 480 [Gutachten betreffend die Förderung des Studiums der preußischen Geschichte, 1866]: 'Für die sogennante allgemeine Bildung – denn von ihr muß noch ein Werth gesagt werden – hat kein Staat mehr getan als der preußische, und er hat unzweifelhaft wohl daran getan. Aber man wird sich der Beobachtung nicht verschließen können, daß das Staatsgefühl in dem preußischen Volk keineswegs mit dieser Bildung gewachsen ist, daß es vielmehr in dem Maaße schlaffer und in cosmopolitischer Weise leerer wird, als sie höher steigt.'

102. Leopold von Ranke. 1928. *Weltgeschichte*, vol. 1: *Die älteste historische Völkergruppe und die Griechen*, Vienna: Gutenberg-Verlag Christensen, 19: 'Die Weltgeschichte würde in Phantasien und Philosopheme ausarten, wenn sie sich von dem festen Boden der Nationalgeschichten losreißen wollte; aber ebensowenig kann sie an diesem Boden haftenbleiben. In den Nationen selbst erscheint die Geschichte der Menschheit.'

103. Dahlmann, *Politik*, 39: 'Wir glauben an ein großes gemeinsames Werk der Menschheit, zu welchen das einzelne Staatenleben nur die Vorarbeiten liefert, an eine auch äußerliche Vollendung der menschlichen Dinge am Ende der Geschichte.'

104. Droysen, *Freiheitskriege* 2: 199–200: 'Die Aufklärung! Wie waren die zwei, drei Jahrzehnte vor der Revolution reich und schön, voll edler Schwärmerei und Menschenliebe, voller Vertrauen auf das siegende Fortschreiten der Humanität, der Wahrheit, des Menschenwohles gewesen. Und nun? Trauernd mochte der Menschenfreund den Blick hinwegwenden von dem wachsenden Unheil, seines Glaubens an die Menschheit enttäuscht. Wie geschändet waren jenen hehren Ideen der Menschenrechte, der Vernunftsherrschaft, der Bruderliebe aller Menschen; und wieder die Frevel, die unter ihren Namen geübt worden, weckten den nicht minder heftigen Gegenschlag.' To be sure, Droysen's view was based on an undifferentiated assessment of the philosophy of the Enlightenment, for he equated the latter with a 'stripped rationalism'. Also see Droysen, *Historik* 2: 204 [Über die deutsche Geistesgeschichte von Kant bis auf Schleiermacher]. Ultimately, Droysen viewed 'die Aufklärung' as historical thought's number one enemy: 'Man kann nicht sagen, daß die aus der mathematischen und metaphysischen Alternative erwachsene Aufklärung dem Verständnis der Historie sehr günstig war' (Droysen, *Historik* 1: 50 [Vorlesungstext, 1857]).

Nineteenth-century general criticism of the Enlightenment was, however, as Ernst Cassirer argued, frequently based on pure prejudice, which blurred the large continuities that mark the intellectual history of both the eighteenth and the nineteenth centuries in the German space. See Ernst Cassirer. 2003. *Die Philosophie der Aufklärung*, Hamburg: Meiner, 206–244. This shows why, despite the nineteenth century's negative appreciation of the Enlightenment, it would be wrong to infer that the concept of humankind that was typical of the Enlightenment era directly opposes the anthropological notions developed within the framework of romanticism and, more generally, historicism. Droysen's assessment of this issue is, therefore, simply misleading. It conceals that leading German historical thinkers' emphasis upon national individuality, at least during the first two thirds of the nineteenth century, was ultimately a way to fulfil and enhance the Enlightenment's universal idea of humankind. It also obliterates the fact that many important traits of the modern historical perspective were actually established by Enlightenment thinkers. See Jaeger and Rüsen, *Geschichte des Historismus*, 51; Levinger, *Enlightened Nationalism*, 5, 99, 223–226; Reill, *The German Enlightenment and the Rise of Historicism*, 2–3; Jörn Rüsen. 1984. "Von der Aufklärung zum Historismus. Idealtypische Perspektiven eines Strukturwandels", in Horst Walter Blanke and Jörn Rüsen (eds), *Von der Aufklärung zum Historismus. Zum Strukturwandel des historischen Denkens*, Paderborn: Schöningh, 43–48.

105. Pandel, *Historik und Didaktik*, 234.

106. Droysen, *Historik* 1: 235 [Vorlesungstext, 1857]: 'Anderen Nationen, die weniger als die deutsche von weltgeschichtlichen Dispositionen beherrscht und einseitiger national sind, wird die erzählende Darstellung darum stets besser gelingen.'

107. See Chapter 3.

108. Meinecke, 'Johann Gustav Droysen', 276: 'Aber in der Zielstrebigkeit seines deutsch-preußischen Wollens und Denkens hatte sich die frühere universalhistorische Weite seines Interesses, zwar nicht in seinem Geiste, aber in seiner praktischen Arbeit verengt.'

109. Nippel, *Johann Gustav Droysen*, 219–238, 309.

110. Andreas Greiert. 2011. '"Viele sind berufen, aber wenige auserwählt". Geschichtstheorie, Politik und sittlicher Kosmos bei Johann Gustav Droysen', *Historische Zeitschrift* 292(2): 414.

111. Welskopp, 'Der "echte Historiker" als "richtiger Kerl"', 398.

112. Herman Paul. 2011. 'Performing History: How Historical Scholarship Is Shaped by Epistemic Virtues', *History and Theory* 50(1): 5–7, 18.

113. Christian-Georg Schuppe. 1997. *Der andere Droysen. Neue Aspekte seiner Theorie der Geschichtswissenschaft*, Stuttgart: Franz Steiner.

114. Droysen, *Historik. Vorlesungen über Enzyklopädie und Methodologie der Geschichte*, 189: 'Wir fanden, daß das ganze weite Gebiet der menschlichen Welt unserer Wissenscahft zugehört, daß das Gebiet der historischen Methode der Kosmos der sittlichen Welt ist.'

115. Droysen, *Historik* 1: 361 [Vorlesungstext, 1857]: 'Wir können es nicht leugnen, daß jede Gestaltung in diesen Sphären geschichtlicher Natur und damit ja auch geeignet zur historischen Erforschung ist.'

116. Droysen, *Historik* 1: 366 [Vorlesungstext, 1857]: 'Wir haben, und mit vollem Recht, geltend gemacht, daß die geschichtliche Welt eigentlich die sittliche Welt ist.'

117. Droysen, *Historik* 1: 368–369 [Vorlesungstext, 1857].

118. Droysen, *Historik* 1: 367 [Vorlesungstext, 1857]: 'Ist einmal zugestanden, daß die noch so kleinen geschichtlichen Bildungen für den Kreis der Beteiligten von geschichtlichem Interesse sind, so ist damit eigentlich zugestanden, daß das Gebiet des Geschichtlichen ohne alle Grenze ist, d.h. daß eben jedes menschliche Verhältnis in geschichtlicher Weise betrachtet und der Erninnerung wert gehalten werden kann.'

119. Droysen, *Historik* 1: 11–12 [Vorlesungstext, 1857]: 'Unsere Wissenschaft muß den großen Schritt tun, ihre Aufgabe anders und tiefer zu fassen, ihren Forschungen einen durchaus anderen und großartigeren Umfang zu geben, einen Umfang, in dem erst die Wissenschaft zu ihrem Recht und zu ihrer ganzen Bedeutung zu gelangen vermag. Es ist nur ein Teilchen Geschichte, was von den Geschichtsschreibern berichtet wird, nur ein Teichen der Geschichte, was etwa Krieg und Frieden, über staatliche und kirchliche Verhältnisse in den Archiven beruht; wenigstens theoretisch beginnt man es anzuerkennen, daß die Geschichte auch die sozialen und rechtlichen, die intellektuellen und ästhetischen, die religiösen und technischen Bildungen des Menschengeschlechtes zu umfassen hat, daß sie sich gegenseitig bedingen und erläutern, ja daß in einzelnen derartigen Momenten historische Zeugnisse aus Zeitaltern vorliegen, welche über jede Überlieferung hinaufreichen; so ist die Sprache der menschlichen Stämme Äonen weit rückwärts führend, weit über alle historische Aufzeichnung hinauf, so klingen in unseren Märchen von Frau Holle oder Schneewittchen Mythologeme nach, die eine Zeit angehörten, in der sich die germanischen Stämme noch nicht von den indischen Ariern getrennt hatten.'

120. Charles-Olivier Carbonell. 1978. 'L'histoire dite "positiviste" en France', *Romantisme* 8(21–22): 179. A good example is Fustel de Coulanges, who in 1864 developed an argument very close to Droysen's, favouring a source-based reconstruction of cultural meanings, rather than political facts: 'Fortunately, the past never completely dies for man. Man may forget it, but he always preserves it within him.… The contemporary of Cicero speaks a language whose roots are very ancient; this language, in expressing the thoughts of ancient ages, has been modelled upon them, and it has kept the impression, and transmits it from century to century. The primary sense of a root will sometimes reveal an ancient opinion or an ancient usage; ideas have been transformed,

and the recollections of them have vanished; but the words have remained, immutable witnesses of beliefs that have disappeared.' (Numa Denis Fustel de Coulanges. 1882. *The Ancient City: A Study on the Religion, Laws, and Institutions of Greece and Rome,* Boston: Lee and Shepard, 14–15).

121. Sebastian Manhart. 2009. 'Was wird werden, wenn man weiß, was wird? Geschichts-schreibung und Staatswissenschaft als Interventionen in sich selbst hervorbringende Systeme im vormärzlichen Diskurs und bei Johann Gustav Droysen', in Horst Walter Blanke (ed.), *Historie und Historik. 200 Jahre Johann Gustav Droysen. Festschrift für Jörn Rüsen zum 70. Geburtstag,* Cologne: Böhlau, 66.

Conclusion

The general thesis underpinning the preceding chapters is that a particular notion from Droysen's historical theory summarizes his alternative to the exemplar theory of history: the notion of historical thinking. As I have attempted to show, many times in his theoretical texts Droysen suggested that historiography's main task should be to stimulate the reader's learning of historical thinking. My main argument was that the didactics implied in this formulation, despite its pragmatic orientation, substantially differs from an older form of didactics centred on historical examples. In Chapters 2, 3 and 4, which I will briefly recapitulate below, I have characterized some implications surrounding this new historical didactics developed by Droysen. Each chapter is dedicated to the survey of a different moment involved in his concept of historical thinking: the didactic moment, the historical-philosophical and the political.

From the perspective of this study, the first moment – the didactic – is the most important. Droysen's historical theory turns into a didactics inasmuch as it assumes that historical thinking is a subjective competence that may and should be learned. This didactic character is only reinforced by his plea that the producers of historical knowledge be aware of their educational task. The main claim put forth here is that Droysen's didactic emphasis is entirely consistent with his well-studied hermeneutical methodology. By analysing the way Droysen employed hermeneutical concepts such as 'historical interpretation' and 'understanding', and by relating these concepts to notions such as 'sense of reality', '*Bildung*', and 'identity', I have attempted to specify the inner link between methodology and didactics underlying his theory of historical science.

The perception of this link leads to two conclusions concerning the theoretical design of the notion of historical thinking. On the one hand, Droysen stresses that the professional historian is the one who, by being able to think historically, can investigate the genetic relationship between past and present. In short, the historian is someone who has the methodical skills to disclose the present's historicity, and to give expression to it. On the other hand, Droysen states that the ultimate purpose behind the production of historical knowledge consists in making the readership acquainted with the historian's way of thinking. In other words, he suggests that besides the historians, daily-life actors can and should learn how to think historically. As a result, he assumes that human agency can benefit from the enhancement of the individual capacity to perceive the historicity inherent in the conditions of action in their present.

The second moment involved in Droysen's notion of historical thinking relates to the substantive interpretations of history it is built upon. I decided to analytically explore this second moment because I was convinced of the need to complement the analysis of Droysen's didactics of historical thinking with an examination of the concrete ways in which he actually thought historically. Bearing this in mind, I turned to Droysen's texts in search of the guidelines that coordinate his macro-interpretation of world history and his cultural critique of his contemporary times. I have reconstructed Droysen's view on classical Greece, Hellenism, Early Christianity, the Reformation, the age of the revolutions, capitalism and modern materialism. I stressed that the closer Droysen's macro-interpretation comes to his own present, the more it changes into a cultural critique. In fact, I have suggested that, particularly during the years between 1848 and 1871, Droysen combined a toned-down historical necessitarianism with a specific interpretation of the history of his present that was loaded with expectations and anxieties regarding the future.

After a detailed consideration of Droysen's history of the present, I returned to his theory of historical thinking in possession of a new analytical key. I then concluded that Droysen ascribed to historiography the function of sponsoring the learning of historical thinking also as a means to counter the cultural threat he associated with the popularization of what he called materialism – a term pointing to different cultural tendencies such as scientism, positivism, rationalism and atheism, as well as capitalism and European republicanism. Having assessed Droysen's critical view of the spread of materialism, I perceived that he invested the notion of historical thinking with such crucial significance because he thought of it as a good response to what he regarded as a menace to the continuation of the historical process. Droysen felt that materialism was engaged in an emancipatory project that would entail an undesirable 'liberation from history'. In contrast, he proposed a different model for human emancipation that favoured a 'liberation to history'. He assumed that this gradualist ideal of social development could only be achieved if social actors were able to perceive history as a long road leading to the expansion of human freedom. To achieve that effect, Droysen claimed, the diffusion of historical thinking was nothing less than mandatory.

The third and last moment encompassed by Droysen's notion of historical thinking is the political. My main argument here pointed out significant tensions between Droysen's didactic universalism and his particularistic political creed. I have suggested that above all, Droysen ardently wished to see the edification of a unified German state under Prussian leadership, and I have explored the way this political expectation permeates his actual historiography. In doing this, my purpose was to show that Droysen's didactics of historical thinking was not immune to the general tendency towards over-politicization that marked his general conceptions of history and historiography. This practical feature neutralized parts of his theoretical universalism and even led him to a surprising return to the exemplary model of historiography, the very model he critiqued from a theoretical viewpoint.

It is easy to see that my interpretation argued not only that Droysen's ideas about the function of historiography were relatively new when they came about, but also that some of them are still relevant to the contemporary reflection on history and historiography. If we accept that it is important for historians to be able to explain the rationale that justifies their professional practice within extra-disciplinary contexts, and if we concur that a reflexive attitude towards researching, writing and teaching history can still be underscored as an important aspiration, then we can easily agree that Droysen's ideas remain valuable. At the very least, this is so for a reason that has nothing to do with the ultimate merits of his historical theory: traditionally, historians have tended to keep their distance from the question of why it is important to write and read histories. This circumstance alone makes any serious attempt to answer the question an answer worth knowing, and Droysen's doubtless was one of them.

But a more difficult question is the extent to which it is still meaningful today to resort to Droysen's notion of historical thinking in order to define the value and function of historiography. Something to bear in mind while addressing this issue is the trivial fact that more than one and a half centuries have passed since Droysen first talked about it. The differences between today's and Droysen's intellectual, cultural, social and political worlds are self-evident, and I will spare readers any comprehensive attempt to discuss them. But at least some special differences deserve close attention.

Droysen had, first of all, many reasons to enthuse about living to see the achievement of what was, by far, the main goal of his political activism – the unification of the German state under Prussian lead. But the very realization of his expectations also represented the slide into obsolescence of his own political agenda, which from 1871 on would increasingly stop corresponding to contemporary social, economic and political challenges in Germany and abroad. The decline of the appeal of Droysen's political historiography was curiously a direct consequence of the high significance it had previously enjoyed.[1] From today's perspective, Droysen's anti-democratic, almost anti-liberal positions seem bound to a very different epoch and could hardly be sustained in the political arena. The same applies to the field of history-education theory, where the established consensus is that history classes in schools and historical learning in general should primarily serve not the interests of states, but those of the learners.[2]

Second, unlike Droysen, whose contemporary historiography was almost monocentrically dedicated to the development of the Prussian state, present historians tend to see no reason to prioritize political events and subjects. Even though the importance of political history is still largely recognized, since Droysen's time historiography has unquestionably experienced an increasing pluralization of research approaches that has forced political events out of the privileged position they used to occupy. Historiography is depoliticized in the sense that political phenomena have lost centrality within the framework of historical investigation. Politics remains legitimately the main subject of many historians, but from a general disciplinary perspective, it is only one of many thematic realms a historian may pass through.

Third, and more important: Droysen's tendency to over-politicize historical research and writing contrasts starkly with what I see as a more reasonable way to relate historiography to politics. Unlike Droysen, many important historians and historical theorists of different political orientations have refused to try to interfere directly in political issues. A key benchmark in this development is surely Max Weber's argument on the inconvenience of drawing a direct line between scientific knowledge and ultimate values, which features in his conference on 'Science as a Vocation', published in text form in 1919. Weber assumes that the ultimate values governing the individual's sense of the true, the beautiful, the good and the sacred are in endless conflict. They are frequently irreconcilable: the beautiful, for instance, can simultaneously be bad, or the sacred, false. Sacred norms can conflict with secularly sanctioned forms of conduct, as in the case of the old opposition between the Christian precept to 'turn the other cheek' and the sense – typical of the Western masculine world – that physical aggression must be countered. Going beyond Weber's text, one may recall the more modern dilemma between human rights and the notion of national sovereignty that has re-emerged in different shapes in nearly every international conflict since at least 1948. With these kinds of conflicts in mind, Weber speaks of a 'polytheism of values' – an eternal battle of values that cannot be pacified by resorting to scientific knowledge, since here science and truth are not the referees but two of the contenders themselves.[3]

Because of this, science – and hence, for Weber, historical studies, too – cannot determine once and for all what decision is right in each present situation.[4] Certainly Weber's arguments are modulated in a tragic tone echoing the uncertainties and frustrations of a generation of intellectuals that sensed that the historicization of the world carried on by nineteenth-century historical studies had weakened the possibility of claiming absolute validity for beliefs, values and forms of life. In Germany, that sense was only amplified by the turbulent years of the First World War and its immediate aftermath.[5] But despite his dramatic pathos, Weber does not go as far as arguing that knowledge has no impact at all on political, moral and religious decisions and actions, or that there can be no bridge between scientific knowledge and practical life. For according to him, the fact that human sciences per se cannot establish the ultimate values one should choose to live by does not render humanistic knowledge useless. Quite the contrary, it necessarily remains a useful knowledge, because among other things it can clarify what is at stake in situations in which one's choices refer to ultimate values.[6] Hence, for Weber, science cannot turn the 'polytheism of values' back into 'monotheism', but it can bring about a formal rationalization of the process of decision-making that prevents it from falling into pure decisionism. And whereas science cannot definitively solve a value problem, it can still clarify it.[7]

It is difficult to endorse all the logical, moral and ethical consequences of Weber's 'polytheism of values', and I myself am unsure how far I would adhere to his strict separation between the stances of the 'is' and 'ought'.[8] But the fact is that by pointing out the tensions between science and values, Weber also accomplished a differentiation between science and politics that is directly applicable to the relationship between historiography and politics. This opened a gap between his way of thinking about the issue of the function of the human sciences, and the intellectual universe Droysen had inhabited two or three generations before.[9] Weber's considerations mark the beginnings of a new intellectual attitude towards politics that I see as desirable. This attitude does not request that historians turn their backs on political and ethical issues, but rather creates the possibility of referring to such issues in a new way. It does not hold simply that historiography should be entirely isolated from politics, or that it has nothing to do with what Kant called 'practical reason'. Actually it encompasses a new form of political engagement, something Raymond Aron would later define using the term 'engaged observer'.[10]

Droysen was by no means an engaged observer of the political game of his time, but rather an active player whose authority in the sphere of political values derived mainly from his scholarly expertise and prestige. Whereas Weber argues for a certain separation between science and politics, Droysen's historical theory is structured upon what Friedrich Meinecke called a 'symbiosis' between the two.[11] This kind of symbiosis has proved itself as disagreeable as its contrary, namely, the total depoliticization of historical understanding. I think Weber wisely paved a middle way that avoids both de- and over-politicization.

* * * * *

In the cultural context in which Droysen developed his understanding of the didactic value of historiography, historical knowledge and education played a much more central role than they do nowadays. In mid nineteenth-century German society, history comprised both a kind of knowledge and a way of thinking that were crucial to the social identity of the educated middle class. The historical approach was not exclusive to scholars who identified themselves as historians; in fact, a good many other disciplines belonging to German faculties of arts (*Philosophische Fakultäten*) – such as, among others, the many specialized philologies, jurisprudence, political economy and philosophy itself – had evolved into 'historical' disciplines.

In the last quarter of the nineteenth century, however, this situation started to change. The framework within which this change took place was that of the so-called crisis of historicism, which is traditionally read as a crisis of historical knowledge's power as a source of cultural orientation and of social norms and values. By this time on the German intellectual scene, authors from such various fields as economy, jurisprudence, philosophy and theology had begun to deplore what they regarded as 'the problem of historicism'. They realized that the proliferation of historical knowledge indicating the relativity of past values and cultures was generating the impression that absolute values were no longer tenable in the present. According to a then existing perception, this situation would have a paralysing effect on human action. Addressing the problem of historicism thus frequently meant underscoring Friedrich Nietzsche's suggestion that an excess of historical knowledge could indeed be a disadvantage for life. In a nutshell: the problem of historicism was the problem of relativism.[12] As a result of this and other developments, many of the old humanistic disciplines had been 'de-historicized' by the end of the First World War. A series of non- or anti-historical paradigms now emerged in the human sciences, particularly within the fields of cultural anthropology, economics, linguistics, political science, psychology and sociology. Thereby, concepts such as culture, economy, language, state, individual and society started to undermine history's central position as a central humanistic concept. The consequence was a certain detachment of history not only from the other human or social sciences, but also from the political and social worlds.[13]

From then on, a few differing ways became available to explain why histories should be written or read, and not all of them could be related to Droysen's notion of historical thinking. Nowadays, some analysts even doubt whether historiography has any practical role in the contemporary world. Hayden White, for instance, has maintained that after several decades of unavailing pursuit of the ideal of objectivity, current professional historiography has 'sold out any claim to relevance to present existential concerns in the societies in which it is practiced'.[14] Hans Ulrich Gumbrecht, for his part, has come to a similar conclusion. According to him, as historical knowledge loses the practical value it possessed in previous centuries, 'legitimizing discourses about the functions of history have degenerated into ossified rituals'. Based on this reading, Gumbrecht attempts to unearth a new cultural role for historiography. He argues that it should break with hermeneutics and focus on the surfaces rather than the depths of its subject matter. In other words, historians should radically break with their traditional knowledge-perspective to try to fulfil the widespread desire for sensual experiences of the past, an abiding wish that in current historical cultures has hitherto been addressed only by other media, for example, movies and museums.[15]

Readers who entirely agree with White's criticism of existing professional historiography, or who subscribe to Gumbrecht's proposal that historiography should stick to the 'presence effects' of things past (rather than to their meanings) are likely to disapprove of both my subject choice and my analytical perspective. Nevertheless, as far as an author can prophesy the reception of his own text, I presume that readers who think a good reason for writing and studying history is to promote frameworks for thinking and action, such as historical consciousness or historical identity, will tend to a more favourable opinion, and I suppose this last standpoint is still broadly shared.

From the late 1970s on, theorists such as Emil Angehrn, David Carr, Hermann Lübbe, Paul Ricoeur and Jörn Rüsen have reassessed the thesis that a chief existential reason links human beings to history.[16] Those authors start with the insight that in ordinary life one can define who one is only by telling oneself or others who one was or became – in other words, by turning experience into historical narrative. Histories, therefore, are vehicles of personal and collective identities. Their function is to guarantee that the human self, which is constantly exposed to its own change and to the influence of others, as well as to various external contingencies, retains a minimum of self-coherence over the course of time. Rüsen quite clearly states this pragmatic, though non-exemplary, definition of historiography's function: 'If we are not able to take along what we were and became into the future towards which we want to direct our lives, then we will lose ourselves in the future.... Hence it would not be a future *for* us, but rather a future *against* us.'[17] According to him, all kinds of stories can take on this role of stabilizing identities, including, of course, those produced by professional historians. Following the traits shared by Angehrn, Carr, Lübbe, Ricoeur and Rüsen, we would conclude that historiography is intertwined with the dynamics of subjectivity, and that one of its most important cultural functions is to advance the individual's quest for self- and collective identities.

This position links to another, prevalent in the field of history education research, that points to the formal underpinnings of historical identities. Leading authors in that field have long agreed that the most important thing learned from studying history is neither a canon of facts, nor a set of historical contents, nor an assortment of good and bad historical examples. The audience's apprehension of factual details, they argue, should not be the primary aim in conveying history. As Sam Wineburg noted, what history is bound to promote in its students is a 'literacy not of dates and names but of discernment, judgement and caution'.[18] It is therefore a way of thinking about time and a capacity for evaluating contexts, taking reasonable decisions and acting accordingly. The most frequent designation for that formal competence is 'historical consciousness', but in this context several authors also resort to a term that leads back to Droysen: 'historical thinking'.[19] According to Bodo von Borries, historical thinking is a 'categorical and methodical way of accessing the world and the self'. For him, historical thinking, as a basal form of knowledge grounded in the most fundamental conditions of human existence, can only be taken as the general aim of history education.[20] Klaus Bergmann revealed the same opinion in his reasoning that, vis-à-vis the contemporary 'ubiquity of history', histories' and historical education's best teaching is on how to think historically.[21]

I am quoting history education theorists here because they, much more than ordinary historians and historical theorists, cannot bypass the problem of finding a positive non-exemplary and non-factualistic definition of the meaning of writing and studying history. Most of them will likely have no problem regarding themselves as continuators of the neo-pragmatic approach to the issue of the function of history, an approach whose most important theorist in the nineteenth century was Droysen himself. While studying Droysen's historical theory, I constantly had the impression that I was nearing the root of the notion that the study of history provides people with tools for making sense of situations and environments that were historically shaped – that is, which developed into their current form through processes of change and development we usually call historical. Curiously, though, because of the reductionist tendency to portray nineteenth-century historiography as fundamentally marked by a 'fetishism of facts',[22] Droysen's non-factualistic (and non-exemplary) definition of the function of historical knowledge may sound surprising to many nowadays. If the chapters above have managed to somehow attenuate that sense of surprise, then I have achieved my most important goal.

Notes

1. Manhart, 'Was wird werden, wenn man weiß, was wird?' 40.
2. Klaus Bergmann. 2000. *Multiperspektivität. Geschichte selber denken,* Schwalbach am Taunus: Wochenschau, 22.
3. Weber, *Gesammelte Aufsätze zur Wissenschaftslehre,* 603–604.
4. Genuine scientific knowledge does not answer important questions such as 'What should we do? How should we live?' This is so because, according to Weber, modern science sees itself as separate from issues of meaning. It is not a path to true art, to true nature or to God, as were the ideals of science that characterized the Middle Ages or the Renaissance. Physicians trained according to the standards of up-to-date scientific medicine, for instance, would not ask whether the lives they are supposed to save are worth living or not. For Weber, physicians cannot and do

not need to answer that kind of question, as long as they remain practitioners of a science-based activity. More or less the same is true of the study of religious, moral and political phenomena. Here, knowledge of systems of beliefs or past political events will not be directly applicable to decisions concerning ultimate values, because of the very fact that whereas scientific knowledge is possible, 'scientific' decision-making is not. Weber, *Gesammelte Aufsätze zur Wissenschaftslehre*, 597–598.

5. A counterpoint to Weber is the late Ernst Troeltsch, who in his inaugural lecture in Berlin in 1915 declared that he was undertaking his professorship in the field of philosophy of history 'to put an end to the anarchy of values' (quoted in Karl Acham. 1995. *Geschichte und Sozialtheorie. Zur Komplementarität kulturwissenschaftlicher Erkenntnisorientierungen*, Freiburg: Alber, 183). One cannot say that Troeltsch entirely succeeded in this, but in any case his idea of 'overcoming history with history' and his (unfinished) attempt to work out a new kind of substantial philosophy of history are quite remarkable. See Eugene Lyman. 1932. 'Ernst Troeltsch's Philosophy of History', *The Philosophical Review* 41(5): 443–465; Acham, *Geschichte und Sozialtheorie*, 171–186.

6. In addition, according to Weber, reliable information produced by cultural and social sciences can prove crucial to political actors, who can resort to scientific knowledge to acquire effective means to achieve predetermined goals. See Edward Portis. 1980. 'Political Action and Social Science: Max Weber's Two Arguments for Objectivity', *Polity* 12(3): 426–427. Furthermore, historiography and the other sciences alike can indeed help people make reasonable decisions by conditioning them to an organized form of thinking, and especially by bringing clarity to the relationship between means and ends, techniques and ultimate values. Weber, *Gesammelte Aufsätze zur Wissenschaftslehre*, 607–608.

7. Wolfgang Schluchter. 1997. 'Polytheismus der Werte. Überlegungen im Anschluß an Max Weber', in Christoph Jamme (ed.), *Grundlinien der Vernunftkritik*, Frankfurt am Main: Suhrkamp; Wilhelm Hennis. 1994. 'The Meaning of "Wertfreiheit" on the Background and Motives of Max Weber's "Postulate"', *Sociological Theory* 12(2): 113–125. For the argument that the well-known supporter of political decisionism Carl Schmitt misinterpreted Weber's thesis on the polytheism of values, see also Arthur Mitzman. 1985. *The Iron Cage: An Historical Interpretation of Max Weber*, New Brunswick: Transaction, 229.

8. For fundamental criticisms of Weber's arguments on values and norms, see Jaeger, *Bürgerliche Modernisierungskrise und historische Sinnbildung*, 222–224; Alasdair MacIntyre. 2007. *After Virtue: A Study in Moral Theory*, Notre Dame: University of Notre Dame Press, 26–29; Sérgio da Mata. 2010. '"O dever-ser é coisa do Diabo"? Sobre o problema da neutralidade axiológica em Max Weber', *Dimensões* 24: 262–283; Walter Runciman. 1978. *A Critique of Max Weber's Philosophy of Social Science*, Cambridge: Cambridge University Press, 49–60.

9. Wolfgang Hardtwig. 1991. 'Geschichtsreligion – Wissenschaft als Arbeit – Objektivität. Der Historismus in neuer Sicht', *Historische Zeitschrift* 252: 17.

10. Raymond Aron. 2005. *Le spectateur engagé. Entretiens avec Jean-Louis Missika et Dominique Wolton*, Paris: Librairie générale française, 430.

11. Meinecke, 'Johann Gustav Droysen', 249.

12. Jaeger, 'Historismus', 532; Georg Iggers. 1995. 'Historicism: The History and the Meaning of the Term', *Journal of the History of Ideas* 56: 133–134; Nietzsche, 'Von Nutzen und Nachteile der Historie für das Leben'; Ringer, *The Decline of the German Mandarins*, 340–347; Gunter Scholtz. 1991. *Zwischen Wissenschaftsanspruch und Orientierungsbedürfnis. Zu Grundlage und Wandel der Geisteswissenschaften*, Frankfurt am Main: Suhrkamp, 130–135; Annette Wittkau. 1994. *Historismus. Zur Geschichte des Begriffs und des Problems*, Göttingen: Vandenhoeck & Ruprecht, 14–20.

13. Reinhart Koselleck. 1990. 'Wozu noch Historie?' in Wolfgang Hardtwig (ed.), *Über das Studium der Geschichte*, Munich: DTV, 348–351.

14. Hayden White. 2005. 'The Public Relevance of Historical Studies: A Reply to Dirk Moses', *History and Theory* 44(3): 336.

15. Hans Ulrich Gumbrecht. 1997. 'After Learning from History', in Hans Ulrich Gumbrecht, *In 1926: Living at the Edge of Time*, Cambridge: Harvard University Press, 411; see also Hans Ulrich Gumbrecht. 2006. 'Presence Achieved in Language', *History and Theory* 45(3): 317–327.

16. Emil Angehrn. 1985. *Geschichte und Identität*, Berlin: Walter de Gruyter; David Carr. 1991. *Time, Narrative, and History*, Bloomington: Indiana University Press; Lübbe, *Geschichtsbegriff und Geschichtsinteresse*; Paul Ricoeur. 1994. *Oneself as Another*, Chicago: The Chicago University Press, 113–168; Rüsen, *Historische Vernunft*; Rüsen, *Lebendige Geschichte*. See also Chris Lorenz. 1997. *Konstruktion der Vergangenheit. Eine Einführung in die Geschichtstheorie*. Cologne: Böhlau, 400–414; MacIntyre, *After Virtue*, 204–225.

17. Jörn Rüsen. 2001. *Zerbrechende Zeit. Über den Sinn der Geschichte*. Cologne: Böhlau, 133: 'Wenn wir nicht das, was wir geworden sind, in die Zukunft hinein mitnehmen können, in die hinein wir unser Leben führen wollen, dann verlieren wir uns in der Zukunft und haben sie nicht. Im schlimmsten Fall hat sie uns, ohne daß wir uns selber in ihr haben können. Dann aber wäre es keine Zukunft für uns, sondern eher gegen uns.'

18. Sam Wineburg. 2001. *Historical Thinking and Other Unnatural Acts: Charting the Future of Teaching the Past*, Philadelphia: Temple University Press, ix. With his thesis that historical thinking is not something that springs automatically from psychological developments, Wineburg has called attention to the difficulties of attaining that learning goal. The achievement of historical thinking, he concludes, 'actually goes against the grain of how we ordinarily think, one of the reasons why it is much easier to learn names, dates, and stories than it is to change the basic mental structures we use to grasp the meaning of the past' (7).

19. Klaus Bergmann. 2000. *Geschichtsdidaktik. Beiträge zu einer Theorie des historischen Lernens*, Schwalbach am Taunus: Wochenschau; Bodo von Borries. 2008. *Historisch Denken Lernen – Welterschließung statt Epochenüberblick. Geschichte als Unterrichtsfach und Bildungsaufgabe*, Opladen: Barbara Budrich; Karl-Ernst Jeismann. 1997. 'Geschichtsbewußtsein – Theorie', in Klaus Bergmann et al. (eds), *Handbuch der Geschichtsdidaktik*, Seelze-Velber: Kallmeyer, 42–45; Hans-Jürgen Pandel. 2007. *Geschichtsunterricht nach PISA. Kompetenzen, Bildungsstandards und Kerncurricula*, Schwalbach am Taunus: Wochenschau; Jörn Rüsen. 1994. *Historisches Lernen. Grundlagen und Paradigmen*, Cologne: Böhlau; Waltraud Schreiber et al. 2006. *Historisches Denken. Ein Kompetenz-Struktur Modell*, Neuried: Ars una; Peter Seixas. 2006. 'Historical Consciousness: The Progress of Knowledge in a Postprogressive Age', in Jürgen Straub (ed.), *Narration, Identity, and Historical Consciousness*, New York: Berghahn Books, 141–156.

20. Borries, *Historisch Denken Lernen*, 10: 'Tatsächlich lässt sich "Historisches Denken" nur als kategorialer und methodischer Zugriff auf Welt und Selbst verstehen; als solcher tritt es neben andere Erkenntnisweisen, von denen es nicht ersetzt werden kann. Basale Formen ergeben sich anthropologisch.'

21. Bergmann, *Geschichtsdidaktik*, 24: 'Mir scheinen in diesem Zusammenhang zwei Gesichtspunkte besonders wichtig zu sein Erstens ist es notwendig, daß Kinder im Geschichtsunterricht vor allem anderen "historisches Denken" lernen und daß das Erlernen des "historischen Denkens" einen unbestrittenen Vorrang vor anderen Möglichkeiten, im Geschichtsunterricht etwas zu lernen, erhält.'

22. Edward H. Carr. 1961. *What Is History?* New York: Vintage, 14.

Appendix
Droysen and His Theory of History

Biographical Note

A frequently repeated cliché states that the most important social institution in German nineteenth-century cultural and intellectual life was the evangelical rectory (*Pfarrhaus*).[1] Like every cliché, this one is surely exaggerated, but the truth behind the hyperbole here is that many important German writers, artists, philosophers and historians were indeed sons of evangelical pastors and thus grew up in highly religious surroundings.[2] Droysen's case tends to confirm the rule. He was born on 6 July 1808 in Treptow an der Rega in Pomerania (a Prussian town that would be incorporated into Poland after 1945 and renamed Trzebiatów), the third son of Anna Dorothea Friederica Droysen (1777–1827), née Casten, and the army chaplain Johann Christoph Droysen (1773–1816). The latter died when Droysen was only seven, and the family consequently fell into financial hardship. Droysen's education at the Marienstiftsgymnasium in Stettin (1820–1826) was only possible because his deceased father's friends and former university colleagues jointly contributed to young Droysen's upkeep.[3]

In the summer of 1826, at the age of seventeen, he registered at the University of Berlin, focusing his studies on classical philology. From the beginning of his studies he was a devoted student of August Böckh (1785–1867), in whose research seminar he took part. But he also obtained a strong philosophical background, attending no fewer than six courses offered by Hegel, who at the time was a very popular member of Berlin's faculty. In addition, he attended three lecture courses by Carl Ritter (1779–1859), one of the founders of modern geography. Ritter is surely the source of the attentiveness to geographical aspects that is particularly evident in Droysen's texts on ancient history. Interestingly enough, however, Droysen did not attend many courses offered by *stricto sensu* history professors. Ranke taught at the University of

Berlin as of 1824, but Droysen enrolled only in his 1827 lectures on the history of literature of the eighteenth and nineteenth centuries.[4] In any case, Droysen concluded the then usual cycle of three years of study – the *triennium* – in early 1829, obtaining a certificate that allowed him to teach at secondary schools. In the summer of 1831, he defended his Ph.D. dissertation on Hellenistic Egypt, written under Böckh's supervision.[5] In the first semester of 1833, he obtained his *Habilitation* and started to deliver lectures as a *Privatdozent* at the University of Berlin. In early 1835, he was appointed extraordinary professor for classical philology and ancient history, though still without pay. His survival was assured by his earnings from teaching secondary school, especially at the *Grauenkloster Gymnasium,* where he began teaching in 1829.

It is fairly difficult to access and reconstruct events related to Droysen's private life. Save for a few exceptions, the letters he exchanged with his closest relatives are not known and indeed may have been lost.[6] Moreover, the editor of his *Correspondence,* grandson Rudolf Hübner (1864–1945), did not prioritize private issues in selecting materials for the 1929 publication.[7] Still, Droysen's friendship with Felix Mendelsohn-Bartholdy (1809–1847), which began in 1827, is worth mention. Droysen became a frequent visitor at the house of the Mendelsohn-Bartholdys, a family of convert Jews whose patriarch was directly descended from the philosopher Moses Mendelsohn (1729–1786). In Berlin, the young Droysen was also a frequent visitor to the house of another family of Jewish origins, the Friedländers, where he became acquainted with his future wife, Marie Mendheim (1820–1847), a granddaughter of Benoni and Rebeca Friedländer who was living with her grandparents after her mother's death. Droysen and Marie Mendheim married in 1836, when she was sixteen and he was in his late twenties, and they had four children: Gustav (1838–1908) (his future biographer), Marie (1839–1896), Anna (1842–1918) and Ernst Droysen (1844–1874).

In the 1830s, despite having to spend at least two dozen hours of his working week in classrooms,[8] Droysen authored an incredible number of texts. By the time he earned his Ph.D., he had finished the translation of Aeschylus' tragedies (which would be published three years later, in 1832).[9] Between 1835 and 1838 he moreover published translations of Aristophanes' comedies.[10] Droysen's translations of Greek drama were quite successful in his lifetime and continue to be republished,[11] but his best known book from the phase in question is nonetheless his *History of Alexander the Great.* Published in 1833, it was continued by the two volumes of the *History of Hellenism* (1836, 1843).[12] In these three books covering essentially the political history of the period 356–221 BC, Droysen connected the results of philological research with a universal-historical perspective that he had constructively assimilated from Hegel's philosophy of history.[13] In addition, he introduced a re-signification of the term Hellenism, which he uses to generally refer to the Greek-speaking civilization that emerged in the Mediterranean world with and after Alexander, rather than only to the Greek-speaking Jews of the post-classic world as was usual among scholars of the seventeenth and eighteenth centuries.[14] In these books, Droysen's main assumption was therefore that Hellenism subsumed 'the period of three centuries in which Greeks and Orientals met and made Christianity possible'.[15] He did not explicitly justify his conceptual innovation, and he used the term Hellenism rather ambiguously. Nevertheless, he can be credited with having established the historical dignity of a period that – not least because of German scholars' preoccupation with classical Greece – was previously looked upon with disfavour and had consequently remained understudied.[16]

Droysen would never fully accomplish his original plan of expanding the argument of the *History of Hellenism* into a history of Christianity until the time of Julius Caesar,[17] and some scholars have attempted to uncover the reasons behind the interruption of the project. Wilfried Nippel suggests that it was connected to Droysen's increasing distrust of traditional philology, a distrust that he would have started cultivating partly in reaction to the criticism many textual philologists had levelled against his texts on ancient history.[18] Nippel also argues that the assumptions related to a substantive philosophy of history that underscored Droysen's project were incompatible with source-based historiography, and that therefore such a plan could never be accomplished in its entirety.[19] Arnaldo Momigliano states that over the course of research, Droysen would have sensed that his intended interpretation of the origins of Christianity would have to refer strongly to the influence of Judaism. As Droysen was attached by marriage and friendship to Jewish converts, Momigliano argues, he would have felt himself increasingly closer to a social taboo and hence preferred to be silent about it.[20]

In any case, Droysen's explanation, which mentions a change in his personal 'external situation' (*äußeren Lage*), is also to be taken seriously.[21] It referred to his new professional situation following his appointment as a history professor at the University of Kiel in 1840. The move to Holstein – then a duchy linked by personal union to the Danish monarchy – coincides with a new phase of Droysen's intellectual biography. An intimate connection between historical research/writing and political activism, which had already characterized Droysen's works on ancient history, would become increasingly pronounced from then on. In Kiel, Droysen continued teaching ancient history, but he also started to teach and publish on contemporary issues.[22] The most important register of his move into contemporary history is the *Lectures on the Wars of Freedom,* delivered in 1842–43 and then published in 1846.[23] In this text, Droysen addressed Western political history from the independence of the United States (1776) until the end of the Congress of Vienna (1815). As his purpose was to contribute to political education rather than to the progress of academic scholarship, he saw no problems in relying on existing historiography in lieu of conducting original source research.[24] Nonetheless, the broad (universal-historical) perspective within which he framed his interpretation is quite remarkable. Droysen recalls and explains a myriad of political events that took place in several countries of Europe and the Americas during the late 1700s and early 1800s. He presents the era of the revolutions as characterized by a struggle for the expansion of human freedom. Ultimately, he resorts here to the same general framework concerning the history of humankind that had permeated his texts on ancient history.[25]

During the 1840s, Droysen would even cross the boundary between political scholarship and hard-core politics. He engaged himself in the conflict between German and Danish nationalisms over the duchies of Schleswig and Holstein, and by the end of the decade had catapulted into the main theatre of German national politics. The Revolution of 1848 led to the constitution of a provisional (pro-German) government in Holstein, which sent Droysen as its official representative to the Bundestag in Frankfurt. He then became member of the so-called Siebzehnerausschuss (30 March to 8 May), the commission established by the parliament after the revolution with the purpose of drafting a national constitution. Further, in 1848 he was elected deputy to the Frankfurt National Assembly,[26] where he again took part in the constitutional committee (*Verfassungsausschuss*) as its secretary.[27] Droysen never delivered a speech to the National Assembly, but backstage he was very influential indeed. As a top-ranked member of the centre-right Casino Party, he tried in general to direct attention to power issues, especially those concerning the relationship between the (projected) new central power and the pre-existing states – particularly Austria.[28]

The failure of the National Assembly's unification project propelled Droysen back into academic life,[29] and he returned to Kiel. His first wife, Marie, had died in 1847, and he married Emma Michaellis (1829–1881), a relative of a friend of his, the orientalist Justus Olshausen (1800–1882). In 1852, Droysen moved to the University of Jena, where he found an intellectual refuge in a time of political reaction in Prussia.[30] The decade Droysen spent in Jena was extremely fruitful in publications and academic activities. It is also remarkable that the stay in Jena represented the *Historik*'s conception phase, which ranged from 1852, when Droysen first announced his intention to lecture on the principles of historical knowledge, to the winter semester of 1857, when he first really lectured on it.[31]

After 1848–49, now lacking a political mandate, Droysen channelled his political energies into intellectual enterprises, such as researching and writing on Prussian national history. In the works produced during the last thirty years of his lifetime, the general perspective that had characterized the *Lectures on the*

Wars of Freedom was clearly narrowed.[32] The first major example of this phase is *The Life of Field Marshal Count York von Wartenburg,* one of the Prussian commanders in the war against the Napoleonic domination (1813–1815).[33] The one-sided nationalistic and militaristic perspective found in that text prevailed also in the work that Droysen considered his magnum opus, the *History of Prussian Politics.*[34] This turned out to be an unfinished mammoth project whose fourteen actually published volumes covered the period between the fifteenth century and the beginning of the Seven Years' War (1756). The argument that Droysen intended to empirically illustrate in the *History of Prussian Politics* (as well as in almost all his other texts on modern and contemporary history) is both ideological and teleological. Droysen argued that Prussia had a 'German vocation', that is, that its historical destiny was to accomplish the re-foundation of the German Empire. Although the text was based upon very extensive research of primary sources, its cognitive value is considerably undermined by Droysen's deliberate choice to work only with Prussian documents and his unconditional retrospective partisanship for Prussia.[35]

Droysen's loyalty to Prussia was eventually rewarded subsequent to the political turnaround initiated by Prince Wilhelm's regency while his brother, the conservative Friedrich Wilhelm IV– the ruler who in 1849 had rejected the unification as proposed by the National Assembly – was facing severe health problems. In 1859 Droysen was finally awarded a chair at the University of Berlin. While he was teaching at the Berlin Faculty of Arts (Philosophische Fakultät), his colleagues included prominent historians such as, for instance, Leopold von Ranke, Ernst Curtius (1814–1896), Theodor Mommsen (1817–1903) and Heinrich von Treitschke. In Berlin, furthermore, Droysen was elected to the Prussian Academy of Sciences in 1866. Another index of his political prestige is his appointment as official historiographer of the state of Brandenburg, an honorary title that gave him free access to this state's official files – but not to the Prussian ones, as Ranke was Prussia's official historian.

Droysen's biographers tend not to concentrate on his later years in Berlin for several reasons that Wilfried Nippel has well explained. First of all, the move to Berlin did not affect the intellectual direction that Droysen had been taking since 1848; therefore many analyses centred either on his *Life of York* or on the first volumes of the *History of Prussian Politics* (published when he was still in Jena) are also valid for this subsequent phase. Additionally, as several of his contacts either lived in or would move to Berlin, his correspondence diminished markedly in comparison to other phases of his career. Moreover, being in the centre of the Prussian (and, some years later, of the German) state led him to give up his previously prolific role as a publicist (which he kept mostly anonymous, as was typical at the time).[36] Droysen's retreat from the political newspapers was surely influenced by the new possibility of exerting direct influence over Prussian and German politics through either internal memoranda or personal conversations with high-ranking politicians and members of the royal family.

Droysen's later decades thus reveal an increasing withdrawal from political discussion and decision-making in favour of immersion in academic work, though the latter continued to be thoroughly permeated by political values and aims. Over his twenty-five years of teaching at the University of Berlin, he continued to lecture mostly on Greek and contemporary history, as well as historical theory and methodology. Interestingly, Droysen's *Historik* lectures were attended by students such as Wilhelm Dilthey (1833–1911), Georg Simmel (1858–1918) and Friedrich Meinecke (1862–1954), who themselves would eventually develop prominent works in the history and theory of the human sciences.[37] In Jena and again in Berlin, Droysen also founded historical seminars that proved very productive efforts towards the training of young and junior modern and contemporary historians in Germany. Academics such as Alfred Dove (1844–1916), Gustav Droysen, Bernhard Erdmannsdörffer (1833–1901), Otto Hintze (1861–1940) and Reinhold Koser (1852–1914), among many others, took part in the activities offered by Droysen's seminar.[38] Through the last months of his life, Droysen would keep on teaching, researching Prussian archives, writing his *History of Prussian Politics* (and other, shorter historical texts) and revising former works for new editions.[39] He died on 19 June 1884 at the age of 75, three years after the death of his second wife, Emma.[40]

A Portrait of the *Historik*

According to Friedrich Meinecke, three different (albeit interwoven) moments are discernible in Droysen's academic biography, two of them characterized by the already mentioned interest in Hellenistic and Prussian history. The third moment is, of course, that of the theory of history.[41] It is ultimately because of his works on historical theory that both philosophically minded historians and historically minded philosophers frequently regard Droysen as a classic author.[42] Hannah Arendt, for instance, remarked that he was 'perhaps the most thoughtful of the nineteenth-century historians'.[43] Hans-Georg Gadamer, on his part, more than once called Droysen 'a penetrating [*scharf*] methodologist'.[44] The philosopher Erich Rothacker spoke of Droysen's *Historik* as 'the most influential [*wirkungsreichste*] document on the logic of the science of history'.[45] For the historian Thomas Nipperdey, Droysen was 'historicism's great theorist'.[46] Jörn Rüsen goes in the same direction, claiming that Droysen's *Historik* is 'one of the most significant texts on the theory of the science of history, or probably the most significant one'.[47] The same holds for Wolfgang Hardtwig, who regarded Droysen as 'undoubtedly the most significant German-speaking historical theorist'.[48]

All these authors agree on one point: that among the German nineteenth-century historians, Droysen was the one who most impressively reasoned on history as a form of knowledge. And in fact, Droysen's reputation as a classic author from the nineteenth-century German tradition of human sciences rests on something other than what he himself deemed as his main intellectual endeavour, namely, both his research activity and his historiographical production concerning Prusso-German political history. Nowadays, the results of those giant scholarly efforts can easily be seen as outdated. Droysen's *History of Prussian Politics,* for instance, only attracts the interest of those few researchers who delve deep into the since downgraded history of the Prussian state. The reason for Droysen's current reputation – that is, his theory and methodology of history – was, hence, only a by-product of his intellectual biography. His theoretical and methodological considerations emerged not from his most elaborate published writings, but rather from his teaching activities. These were developed in the context of lectures designed to convey to young students the general principles of the historian's metier. Droysen delivered those lectures many times between 1857 and 1882–83, in Jena and Berlin, but he seems never to have seriously considered preparing them for publication as a book. As a result, the contents of his lectures in their entirety and depth were long unavailable to the public beyond his circle of students. The *Outlines of Historical Theory (Grundriß der Historik)*, which Droysen indeed published in four editions between 1858 and 1882, only compiled the lectures' outlines.[49] What they offered was actually only a short inventory of Droysen's argumentation rather than fully developed ideas.[50] Only in 1937 – more than forty years after Droysen's death – was a full-text version of the *Historik* lectures published. Furthermore, preparation of the critical edition of Droysen's theoretical texts began only in 1971 and is still on course.[51]

Nevertheless, when Droysen started to lecture on *Historik* in the mid-nineteenth century, he was not beginning something entirely new but rather inserting himself into an intellectual tradition – that of lectures on the principles of historical scholarship – that had begun several decades before.[52] Blanke, Fleischer and Rüsen, having extensively researched this relatively unexplored textual genre, dated its origin to the mid-eighteenth century, when Johann Martin Chladenius delivered his first theoretical lectures and published his *Allgemeine Geschichtswissenschaft* (1752). Advertised under titles such as 'Historische Propedeutik', 'Historische Encyklopädie', or 'Historik', these lectures aimed to give students an overview of the fundamental features and methods that characterize historical research and writing. In the late 1700s and throughout the 1800s, such lectures were quite common at the universities of the German-speaking world. Some were subsequently published as texts in integral or, oftener, abridged form, like Droysen's *Grundriß*. At least in Droysen's case, the lectures were addressed to senior students, for he was of the opinion that such lectures would only excite freshmen's imagination without offering them anything palpable.[53]

All the historians who read these propaedeutic lectures were male, as was the absolute majority of the attending audience, as German universities did not begin to admit women until the end of the nineteenth century. Most of the lecturers also taught about historical issues other than theory and methodology, and in addition devoted most of their research energies to 'non-theoretical' subjects. Yet they nurtured a special interest in theoretical and philosophical issues that was eventually channelled into their lectures on *Historik*. The popularization of this didactical practice ultimately fulfilled a very important role in history's institutionalization as an autonomous discipline in nineteenth-century German universities.[54] Modern German discourse on history and historiography, that is, theory of history, was thus born and developed within the framework of such propaedeutic lectures. Besides Chladenius and Droysen, the most famous historians from the late eighteenth and the nineteenth centuries to contribute lectures, treatises and essays to the tradition of the *Historik* were Johann Christoph Gatterer, August Ludwig Schlözer, Wilhelm Wachsmuth, Georg Gottfried Gervinus, Jacob Burckhardt and Ernst Bernheim.[55]

The main perspective structuring Droysen's *Historik* echoes his goal of explaining the principles that, in his view, tacitly regulate the work of professional historians. Droysen usually opened his lectures with the claim that historians, despite their amazing research successes, had until then remained rather unclear as to the most essential issues concerning their discipline.[56] He chose to think, lecture and write on historical theory following this perception that it was absolutely necessary to methodologically enlighten the historical discipline on its general value, aims and competences. Because of that, Droysen's theory of history is, first and foremost, a theory of the science of history.

In line with this feature, he developed a theory of historical method, that is, a demonstration that the research procedures deployed by historians follow rules that are specific to the historical discipline. He thus accepts the existence of scientific pluralism and, based on this assumption, elaborates a justification for the autonomy of history as an academic field positioned between philosophy and the natural sciences. Droysen's famous assertion that the essence of historical method is 'to understand by means of research' (*forschendes verstehen*) reflects this argument on history's intermediary position between those two other fields. Contrary to philosophy (and theology), history is, on the one hand, a research-based empirical science. But on the other, history fundamentally differs from the natural sciences in the way it makes reference to experience: historians deal not with recurring natural phenomena, but with the singular products of human thinking and action, that is, with the incessantly changing 'ethical world' (*sittliche Welt*).[57] Having presupposed this fundamental difference between the subject matters of history and natural sciences, Droysen claims that the historian's purpose is to understand (or interpret) particular human expressions instead of to explain the empirical world with the aid of general laws.[58]

Droysen's general argument locating history in an intermediary and autonomous position between philosophical speculation and natural-scientific explanation was trailblazing for subsequent theories of the human sciences, the most famous of which is undoubtedly Wilhelm Dilthey's.[59] But Droysen's hermeneutical theory of historical method still comprises a pioneering methodics – a threefold scheme of the phases of historical research that differentiates between heuristics, criticism and interpretation.[60] By means of such differentiations, Droysen countered the notion that source criticism was the quintessential historical procedure. Later on, his argument that the method employed by historians goes far beyond source criticism was also relatively successful. It was assimilated by methodological textbooks of the late nineteenth and early twentieth centuries, most remarkably by Ernst Bernheim's *Lehrbuch der historischen Methode* (1889) and Charles-Victor Langlois (1863–1929) & Charles Seignobos' (1854–1942) *Introduction aux études historiques* (1898).[61] Through the mediation of such texts, Droysen's scheme of historical method helped establish a set of *minimal standards* that, by the end of the long nineteenth century, became the distinctive mark of historical professionalism in many different countries.[62] As historians became familiar with the idea that they used a special method of their own – an idea somewhat traceable to Droysen's methodology – they also became able to conceive of themselves as an autonomous and relatively homogeneous academic group, and their disciplinary identity was much strengthened as a result. The sort of scientific identity offered by the notion of historical method was not unimportant within the framework of a discipline whose practitioners often diverged widely in their thematic research interests, political persuasions and philosophical world views. Furthermore, one should not forget that by the end of the nineteenth century, history was being unsettled by both natural-scientific positivism and the emergence of the social sciences. In this context, the development of a unifying notion of historical method that pointed to both source criticism and interpretation – that is, to methodical procedures that the natural and social sciences either did not use or were unwilling to highlight – served to counterbalance these new orientations' impact on the historical profession.[63]

Droysen's theory of history also comprises a theory on both the possibility of and the presuppositions for historical knowledge, that is, an epistemology. This shows quite clearly how several parts of the *Historik* ultimately extended to issues located beyond the methodology of historical science and its self-justificatory discourse.[64] Not satisfied with the trivial distinction between past and history, Droysen tried to specify the operative criteria that historians apply while transforming 'deeds into history'.[65] The epistemology that came out of his effort is in fact very peculiar. On the one hand, Droysen recognizes that whereas 'deeds' can turn into 'history', they do not automatically bear a historical meaning. Knowing that only subjects of knowledge can perceive past events as historical events, he therefore admits the inherent subjective character of historical knowledge. On the other hand, though, Droysen leaves no room for arguments linking what a subject perceives and interprets as history to arbitrary subjective determinations that can be understood only in terms of aesthetics or psychology. Actually, he defines historical knowledge as something simultaneously subjective and objective. It is neither a restitution nor a re-enactment of past experiences, but rather the product of a subjective conception in which reference to past experiences is methodically controlled: 'Our science is based on the fact that, instead of producing pasts from the still existing [research] materials, we rather want to found, correct, and extend our own idea of those pasts by means of a methodical procedure.'[66]

Droysen's epistemology, however, lives side by side with presuppositions that originated from the substantive philosophy of history that he received and adapted from his philosophical teacher, Hegel. What Droysen really considers to be 'the historical' quality par excellence can only be understood in light of his notion that there is 'a History over all histories' or the 'History of history' (*Geschichte der Geschichte*).[67] These formulations are only seemingly paradoxical. For Droysen, each event in everyday life inherently has a historical character, in the sense that it necessarily takes place within the historical world – the world as resulting from the formative process of history. But this circumstance does not suffice to explain the historical quality that historians ascribe to the events they investigate. To tackle this, Droysen differentiates between particular histories and 'History' in singular form, noting that only the latter concerns humankind as such. In his view, the historian's interest should be rather directed towards History with a capital letter.

Droysen's own division of the *Historik*'s subject matter into three chapters called '*Methodik*', '*Systematik*', and '*Topik*', respectively, already points to something that may further clarify what he actually considered to be the historical quality in that specific sense.[68] Looking briefly to the names of those chapters, one might conclude that the first and the third titles are self-explanatory enough, while the meaning of 'systematics' is much less evident. To understand it, it is worth recalling that Droysen actually discusses under the title '*Systematik*' the issue of what kinds of objects could be studied by means of the methodical procedures he had introduced in the previous chapter (*Methodik*). He synthesizes his position by stating that 'the historical method's field is that of the cosmos of the ethical world'.[69] Droysen thereby suggests that the historical method's field of application is not the entire human past, but only the part of it that might be identified with the 'ethical powers'. The notions of an ethical world and ethical powers stand, hence, for the criteria that specify which past events, realities and processes may become historical – that is, which of them are worthy of the historians' methodical understanding.

In other words, this means that for a 'deed' to become 'history', it must first of all be connectable to the general development of the 'ethical powers'. The history that lies over all histories is thus the history of the constitution of the present world. More precisely, it is history as structured from the general perspective that authors prior to Droysen had already defined as world history, universal history or history of humankind.[70] Droysen sees the histories that come out of this perspective not so much as subjective syntheses of or projections over past events, but rather as registers of the nexus between past and present, inside of which the historian too, as a subject of knowledge, is located. Therefore, the subject of historical knowledge is simultaneously its object, because he or she has already been 'produced' by history. In history – as one may conclude based on Droysen – the subject and object of knowledge largely confound themselves.[71] This assumption is, by the way, the epistemological departing point for a theory of historicity, which is another built-in element of his *Historik*.

So from a purely logical point of view, Droysen regards properly made historiography as the study of the ethical powers in their temporal dynamics – of the ethical world in its development over time. It goes without saying that, in needing to explain how the concrete ethical powers had evolved into their current states, he resorted to a substantive philosophy of history. And as in many other classical philosophies of history, the general conception of the historical process presupposed by Droysen is ultimately anchored in religious assumptions. For him, the process of history is ultimately strongly linked, albeit in a mediated fashion, with the episode of God's creation of the world. Historical science's subject matter, human history, despite its relative opposition to natural history, is nothing but an advanced segment of the history of the world as created by God. Consequently, the last pillar of the science of history is of a religious nature. This is why Droysen could once suggest that '[the science of history's] highest task is the theodicy'.[72]

This statement stresses that ultimately, historical studies do or should indirectly point to the existence of God. More important, they do or should contribute to resolving a tension inherent in Christian thought, one that has been perceived as crucial since the early eighteenth century. That tension, put simply, is that even if God is considered to be good and to have created the world consonantly with his good purposes, the fact remains that in ordinary experience, bad things keep happening. Since Gottfried Wilhelm Leibniz's (1646–1716) famous *Essais de théodicée* (1710) – and his famous postulate that the already existing is the best of all possible worlds – German philosophers had attempted to rationally demonstrate the goodness of God and to harmonize God's goodness with the existence of evil. Throughout the eighteenth century, those attempts became known as 'the problem of theodicy'.[73] Droysen's decided linkage of this philosophical-theological problem with the issue of the function of historical science strongly confirms the centrality of religion in his historical cosmos. Through the mediation of a substantive philosophy of history, Droysen not only conciliates his scientific ideals with his religious beliefs; he also subordinates the former to the latter.[74] In his view, research-based understanding of the past is ultimately motivated by the expectation of catching a glimpse of the meaning of the whole historical process. This is the most accessible path to a partial albeit possible understanding of God. Knowledge of history is therefore, as Dirk Fleischer has pointed out, equal to knowledge of God.[75] 'Our method', Droysen explains, referring to the historian's method, 'does not open up the last mystery.... We cannot conceive the absolute totality, the purpose of the purposes, but we can understand it in one of its expressions, in that one which is for us the most accessible. From history we learn how to understand God, and only in God can we understand history.'[76]

Besides such a substantive philosophy – which, as one can see, ultimately leads to a sort of theology of history – a further aspect of Droysen's historical theory is his typology of historiography, something that is, again, a very peculiar product within the context of nineteenth-century meta-historical reflection. It combines the principles of source criticism then in vogue with the old rhetorical principles around which Western reflections on historiography had previously gravitated. Droysen wanted historiography to be connected to the results of empirical research, but he already knew that such results cannot be merely mirrored by the historical account, and that one can only talk about them after representational mediations and transformations.[77] 'The forms of representation' – as he puts it – 'are determined not according to the segments of the investigated pasts, but to the motives espoused by both the research and the researcher.'[78] The four forms of representation he typologically worked out – investigative, narrative, didactic and discursive – are structured precisely in accordance with the prospective kind of reading that the historical text aims to stimulate. Anyhow, Droysen's representational types run, as Hayden White elegantly remarked, much less to a theory of historical composition but rather to a 'phenomenology of historical reading'.[79]

In addition, one can also extract from Droysen's theory of history arguments related to social and cultural theory. These are especially evident in his discussion of the relationship between 'history's workers' and 'history's forms'. Droysen equates the latter with the 'ethical powers', the communities of the social world that mediate between history's supreme realm, that of humankind, and the real 'historical workers', the single individuals. He considers the relationship between the individual on the one hand, and either society or culture (as expressed in the various ethical spheres) on the other, as a two-way street.[80] For him, 'ethical communities' such as families, languages, arts, sciences, religions, societies, economies and states, indeed condition the individual's socialization and acculturation. But individuals, as 'historical workers', do not necessarily only adhere to the norms of the ethical communities in which they partake. Some individuals eventually break the established norms and, in doing so, help bring about evolutionary transformations in the ethical spheres. Therefore, the fact that individuals are bound by those spheres does not simply cancel the possibility of freedom. According to Droysen, what the long course of human history has proven is quite the reverse: since classical antiquity, free individuals have continuously broken with the established social and moral norms, and dialectically propelled the establishment of new social orders in which more and more individuals became free. Droysen thus regards 'ethical communities' as forms within the historical process that dialectically shape individuals' behaviour and are shaped by the individuals in consequence of their interactions and free actions.

At this juncture, Droysen's historical theory turns into what could be defined as a historical ethics. Broadly speaking, Droysen holds that since the ancient Greeks, the historical process has led to continuous enlargement of the space of freedom in the human world.[81] He moves across traditional ethics as he consciously proposes historical knowledge as a means for expanding freedom, that is, as a means for making human life better. While concluding his first course of lectures on *Historik,* and driven by his strong perception of the historicity of the 'ethical spheres', Droysen even came to suggest that ethics should be expanded into history.[82] This means that he was thinking of historical science as a substitute to traditional ethics. Droysen is less daring in the last version of the *Grundriß der Historik,* but he makes more or less the same point by characterizing ethics and *Historik* as 'coordinates'. Using Immanuel Kant's (1724–1804) concepts, he reinforces the ethical dimension of history, stating that it delivers 'the genesis of the "postulate of practical reason"', a postulate which is not accessible to "pure reason"'.[83] Historical knowledge produces, hence, a sort of genealogy of morals suited to orientating the moral action of human individuals in the present. In doing so, it stimulates an awareness of the historicity of the ethical communities that circumscribe human agents.[84] This argument that history is ultimately very much akin to ethics is ultimately a philosophical justification for the didactic moment of his historical theory.

Droysen relates the ethical-didactic task of historical science to more than a subjective capacity to form and enhance oneself by acquiring knowledge on the historicity of the world one lives in. From the perspective of the science of history, he argues, it is much more important to apply historical thinking as an ethical tool in the 'ethical spheres' within which the historical process takes place. Droysen pointed to one especial 'ethical sphere' in which historical thinking should play a crucial strategic role, namely, the state. This is how politics connects to Droysen's substantive philosophy of history. Distinct from other nineteenth-century German historical thinkers, Droysen espoused a relativized view of the importance of the state, listing it as only one among many other autonomous 'ethical powers'. However, and even trying to avoid a statist conception of history, he still conceded that the state had a leading role to play in the development of all other social spheres.[85] Droysen stuck to this ethical conception of the role of the state throughout his entire life. He also linked these philosophical arguments with the concrete political ideas and projects he endorsed – mostly the quest for German political unification. Indeed, he never stopped using philosophy of history and historical thinking to justify political values and choices that appear highly problematic when seen through today's post-national, democratic lens.

As one may conclude from the depiction above, Droysen's theory of the science of history comprises several highly integrated yet also discrete microtheories: a methodology, a methodics, a simultaneously dialectical and hermeneutical epistemology, a substantive philosophy of history anchored in religious values, a theory of historicity, a typology of historical representation, a sociocultural theory, a historical ethics and a political theory, among others. What led him to bring these disparate theoretical discussions together was not a special preference for eclecticism; nor was it the intention to build a philosophical system that could provide the human sciences with something similar to what Kant's philosophy had brought to the natural sciences – something that Dilthey, for instance, would later have in mind.[86] Droysen's *Historik* is not structured on a philosophical perspective, though it frequently lands at philosophical discussions. Therefore it would be a misunderstanding to characterize his project as an attempt to establish a philosophical foundation for the historical or the human sciences. In fact, this is not the main issue with which he was concerned, even though his methodics – which features the distinction between *Verstehen* and *Erklären* – ended up becoming an important chapter of Western philosophy in the nineteenth century. His thoughts on historiography accrued from the 'inside' of the practice of historical scholarship, rather than from the 'outside' of philosophical tradition.[87] Likewise, the problems he wanted to tackle were practical problems specific to historical inquiry, not the big issues of nineteenth-century philosophy. Droysen's main aim was, in sum, to develop a theoretical framework by reference to which historians could enhance their professional self-reflexivity. He conceived his *Historik* as a means to help his students become less intuitive as regards the nature, the principles and the functions of historiography.

Notes

1. I have compiled most of the biographical information presented in this appendix from the following sources: Gustav Droysen. 1910. *Johann Gustav Droysen,* part 1: *Bis zum Beginn der*

Frankfurter Tätigkeit, Leipzig: B.G. Teubner; Hans-Joachim Gehrke. 1989. 'Johann Gustav Droysen', in Michael Erbe (ed.), *Berlinische Lebensbilder*, vol. 4: *Geisteswissenschaftler*, Berlin Colloquium, 127–142; Hintze, 'Johann Gustav Droysen', 150–213; Friedrich Meinecke. 1930. 'Johann Gustav Droysen. Sein Briefwechsel und seine Geschichtsschreibung', *Historische Zeitschrift* 141: 249–287; Nippel, *Johann Gustav Droysen*; Werner Obermann. 1977. *Der Junge Johann Gustav Droysen. Ein Beitrag zur Entstehungsgeschichte des Historismus*, Ph.D. thesis: Universität Bonn; Jörn Rüsen. 1973. 'Johann Gustav Droysen', in Hans-Ulrich Wehler (ed.), *Deutsche Historiker*, Göttingen: Vandenhoeck & Ruprecht; Schieder, 'Johann Gustav Bernhard Droysen', 115–131. The catalogue of the exhibition organized at the University of Berlin in honour of Droysen's 200th jubilee is a good source of basic information on Droysen's biography, as well as of iconographic material related to him: Christiane Hackel (ed.). 2008. *Philologe – Historiker – Politiker. Johann Gustav Droysen, 1808–1884. Katalog zur Ausstellung des Sonderforschungsbereiches «Transformationen der Antike», Humboldt Universität zu Berlin, 01.07–08.08.2008*, Berlin: G + H. For a short biographical account in English, see Hermann Krüger. 1893. 'Biographical Sketch: Johann Gustav Droysen', in Johann Gustav Droysen, *Outline of the Principles of History*, Boston: Ginn & Company, xv–xxxv.

2. For a historical analysis of the discourse on the cultural importance of the evangelical rectory, see Oliver Janz. 2001. 'Das evangelische Pfarrhaus', in Étienne François and Hagen Schulze (eds), *Deutsche Erinnerungsorte III*, Munich: C.H. Beck, 221–238.

3. Johann Christoph Droysen had studied theology at the University of Halle from 1792 to 1794. After graduating, he worked as a private tutor, and in 1803 he moved to Treptow following his appointment as chaplain of the cuirassier regiment stationed there. In 1804, he married Friederike Casten, daughter of a local grocer. Christiane Hackel and Nadine Wendland. 2008. 'Kindheit im pommerschen Pfarrhaus', in Hackel, *Philologe – Historiker – Politiker*, 9.

4. The other history course Droysen attended was Friedrich Wilken's (1777–1840) lectures on medieval history in the winter semester of 1828–29. For a complete list of lectures attended by Droysen, see Hildegard Astholz. 1933. *Das Problem ‹Geschichte› untersucht bei J. G. Droysen*, Berlin Ebering, 209–210.

5. Johann Gustav Droysen. 1831. *De Lagidarum regno Ptolemaeo IV Philometore rege*, Quam commentationem amplissimi ordinis philosophici Berolinensis auctoritate ad summos in philosophia honores rite capessendos die XXXI Aug. A. MDCCCXXXI publice defendet Johannes Gustavus Droysen Pomeranus, Berlin: Eisendorf. The dissertation covered the period from 180 and 163 BC in the reign of Ptolemy VI, Philometor (191–145 BC), a pharaoh of the second Hellenistic dynasty (which ended when Egypt became a province of Rome in 30 BC).

6. Nippel, *Johann Gustav Droysen*, 12.

7. Rudolph Hübner. 1967. 'Vorwort', in Johann Gustav Droysen, *Briefwechsel*, vol. 1: *1828–1851*, Osnabrück: Biblio, viii.

8. Droysen, *Briefwechsel* 1: 91 [Letter to Karl Freiherr von Stein zum Altenstein, 08 July 1836].

9. Johann Gustav Droysen. 1832. *Des Aischylos Werke*, 2 vols, Berlin: G. Finke.

10. Johann Gustav Droysen. 1835–38. *Des Aristophanes Werke*, 3 vols, Berlin: Veit.

11. On Droysen's translations, see Josefine Kitzbichler. 2008. 'Der Übersetzer', in Hackel, *Philologe – Historiker – Politiker*, 33–38.

12. Johann Gustav Droysen. 1833. *Geschichte Alexander des Großen*, Berlin: G. Finke; Johann Gustav Droysen. 1836. *Geschichte des Hellenismus*, part 1: *Geschichte der Nachfolger Alexanders*. Hamburg: Friedrich Perthes; Johann Gustav Droysen. 1843. *Geschichte des Hellenismus*, part 2: *Geschichte der Bildung des hellenistischen Staatensystems*. Hamburg: Friedrich Perthes. A largely revised version of the *History of Alexander the Great* and the two subsequent volumes on Hellenistic history were published in three volumes under the title *Geschichte des Hellenismus* (Gotha: Friedrich Andreas Perthes, 1877–78).

13. Bravo, 'Hégélianisme et recherche historique dans l'oeuvre de J.G. Droysen', 155–157.

14. Momigliano, 'J. G. Droysen between Greeks and Jews', 142.

15. Momigliano, 'J. G. Droysen between Greeks and Jews', 144.

16. Nippel, *Johann Gustav Droysen,* 39–40, 308.

17. Droysen, *Historik* 2: 445 [Antrittsrede, 1867]: 'Ich hatte in frühen Jahren den Plan gefaßt, denjenigen Zeitraum der alten Geschichte zu erforschen, der zwischen Alexander und Cäsar liegt, der aus dem Griechentum zum Christenthum hinüberführt.' This was, at least, the way the older Droysen in 1867 (in his inaugural speech at Berlin's Academy of Sciences) recalled the research project of his youth. Momigliano also mentions that Droysen had once intended to conclude his Hellenism work with a volume covering the cultural history from the times of Alexander up to the Arab invasion of Egypt and Syria in the seventh century AD. See Momigliano, 'J. G. Droysen between Greeks and Jews', 143.

18. Droysen's texts on Hellenistic history were very much debated and contested immediately after their publication. They were written amidst a quarrel that agitated German classical philologists in the first half of the nineteenth century, in which one of the main disputants was Droysen's teacher, Böckh, who argued for expanding the domain of philological work to material sources beyond conventional textual sources. Böckh's main opponent was Gottfried Hermann (1772–1848), a professor at the University of Leipzig, who for his part advocated for a philology focused on textual criticism, grammar and metrics. See Wilfried Nippel. 1997. 'Philologenstreit und Schulpolitik. Zur Kontroverse zwischen Gottfried Hermann und August Böckh', in Wolfgang Küttler et al. (eds), *Geschichtsdiskurs,* vol. 3: *Die Epoche der Historisierung,* Frankfurt am Main: Fischer, 244–253. Most criticism of Droysen's works on ancient history came from the ranks of Hermann's supporters. See Nippel, *Johann Gustav Droysen,* 29–34.

19. Nippel, *Johann Gustav Droysen,* 33–34, 39.

20. Momigliano, 'J. G. Droysen between Greeks and Jews', 150–151.

21. Droysen, *Historik* 2: 445 [Antrittsrede bei der Berliner Akademie, 1867].

22. In addition, Droysen once delivered lectures on medieval history. See Droysen, *Historik* 2: 167–174 [Vorlesung über die Geschichte des Mittelalters, 1840].

23. Droysen, *Vorlesungen über die Freiheitskriege,* 2 vols.

24. Schieder, 'Johann Gustav Bernhard Droysen', 136.

25. Rüsen, 'Johann Gustav Droysen', 121.

26. The Frankfurt National Assembly, inaugurated on 18 May 1848, was another outcome of the revolution of March 1848. It was the first general parliament in the German states whose members were elected by popular vote. Hosted at St. Paul's Church, it was convoked to prepare and promulgate a federal constitution. It was practically dissolved on 31 May 1849, when the Prussian king Friedrich Wilhelm IV rejected the assembly's proposal to make him the emperor of a constitutional, parliamentarian and little-German (i.e., without Austria) national state. Droysen was elected by the 5th electoral district of the duchy Holstein (Lütjenburg, Oldenburg, Oldsloe, Neustadt, Heiligenhafen). He obtained 4,388 votes, a comfortable victory over his opponent, lawyer Ludolph Bargum, who garnered only 1,890 votes. See Nippel, *Johann Gustav Droysen,* 98.

27. Some of Droysen's unofficial records of the meetings of the constitutional commission had been published by the end of 1849: Johann Gustav Droysen. 1849. *Die Verhandlungen des Verfassungs-Ausschusses der deutschen Nationalversammlung,* part 1, Leipzig: Weidmann. The rest of these records were edited and incorporated into a posthumous publication: Johann Gustav Droysen. 1924. *Aktenstücke und Aufzeichnungen zur Geschichte der Frankfurter Nationalversammlung aus dem Nachlaß von Johann Gustav Droysen,* Stuttgart: Deutsche Verlags-Anstalt.

28. Hintze, 'Johann Gustav Droysen', 168–171.

29. Following his retreat from direct politics, Droysen published a collection of political memoranda: Johann Gustav Droysen. 1849. *Beiträge zur neuesten deutschen Geschichte,* Braunschweig: Friedrich Vieweg und Sohn. He also wrote a text on the conflict over Schleswig-Holstein: Johann Gustav Droysen and Karl Samwer. 1850. *Die Herzogthümer Schleswig-Holstein und das Königreich Dänemark. Aktenmäßige Geschichte der dänischen Politik seit dem Jahre 1806,* Hamburg: Perthes-Besser und Mauke.

30. Stephan Paetrow. 2008. *Johann Gustav Droysen in Jena. Ein Beitrag zur Entstehungsgeschichte von Droysens ‹Historik› und ‹Geschichte der preußischen Politik›,* Saarbrücken: VDM, 58.

31. Paetrow, *Johann Gustav Droysen in Jena*, 76–77.

32. Nippel, *Johann Gustav Droysen*, 177.

33. Johann Gustav Droysen. 1851–52. *Das Leben des Feldmarschalls Grafen York von Wartenburg*, 3 Vols., Berlin Veit & Comp.

34. Johann Gustav Droysen. 1855–86. *Geschichte der Preußischen Politik*, 14 vols, Berlin and Leipzig: Veit.

35. Rüsen, 'Johann Gustav Droysen', 118–119.

36. Nippel, *Johann Gustav Droysen*, 260–262.

37. Christiane Hackel. 2008. 'Der Geschichtstheoretiker', in Hackel (ed.), *Philologe – Historiker – Politiker*, 57.

38. Hintze, 'Johann Gustav Droysen', 178–179, 181; Nippel, *Johann Gustav Droysen*, 291–295; Droysen, *Briefwechsel* 2: 95, fn. 2 [editor's footnote].

39. Droysen, *Briefwechsel* 2: 985–987 [editor's final remarks].

40. One of the oldest summaries of Droysen's intellectual biography is an article by Alfred Dove published on the occasion of Droysen's sixtieth birthday in 1878. For a reprint of this text see Alfred Dove. 1898. 'Johann Gustav Droysen', in Alfred Dove, *Ausgewählte Schriftchen vornehmlich historischen Inhalts*, Leipzig: Duncker & Humblot. Other late nineteenth-century biographical summaries appeared in the form of obituaries published immediately after Droysen's death in 1884. The most famous and often cited is an article written by a friend of Droysen's, the historian Max Duncker. 1884. 'Johann Gustav Droysen', *Preußische Jahrbücher* 54: 134–167. In 1904, a more comprehensive biographical essay was written by Otto Hintze for the *Allgemeine Deutsche Biographie* (for a reprint of this text, see Hintze, 'Johann Gustav Droysen', 150–213). In 1910, a longer biographical account written by Droysen's son Gustav was published. This incomplete work – interrupted by the author's death – covers, however, the period 1808–48 in great detail. See (Gustav) Droysen, *Johann Gustav Droysen*, part 1: *Bis zum Beginn der Frankfurter Tätigkeit*. Other significant sources of biographical information are Friedrich Meinecke's review of Droysen's edited *Correspondence* (see Meinecke, 'Johann Gustav Droysen'). All these initial texts on Droysen still convey important biographical information, and some of them – especially Hintze's and Meinecke's – contain several enlightening interpretations of Droysen's texts and ideas. All these texts tend, however, to excessive eulogy, flagrantly lacking critical distance in relation to many essential points.

Since the 1930s, biographical surveys on Droysen have been rather rare. Two exceptions were Werner Obermann's book on the young Droysen (Obermann, *Der Junge Johann Gustav Droysen*), and Stephan Paetrow's on Droysen's eight years in Jena (Paetrow, *Johann Gustav Droysen in Jena*). A third and most significant exception is the recent biography by Wilfried Nippel. Focusing on Droysen's professional and political trajectories, Nippel successfully undertook the task of elevating the critical level of biographical knowledge on Droysen. His book competently deconstructs a number of myths, brings new facts to light and details several already known pieces of information, therefore constituting an essential reference. See Nippel, *Johann Gustav Droysen*. For a synopsis of Nippel's arguments, see Wilfried Nippel. 2009. 'Droysen-Legenden', in Horst Walter Blanke (ed.), *Historie und Historik. 200 Jahre Johann Gustav Droysen. Festschrift für Jörn Rüsen zum 70. Geburtstag*, Cologne: Böhlau, 158–176.

41. Meinecke, 'Johann Gustav Droysen', 257. It should be noted that Meinecke's statement disregards Droysen's seminal translations of the works of Aeschylus and Aristophanes.

42. It is also important to recall Droysen's well-acknowledged – and already mentioned – role as a sort of intellectual founding father of the field of Hellenistic studies.

43. Hannah Arendt. 1993. *Between Past and Future: Eight Exercises in Political Thought*, New York: Penguin, 75.

44. Hans-Georg Gadamer. 1990. *Wahrheit und Methode. Grundzüge einer philosophischen Hermeneutik*, Tübingen: Mohr Siebeck, 213, 216.

45. Rothacker, 'J.G. Droysens Historik', 90.

46. Nipperdey, *Deutsche Geschichte 1800–1866*, 517.

47. Rüsen, *Konfigurationen des Historismus,* 243: 'Droysens "Historik" ist einer der bedeutendsten, wenn nicht gar der bedeutendste Text zur Theorie der Geschichtswissenschaft'.

48. Wolfgang Hardtwig. 1990. 'Johann Gustav Droysen', in Wolfgang Hardtwig (ed.), *Über das Studium der Geschichte.* Munich: DTV, 83: 'Johann Gustav Droysen ist unzweifelhaft der bedeutendste Geschichtstheoretiker deutscher Sprache'.

49. Droysen printed the first version of the *Grundriß der Historik* in 1858 and handed it out to students and some colleagues. The first commercial edition of the text, however, appeared only in 1868, when Droysen augmented the outlines of his *Historik* lectures with three essays: *The Elevation of History to the Rank of a Science* (1863), *Nature and History* (1866), and *Art and Method* (1867). Droysen republished the *Grundriß* twice more, in 1875 and 1882, and in both cases he made some corrections and changes to the text. The 1882 edition was reprinted, first in 1925 by Erich Rothacker, then in 1937 by Rudolf Hübner, and finally in 1977 by Peter Leyh. The text, last revised in 1882, was also translated into both French and English towards the end of the nineteenth century: *Précis de la Science de l'Histoire,* trans. P.-A. Dormoy, Paris: E. Leroux (1887); *Outline of the Principles of History,* trans. E. Benjamin Andrews, Boston: Ginn (1893). Further translations of the text include 史学綱要 (*Shigaku Kouyou*), trans. Toshio Kanba, Tokyo: Toukou Shyoin (1937); *Sommario di istorica,* trans. Delio Cantimori, Florence: Sansoni (1943); *Compendio di istorica* (Prima versione manoscritta completa, 1857–1858), trans. Silvia Caianiello, *Archivio di storia della cultura* 2 (1989), 325–339 (from the 1858 edition); *Précis de théorie d'histoire,* trans. Alexandre Escudier, Paris: Ed. du Cerf (2002); *Manual de teoria da história,* trans. Sara Baldus and Júlio Bentivoglio, Petrópolis: Vozes (2009). For more detailed information on Droysen's publications and their editorial history, see Johann Gustav Droysen. 2008. *Historik. Supplement: Droysen Bibliographie,* edited by Horst Walter Blanke, Stuttgart: Frommann-Holzboog (2008).

50. Presenting the 1867 edition of the *Grundriß der Historik,* Droysen explained quite clearly the context in which his theoretical writings had originated: 'Lectures upon Encyclopaedia and Methodology of History which I delivered from time to time, beginning with 1857, led me to write down the skeleton of the same in order to give my auditors a basis for my oral amplification.' Droysen, *Outline of the Principles of History,* ix.

51. The appearance of the first full-text version of the *Historik* lectures in 1937 was due to the editorial efforts of Droysen's grandson, Rudolf Hübner. This publication was mostly a reconstruction of the last course of lectures delivered by Droysen in the winter semester of 1882–83 (Droysen, *Historik. Vorlesungen über Enzyklopädie und Methodologie der Geschichte*). The textual-philological deficiencies of the Hübner edition subsequently justified the enterprise of assembling a critical edition of Droysen's theoretical texts, which began in 1971 with Peter Leyh's reconstruction of the first course of the *Historik* lectures (delivered in the summer semester of 1857) (Droysen, *Historik* 1). In recent years, the critical edition of Droysen's *Historik* has continued, now under the coordination of Horst Walter Blanke. In 2007, he edited two volumes containing short texts by Droysen under the title *Texts within the Historik's Perimeter* (Droysen, *Historik* 2). In 2008, there followed a cautiously researched supplementary volume, in which Blanke organized extensive information on the editorial history of Droysen's texts. In this publication, Blanke also presented a good list of the most relevant studies on Droysen's life and oeuvre (Droysen, *Historik. Supplement*). A critical reconstruction of the final course of the *Historik* lectures is in preparation and will be published soon.

Hübner's edition of the full text of Droysen's *Historik* has been translated into Italian, Spanish and Russian: *Istorica. Lezioni sulla enciclopedia e metodologia della storia,* trans. Luigi Emery, Milano: Ricciardi (1966); *Histórica. Lecciones sobre la enciclopedia y metodología de la historia,* trans. Ernesto Garzón Valdés and Rafael Gutiérrez Girardot, Barcelona: Alfa (1983); *Историка* (Istorika), trans. G.I. Federov, Saint Petersburg: Vladimir Dal' (2004). The Leyh full-text edition boasts an Italian translation: *Istorica. Lezioni di enciclopedia e metodologia della storia,* trans. Silvia Caianiello, Napoli: Guida (1994). Moreover, selected parts of the Leyh edition were published in both Taiwan and continental China: 歷史知識的理論 (Lìshǐ Zhīshì de Lǐlùn), trans. Hu Chang-Tze, Taipei: Linkingbooks (1986); the same edition was also published in Peking: Peking University Press (2006).

52. Christiane Hackel has shown that another tradition of academic lectures also influenced the development of Droysen's lectures on *Historik*, namely the *Enzyklopädie* lectures. Famous representatives of this wide and cross-disciplinary genre of 'encyclopaedias' include Friedrich Wolf's *Enzyklopädie und Methodologie der Studien des Altertums* (1785; first lecture), Schleiermacher's *Einführung in die Grundlage der Theologie* (1805), Böckh's *Encyklopädie und Methodologie der philologischen Wissenschaften* (1809) and Hegel's *Enzyklopädie der philosophischen Wissenschaften im Grundrisse* (1817). See Christiane Hackel. 2006. *Die Bedeutung August Boeckhs für den Geschichtstheoretiker Johann Gustav Droysen. Die Enzyklopädie-Vorlesungen im Vergleich,* Würzburg: Könighausen und Neumann, 21–27.

53. Droysen, *Historik* 2: 502–503 [Über die wissenschaftlich-praktischen Studien, 1869]: 'Wer mit der Absicht, Geschichte zu studieren, zur Universität kommt, hat – wie ähnlich in allen anderen Fächern – vom Wesen und Umfang dieser Disciplin eine nur abstracte und undeutliche Vorstellung. Es würde thöricht sein, wenn man damit beginnen wollte, ihm in theoretischer Weise den Umfang, die Art und Weise seines Studiums darzulegen; es würde nur die Phantasie erregen, ohne dem Verstande, dem eigene Erfahrung noch kein Maaß und keinen Anhalt giebt, Faßbares zu bieten. Eine solche Encyclopädie und Methodologie der Geschichte ist der Schluß des Studiums; erst dann ist das Verständniß der großen und schwierigen Fragen, um die es sich da handelt, möglich und Bedürfniß.'

54. Horst Walter Blanke, Dirk Fleischer and Jörn Rüsen. 1984. 'Theory of History in Historical Lectures: The German Tradition of Historik, 1750–1900', *History and Theory* 23(3): 334. For some additional detail on these lectures, see also Ulrich Muhlack. 1990. 'Johann Gustav Droysen: "Historik" et "Hermeneutique"', in André Laks and Ada Neschke (eds), *La naissance du paradigme herméneutique. Schleiermacher, Humboldt, Boeckh, Droysen,* Lille: Presses Universitaires de Lille, 361–362.

55. On the general features of historical teaching and research at German universities in the nineteenth century, see Hans-Jürgen Pandel. 1993. 'Wer ist ein Historiker? Forschung und Lehre als Bestimmungsfaktoren in der Geschichtswissenschaft des 19. Jahrhunderts', in Wolfgang Küttler et al. (eds), *Geschichtsdiskurs,* vol. 1: *Grundlagen und Methoden der Historiographiegeschichte,* Frankfurt am Main: Fischer.

56. Droysen, *Historik* 1: 3 [Vorlesungstext, 1857], 417 [Grundriß der Historik, 1882].

57. MacLean, 'History in a Two-Cultures World', 485.

58. Droysen, *Historik* 1: 461 [Erhebung der Geschichte zum Rang einer Wissenschaft, 1863].

59. Rothacker. 'J.G. Droysens Historik', 89: 'Droysen ist damit unverkennbar der Anreger der Diltheyschen Versuche zu einer Grundlegung der Geisteswissenschaften geworden.... Im besonderen aber ist er der Ahnherr des Diltheyschen Versuchs, die Logik der Geisteswissenschaften auf eine Logik des "Verstehens" zu gründen.' On the many theoretical presuppositions shared by Droysen and Dilthey, see Massimo Mezzanzanica. 2009. 'Expérience historique et théorie de la comprehension: Droysen et Dilthey', in Jean-Claude Gens (ed.), *Johann Gustav Droysen: L'avénement du paradigme herméneutique dans les sciences humaines,* Argenteuil: Le Cercle herméneutique, 205–221. In several of his earlier writings, Dilthey directly referenced Droysen's theoretical and historical texts. From the early 1870s onwards, however, he kept his distance from Droysen and what he called 'the historical school'. Hence, references to Droysen in his most important texts, such as the *Einleitung in die Geisteswissenschaften* (1881) and *Der Aufbau der geschichtlichen Welt in den Geisteswissenschaften* (1910), are scarce. On this issue, see: Guy van Kerckhoven. 2009. 'Geschichtlichkeit chez Droysen et Dilthey', also in Gens, *Johann Gustav Droysen,* 173–203. Droysen's opinion on Dilthey's theory of the human sciences, on the other hand, was far from enthusiastic. In 1883, shortly after the publication of Dilthey's *Einleitung,* he wrote to his son Gustav that 'Von Diltheys Buch über die Geisteswissenschaften habe ich wohl schon geschrieben? Schmoller hätte es sich ersparen können, darüber eine Fanfare zu blasen. Ich kann ja sagen, da ich das ästhetisch kokette Buch ganz und genau gelesen habe.' Droysen, *Briefwechsel* 2: 970 [Letter to Gustav Droysen, 24 September 1883].

60. In former versions of the *Historik* lectures, Droysen had added to these three a fourth methodical operation: the writing of the historical text, which he called *Apodeixis*. In latter versions of the *Historik*, he transferred the discussion on representation to a third new major section (besides the *Methodik* and the *Systematik*) that he designated as *Topik*.

61. Bernheim indeed recognized that he had borrowed his scheme of historical method from Droysen's *Grundriß der Historik*. In a remark he made in the first edition of the *Lehrbuch* (which is absent in later editions), Bernheim admits that Droysen's handbook was 'the only theoretical and methodological overview that did justice to the then contemporary progresses of historical science'. Ernst Bernheim. 1889. *Lehrbuch der historischen Methode*. Leipzig: Duncker & Humblot, 149. Moreover, after distinguishing the four operations of his methodology – heuristics, criticism, conception and representation – Bernheim explains in a footnote that he made that classification 'as Droysen was the first to do in his *Grundriß*'. Bernheim, *Lehrbuch der historischen Methode und der Geschichtsphilosophie*, 250–251 [5th and 6th rev. and exp. editions, 1908]. Langlois and Seignobos's methodical scheme resembles Bernheim's tremendously – which is no surprise, as they admit in their introductory literature review that they had largely drawn heavily on Bernheim's manual. Charles Langlois and Charles Seignobos. 1909. *Introduction to the Study of History,* New York: Henry Holt, 10–11. On the relationship between the conceptions of historical method developed by Droysen, Bernheim, and Langlois and Seignobos, see Rolf Torstendahl. 2003. 'Fact, Truth and Text: The Quest for a Firm Basis for Historical Knowledge around 1900', *History and Theory* 42(3): 305–331.

62. Lutz Raphael, *Geschichtswissenschaft im Zeitalter der Extreme,* 40–41; Gabriele Lingelbach. 2003. *Klio macht Karriere. Die Institutionalisierung der Geschichtswissenschaft in Frankreich und den USA in der zweiten Hälfte des 19. Jahrhunderts,* Göttingen: Vandenhoeck & Ruprecht, 386–387.

63. See Lingelbach, *Klio macht Karriere,* 386; Torstendahl, 'Fact, Truth and Text', 309.

64. Droysen himself recognized that he was attracted to issues that went far beyond ordinary methodical problems related to the practice of the science of history. See Droysen, *Historik* 1: 4 [Vorlesungstext].

65. Droysen, *Historik. Vorlesungen über Enzyklopädie und Methodologie der Geschichte,* 183: 'Was der einzelne will und tut und schafft, ist sein Geschäft und auf seine Gegenwart gerichtet, ist nicht Geschichte, sondern wird erst Geschichte durch die Art der Betrachtung, in die wir es stellen und auffassen.'

66. Droysen, *Historik. Vorlesungen über Enzyklopädie und Methodologie der Geschichte,* 20: 'Unsere Wissenschaft beruht darauf, daß wir aus solchen noch gegenwärtigen Materialien nicht die Vergangenheiten herstellen, sondern unsere Vorstellungen von ihnen begründen, berichtigen, erweitern wollen, und zwar durch ein methodisches Verfahren [...]'.

67. Droysen, *Outline of the Principles of History,* 44: 'Even the narrow, the very narrowest of human relations, strivings, activities, etc., have a process, a history, and are for the persons involved, historical. So family histories, local histories, special histories. But over all these and such histories there is History'; see also Droysen, *Historik. Vorlesungen über Enzyklopädie und Methodologie der Geschichte,* 221; Droysen, *Historik* 1: 369 [Vorlesungstext, 1857].

68. Once again, it is important to note that the *Topik* chapter did not exist in the first version of Droysen's *Historik*.

69. Droysen, *Historik. Vorlesungen über Enzyklopädie und Methodologie der Geschichte,* 189: 'Wir fanden, daß das ganze weite Gebiet der menschlichen Welt unserer Wissenscahft zugehört, daß das Gebiet der historischen Methode der Kosmos der sittlichen Welt ist.'

70. Droysen, *Historik* 1: 368 [Vorlesungstext, 1857].

71. Droysen, *Historik* 1: 369 [Vorlesungstext, 1857]: 'Ist nun das generelle Ich, d.h. der Mensch, das Subjekt dieser Geschichte, wie er zugleich ihr Objekt ist, hier zugleich der Zweck und das Mittel, ihn zu verwirklichen, und das Mittel erfüllt und bewegt von dem Zweck, um dessen[t]willen und in dem die Geschichte ist, wird der Mensch in eben dieser Geschichte, die, mit Goethe zu sprechen, "Dich zeugte, da Du zeugtest" so ist klar, wie gerade diese Sphäre, wenn ich so sagen darf, die Geschichte der Geschichte enthalten wird.'

72. Droysen, *Historik* 2: 228 [Privatvorrede, 1843].

73. Thomas Pröpper and Magnus Striet. 2000. 'Theodizee', in Walter Kasper et al. (eds), *Lexikon für Theologie und Kirche,* vol. 9, Freiburg im Breisgau: Herder, 1396.

74. See Hardtwig, 'Geschichtsreligion – Wissenschaft als Arbeit – Objektivität', 6. On the role of religion in Droysen's historical theory, see also Uwe Barrelmeyer. 1997. *Geschichtliche Wirklichkeit als Problem. Untersuchungen zu geschichtstheoretischen Begründungen historischen Wissens bei Johann Gustav Droysen, Georg Simmel und Max Weber.* Münster: LIT, 43–52.

75. Dirk Fleischer. 2009. '"Geschichtserkenntnis als Goterkenntnis". Das theologische Fundament der Geschichtstheorie Johann Gustav Droysens', in Horst Walter Blanke (ed.), *Historie und Historik. 200 Jahre Johann Gustav Droysen. Festschrift für Jörn Rüsen zum 70. Geburtstag.* Cologne: Böhlau, 73–89.

76. Droysen, *Historik* 1: 30 [Vorlesungstext, 1857]: 'Nicht das letzte Geheimnis erschließt unsere Methode, wenn auch einen Weg dazu, wenn auch den Eingang zum Tempel. Nicht die absolute Totalität, den Zweck der Zwecke, erfassen wir, aber in einer ihrer Äußerungen, in der uns verständlichsten, verstehen wir sie. Aus der Geschichte lernen wir Gott verstehen und in Gott können wir die Geschichte verstehen.'

77. Rüsen, *Konfigurationen des Historismus,* 269.

78. Droysen, *Historik* 1: 405 [Grundriß der Historik, 1857]: 'Die Formen der Darstellung bestimmen sich nicht nach den erforschten Vergangenheiten, sondern aus Motiven der Forschung oder des Forschers.'

79. White, 'Droysen's Historik', 88.

80. Droysen, *Historik* 1: 290 [Vorlesungstext, 1857].

81. Droysen, *Historik. Vorlesungen über Enzyklopädie und Methodologie der Geschichte,* 243: 'Ich habe bisher das Wort Freiheit absichtlich wenig oder nicht gebraucht. Nicht als wenn ich nicht wüßte und anerkennte, daß die Freiheit wie das Samenkorn so die Frucht der Sittlichkeit, der Geschichte ist.'

82. Droysen, *Historik* 1: 393 [Vorlesungstext, 1857]: 'Wir werden sagen dürfen, die Ethik hat sich zur Geschichte zu erweitern, erst in dieser größeren Gestaltung, erst als Geschichte begriffen, hat die Ethik das Recht, zwischen Logik und Physik zu stehen.'

83. Droysen, *Historik* 1: 444 [Grundriß der Historik, 1882]: 'Ethik und Historik sind gleichsam Koordinaten. Denn die Geschichte gibt die Genesis des "Postulats der praktischen Vernunft", das der "reinen Vernunft" unfindbar blieb.'

84. On the relationship between history and ethics in Droysen's *Historik,* see Escudier, 'Présentation', 21–24; Riedel, *Verstehen oder Erklären,* 132.

85. Droysen, *Historik* 1: 357 [Vorlesungstext, 1857]: 'Gewiß kann man die Macht bis zu einen gewissen Grad über jene anderen sittlichen Sphären bestimmend einwirken, aber auch nur bis zu einem bestimmten Grad; diesen würde sie ungestraft nicht überschreiten.'

86. Cf. Röd, Schmidinger and Thurnher, *Die Philosophie des ausgehenden 19. und des 20. Jahrhunderts,* vol. 3, 114–115.

87. Droysen, *Historik. Vorlesungen über Enzyklopädie und Methodologie der Geschichte,* 3: 'Ich will Ihnen nicht eine Übersicht der einzelnen Disziplinen geben, die zum Studium der Geschichte gerechnet zu werden pflegen…. Mein Zweck ist ein anderer, ein in anderem Sinn praktischer…. Es scheint mir für jeden, der sich diesen Studien zuwenden will, von Interesse zu sein, darüber ins klare zu kommen, diese Studien nach ihre Rechtfertigung, nach ihrem Verhältnis zu anderen Formen und Richtungen der menschlichen Erkenntnis, nach der Eigenartigkeit ihrer Aufgabe, nach der Begründung ihres Verfahrens zu fragen.'

Bibliography

Primary Sources

Droysen's Texts

2008. *Historik. Supplement: Droysen Bibliographie,* edited by Horst Walter Blanke. Stuttgart: Frommann-Holzboog.

2007. *Historik,* vol. 2: *Texte im Umkreis der Historik (1826–1882),* edited by Horst Walter Blanke. Stuttgart: Frommann-Holzboog.

1980. *Geschichte des Hellenismus,* vol. 1: *Geschichte Alexander des Großen,* 2nd ed. [1877–78], edited by Erich Bayer. Munich: DTV [1st ed., 1833, as *Geschichte Alexander des Großen*].

1980. *Geschichte des Hellenismus,* vol. 2: *Geschichte der Diadochen,* 2nd ed. [1877–78], edited by Erich Bayer. Munich: DTV [1st ed., 1836, as *Geschichte des Hellenismus I*].

1980. *Geschichte des Hellenismus,* vol. 3: *Geschichte der Epigonen,* 2nd ed. [1877–78], edited by Erich Bayer. Darmstadt: Wissenschaftliche Buchgesellschaft [1st ed., 1843, as *Geschichte des Hellenismus II*].

1977. *Historik,* vol. 1: *Rekonstruktion der ersten vollständigen Fassung der Vorlesungen (1857); Grundriß der Historik in der ersten handschriftlichen (1857/58) und in der letzten gedruckten Fassung (1882),* edited by Peter Leyh. Stuttgart: Frommann-Holzboog.

1971. *Historik. Vorlesungen über Enzyklopädie und Methodologie der Geschichte,* 6th unaltered ed., edited by Rudolf Hübner. Munich: R. Oldenbourg [1937].

1967. *Briefwechsel,* vol. 1: *1828–1851,* edited by Rudolf Hübner. Osnabrück: Biblio [1929].

1967. *Briefwechsel,* vol. 2: *1851–1884,* edited by Rudolf Hübner. Osnabrück: Biblio [1929].

1933. *Politische Schriften,* edited by Felix Gilbert. Munich: R. Oldenbourg.

1932. *Geschichte Alexanders des Großen,* Neudruck der Urausgabe, edited by Helmut Berve. Leipzig: Alfred Kröner [1833].

1924. *Aktenstücke und Aufzeichnungen zur Geschichte der Frankfurter Nationalversammlung aus dem Nachlaß von Johann Gustav Droysen,* edited by Rudolf Hübner. Stuttgart, Berlin, Leipzig: Deutsche Verlags-Anstalt.

1894. *Kleine Schriften zur alten Geschichte,* 2 vols. Leipzig: Veit.

1893. *Outline of the Principles of History,* trans. E. Benjamin Andrews. Boston: Ginn.

1868. *Geschichte der Preußischen Politik,* part 1: *Die Gründung,* 2nd ed. Leipzig: Veit [1855].

1855–86. *Geschichte der Preußischen Politik,* 14 vols. Berlin and Leipzig: Veit.

1851–52. *Das Leben des Feldmarschalls Grafen York von Wartenburg,* 3 vols. Berlin: Veit.

1850. *Die Herzogthümer Schleswig-Holstein und das Königreich Dänemark. Aktenmäßige Geschichte der dänischen Politik seit dem Jahre 1806,* co-authored by Karl Samwer. Hamburg: Perthes-Besser und Mauke.

1849. *Beiträge zur neuesten deutschen Geschichte*. Braunschweig: Friedrich Vieweg und Sohn.
1849. *Die Verhandlungen des Verfassungs-Ausschusses der deutschen Nationalversammlung*, part 1. Leipzig: Weidmann.
1846. *Vorlesungen über die Freiheitskriege*, 2 vols. Kiel: Universitäts-Buchhandlung.
1843. *Geschichte des Hellenismus*, part 2: *Geschichte der Bildung des hellenistischen Staatensystems*. Hamburg: Friedrich Perthes.
1836. *Geschichte des Hellenismus*, part 1: *Geschichte der Nachfolger Alexanders*. Hamburg: Friedrich Perthes.
1835–38. *Des Aristophanes Werke*, 3 vols. Berlin: Veit.
1833. *Geschichte Alexander des Großen*. Berlin: G. Finke.
1832. *Des Aischylos Werkes*, 2 vols. Berlin: G. Finke.
1831. *De Lagidarum regno Ptolemaeo IV Philometore rege*. Quam commentationen amplissimi ordinis philosophici Berolinensis auctoritate ad summos in philosophia honores rite capessendos die XXXI Aug. A. MDCCCXXXI publice defendet Johannes Gustavus Droysen Pomeranus, Berlin: Eisendorf.

Texts by Other Authors

Bede. 2007. *The Ecclesiastical History of the English Nation*, trans. L.C. Jane. New York: Cosimo [ca. 731].
Bernheim, Ernst. 1908. *Lehrbuch der historischen Methode und der Geschichtsphilosophie*, 5th and 6th rev. and exp. eds. Leipzig: Duncker & Humblot.
———. 1889. *Lehrbuch der historischen Methode*. Leipzig: Duncker & Humblot.
Bolingbroke, Lord (Henry St-John). 1791. *Letters on the Study and Use of History*, 8th ed. Basel: J. J. Tourneisen [1735].
Bossuet, Jacques-Bénigne. 1991. 'Discourse on Universal History (Fragment)', trans. Elborg Forster, in Donald Kelley (ed.), *Versions of History: From Antiquity to the Enlightenment*. New Haven, CT: Yale University Press, 425–434 [1681].
Buckle, Henry Thomas. 1866. *The History of Civilization in England*, vol. 1, 2nd ed. New York: Appleton [1857].
Burckhardt, Jacob. 1979. *Reflections on History*, trans. M.D. Hottinger. Indianapolis: Liberty Fund [1868/72].
Burke, Edmund. 1790. *Reflections on the Revolution in France*, 2nd ed. London: J. Dodsley.
Cicero, Marcus Tullius. 1942. *De oratore*, books I–II, trans. E.W. Sutton. London: Heinemann; Cambridge, MA: Harvard University Press [55 BC].
Dahlmann, Friedrich Christoph. 1968. *Die Politik*. Frankfurt am Main: Suhrkamp [1835].
Diodorus of Sicily. 1933. *Library of History*, vol. 1: *Books 1–2.34*, trans. C.H. Oldfather. Cambridge, MA: Harvard University Press [1st century BC].
Fichte, Johann Gottlieb. 1808. *Reden an die deutsche Nation*. Berlin: In der Realschulbuchhandlung.
Fustel de Coulanges, Numa Denis. 1882. *The Ancient City: A Study on the Religion, Laws, and Institutions of Greece and Rome*, trans. Willard Small. Boston: Lee and Shepard [1864].
Goethe, Johann Wolfgang. 1986. 'Faust. Eine Tragödie', in *Goethes Werke*, vol. 3, 13th ed., edited by Erich Trunz. Munich: C.H. Beck [1808].
Guicciardini, Francesco. 1890. *Consels and Reflections*, trans. Ninian Hill Thomson. London: Kegan Paul [1512–1530].
Hegel, Georg Wilhelm Friedrich. 2001. *The Philosophy of History*, trans. J. Sibree. Kitchener: Batoche [1822/30].
———. 1986. 'Rechts-, Pflichten-, und Religionslehre für die Unterklasse', in Georg Hegel, *Werke in 20 Bänden*, vol. 4: *Nürnberger und Heidelberger Schriften, 1808–1817*. Frankfurt am Main: Suhrkamp, 204–275 [1810].
———. 1955. *Die Vernunft in der Geschichte*, 5th ed., edited by Johannes Hoffmeister. Hamburg: Felix Meiner [1822/30].

Humboldt, Wilhelm von. 1967. 'On the Historian's Task', *History and Theory* 6(1): 57–71 [1821].

———. 1964. 'Der königsberger Schulplan', in Wilhelm von Humboldt, *Bildung des Menschen in Schule und Universität*. Heidelberg: Quelle & Meyer, 11–22 [1810].

———. 1841. 'Über die Aufgabe des Geschichtsschreibers', in Wilhelm von Humboldt, *Gesammelte Werke*, vol. 1. Berlin: G. Reimer, 1–25 [1821].

Ibn Khaldūn, Abū Zayd. 1967. *The Muqaddimah: An Introduction to History*, vol. 1, trans. Franz Rosenthal. Princeton, NJ: Princeton University Press [1377].

Isidore of Seville. 1912. 'The Etymologies', in Ernest Brehaut (ed.), *An Encyclopedist of the Dark Ages: Isidore of Seville*. New York: Columbia University Press, 89–264 [ca. 630].

Josephus, Flavius. 1991. 'Jewish Antiquities (Fragment)', trans. H.S.J. Thackery, in Donald Kelley (ed.), *Versions of History: From Antiquity to the Enlightenment*. New Haven, CT: Yale University Press, 131–134 [ca. 93].

Lessing, Gotthold Ephraim. 1855. 'Die Erziehung des Menschengeschlechtes', in Gotthold E. Lessing, *Gesammelte Werke in 2 Bände*, vol. 2. Leipzig: Göschen, 358–355 [1780].

Livy. 2006. *The History of Rome*, books 1–5, trans. with introduction and notes by Valerie M. Warrior. Indianapolis: Hackett [27–25 BC].

Luther, Martin. 1991. 'Preface to Galeatius Capella's History', trans. Lewis Spitz, in Donald Kelley (ed.), *Versions of History: From Antiquity to the Enlightenment*. New Haven, CT: Yale University Press, 314–317 [1538].

Machiavelli, Niccolò. 1901. *History of Florence*. New York: The Colonial Press [1525].

———. 1893. *Discourses on the First Decade of Titus Livius*, trans. Ninian Hill Thompson. London: Kegan Paul [ca. 1517].

Marx, Karl and Friedrich Engels. 2002. *The Communist Manifesto*, edited by Gareth Stedman Jones. London: Penguin Classics [1848].

Mexía, Pero. 1545. *Historia imperial y cesárea: en la que en suma se contiene las vidas y hechos de todos los césares emperadores de Roma*. Seville: Sebastian Trugillo.

Nietzsche, Friedrich. 2000. 'Von Nutzen und Nachteile der Historie für das Leben', in Friedrich Nietzsche, *Unzeitgemäße Betrachtungen*. Frankfurt am Main: Insel, 95–184 [1874].

———. 1983. 'On the Uses and Disadvantages of History for Life', in Friedrich Nietzsche, *Untimely Meditations*, trans. R.J. Hollingdale. Cambridge: Cambridge University Press, 57–124 [1874].

Polybius. 1889. *Histories*, trans. Evelyn S. Shuckburgh. London: Macmillan [ca. 150 BC].

Procopius of Caesarea. 1991. 'History of the Wars (Fragment)', trans. B.H. Dewing, in Donald Kelley (ed.), *Versions of History: From Antiquity to the Enlightenment*. New Haven, CT: Yale University Press, 107–108 [ca. 550].

Pufendorf, Samuel. 1991. 'An Introduction to the History of the Principal Kingdoms and States of Europe (Fragment)', in Donald Kelley (ed.), *Versions of History: From Antiquity to the Enlightenment*. New Haven, CT: Yale University Press, 435–438 [1684].

Ranke, Leopold von. 1990. 'Vorwort zu den ‹Geschichten der romanischen und germanischen Völker von 1494 bis 1535›', in Wolfgang Hardtwig (ed.), *Über das Studium der Geschichte*. Munich: DTV, 44–46 [1824].

———. 1975. 'Einleitung zu einer Vorlesung über neure Geschichte', in Leopold von Ranke, *Aus Werk und Nachlass*, vol. 4: *Vorlesungseinleitungen*, edited by Volker Dotterweich and Walther Peter Fuchs. Munich: Oldenbourg, 294–298 [1859–61].

———. 1971. *Aus Werk und Nachlass*, vol. 2: *Über die Epochen der neuren Geschichte. Historisch-kritische Ausgabe*, edited by Theodor Schieder and Helmut Berding. Munich: Oldenbourg [1854].

———. 1928. *Weltgeschichte*, vol. 1: *Die älteste historische Völkergruppe und die Griechen*, edited by Horst Michael. Vienna: Gutenberg-Verlag Christensen, 1928 [1881].

———. 1860. *Englische Geschichte, vornehmlich im 16. und 17. Jahrhundert*, vol. 2. Berlin: Duncker & Humblot.

———. 1859. *Englische Geschichte, vornehmlich im 16. und 17. Jahrhundert*, vol. 1. Berlin: Duncker & Humblot.

Rotteck, Karl von. 1851. *Allgemeine Geschichte: von Anfang der historischen Kenntniß auf unsere Zeiten,* vol. 1. Braunschweig: George Westermann.

Savigny, Friedrich Carl von. 1850. *Vermischte Schriften,* vol. 1, Berlin: Veit.

Schlözer, August Ludwig. 1997. *Vorstellung seiner Universal-Historie,* edited by Horst Walter Blanke. Waltrop: Hartmut Spenner [1772/73].

Sybel, Heinrich von. 1925. 'Brief an Hermann Baumgarten, 27.01.1871', in Julius Heyderhoff (ed.), *Die Sturmjahre der preußisch-deutschen Einigung 1859–1870. Politische Briefe aus dem Nachlaß liberaler Parteiführer,* vol. 1. Bonn: Kurt Schroeder, 494.

Tocqueville, Alexis de. 2004. *Democracy in America,* trans. Arthur Goldhammer. New York: The Library of America.

Treitschke, Heinrich von. 1879. 'Unsere Aussichten', *Preussische Jahrbücher* 44: 559–576.

Vico, Giambattista. 1948. *The New Science of Giambattista Vico,* trans. Thomas G. Bergin and Max Harold Fisch. Ithaca, NY: Cornell University Press [1744].

Secondary Literature

Acham, Karl. 1995. *Geschichte und Sozialtheorie. Zur Komplementarität kulturwissenschaftlicher Erkenntnisorientierungen.* Freiburg: Alber.

Acton, John Dalberg. 1930. *Lectures on Modern History.* London: Macmillan.

Allan, David. 1993. *Virtue, Learning and the Scottish Enlightenment: Ideas of Scholarship in Early Modern History.* Edinburgh: Edinburgh University Press.

Angehrn, Emil. 1985. *Geschichte und Identität.* Berlin: Walter de Gruyter.

Araújo, André de Melo. 2012. *Weltgeschichte in Göttingen. Eine Studie über das spätaufklärerische universalhistorische Denken, 1756-1815.* Bielefeld: Transcript.

Arendt, Hannah. 1993. *Between Past and Future: Eight Exercises in Political Thought.* New York: Penguin.

Aron, Raymond. 2005. *Le spectateur engagé. Entretiens avec Jean-Louis Missika et Dominique Wolton.* Paris: Librairie générale française.

Assmann, Aleida. 1993. *Arbeit am nationalen Gedächtnis. Eine kurze Geschichte der deutschen Bildungsidee.* Frankfurt am Main and New York: Campus.

Astholz, Hildegard. 1933. *Das Problem ‹Geschichte› untersucht bei J.G. Droysen.* Berlin: Ebering.

Auerbach, Erich. 1952. 'Typological Symbolism in Medieval Literature', *Yale French Studies* 9: 3–10.

Aylmer, Gerald. 1997. 'Introductory Survey: From the Renaissance to the Eighteenth Century', in Michael Bentley (ed.), *Companion to Historiography.* London: Routledge, 236–267.

Bauer, Christoph Johannes. 2001. *‹Das Geheimnis aller Bewegung ist ihr Zweck›. Geschichtsphilosophie bei Hegel und Droysen.* Hamburg: Meiner.

Barrelmeyer, Uwe. 1997. *Geschichtliche Wirklichkeit als Problem. Untersuchungen zu geschichtstheoretischen Begründungen historischen Wissens bei Johann Gustav Droysen, Georg Simmel und Max Weber.* Münster: LIT.

Beiser, Frederick. 2011. *The German Historicist Tradition.* Oxford: Oxford University Press.

Bergmann, Klaus. 2000. *Geschichtsdidaktik. Beiträge zu einer Theorie des historischen Lernens.* Schwalbach am Taunus: Wochenschau.

———. 2000. *Multiperspektivität. Geschichte selber denken.* Schwalbach am Taunus: Wochenschau.

Birtsch, Günter. 1964. *Die Nation als sittliche Idee. Der Nationalstaatsbegriff in Geschichtsschreibung und politischer Gedankenwelt Johann Gustav Droysens.* Cologne: Böhlau.

Blanke, Horst Walter. 1996. 'Aufklärungshistorie und Historismus: Bruch und Kontinuität', in Otto Gerhard Oexle and Jörn Rüsen (eds), *Historismus in den Kulturwissenschaften. Geschichtskonzepte, historische Einschätzungen, Grundlagenprobleme.* Cologne: Böhlau, 69–98.

———. 1991. *Historiographiegeschichte als Historik.* Stuttgart: Frommann-Holzboog.

Blanke, Horst Walter, Dirk Fleischer and Jörn Rüsen. 1984. 'Theory of History in Historical Lectures: The German Tradition of Historik, 1750–1900', *History and Theory* 23(3): 331–356.

Blankertz, Herwig. 1992. *Die Geschichte der Pädagogik. Von der Aufklärung bis zur Gegenwart.* Wetzlar: Büchse der Pandora.

Bleek, Wilhelm. 2001. *Geschichte der Politikwissenschaft in Deutschland.* München: C.H. Beck.

Blumenthal, Hermann. 1933. 'Johann Gustav Droysens Auseinandersetzung mit dem Idealismus', *Neue Jahrbücher für Wissenschaft und Jugendbildung* 9: 344–355.

Bobbio, Norberto. 2005. *Liberalism and Democracy,* trans. Martin Ryle and Kate Soper. London: Verso.

Boia, Lucian. 1991. 'Henry Thomas Buckle', in Lucian Boia (ed.), *Great Historians of the Modern Age: An International Dictionary.* Westport, CT: Greenwood, 187–188.

Bollenbeck, Georg. 1996. *Bildung und Kultur. Glanz und Elend eines deutschen Deutungsmusters.* Frankfurt am Main: Suhrkamp.

Borries, Bodo von. 2008. *Historisch Denken Lernen – Welterschließung statt Epochenüberblick. Geschichte als Unterrichtsfach und Bildungsaufgabe.* Opladen: Barbara Budrich.

Bravo, Benedetto. 1966. 'Hégélianisme et recherche historique dans l'oeuvre de J.G. Droysen', in Jan Burian and Ladislav Vidman (eds), *Antiquitas graeco-romana ac tempora nostra. Acta congressus internationalis habiti Brunae diebus 12–16 mensis Aprilis.* Prague: Academia, 151–159.

Brobjer, Thomas. 2007. 'Nietzsche's Relation to Historical Methods and Nineteenth Century German Historiography', *History and Theory* 46(2): 155–179.

———. 2004. 'Nietzsche's View of the Value of Historical Studies and Methods', *Journal of the History of Ideas* 65(2): 301–322.

Bruford, Walter Horace. 1975. *The German Tradition of Self-Cultivation:* Bildung *from Humboldt to Thomas Mann.* Cambridge: Cambridge University Press.

Buck, Günther. 1981. *Hermeneutik und Bildung. Elemente einer verstehenden Bildungslehre.* Munich: Wilhelm Fink.

Burger, Thomas. 1977. 'Droysen's Defense of Historiography: A Note', *History and Theory* 16(2): 168–173.

Burrow, John. 2009. *A History of Histories: Epics, Chronicles, Romances and Inquiries from Herodotus and Thucydides to the Twentieth Century.* New York: Vintage.

Butterfield, Herbert. 1974. 'History of Historiography', in Philip Viennaer (ed.), *Dictionary of the History of Ideas: Studies of Selected Pivotal Ideas,* vol. 2. New York: Charles Scribner's Sons, 465–498.

Caianiello, Silvia. 1999. *La ‹duplice natura› dell'uomo. La polarità come matrice del mondo storico in Humboldt e in Droysen.* Soveria Mannelli: Rubbettino.

Caldas, Pedro S.P. 2006. 'O limite do historismo: Johann Gustav Droysen e a importância do conceito de *Bildung* na consciência histórica alemã do século XIX', *Revista Filosófica de Coimbra* 29: 139–160.

———. 2004. *Que significa pensar historicamente: uma interpretação da teoria da história de Johann Gustav Droysen,* Ph.D. Thesis. Pontifícia Universidade Católica do Rio de Janeiro.

Carbonell, Charles-Olivier. 1978. 'L'histoire dite ‹positiviste› en France', *Romantisme* 8(21–22): 173–185.

Carr, David. 1991. *Time, Narrative, and History.* Bloomington: Indiana University Press.

Carr, Edward H. 1961. *What Is History?* New York: Vintage.

Cassirer, Ernst. 2003. *Die Philosophie der Aufklärung.* Hamburg: Meiner.

Clark, Christopher. 2008. *Iron Kingdom: The Rise and Downfall of Prussia, 1600–1947.* Cambridge: Harvard University Press.

———. 1996. 'The Wars of Liberation in Prussian Memory: Reflections on the Memorialization of War in Early Nineteenth-century Germany', *The Journal of Modern History* 68(3): 550–576.

Collingwood, Robin G. 1999. *The Principles of History: And Other Writings in Philosophy of History,* edited by William Dray and Jan van der Dussen. Oxford: Oxford University Press.

Copleston, Frederick. 1985. *A History of Philosophy,* vol. 7: *Fichte to Nietzsche.* New York: Image.

Corradini, Piero. 1994. 'History and Historiography in China', in *The East and the Meaning of History: Proceedings of the International Conference, November, 1992.* Rome: Bardi, 425–434.

Croce, Benedetto. 2000. *History as the Story of Liberty,* trans. Sylvia Sprigge. Indianapolis: Liberty Fund.

Dilthey, Wilhelm. 1981. *Der Aufbau der geschichtlichen Welt in den Geisteswissenschaften.* Frankfurt: Suhrkamp [1910].

Dobson, J.F. 1919. *The Greek Orators.* London: Methuen.

Dove, Alfred. 1898. 'Johann Gustav Droysen', in Alfred Dove, *Ausgewählte Schriftchen vornehmlich historischen Inhalts.* Leipzig: Duncker & Humblot, 369–382.

Dray, William. 1964. *Philosophy of History.* Englewood Cliffs, NJ: Prentice-Hall.

Droysen, Gustav. 1910. *Johann Gustav Droysen,* part 1: *Bis zum Beginn der Frankfurter Tätigkeit.* Leipzig: B.G. Teubner.

Duncker, Max. 1884. 'Johann Gustav Droysen', *Preußische Jahrbücher* 54: 134–167.

Eibach, Joachim. 2008. 'Rezension zu: "Nippel, Wilfried: Johann Gustav Droysen. Ein Leben zwischen Wissenschaft und Politik. Munich 2008"', *H-Soz-u-Kult,* 12 December. Retrieved from http://hsozkult.geschichte.hu-berlin.de/rezensionen/2008-4-226

Escher, Felix. 1989. 'Leopold Ranke', in Michael Erbe (ed.). *Berlinische Lebensbilder,* vol. 4: *Geisteswissenschaftler.* Berlin: Colloquium, 109–125.

Escudier, Alexandre. 2006. 'Theory and Methodology of History from Chladenius to Droysen: A Historiographical Essay', in Christopher Ligota and Jean-Louis Quantin (eds), *History of Scholarship: A Selection of Papers from the Seminar on the History of Scholarship Held Annually at the Warburg Institute.* Oxford: Oxford University Press, 437–486.

———. 2002. 'Présentation: Refonder les sciences historiques. L'odyssée du monde éthique chez Droysen', in Johann Gustav Droysen, *Précis de theorie de l'histoire.* Paris: Les Éditions du Cerf, 7–28.

Evans, G.R. 1993. *Philosophy and Theology in the Middle Ages.* London: Routledge.

Fenske, Walter. 1930. *Johann Gustav Droysen und das deutsche Nationalstaatsproblem. Ein Beitrag zur Geschichte der Frankfurter Nationalversammlung von 1848/49.* Erlangen: Palm & Enke.

Fleischer, Dirk. 2009. '"Geschichtserkenntnis als Goterkenntnis". Das theologische Fundament der Geschichtstheorie Johann Gustav Droysens', in Horst Walter Blanke (ed.), *Historie und Historik. 200 Jahre Johann Gustav Droysen. Festschrift für Jörn Rüsen zum 70. Geburtstag.* Cologne: Böhlau, 73–89.

Force, Pierre. 2009. 'Voltaire and the Necessity of Modern History', *Modern Intellectual History* 6(3): 457–484.

Franke, Ursula. 2000. 'Bildung/Erziehung, ästhetische', in Karlheinz Barck et al. (eds), *Ästhetische Grundbegriffe.* Stuttgart: J.B. Metzler, 696–726.

Fryde, E.B. 1983. *Humanism and Renaissance Historiography.* London: The Hambledon.

Fuchs, Eckhardt. 1997. 'Positivistischer Szientismus in vergleichender Perspektive: Zum nomothetischen Wissenschaftsverständnis in der englischen, amerikanischen und deutschen Geschichtsschreibung', in Wolfgang Küttler et al. (eds), *Geschichtsdiskurs,* vol. 3: *Die Epoche der Historisierung.* Frankfurt am Main: Fischer, 396–423.

Fueter, Eduard. 1936. *Geschichte der neueren Historiographie.* Munich: R. Oldenbourg [1911].

Fulbrook, Mary. 2010. *A Concise History of Germany.* Cambridge: Cambridge University Press.

Fulda, Daniel. 2006. 'Rex ex historia. Komödienzeit und verzeitlichte Zeit in "Minna von Barnhelm"', in *Das achtzehnte Jahrhundert* 30(2): 179–192 [Themenheft: *Zeitkonzepte. Zur Pluralisierung des Zeitdiskurses im langen 18. Jahrhundert,* ed. Stefanie Stockhorst].

———. 1996. *Wissenschaft aus Kunst. Die Entstehung der modernen deutschen Geschichtsschreibung, 1760–1860.* Berlin: Walter de Gruyter.

Fulda, Friedrich. 1974. 'Der Begriff des Geistes bei Hegel und seine Wirkungsgeschichte', in Joachim Ritter (ed.), *Historisches Wörterbuch der Philosophie,* vol. 3. Basel: Schwabe, 191–199.

Gadamer, Hans-Georg. 1990. *Wahrheit und Methode. Grundzüge einer philosophischen Hermeneutik,* 6th ed. Tübingen: Mohr Siebeck.

Gehrke, Hans-Joachim. 2003. *Geschichte des Hellenismus.* Munich: Oldenbourg.

———. 1989. 'Johann Gustav Droysen', in Michael Erbe (ed.), *Berlinische Lebensbilder,* vol. 4: *Geisteswissenschaftler.* Berlin: Colloquium, 127–142.

Geuss, Raymond. 1996. 'Kultur, Bildung, Geist', *History and Theory* 35(2): 152–164.

Gilbert, Felix. 1973. *Machiavelli and Guicciardini: Politics and History in Sixteenth Century Florence.* Princeton, NJ: Princeton University Press.

Ginzburg, Carlo. 1999. 'Lorenzo Valla and the "Donation of Constantine"', in Carlo Ginzburg, *History, Rhetoric, and Proof.* Hanover, NH: University Press of New England, 54–70.

Goetz, Hans-Werner. 1989. 'Von der "res gestae" zur "narratio rerum gestarum". Anmerkungen zu Methoden und Hilfswissenschaften des mittelalterlichen Geschichtsschreibers', *Revue belge de philologie et d'histoire* 67(4): 695–713.

Grafton, Anthony. 2007. *What Was History? The Art of History in Early Modern Europe,* Cambridge: Cambridge University Press.

———. 1999. *The Footnote. A Curious History,* Cambridge: Harvard University Press.

Grant, Edward. 1996. *The Foundations of Modern Science in the Middle Ages. Their Religious, Institutional, and Intellectual Contexts,* Cambridge: Cambridge University Press.

Greiert, Andreas. 2011. '"Viele sind berufen, aber wenige auserwählt". Geschichtstheorie, Politik und sittlicher Kosmos bei Johann Gustav Droysen', *Historische Zeitschrift* 292(2): 397–423.

Guenée, Bernard. 1973. 'Histoires, annales, chroniques. Essai sur les genres historiques au Moyen Âge', *Annales. Économies, Sociétés, Civilisations* 28(4): 997–1016.

Gumbrecht, Hans Ulrich. 2006. 'Presence Achieved in Language', *History and Theory* 45(3): 317–327.

———. 1997. 'After Learning from History', in Hans Ulrich Gumbrecht, *In 1926: Living at the Edge of Time.* Cambridge: Harvard University Press, 411–436.

Günther, Horst. 1979. 'Geschichte, Historie. IV. Historisches Denken in der frühen Neuzeit', in Otto Brunner et al. (eds), *Geschichtliche Grundbegriffe. Historisches Lexikon zur politisch-sozialen Sprache in Deutschland,* vol. 2. Stuttgart: Klett-Cotta, 625–647.

Hackel, Christiane. 2008. 'Der Geschichtstheoretiker', in Christiane Hackel (ed.), *Philologe – Historiker – Politiker. Johann Gustav Droysen, 1808–1884. Katalog zur Ausstellung des Sonderforschungsbereiches «Transformationen der Antike», Humboldt Universität zu Berlin, 01.07–08.08.2008.* Berlin: G + H, 57–62.

———. 2008. 'Studium an der Berliner Universität', in Christiane Hackel (ed.), *Philologe – Historiker – Politiker. Johann Gustav Droysen, 1808–1884. Katalog zur Ausstellung des Sonderforschungsbereiches «Transformationen der Antike», Humboldt Universität zu Berlin, 01.07–08.08.2008.* Berlin: G + H, 15–22.

———. 2006. *Die Bedeutung August Boeckhs für den Geschichtstheoretiker Johann Gustav Droysen. Die Enzyklopädie-Vorlesungen im Vergleich.* Würzburg: Königshausen und Neumann.

Hackel, Christiane (ed.). 2008. *Philologe – Historiker – Politiker. Johann Gustav Droysen, 1808–1884. Katalog zur Ausstellung des Sonderforschungsbereiches «Transformationen der Antike», Humboldt Universität zu Berlin, 01.07–08.08.2008.* Berlin: G + H.

Hackel, Christiane and Nadine Wendland. 2008. 'Kindheit im pommerschen Pfarrhaus', in Christiane Hackel (ed.), *Philologe – Historiker – Politiker. Johann Gustav Droysen, 1808–1884. Katalog zur Ausstellung des Sonderforschungsbereiches «Transformationen der Antike», Humboldt Universität zu Berlin, 01.07–08.08.2008.* Berlin: G + H, 9–14.

Handy, Robert Henry. 1966. *J.G. Droysen: The Historian and German Politics in the Nineteenth Century,* Ph.D. thesis. Georgetown University: Washington, D.C.

Hardtwig, Wolfgang. 1991. 'Geschichtsreligion – Wissenschaft als Arbeit – Objektivität Der Historismus in neuer Sicht', *Historische Zeitschrift* 252: 1–32.

———. 1990. 'Johann Gustav Droysen', in Wolfgang Hardtwig (ed.), *Über das Studium der Geschichte.* München: DTV, 83–85.

Harrison, Robert, Aled Jones and Peter Lambert. 2004. 'The Institutionalisation and Organisation of History', in Peter Lambert and Phillip Schofield (eds), *Making History: An Introduction to the History and Practices of a Discipline.* London: Routledge, 9–25.

Hartog, François. 2003. 'O caso grego: do ktêma ao exemplum, passando pela arqueologia', in François Hartog, *Os antigos, o passado e o presente,* edited by José Otávio Guimarães, trans. Sonia Lacerda, Marcos Veneu and José Otávio Guimarães. Brasília: Ed. UnB, 53–70.

———. 2001. 'Como se escreveu a história na Grécia e em Roma', in François Hartog (ed.), *A história. De Homero a Santo Agostinho: Prefácios de historiadores e textos sobre história reunidos e comentados,* trans. Jacyntho Lins Brandão. Belo Horizonte: Ed. UFMG.

———. 2000. 'The Invention of History: The Pre-History of a Concept from Homer to Herodotus', *History and Theory* 39(3): 384–395.

Heath, Malcolm. 2003. 'Pseudo-Dionysius Art of Rhetoric 8–11: Figured Speech, Declamation and Criticism', *American Journal of Philology* 124: 81–105.

Hedinger, H.-W. 1974. 'Historik, ars historica', in Joachim Ritter (ed.), *Historisches Wörterbuch der Philosophie,* vol. 3. Basel: Schwabe, 1131–1138.

Hennis, Wilhelm. 1994. 'The Meaning of "Wertfreiheit" on the Background and Motives of Max Weber's "Postulate"', *Sociological Theory* 12(2): 113–125.

Hintze, Otto. 1942. 'Johann Gustav Droysen', in Otto Hintze, *Zur Theorie der Geschichte. Gesammelte Abhandlungen,* edited by Fritz Hartung. Leipzig: Koehler & Amelang, 150–213.

Huber, Jürgen. 2004. *Guicciardinis Kritik an Machiavelli. Streit um Staat, Gesellschaft und Geschichte im frühneuzeitlichen Italien.* Wiesbaden: DUV.

Hübinger, Gangolf. 2006. *Gelehrte, Politik und Öffentlichkeit. Eine Intellektuellengeschichte.* Göttingen: Vandenhoeck & Ruprecht.

———. 1984. *Georg Gottfried Gervinus. Historisches Urteil und politische Kritik.* Göttingen: Vandenhoeck & Ruprecht.

Hübner, Rudolph. 1967. 'Vorwort', in Johann Gustav Droysen, *Briefwechsel,* vol. 1: *1828–1851,* edited by Rudolf Hübner. Osnabrück: Biblio, vii–xv.

———. 1917. 'Johann Gustav Droysens Vorlesungen über die Politik', *Zeitschrift für Politik* 10: 325–376.

Huppert, George. 1970. *The Idea of Perfect History: Historical Erudition and Historical Philosophy in Renaissance France.* Urbana: The University of Illinois Press.

Iggers, Georg. 1997. *Historiography in the Twentieth Century: From Scientific Objectivity to the Postmodern Challenge.* Middletown, CT: Wesleyan University Press.

———. 1995. 'Historicism: The History and the Meaning of the Term', *Journal of the History of Ideas* 56: 129–152.

———. 1994. 'Ist es in der Tat in Deutschland früher zur Verwissenschaftlichung der Geschichte gekommen als in anderen europäischen Ländern?' in Wolfgang Küttler et al. (eds), *Geschichtsdiskurs,* vol. 2: *Anfänge modernen historischen Denkens.* Frankfurt am Main: Fischer, 73–86.

Iggers, Georg and Edward Wang. 2008. *A Global History of Modern Historiography.* Harlow: Pearson.

Inwood, Michael. 1992. *A Hegel Dictionary.* Oxford: Blackwell.

Jaeger, Friedrich. 2010. 'Die Neuere Geschichte bei Johann Gustav Droysen', in Horst Walter Blanke (ed.), *Historie und Historik. 200 Jahre Johann Gustav Droysen. Festschrift für Jörn Rüsen zum 70. Geburtstag.* Cologne: Böhlau, 106–129.

———. 2007. 'Historismus', in Friedrich Jaeger (ed.), *Enzyklopädie der Neuzeit,* vol. 5. Stuttgart: J.B. Metzler, 532–539.

———. 1997. 'Geschichtsphilosophie, Hermeneutik und Kontingenz in der Geschichte des Historismus', in Wolfgang Küttler et al. (eds), *Geschichtsdiskurs,* vol. 3: *Die Epoche der Historisierung.* Frankfurt am Main: Fischer, 45–79.

———. 1994. *Bürgerliche Modernisierungskrise und historische Sinnbildung. Kulturgeschichte bei Droysen, Burckhardt und Max Weber.* Göttingen: Vanderhoeck & Ruprecht.

Jaeger, Friedrich and Jörn Rüsen. 1992. *Geschichte des Historismus. Eine Einführung.* Munich: C.H. Beck.

Janz, Oliver. 2001. 'Das evangelische Pfarrhaus', in Étienne François and Hagen Schulze (eds), *Deutsche Erinnerungsorte III.* Munich: C.H. Beck, 221–238.

Jasmin, Marcelo. 2005. *Alexis de Tocqueville. A historiografia como ciência da política.* Belo Horizonte: Ed. UFMG.

Jay, Jennifer W. 1999. 'Sima Guang', in Kelly Bord (ed.), *Encyclopedia of Historians and Historical Writing*, vol. 2. London: Fitzroy Dearborn, 1092–1093.

Jeanneret, Michel. 1998. 'The Vagaries of Exemplarity: Distortion or Dismissal?' *Journal of the History of Ideas* 59(4): 565–579.

Jefferies, Matthew. 2006. 'The Age of Historism', in Stefan Berger (ed.), *A Companion to Nineteenth-Century Europe.* Malden, MA: Blackwell, 316–332.

Jeismann, Karl-Ernst. 1997. 'Geschichtsbewußtsein – Theorie', in Klaus Bergmann et al. (eds), *Handbuch der Geschichtsdidaktik*, 5th rev. ed. Seelze-Velber: Kallmeyer, 42–45.

———. 1987. 'Zur Bedeutung der "Bildung" im 19. Jahrhundert', in Karl-Ernst Jeismann and Peter Lundgreen (eds), *Handbuch der deutschen Bildungsgeschichte*, vol. 3: *1800–1870: Von der Neuordnung Deutschlands bis zur Gründung des Deutschen Reiches.* Munich: C.H. Beck, 1–23.

Jenkins, Rommily. 1963. 'The Hellenistic Origins of Byzantine Literature', *Dumbarton Oaks Papers* 17: 37–52.

Jordan, Stefan. 1999. *Geschichtstheorie in der ersten Hälfte des 19. Jahrhunderts. Die Schwellenzeit zwischen Pragmatismus und Klassischem Historismus.* Frankfurt am Main: Campus.

———. 1995. 'G. W. F. Hegels Einfluss auf das philologische und altertumswissenschaftliche Schaffen Johann Gustav Droysens', in Helmut Schneider (ed.), *Jahrbuch für Hegelforschung.* Sankt Augustin: Academia, 141–155.

Jung, Theo. 2010–11. 'Das Neue der Neuzeit ist ihre Zeit. Reinhart Kosellecks Theorie der Verzeitlichung und ihre Kritiker', *Moderne Kulturwissenschaftliches Jahrbuch* 6: 172–184.

Kerckhoven, Guy van. 2009. 'Geschichtlichkeit chez Droysen et Dilthey', in Jean-Claude Gens (ed.), *Johann Gustav Droysen: L'avènement du paradigme herméneutique dans les sciences humaines.* Argenteuil: Le Cercle herméneutique, 173–203.

Kersting, Wolfgang. 1995. 'Sittlichkeit; Sittenlehre', in Joachim Ritter and Karlfried Gründer (eds), *Historisches Wörterbuch der Philosophie*, vol. 9. Basel: Schwabe, 907–923.

Kessler, Eckhard. 1971. 'Geschichte: Menschliche Praxis oder kritische Wissenschaft? Zur Theorie der humanistischen Geschichtsschreibung', in Ekhard Kessler (ed.), *Theoretiker humanistischer Geschichtsschreibung. Nachdruck exemplarischer Texte aus dem 16. Jahrhundert.* Munich: Wilhelm Fink, 7–47.

Kitzbichler, Josefine. 2008. 'Der Übersetzer', in Christiane Hackel (ed.), *Philologe – Historiker – Politiker. Johann Gustav Droysen, 1808–1884. Katalog zur Ausstellung des Sonderforschungsbereiches «Transformationen der Antike»*, *Humboldt Universität zu Berlin, 01.07–08.08.2008.* Berlin: G + H, 33–38.

Kohlstrunk, Irene. 1980. *Logik und Historie in Droysens Geschichtstheorie. Eine Analyse von Genese und Konstitutionsprinzipien seiner ‹Historik›.* Wiesbaden: Franz Steiner.

Koselleck, Reinhart. 2004. *Futures Past: On the Semantics of Historical Time,* trans. Keith Tribe. New York: Columbia University Press.

———. 2003. *Vergangene Zukunft. Zur Semantik geschichtlicher Zeiten.* Frankfurt am Main: Suhrkamp.

———. 2003. *Zeitschichten. Studien zur Historik.* Frankfurt am Main: Suhrkamp.

———. 1990. 'Wozu noch Historie?' in Wolfgang Hardtwig (ed.), *Über das Studium der Geschichte.* Munich: DTV, 347–365.

———. 1990. 'Zur anthropologischen und semantischen Struktur der Bildung', in Reinhart Koselleck (ed.), *Bildungsbürgertum im 19. Jahrhundert*, part 2: *Bildungsgüter und Bildungswissen.* Stuttgart: Klett-Cotta, 11–46.

————. 1984. '‹Revolution› und ihre Gegenbegriffe in geschichtsphilosophischer Perspektive', in Otto Brunner et al. (eds), *Geschichtliche Grundbegriffe. Historisches Lexikon zur politisch-sozialen Sprache in Deutschland*, vol. 5. Stuttgart: Klett-Cotta, 739–788.

————. 1979. 'Geschichte, Historie. I. Einleitung', in Otto Brunner et al. (eds), *Geschichtliche Grundbegriffe. Historisches Lexikon zur politisch-sozialen Sprache in Deutschland*, vol. 2. Stuttgart: Klett-Cotta, 593–595.

————. 1979. 'Geschichte, Historie. V. Die Herausbildung des modernen Geschichtsbegriffs', in Otto Brunner et al. (eds), *Geschichtliche Grundbegriffe. Historisches Lexikon zur politisch-sozialen Sprache in Deutschland*, vol. 2. Stuttgart: Klett-Cotta, 647–717.

————. 1972. 'Einleitung', in Otto Brunner et al. (eds). *Geschichtliche Grundbegriffe. Historisches Lexikon zur politisch-sozialen Sprache in Deutschland*, vol. 1. Stuttgart: Klett-Cotta, xiii–xxvii.

————. 1967. 'Richtlinien für das Lexikon politisch-sozialer Begriffe der Neuzeit', *Archiv für Begriffsgeschichte* 11: 81–99.

Krieger, Leonard. 1977. *Ranke: The Meaning of History*. Chicago: University of Chicago Press.

Kristeller, Paul Oskar. 1961. *Renaissance Thought: The Classic, Scholastic and Humanist Strains*. New York: Harper & Row.

Krüger, Hermann. 1893. 'Biographical Sketch: Johann Gustav Droysen', in Johann Gustav Droysen, *Outline of the Principles of History*, trans. E. Benjamin Andrews. Boston: Ginn, xv–xxxv.

Landfester, Rüdiger. 1972. *Historia Magistra Vitae. Untersuchungen zur humanistischen Geschichtstheorie des 14. bis 16. Jahrhunderts*. Geneva: Librairie Droz.

Langlois, Charles Victor and Charles Seignobos. 1909. *Introduction to the Study of History*, trans. G.G. Berry. New York: Henry Holt [1898].

Lemon, Michael. 2003. *Philosophy of History: A Guide for Students*. London: Routledge.

Lessing, Hans-Ulrich. 2006. 'Das Wahrheitsproblem im Historismus: Droysen und Dilthey', in Markus Enders and Jan Szaif (eds), *Die Geschichte des philosophischen Begriffs der Wahrheit*. Berlin Walter de Gruyter, 275–286.

Levinger, Matthew. 2000. *Enlightened Nationalism: The Transformation of Prussian Political Culture, 1806–1848*. New York: Oxford University Press.

Lewark, Sybille. 1975. *Das politische Denken Johann Gustav Droysens*, Ph.D. Thesis. Eberhard-Karls-Universität zu Tübingen.

Leyh, Peter. 1977. 'Vorwort des Herausgebers', in Johann Gustav Droysen, *Historik*, vol. 1: *Rekonstruktion der ersten vollständigen Fassung der Vorlesungen (1857); Grundriß der Historik in der ersten handschriftlichen (1857/58) und in der letzten gedruckten Fassung (1882)*, edited by Peter Leyh. Stuttgart: Frommann-Holzboog, ix–xxix.

Liebersohn, Harry. 2007. 'German Historical Writing from Ranke to Weber: The Primacy of Politics', in Lloyd Kramer and Sarah Maza (eds), *A Companion to Western Historical Thought*. Malden, MA: Blackwell, 166–184.

Liechtenstein, Ernst. 1971. 'Bildung', in Joachim Ritter (ed.), *Historisches Wörterbuch der Philosophie*. Basel: Schwabe, 921–937.

Lingelbach, Gabriele. 2003. *Klio macht Karriere. Die Institutionalisierung der Geschichtswissenschaft in Frankreich und den USA in der zweiten Hälfte des 19. Jahrhunderts*. Göttingen: Vandenhoeck & Ruprecht.

Lorenz, Chris. 1998. 'Can Histories Be True? Narrativism, Positivism and the "Metaphorical Turn"', *History and Theory* 37(3): 309–329.

————. 1997. *Konstruktion der Vergangenheit. Eine Einführung in die Geschichtstheorie*, trans. Annegret Böttner. Cologne: Böhlau.

Löwith, Karl. 2004. *Meaning and History: The Theological Implications of the Philosophy of History*. Chicago: University of Chicago Press.

Lübbe, Hermann. 1977. *Geschichtsbegriff und Geschichtsinteresse. Analytik und Pragmatik der Historie*. Basel: Schwabe.

Lyman, Eugene. 1932. 'Ernst Troeltsch's Philosophy of History', *The Philosophical Review* 41(5): 443–465.

MacIntyre, Alasdair. 2007. *After Virtue: A Study in Moral Theory*. Notre Dame, IN: University of Notre Dame Press.

MacLean, Michael. 1988. 'History in a Two-cultures World: The Case of the German Historians', *Journal of the History of Ideas* 49(3): 473–494.

————. 1982. 'Johann Gustav Droysen and the Development of Historical Hermeneutics', *History and Theory* 21(3): 347–365.

Manhart, Sebastian. 2009. 'Was wird werden, wenn man weiß, was wird? Geschichtsschreibung und Staatswissenschaft als Interventionen in sich selbst hervorbringende Systeme im vormärzlichen Diskurs und bei Johann Gustav Droysen', in Horst Walter Blanke (ed.), *Historie und Historik. 200 Jahre Johann Gustav Droysen. Festschrift für Jörn Rüsen zum 70. Geburtstag.* Cologne: Böhlau, 38–72.

Marcuse, Herbert. 1937. 'Rezension von J. G. Droysens "*Historik*", Hrsg. v. R. Hübner', *Zeitschrift für Sozialforschung* 6: 421–422.

Marrou, Henri-Irénée. n.d. *Do conhecimento histórico*, trans. Ruy Belo. Lisbon: Aster.

Mata, Sérgio da. 2010. '"O dever-ser é coisa do Diabo"? Sobre o problema da neutralidade axiológica em Max Weber', *Dimensões* 24: 262–283.

McGlew, James. 1984. 'J. G. Droysen and the Aeschylean Hero', *Classical Philology* 79(1): 1–14.

Megill, Alan. 1987. *Prophets of Extremity: Nietzsche, Heidegger, Foucault, Derrida*. Berkeley: University of California Press.

Meier, Christian. 1979. 'Geschichte, Historie. II. Antike', in Otto Brunner et al. (eds), *Geschichtliche Grundbegriffe. Historisches Lexikon zur politisch-sozialen Sprache in Deutschland*, vol. 2. Stuttgart: Klett-Cotta, 595–610.

Meinecke, Friedrich. 1930. 'Johann Gustav Droysen. Sein Briefwechsel und seine Geschichtsschreibung', *Historische Zeitschrift* 141: 249–287.

Merquior, José Guilherme. 1988. 'Philosophy of History: Thoughts on a Possible Revival', *History of the Human Sciences* 1(1): 23–31.

Mezzanzanica, Massimo. 2009. 'Expérience historique et théorie de la comprehension: Droysen et Dilthey', in Jean-Claude Gens (ed.), *Johann Gustav Droysen: L'avénement du paradigme herméneutique dans les sciences humaines.* Argenteuil: Le Cercle herméneutique, 205–221.

Mitzman, Arthur. 1985. *The Iron Cage: An Historical Interpretation of Max Weber.* New Brunswick, NJ: Transaction.

Momigliano, Arnaldo. 2000. 'Die Geschichte der Entstehung und die heutige Funktion des Begriffs des Hellenismus', in Arnaldo Momigilano, *Ausgewählte Schriften zur Geschichte und Geschichtsschreibung*, vol. 3: *Die moderne Geschichtsschreibung der alten Welt*, edited by Glenn Most, trans. Kai Brodersen and Andreas Wittenburg. Stuttgart: J.B. Metzler, 113–142.

————. 1980. 'Historicism Revisited', in Arnaldo Momigliano, *Sesto contributo alla storia degli studi classici e del mondo antico*, vol. 1. Rome: Edizioni di Storia e Letteratura, 23–32.

————. 1970. 'J. G. Droysen between Greeks and Jews', *History and Theory* 9(1): 139–153.

————. 1966. 'Time in Ancient Historiography', *History and Theory* 6(6): 1–23.

Mommsen, Theodore Ernst. 1942. 'Petrarch's Conception of the "Dark Ages"', *Speculum* 17(2): 226–242.

Moos, Peter von. 1996. *Geschichte als Topik. Das rhetorische Exemplum von der Antike zur Neuzeit und die historiae in ‹Policraticus› Johanns von Salisbury.* Hildesheim: Olms.

Muhlack, Ulrich. 1991. *Geschichtswissenschaft im Humanismus und in der Aufklärung. Die Vorgeschichte des Historismus.* Munich: C.H. Beck.

————. 1990. 'Bildung zwischen Neuhumanismus und Historismus', in Reinhart Koselleck (ed.), *Bildungsbürgertum im 19. Jahrhundert*, part 2: *Bildungsgüter und Bildungswissen.* Stuttgart: Klett-Cotta, 80–105.

————. 1990. 'Johann Gustav Droysen: "Historik" et " Hermeneutique"', in André Laks and Ada Neschke (eds), *La naissance du paradigme hermeneutique. Schleiermacher, Humboldt, Boeckh, Droysen.* Lille: Presses Universitaires de Lille, 359–380.

Mutschler, Fritz-Heiner. 2003. 'Zur Sinnhorizont und Funktion griechischer, römischer und altchinesischer Geschichtsschreibung', in Karl-Joachim Hölkeskamp et al. (eds), *Sinn (in) der Antike. Orientierungssysteme, Leitbilder und Wertkonzepte im Altertum.* Mainz: Phillip von Zabern, 33–54.

Nadel, George H. 1964. 'Philosophy of History before Historicism', *History and Theory* 3(3): 291–315.

———. 1962. 'New Light on Bolingbroke's Letters on History', *Journal of the History of Ideas* 23(4): 550–557.

Navarro, Jorge. 1997. 'Fichte, Humboldt y Ranke sobre la idea y las ideas historicas (con un apendice sobre Hegel y Droysen)', *Anuario Filosofico* 30: 405–426.

Nippel, Wilfried. 2009. 'Droysen-Legenden', in Horst Walter Blanke (ed.), *Historie und Historik. 200 Jahre Johann Gustav Droysen. Festschrift für Jörn Rüsen zum 70. Geburtstag.* Cologne: Böhlau, 158–176.

———. 2008. *Johann Gustav Droysen. Ein Leben zwischen Wissenschaft und Politik.* Munich: C. H. Beck.

———. 1997. 'Philologenstreit und Schulpolitik. Zur Kontroverse zwischen Gottfried Hermann und August Böckh', in Wolfgang Küttler et al. (eds), *Geschichtsdiskurs*, vol. 3: *Die Epoche der Historisierung.* Frankfurt am Main: Fischer, 244–253.

Nipperdey, Thomas. 1998. *Deutsche Geschichte 1800–1866. Bürgerwelt und starker Staat.* Munich: C.H. Beck.

———. 1998. *Deutsche Geschichte 1866–1918,* vol. 2: *Machtstaat vor der Demokratie.* Munich: C.H. Beck.

Obermann, Werner. 1977. *Der Junge Johann Gustav Droysen. Ein Beitrag zur Entstehungsgeschichte des Historismus,* Ph.D. Thesis. Universität Bonn.

Oexle, Otto Gerhard. 1996. *Geschichtswissenschaft im Zeichen des Historismus: Studien zu Problemgeschichten der Moderne.* Göttingen: Vandenhoeck und Ruprecht.

Olsen, Niklas. 2012. *History in the Plural: An Introduction to the Work of Reinhart Koselleck.* New York: Berghahn Books.

Paetrow, Stephan. 2008. *Johann Gustav Droysen in Jena. Ein Beitrag zur Entstehungsgeschichte von Droysens ‹Historik› und ‹Geschichte der preußischen Politik›.* Saarbrücken: VDM.

Pandel, Hans-Jürgen. 2007. *Geschichtsunterricht nach PISA. Kompetenzen, Bildungsstandards und Kerncurricula.* Schwalbach am Taunus: Wochenschau.

———. 1993. 'Wer ist ein Historiker? Forschung und Lehre als Bestimmungsfaktoren in der Geschichtswissenschaft des 19. Jahrhunderts', in Wolfgang Küttler et al. (eds), *Geschichtsdiskurs,* vol. 1: *Grundlagen und Methoden der Historiographiegeschichte,* Frankfurt am Main: Fischer, 346–354.

———. 1990. *Historik und Didaktik. Das Problem der Distribution historiographisch erzeugten Wissens in der deutschen Geschichtswissenschaft von der Spätaufklärung zum Frühhistorismus (1765–1830).* Stuttgart: Frommann-Holzboog.

Paul, Herman. 2011. 'Distance and Self-Distanciation: Intellectual Virtue and Historical Method around 1900', *History and Theory* 50(4): 104–116.

———. 2011. 'Performing History: How Historical Scholarship Is Shaped by Epistemic Virtues', *History and Theory* 50(1): 1–19.

Paulsen, Friedrich. 1885. *Geschichte des gelehrten Unterichts auf den deutschen Schulen und Universitäten. Vom Ausgang des Mittelalters bis zur Gegenwart.* Leipzig: Veit.

Peters, Martin. 2003. *Altes Reich und Europa: Der Historiker, Statistiker und Publizist August Ludwig (v.) Schlözer (1735–1809).* Berlin LIT.

Phillips, Mark. 1989. 'Macaulay, Scott, and the Literary Challenge to Historiography', *Journal of the History of Ideas* 50(1): 117–133.

———. 1977. *Francesco Guicciardini: The Historian's Craft.* Toronto: Manchester University Press.

Pittock, Murray. 2003. 'Historiography', in Alexander Broadie (ed.), *The Cambridge Companion to the Scottish Enlightenment.* Cambridge: Cambridge University Press, 258–279.

Popper, Karl. 2002. *The Poverty of Historicism*. London: Routledge.

Portis, Edward. 1980. 'Political Action and Social Science: Max Weber's Two Arguments for Objectivity', *Polity* 12(3): 409–427.

Pröpper, Thomas and Magnus Striet. 2000. 'Theodizee', in Walter Kasper et al. (eds), *Lexikon für Theologie und Kirche*, vol. 9. Freiburg im Breisgau: Herder, 1396–1398.

Raphael, Lutz. 2003. *Geschichtswissenschaft im Zeitalter der Extreme. Theorien, Methoden, Tendenzen von 1900 bis zur Gegenwart*. Munich: C.H. Beck.

Reill, Peter Hanns. 1994. 'Science and the Construction of the Cultural Sciences in Late Enlightenment Germany: The Case of Wilhelm von Humboldt', *History and Theory* 33(3): 345–366.

———. 1986. 'Science and the Science of History in the Spätaufklärung', in Hans Erich Bödecker et al. (eds), *Aufklärung und Geschichte. Studien zur deutschen Geschichtswissenschaft im 18. Jahrhundert*. Göttingen: Vanderhoeck & Ruprecht, 430–449.

———. 1975. *The German Enlightenment and the Rise of Historicism*. Berkeley: University of California Press.

Reinhard, Wolfgang. 2006. 'The Idea of Early-Modern History', in Michael Bentley (ed.), *A Companion to Historiography*. London: Routledge, 268–280.

Reynolds, Beatrice. 1953. 'Shifting Currents in Historical Criticism', *Journal of the History of Ideas* 14(4): 471–492.

Ricoeur, Paul. 1994. *Oneself as Another*, trans. Kathleen Blamey. Chicago: The Chicago University Press.

Riedel, Manfred. 1978. *Verstehen oder Erklären. Zur Theorie und Geschichte der hermeneutischen Wissenschaften*. Stuttgart: Klett-Cotta.

———. 1973. 'Aristotelismus und Humanismus: Der Einfluß der humanistishen Aristotelesrezeption auf die politische Sprache der neuzeitlichen Philosophie', *Zeitschrift für philosophische Forschung* 27(3): 367–376.

Rigolot, François. 1998. 'The Renaissance Crisis of Exemplarity', *Journal of the History of Ideas* 59(4): 557–563.

Ringer, Fritz. 1990. *The Decline of the German Mandarins: The German Academic Community, 1890–1933*. Cambridge: Harvard University Press.

Röd, Wolfgang; Heinrich Schmidinger and Rainer Thurnher. 2002. *Die Philosophie des ausgehenden 19. und des 20. Jahrhunderts*, vol. 3: *Lebensphilosophie und Existezphilosophie*. Munich: C.H. Beck.

Rohbeck, Johannes. 2001. 'Verzeitlichung', in Joachim Ritter et al. (ed.), *Historisches Wörterbuch der Philosophie*, vol. 11. Basel: Schwabe, 1026–1028.

Rosa, Hartmut. 2005. *Beschleunigung. Die Veränderung der Zeitstrukturen in der Moderne*. Frankfurt am Main: Suhrkamp.

Rothacker, Erich. 1972. *Einleitung in die Geisteswissenschaften*. Darmstadt: Wissenschaftliche Buchgesellschaft.

———. 1940. 'J.G. Droysens Historik', *Historische Zeitschrift* 161: 84–92.

Runciman, Walter. 1978. *A Critique of Max Weber's Philosophy of Social Science*. Cambridge: Cambridge University Press.

Rüsen, Jörn. 2008. 'J. G. Droysen, Dämon der Machtbesessenheit. Rezension zu Wilfried Nippels "Johann Gustav Droysen: Ein Leben zwischen Wissenschaft und Politik"', *Die Welt*, 5 April 2008, Literarische Welt, 3.

———. 2005. 'Droysen heute – Plädoyer zum Bedenken verlorener Themen der Historik', in Lutz Niethammer (ed.), *Droysen-Vorlesungen*. Jena: Universität Jena, Philosophische Fakultät, Historisches Institut, 177–200.

———. 2003. 'Die Kultur der Zeit. Versuch einer Typologie temporaler Sinnbildungen', in Jörn Rüsen (ed.), *Zeit deuten. Perspektiven – Epochen – Paradigmen*. Bielefeld: Transcript, 23–53.

———. 2002. 'Historische Methode als religiöser Sinn. Dialektische Bewegungen in der Neuzeit', in Jörn Rüsen, *Geschichte im Kulturprozess*. Cologne: Böhlau, 9–41.

———. 2001. *Zerbrechende Zeit. Über den Sinn der Geschichte.* Cologne: Böhlau.

———. 1994. *Historisches Lernen. Grundlagen und Paradigmen.* Cologne: Böhlau.

———. 1993. *Konfigurationen des Historismus. Studien zur deutschen Wissenschaftskultur.* Frankfurt am Main: Suhrkamp.

———. 1989. *Lebendige Geschichte: Grundzüge einer Historik III: Formen und Funktionen des historischen Wissens.* Göttingen: Vanderhoeck & Ruprecht.

———. 1986. *Rekonstruktion der Vergangenheit: Grundzüge einer Historik II: Die Prinzipien der historischen Forschung.* Göttingen: Vanderhoeck & Ruprecht.

———. 1984. 'Von der Aufklärung zum Historismus. Idealtypische Perspektiven eines Strukturwandels', in Horst Walter Blanke and Jörn Rüsen (eds), *Von der Aufklärung zum Historismus. Zum Strukturwandel des historischen Denkens.* Paderborn: Schöningh, 15–58.

———. 1983. *Historische Vernunft. Grundzüge einer Historik I: Die Grundlagen der Geschichtswissenschaft.* Göttingen: Vandenhoeck & Ruprecht.

———. 1973. 'Johann Gustav Droysen', in Hans-Ulrich Wehler (ed.), *Deutsche Historiker.* Göttingen: Vandenhoeck & Ruprecht, 115–131.

———. 1969. *Begriffene Geschichte. Genesis und Begründung der Geschichtstheorie J. G. Droysens.* Paderborn: Ferdinand Schöningh.

———. 1968. 'Politisches Denken und Geschichtswissenschaft bei J. G. Droysen', in Kurt Kluxen and Wolfgang Mommsen (eds), *Politische Ideologien und Nationalstaatliche Ordnung. Studien zur Geschichte des 19. und 20. Jahrhunderts. Festschrift für Theodor Schieder.* Munich: Oldenbourg, 171–187.

Sawilla, Jan Marco. 2011. 'Geschichte und Geschichten zwischen Providenz und Machbarkeit. Überlegungen zu Reinhart Kosellecks Semantik historischer Zeiten', in Hans Joas and Peter Vogt (eds), *Begriffene Geschichte. Beiträge zum Werk Reinhart Kosellecks.* Frankfurt am Main: Suhrkamp, 387–422.

———. 2004. '"Geschichte": Ein Produkt der deutschen Aufklärung? Eine Kritik an Reinhart Kosellecks Begriffs des "Kollektivsingulars" Geschichte', *Zeitschrift für historische Forschung* 31: 381–428.

Schieder, Theodor. 1959. 'Johann Gustav Bernhard Droysen', in *Neue Deutsche Biographie,* vol. 4. Berlin: Duncker & Humblot [Reprinted in 1971 by Fotokop Wilhelm Weihert, Darmstadt].

Schiffman, Zachary. 1985. 'Renaissance Historicism Reconsidered', *History and Theory* 24(2): 170–182.

Schluchter, Wolfgang. 1997. 'Polytheismus der Werte. Überlegungen im Anschluß an Max Weber', in Christoph Jamme (ed.), *Grundlinien der Vernunftkritik.* Frankfurt am Main.: Suhrkamp, 307–339.

Schnädelbach, Herbert. 1974. *Geschichtsphilosophie nach Hegel. Die Probleme des Historismus.* Freiburg and Munich: Karl Alber.

Schnicke, Falko. 2010. *Prinzipien der Entindividualisierung. Theorie und Praxis biographischer Studien bei Johann Gustav Droysen.* Cologne: Böhlau.

Scholtz, Gunther. 1991. *Zwischen Wissenschaftsanspruch und Orientierungsbedürfnis. Zu Grundlage und Wandel der Geisteswissenschaften.* Frankfurt am Main Suhrkamp.

Schreiber, Waltraud et al. 2006. *Historisches Denken. Ein Kompetenz-Struktur Modell,* 2nd ed. Neuried: Ars una.

Schulze, Hagen. 1998. *Gibt es überhaupt eine deutsche Geschichte?* Stuttgart: Reclam.

Schuppe, Christian-Georg. 1997. *Der andere Droysen. Neue Aspekte seiner Theorie der Geschichtswissenschaft.* Stuttgart: Franz Steiner.

Sebastián, Javiér Fernández and Juan Francisco Fuentes. 2006. 'Conceptual History, Memory, and Identity: An Interview with Reinhart Koselleck', *Contributions to the History of Concepts* 2(1): 99–127.

Seixas, Peter. 2006. 'Historical Consciousness: The Progress of Knowledge in a Postprogressive Age', in Jürgen Straub (ed.), *Narration, Identity, and Historical Consciousness.* New York: Berghahn Books, 141–156.

Sheehan, James. 2009. 'A Political Professor: A New Biography of J.G. Droysen', *German History* 27(4): 580–582.

———. 1983. *German Liberalism in the Nineteenth Century.* Chicago: The University of Chicago Press.

Skinner, Quentin. 2000. *Machiavelli: A Very Short Introduction.* Oxford: Oxford University Press.

Smith, Bonnie G. 1995. 'Gender and the Practices of Scientific History: The Seminar and Archival Research in the Nineteenth Century', *American Historical Review* 100(4): 1150–1176.

Southard, Robert. 1995. *Droysen and the Prussian School of History.* Lexington: University Press of Kentucky.

———. 1979. 'Theology in Droysen's Early Political Historiography: Free Will, Necessity, and the Historian', *History and Theory* 18(3): 378–396.

Spiegel, Gabrielle. 2007. 'Historical Thought in Medieval Europe', in Lloyd Kramer and Sarah Maza (eds), *A Companion to Western Historical Thought.* Malden, MA: Blackwell, 78–98.

———. 1975. 'Political Utility in Medieval Historiography: A Sketch', *History and Theory* 14(3): 314–325.

Spieler, Karl-Heinz. 1970. *Untersuchungen zu Johann Gustav Droysens ‹Historik›.* Berlin: Duncker & Humblot.

Stack, George. 1998. 'Materialism', in Edward Craig (ed.), *Routledge Encyclopaedia of Philosophy.* London: Routledge, 170–173.

Stockhorst, Stefanie. 2001. 'Novus ordo temporum. Reinhart Kosellecks These von der Verzeitlichung des Geschichtsbewußtseins durch die Aufklärungshistoriographie in methodenkritischer Perspektive', in Hans Joas and Peter Vogt (eds), *Begriffene Geschichte. Beiträge zum Werk Reinhart Kosellecks.* Frankfurt am Main: Suhrkamp, 359–386.

Summerell, Orrin. 1996. 'Geist', in Peter Prechtl and Franz-Peter Burkard (eds), *Metzler Philosophie Lexikon.* Stuttgart: J.B. Metzler, 180–181.

Telman, Jeremy. 1994. 'Review Essay', *History and Theory* 33(2): 249–265.

Thapar, Romila. 2006. 'The Tradition of Historical Writing in Early India', in Romila Thapar, *Ancient Indian Social History: Some Interpretations.* New Delhi: Orient Blackswan, 237–258.

Thornhill, Chris. 2007. *German Political Philosophy. The Metaphysics of Law.* London: Routledge.

Torstendahl, Rolf. 2003. 'Fact, Truth and Text: The Quest for a Firm Basis for Historical Knowledge around 1900', *History and Theory* 42(3): 305–331.

Troeltsch, Ernst. 1961. *Der Historismus und seine Probleme,* book 1: *Das logische Problem der Geschichtsphilosophie.* Aalen: Scientia [1922].

Unger, Rudolf. 1971. 'The Problem of Historical Objectivity: A Sketch of its Development to the Time of Hegel', *History and Theory* 11(4): 60–86.

Veyne, Paul. 1984. *Writing History: Essay on Epistemology,* trans. Mina Moore-Rinvolucri. Middletown, CT: Wesleyan University Press.

Vierhaus, Rudolf. 1979. 'Bildung', in Otto Brunner et al. (eds), *Geschichtliche Grundbegriffe: Historisches Lexikon zur politisch-sozialen Sprache in Deutschland,* vol. 1. Stuttgart: Klett-Cotta, 508–551.

Wach, Joachim. 1984. *Das Verstehen. Grundzüge einer Geschichte der hermeneutischen Theorie im 19. Jahrhundert,* 3 vols. Hildesheim: Georg Olms.

Walbank, Frank. 1990. *Polybius.* Berkeley: University of California Press.

Watkins, Carl. 2007. *History and the Supernatural in Medieval England.* Cambridge: Cambridge University Press.

Weber, Max. 1988. *Gesammelte Aufsätze zur Wissenschaftslehre,* edited by Johannes Winckelmann. Tübingen: J.C.B. Mohr [1951].

Welskopp, Thomas. 2009. 'Der echte Historiker als "richtiger Kerl". Neue Veröffentlichungen (nicht nur) zum 200. Geburtstag von Johann Gustav Droysen', *Historische Zeitschrift* 288(2): 385–407.

White, Hayden. 2005. 'The Public Relevance of Historical Studies: A Reply to Dirk Moses', *History and Theory* 44(3): 333–338.

————. 1987. 'Droysen's Historik: Historical Writing as a Bourgeois Science', in Hayden White, *The Content of the Form: Narrative Discourse and Historical Representation*. Baltimore: The John Hopkins University Press, 83–103.

Wineburg, Sam. 2001. *Historical Thinking and Other Unnatural Acts: Charting the Future of Teaching the Past*. Philadelphia: Temple University Press.

Witschi-Bernz, Astrid. 1972. 'Main Trends in Historical-Method Literature: Sixteenth to Eighteenth Centuries', *History and Theory* 12(supplement 12: *Bibliography of Works in the Philosophy of History, 1500–1800*): 51–90.

Wittkau-Horgby, Annette. 2005. 'Droysen and Nietzsche: Two Different Answers to the Discovery of Historicity', in Peter Koslowski (ed.), *The Discovery of Historicity in German Idealism and Historism*. Berlin: Springer, 59–76.

Wittkau, Annette. 1994. *Historismus. Zur Geschichte des Begriffs und des Problems*, 2nd ed. Göttingen: Vandenhoeck & Ruprecht.

Woolf, Daniel. 2005. 'Historiography', in Maryanne Horowitz (ed.), *New Dictionary of the History of Ideas*, vol. 1. Detroit: Thomson Gale, xxxv–lxxxviii.

Wright, Johnson Kent. 2007. 'The Historical Thought of the Enlightenment', in Lloyd Kramer and Sarah Maza, *A Companion to Western Historical Thought*. Malden, MA: Blackwell, 123–142.

Yü, Ying-shih. 2002. 'Reflections on Chinese Historical Thinking', in Jörn Rüsen (ed.), *Western Historical Thinking: An Intercultural Debate*. New York: Berghahn Books, 152–17.

Index

MAKING SENSE OF HISTORY
Studies in Historical Cultures
General Editor: Stefan Berger
Founding Editor: Jörn Rüsen

Bridging the gap between historical theory and the study of historical memory, this series crosses the boundaries between both academic disciplines and cultural, social, political and historical contexts. In an age of rapid globalization, which tends to manifest itself on an economic and political level, locating the cultural practices involved in generating its underlying historical sense is an increasingly urgent task.

Printed in the USA
CPSIA information can be obtained
at www.ICGtesting.com
CBHW072347130724
11570CB00012B/607

9 781785 333347